PRIVATE EYE

THE FIRST
50
YEARS

For my mum and dad,
Sandra and James Macqueen,
for always encouraging me
never to get a proper job.

Published by Private Eye Productions Limited 2011

10 9 8 7 6 5 4 3 2

Copyright © Private Eye Productions Limited and Adam Macqueen 2011

Adam Macqueen has asserted his right to be identified as the author of this work
under the Copyright, Designs and Patents Act 1988

First published in Great Britain by Private Eye Productions Limited 2011

6 Carlisle Street
London W1D 3BN

www.private-eye.co.uk

A CIP catalogue record for this book is available from the British Library

ISBN 978-1-901784-56-5

Mixed Sources
Product group from well-managed
forests and other controlled sources
www.fsc.org Cert no. TT-COC-2139
© 1996 Forest Stewardship Council

FSC

Designed by Peter Ward
Printed and bound in Great Britain by Butler Tanner & Dennis Ltd, Frome, Somerset

PRIVATE EYE

THE FIRST

50

YEARS

AN A-Z BY ADAM MACQUEEN

You can read this book in a number of different ways.
Start at A and work all the way through to Z.
Read about the key events in the magazine's history in
chronological order by following the timeline below . . .

1950 – Thirteen-year-olds Richard Ingrams and William Rushton arrive at Shrewsbury School, where they are joined a few terms later by Christopher Booker and Paul Foot (☞ p. 259). All four go on to work on the school magazine, the *Salopian*.

1958 – Following national service (p. 202), Ingrams and Foot are reunited at Oxford University. They co-edit student magazine *Parson's Pleasure* (p. 224). They and Rushton are then recruited by Peter Usborne along with John Wells to work on *Mesopotamia* (p.186).

1961 – Usborne persuades Andrew Osmond to invest £450 in a new magazine, a "fortnightly lampoon" called *Private Eye* (p. 217). The first issue appears on 25 October 1961 (p. 96). Christopher Booker is editor (p. 36). They set up a company called Pressdram to publish it (p. 230).

May 1962 – Osmond sells *Private Eye* to comedian Peter Cook (p. 248).

November 1962 – *Eye* receives first libel writ (p. 300).

August 1963 – Claud Cockburn joins, and introduces investigative journalism to magazine (p. 51) alongside the jokes.

September 1963 – Booker sacked as editor. Richard Ingrams takes over (p. 38).

1964 – "Mrs Wilson's Diary", the first in a long-running series of prime ministerial parodies, begins. It is written by Richard Ingrams and John Wells (p. 196).

1965 – First libel case to reach court, brought by Lord Russell of Liverpool. *Eye* loses (p. 49).

1967 – Paul Foot joins staff (p. 101).

1970 – Auberon Waugh joins (p. 140). His "Diary" starts two years later (p. 78).

1972 – Home secretary Reginald Maudling resigns after long series of *Eye* stories chronicling his dodgy business associates (p. 229). First appeal to readers for help with legal costs, the Ballsoff Fund, launched (p. 30).

1976 – Sir James Goldsmith issues sixty-three writs against magazine and attempts to bring criminal libel case (p. 117) against Ingrams and journalist Patrick Marnham.

1978 – Magazine reveals that police wish to arrest Liberal leader Jeremy Thorpe for conspiracy to murder. He sues, but is arrested two weeks later (p. 81).

. . . Look up your favourite features from the magazine, and see where the cross-references take you. Or do what most people do with their copies of *Private Eye* each fortnight, and leave it by the loo for a while to dip into at random. Then wash your hands.

1979 – "Dear Bill", the letters of Denis Thatcher as imagined by Ingrams and Wells, begins (p. 72).

1981 – Twenty-one-year-old Ian Hislop joins magazine as joke-writer and journalist (p. 137).

1986 – Richard Ingrams unexpectedly announces his resignation as editor in favour of Ian Hislop (p. 145) at leaving lunch for Auberon Waugh (p. 246) Revolt by former staff (p. 298). *Eye* suffers libel defeat by Robert Maxwell (p. 181). Nick Newman, who has been contributing cartoons since 1981, joins the main joke-writing team (p. 204).

1987 – Francis Wheen recruited as hack (p. 294).

1988 – Craig Brown recruited to write the regular celebrity diary (p. 44).

1989 – Sonia Sutcliffe, wife of Yorkshire Ripper, awarded £600,000 in libel damages, nearly putting *Eye* out of business. Editor declares self banana (p. 30)

1992 – M.D., alias Dr Phil Hammond, one of a number of specialist columnists recruited by Hislop, first reveals what will become known as Bristol Heart Scandal. A public inquiry finally reports in 2001 (p. 42).

1993 – Paul Foot, who has continued to contribute to the *Eye* while working for the *Daily Mirror*, rejoins the staff permanently (p. 105).

1995 – Death of proprietor Peter Cook (p. 62).

1997 – Death of Princess Diana. *Private Eye* removed from shops as period of national hysteria declared (p. 75).

1999 – Nev Fountain and Tom Jamieson begin contributing to jokes section (p. 198).

2001 – *Eye* celebrates victory in million-pound, ten-year libel action brought with assistance of long-time foes Carter-Fuck (p. 188).

2009 – Two legal victories for the *Eye* as injunctions brought by oil company Trafigura (p. 282) and lawyer Michael Napier (p. 148) on grounds of privacy, as opposed to libel, are overturned.

2011 – *Private Eye* reaches age of fifty with its highest circulation in eighteen years. It is still put together each fortnight in pretty much the same way it always has been (p. 6).

INTRODUCTION: A PRESS DAY IN THE LIFE OF . . .

Monday 14 September 2010

Tony Blair's memoirs are breaking all sales records, Pope Benedict is about to arrive on a state visit to Britain, and Downing Street spin doctor Andy Coulson continues unconvincingly to deny knowing anything about phone-hacking at the *News of the World*.

And the 1271st edition of *Private Eye* is due at the printers at half-past six this evening.

9.00am Editorial secretary Hilary Lowinger is sorting through the hundreds of emails which have come in over the weekend. They include this fortnight's offerings from columnists Gavel Basher and Remote Controller, and a note from "Rotten Boroughs" editor Tim Minogue amending the copy he filed the previous Thursday: "One of the principal characters in the Cotswold story dropped dead on Friday night, and we must get that in."

Lowinger is simultaneously manning the phones, answering each call with scrupulous politeness. Sometimes, to the never-ending delight of her colleagues, she uses the same crisply enunciated tones to use the C-word to describe the caller the second she puts the receiver down.

On the adjoining desk in the front office, Sue Roccelli is sorting through the photos enterprising picture agencies have sent over in the hope they might make the magazine's cover. These divide into two categories: pictures of key figures in the week's headlines, and pictures of politicians looking silly – i.e. lots of Boris Johnson.

Next door in the production studio, Sally Farrimond is downloading the cartoons which have arrived over the weekend. Editor Ian Hislop selected his favourites from a selection of possible roughs which the artists sent over the week before: these are the finished inked and coloured versions of regular strips like "The Premiershits" and "Dave Snooty", ready to go on the page.

9.30am Chief sub-editor Tristan Davies wheels his bike into the production studio and forecasts a long day. The "In the Back" section is usually finalised on the Friday before press day, but "Ian didn't manage to do it, so we're behind already."

The magazine goes to press on Mondays in order to have it on sale for the maximum number of working days that the joke on the cover still feels topical. "So much depends on the cover," says Nick Newman, who is part of the team behind the trademark speech bubbles. "Ian agonizes about the cover because when you look at the figures, if you have a really strong joke on the cover it sells another 20,000 copies or something like that." Pleasingly, the same rule used to apply to *Private Eye* as to women's magazines – put Princess Di on the cover and circulation will go up (it didn't work straight after her death, mind).

9.40am Ian Hislop arrives, and settles into the handsome leather chair in the front office to work his way through the post, emails and cartoons awaiting him in the four in-trays on Lowinger's desk. His is far from the first famous bottom to grace this chair – it used to belong to the *Eye*'s arch-enemy Robert Maxwell, and was donated to the office by a reader who bought it in the fire sale which followed the fat fraudster's death.

Hilary Lowinger mans the phones . . . and a cartoonist's eye view of her and her colleague Sue Roccelli by Tony Husband

That Husband only comes in to use the fuckin' fax

9.55am Hislop and Davies have a quick pow-wow about the "In the Back" pages: "Turn these two into one, at about a third of the space. It's a single story about inquests."

10.00am To Hislop's spectacularly untidy office for the morning editorial meeting with hacks Francis Wheen, Jane Mackenzie, Andy Murray and me. There is much glee over this morning's *Daily Mail*, which has splashed with the tale of wrongdoing at the Commonwealth Development Corporation, a tale much documented in the *Eye* over the past three years and the subject of a seven-page special report by Richard Brooks in the previous issue. "Did you see their editorial?" demands Wheen, leafing through the paper. "'Today's revelations will be the first most people have heard of CDC'!"

A handful of hacks – clockwise from far left, Francis Wheen, Tim Minogue, Jane Mackenzie and Heather Mills

The editor instructs him to bash out one of the magazine's increasingly regular "*Eye* Told You So" features for the front page. "I'd get Richard to do it himself, but he'll probably try to be modest, and that's no good." He also notes that the story of Andrew Symeou, a miscarriage of justice which investigative hack Heather Mills has been following for several years, has suddenly burst into the nationals, and that the abject failure of the government's outsourced "Pathways to Work" scheme, as documented by Mackenzie, has been recognised by a parliamentary committee.

Hacks Adam Macqueen and Richard Brooks

Far right: Former editor Richard Ingrams talks to art director Tony Rushton

10.30am Editor emeritus Richard Ingrams has arrived for the morning joke-writing session, but first, there are more important things to be organised: who he is going to have lunch with. "Hello Tariq, it's Ingo," he booms into the phone from the depths of Maxwell's chair.

Hislop works his way through a notebook in which he has noted down any stories that particularly exercised him over the weekend and which he feels the *Eye* ought to have a take on, and then asks for suggestions from the hacks. If you've got a really good story, this is the point to spring it on him. There is a similar meeting the previous Wednesday which kicks off the editorial cycle (known on the fortnightly magazine as the "on-week") for the issue: give him a good story then and he has five full days to get bored with it and decide not to put it in. "The beginning of the on-week is enthusiasm, it's 'I like this, that'll be good, that'll be good,' and then towards the end of the week it's 'Oh fuck, this is boring, why's this been submitted?'" admits Hislop. "And I do it every issue and I can see myself doing it, but that seems to be how I work."

The meeting is brief, and often followed by further informal session where smaller groups of hacks get together sans editor and try to work out what story he was actually talking about when they were nodding knowledgeably and promising to follow up.

10.45am The last joke-writing session for the issue in Hislop's office. Various different combinations of jokesmiths have met up during the past week: Hislop, Ingrams, Barry Fantoni and the even-more-emeritus editor Christopher Booker on Wednesday morning, Hislop and Newman on Thursday afternoon, and Tom Jamieson and Nev Fountain in two sessions on Tuesday and Friday, but it is on the Monday morning, that, in Hislop's words, "a lot of it gets done".

How do the writing sessions work? "God knows," says the editor. "It seems to be quite a lot of just chat. My job for a long time has been to orchestrate them." Whereas Booker wields the biro at the Wednesday session, on Mondays it is Hislop who scribbles the best lines that fly around the room on to sheaves of pink paper. "It's all done in longhand and I think that gives you just enough time to mentally edit," he says. "You've got to keep up, which is very difficult, because everyone's shouting, and essentially you're going for creating a flow out of the best jokes, and sort of editing to make it prose at the same time, which Booker is very good at."

THOSE STIGS
FG Cond. U/L   —22—
IN FULL

→ The Eye's handy cut-out-and-
FG 10 on 12   —22—
throw away guide to ~~the stigs again~~
the stig's they are all talking about.

The Stig
FG demi

recognisable
head
v. small

The Stig
Mystery racing driver who is
FG 8 on 9 unj 10.5
in fact someone you have
never heard of.

stig Larsson

Stig Larsson
Mystery swedish novelist
who turns out to be
dead.

—22—
Fette Fraktur U/L
v
NUREMBERG TIMES
FINE LINE

T. New R Bold → **COULSON**
COND.   *1 line*
   —22—
ON
TRIAL
by our crime
staff A. Hack   *Times Small Caps*
   —22—

COL WIDTH PIC
top Col 2

T. New R
9 on 10 → The former Head of Propaganda
10.5 for the Nasty Party. Oberspinner
meisterfuhrer *Andy* Coulson denied
any knowledge of the
thousands of victims of
the infamous Phone Tapping
which had taken place under

Booker was famously sacked in 1963. But little things like that aren't allowed to get in the way at the *Eye*. They've sacked Tony Rushton, the art director, at least once, and it never stopped him coming in.

Each joke-writer brings something different to the mix. "Richard always has fully formed ideas, and I'm like him," says Hislop. "Once you've got the idea, they kind of write themselves," says Ingrams. "I had this idea – this comes into my head as an example – there was a story in the paper that Tony Blair had always wanted to become a Catholic but he wasn't able to because he was the prime minister, and I said to Ian, 'Blair admits: I was always a Conservative.' And, immediately you say that, you can just write the piece."

Fantoni is more of a character man. "Barry's fantastic at voices, so you start off writing a 'Glenda' or a tabloid piece and then you just let him go," says Hislop. "He's like Peter Cook: the voice just makes you laugh. He's very good at the 'Glenda' voices and the cabbies, and that's what you get, Barry acting really. When he's on song I just write it down."

Nick Newman provides "a cartoonist's eye. All those things like the 'Nursery Times', you'll find are him. Nick is very like Barry, the quantity of jokes, a plethora. You get a lot of ideas with Nick."

For the past fourteen years I've spent most press days in a neighbouring office, hearing volcanic eruptions of laughter from behind the closed door. "The Monday sessions are an absolute blast," says Newman. "It's great working with the other three. Everybody usually brings something to the party. Richard's still very sharp, and has terrific ideas for pieces. And Barry's stuff is just inspired and mad." Next door, things aren't quite as cheerful. Wheen and I are hammering away at computers, as are Mackenzie and Murray upstairs. The final deadline for copy is – theoretically at least – 12 noon.

The jokes pages as they emerge from the morning writing session. The handwriting is Ian Hislop's, the red annotations by Tony Rushton

The layout table

The production studio

11.35am Hislop breaks from the jokes meeting to deliver the first batch of material to the production staff who will type it up and lay it out downstairs. They are ranged down one side of the vast studio tacked on to the back of the building: Bridget Tisdall, Sally Farrimond, Megan Trudell and Ruth Pallesen-Mustikay, not a public schoolboy among them.

In the far corner huddle the sub-editors, Davies and his deputy Simon Edmond. The bulk of the room, however, is occupied by Tony Rushton, whose desk, drawing table, shelving units and noticeboards take up about as much space as everyone else put together. (He does, to be fair, share this area with a small stuffed dog which used to belong to Auberon Waugh.)

Rushton is also in charge of the enormous layout table in the centre of the room where each page of the magazine is painstakingly assembled from lots of little bits of paper, in a process which used to be commonplace in the magazine business until about, ooh, three decades ago.

"I still find it easier to do it that way," says Hislop. "And part of me really doesn't know whether a piece is interesting or not until it's there, on a white bit of paper and I'm thinking 'Do I care about this enough to put it on the page?' On the screen everything looks fine, but at that moment, that's the bit where you think ..." The process is essentially unchanged since Rushton, the cousin of *Eye* founder Willie, first picked up the scissors five decades ago. "His rather haphazard art-school layout became a sort of visual emblem of the magazine," says

Opening pages from 1964 and 2010

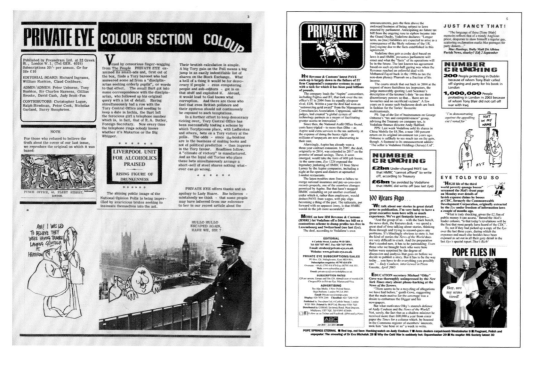

A page as laid out by Hislop, and in its finished form: the "holding" copy for the Dave Snooty slot has been replaced by a new strip

Hislop. "I've always tried to preserve a slight amateurishness about that side of production. I remember when magazines were first laid out on computer, I thought 'They all just look the same.' And if we looked like that, I won't want to read it any more."

There have been some concessions to modernity. The final layout is now done on computer – the pages with their precious load of confetti carried across the room while everyone holds their breath and tries not to sneeze – rather than pasted down and sent off to a repro-house to be photographed, as they still were when I joined in the late 1990s. But only because the EU finally banned Cow Gum for health and safety reasons.

11.45am Cartoonist Henry Davies has just arrived with the artwork for this week's "Dig for LibTory", the regular strip scripted by Fountain and Jamieson, which he transfers from his laptop on to the *Eye*'s system. Davies was recruited to draw their previous strip, "The Broonites", after working on the original Broons in the Scottish *Sunday Post*. "Where we spend about half an hour on a joke, Henry tortures over it for three days," laughs Jamieson.

12.55pm The jokes meeting is over. Hislop comes down with another batch of material. He briefly switches over to serious mode to inspect the reworked "In the Back" pages with their cheery cargo of NHS bullying, tax avoidance, deaths in custody and defence lobbying. Unlike many editors, Hislop personally approves every page before it goes to print.

Hislop makes last-minute adjustments on screen with chief sub-editor Tristan Davies

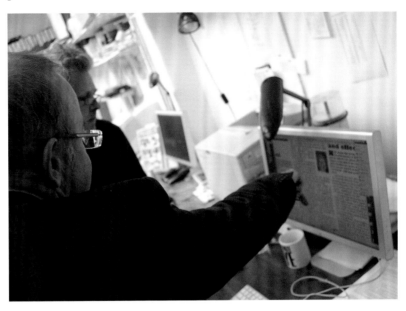

1.05pm "Do we not have a cover yet?" someone inquires. Fantoni and Ingrams have left the building, but Hislop has headed back upstairs for a further session with Newman, who is standing in the middle of the room rocking gently backwards and forwards as he rattles out possible gags. "The problem is, we've used our best Pope joke," confesses Hislop, remembering an issue from April 2010 in which a Vatican crowd pointed out that "In the old days boys wanted to enter the priesthood, rather than the other way round."

1.25pm "Let's try that for a cover." Hislop hands over two photographs of Benedict XVI, each neatly paperclipped to a pink sheet of paper with a hand-drawn speech bubble on it. "And try that one as well – it's very silly, but it might be funny." Rushton leaps into action, sketching out a colour palette for the cover in felt tip – papal purple and cardinal red.

1.30pm Hislop spots a photo of Andy Coulson on one of the computer screens which is not what he wants. "You need the full pic of him with his hands on the desk – have you got that one? And if Ruth could sepia him out so it looks like it's Nuremberg." A tinted

The three vital ingredients that make up a cover

Coulson appears, on trial as senior commandant of the Nasty Party, just minutes later.

Nick Newman has settled at his drawing desk to work on his strip "Snipcock and Tweed".

Occasionally he will screw up something that hasn't worked and throw it at the bin. More often than not they seem to land in Sally Farrimond's nearby handbag. "I could put them all on Ebay," she points out.

2pm Newman has another idea for the cover photo of the Pope with Tony Blair – "something about having a dodgy military past" – and dictates two alternative versions directly on to Bridget Tisdall's screen.

Robin Shaw, the lawyer who reads every issue of the *Eye* before it goes to press to identify libel risks, emerges from the windowless cubbyhole where he spends each press day and lopes into the studio to collect another armful of copy from the sub-editors.

2.30pm Tempers are beginning to fray in the production studio. The team tend to treat Rushton a bit like cheeky schoolchildren do supply teachers. "I will do it with a pencil and paper if it's so difficult," he snaps as the women debate the best way to mock up a masthead for the "Daily Mailograph" on their computers.

Michael Gillard – aka Slicker – files his "In the City" column. He has always filed on press day – "due to his dilatory ways", says Ingrams, who recruited him forty-two years ago – and its arrival generally elicits groans from the already word-blind sub-editors and proof-reader.

2.40pm Hislop drops another idea for the cover on to Tisdall's desk. This one has His Holiness saying to Tony Blair, "I hear you're infallible."

Hislop then stands in the middle of the studio working his way through a great pile of stories printed out on paper, annotating and editing them in biro as he goes. About half are passed to the slightly fraught but ever-capable sub-editors. The other half are dumped straight into the bin.

2.50pm After consultation with Hislop, Newman requests that Tisdall mock up yet another cover, showing the Pope with the Archbishop of Canterbury. "What's the bubble?" she asks. "I don't know yet," admits Newman. Then, on the hoof, "'What about the paedophile priests?' and the Pope saying 'I didn't expect the Spanish Inquisition.'"

The options for the cover, lined up on designer Bridget Tisdall's screen

3pm Hislop is shuffling pieces of paper around on the layout table, a look of intense concentration on his face. Things are moving amazingly fast now: a *Top Gear* joke, "Those Stigs in Full", went from scribbles on paper to fully laid-out and illustrated item within half an hour. Newman has finished the "Snipcock and Tweed" strip and moved on to his topical spot cartoons which will be scattered through the news pages.

3.20pm Sheila Molnar, the *Eye*'s managing director (aka chief boxwallah) arrives from her office to look at the possible covers and laugh encouragingly. Does the Pope sell well? "He can't do worse than David Cameron," she mutters darkly. That said, Cameron was present on the best-selling cover of the previous year, which sold a stonking 227,127 copies.

"It must be SUCH fun working at the *Eye!*": How Michael Heath saw the office, with Sheila Molnar hard at work, in 1983

3.40pm Hislop has just remembered he used the "Apparently you're infallible" joke in 2009. That cover is scrapped. He and Newman stand surveying the five remaining jokes on Tisdall's screen like grim-faced doctors trying to diagnose a terminal condition from a selection of X-rays.

4pm A picture of Nick Clegg with some children is needed to illustrate the "New Coalition Academy" page. Luckily, the staff have been collecting such photos since the latest prime ministerial parody began. "They're in a red file," announces Hislop. Four staff are dispatched to look for it. Maisie Glazebrook finally finds it. It is blue.

4.10pm Upstairs, Francis Wheen is worried. "It's quiet. Too quiet. Is the lawyer even here? I haven't heard a peep out of him."

4.15pm Hislop is back on the layout table, shuffling bits of paper around and occasionally consulting Rushton about which pages are spreads and which are turns. He removes one rectangle of paper out of the mass. "This I don't entirely believe, about shagging the Queen Mother," he announces.

5.30pm Back to the covers. Two – Newman's ideas about not mentioning the war – bite the dust immediately. The Archbishop never really made it off the ground. Hislop adds the caption "Top Catholic Visits Britain" to the one featuring Blair with the Pontiff. It is one of only two left in the running now.

"Stupid or satirical?" ponders the editor. He plumps for satirical, with the silly joke running inside instead.

5.45pm There are just two pages left on the layout table. Hislop and Davies run through the selection of stories for the news section at the front. "We used to care about that," comments the editor, shifting paper about. "*That* might be interesting for five seconds, but we're not that bothered about it … Can I get a rewrite on that one?"

Several stories have joined the Queen Mother one on the "hold" pile and may make it in next fortnight. Several are about PFI (Private Finance Initiative) deals, like a number which have made it in. "There's nothing wrong with the quality of any of it," says Hislop, "but sometimes the amount of financial stuff is just too much – you need a break from it."

The cover is narrowed down to two options

5.50pm Mackenzie, now proof-reading the jokes pages, spots that Ann Widdecombe has been described as "Mrs". Neither she, nor the readers, would let the *Eye* get away with this, and she is swiftly amended to a "Miss". This kicks off a lengthy discussion between Hislop and Newman about how the hierarchy of under-matrons, or "hags", were addressed at their school, which rather undermines the point I was trying to make earlier about the place not being dominated by public schoolboys any more.

6.25pm Against all odds, it looks like the magazine is going to meet the printers' deadline – press days have been known to drag on much later, but Sheila Molnar tends to get jittery even thinking about this. "Anything later than this means we will be late on sale – up to a day late in some places and this has a significant impact on sales. The print run is now a stupendous 280,000-plus, and we need to get 110,000 subscription copies printed, delivered, bagged and sent to the central postal collection by 11am on Tuesday morning – 1pm at the latest or else next day delivery is not guaranteed. So at 6.30 on a Tuesday morning I wait for the phone call to tell me all is well."

The very last story to be approved concerns the recently deceased Cyril Smith, former MP for Rochdale. As the *Eye* is reminding its readers, it revealed in 1979 that he was a keen sexual abuser of children in a local boys' hostel. Hislop gives this some final tweaks. "I just want to be sure that I've got the tone right," he reveals. "To make sure it's not 'Ha ha, we can say this now that he's dead,' but 'Look, we said this while he was alive, and its scandalous that no one followed it up.'" Does he expect outraged letters from readers? "I don't give a fuck about that," he says firmly.

Amendments duly made, Megan Trudell sends the final page through to the printers. The magazine will be in shops across the country within twenty-four hours. The first complaints about its contents will be on their way to the office within forty-eight.

The England Cricket Team
An Apology

IN COMMON with other papers, we last ~~month~~ published an apology for previous ~~assertions~~ that the English cricket team ~~was~~ the greatest team on earth and was ~~destined~~ to retain the Ashes.

We would now like to apologise for our ~~earlier~~ apology, based, as it was, on the dismal ~~performances~~ of what we described as ~~"England's~~ sorry squad of losers".

We now recognise that, far from being the ~~disgraceful~~ bunch of zeroes ever to leave ~~these shores,~~ England's cricketers are the finest ~~sportsmen~~ this country has ever produced

We are sorry for...

Defeated Australian skipper Ricky "Punter" Ponting

...they have ...feeble

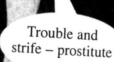

Trouble and strife – prostitute

PRIVATE EYE
~~AY~~ATOLLAH

Have you read the book?

Do you think I'm mad?

ANARCHIST RALLY

"GENTLEMEN, GENTLEMEN! DISORDER, PLEASE, DISORDER!"

~~T~~HIS YEAR'S MUST-HAVE CHRISTMAS TOY

~~W~~OUNDED-IN-~~A~~CTION ~~M~~an

Comes complete with:
- ✓ No hospital facilities
- ✓ No compensation
- ✓ No recognition

Price: Next to nothing.

"Nigel, I think we're going to have an abortion"

PRIVATE EYE
Presents
~~D~~OWNTURN ABBEY

"Excuse me, is this Alcoholics Hieronymous?"

A

dreaming spires

ADVICE to be followed by
Editors of *Private Eye*

Ian Hislop: "I remember Ingrams saying to me when I became editor, 'It is incumbent on you not to shag the secretaries or put your hand in the till. I took that to heart.'"[1]

AESOP REVISITED

"Aesop Revisited" was a feature of the very earliest *Private Eyes*, which took a fashionable figure such as John Osborne or Tony Hancock each fortnight and dissected him in the course of a full-page cartoon strip drawn by Willie Rushton. In their first book *Private Eye on London*, published in 1962, the team extended the treatment to themselves.
☞ MOSS, Stirling; OZ AND UZ; SHREWSBURY; WRITS, First of many

AITKEN, Jonathan, Lying liar

The *Eye* was one of a number of enemies lined up before Jonathan Aitken's "sword of truth and trusty shield of British fair play" in 1995. Seven years later – after the former cabinet minister had been in and out of prison for perjury – the magazine finally scraped back a fraction of its legal costs from his bankruptcy supervisor. And even then the cheque was unsigned, and therefore not worth the paper it was written on.

ANONYMITY, reasons for

Each edition of *Private Eye* until February 1967 carried a full staff list, which reveal such famous names as Peter Sellers, Keith Waterhouse, Bernard Levin and John Bird as one-time contributors. The last of the bylines disappeared not long after all pretence at a co-operative editorial board was dropped and Richard Ingrams was recognised as sole editor and public face of the magazine.

There are all sorts of reasons for this. The Randoph Churchill case (☞ WRITS, First of many), when libel writs were served on everyone "right down to the girls in the office", had demonstrated the potential dangers of having one's name attached to material you might not even have read, let alone written: Ingrams and Hislop alike have always been exemplary in absorbing legal fallout rather than allowing it to shower on junior staff.

The main reason, however, lies in the sort of material that the *Eye* was beginning to print. By mid-1966 they were receiving regular leaks from newspaper offices, the BBC, Scotland Yard and

Bank of Ireland ⬡

BANK HOUSE HIGH ST HAMPTON WICK
KINGSTON UPON THAMES KT1 4DS

30-11-55

Pay *Prendrem ltd*

Date 25/1/02

Furteen thousand two hundred + ninety arl pounds + 70 Pence

£ 14291 —— 70·

For 24 hour banking call 08457 365 333
www.bank-of-ireland.co.uk

LOUISE BRITTAIN SUPERVISOR OF
J W P AITKEN

121201   Serial No.   Branch Code.   Account No.

⑆000012⑆ 30⑈1155⑉ 4228635011⑆ 10

"I've occasionally heard people complain that it's cowardice that people aren't prepared to put their names to stuff, but it means that although it's a disparate group of people there is a collective voice"
Francis Wheen

the inner circle around prime minister Harold Wilson. "The problem about the circulation of real information in our society is that people at all levels of it, especially the top, do not disclose even what they want to disclose. They are worried about their own position as the discloser," said *Eye* hack Paul Foot. "Only when they can be sure that they are safe does the information start to flow. It follows that, as far as the general flow of information goes, protecting the source of a story is more important than the story itself."

Forty-five years on it remains just as vital that some of them stay secret. Frequent contributors to the *Eye* include a number of BBC broadcasters, some well-known authors and a lot of journalists from the daily and Sunday papers, a smattering of them of the "own column with flattering picture byline" variety. I'm not about to tell you who any of them are. It is an article of faith for all journalists that sources remain secret ("We won't hand your precious material back to your head of department just because some jumped-up Master of the Rolls says we have to. If necessary we will lie, cheat and commit contempt of court to protect our precious moles," the *Eye* promised after the *Guardian* grassed up civil servant Sarah Tisdall in 1983). On the *Eye*, it applies to a significant proportion of the writers as well.

Many of the higher-profile regular contributors have acquired their own pseudonyms over the years – Urquhart, Quintus Slide, Remote Controller, Gavel Basher and the like. "Those are people to whom I can offer a soubriquet," explains Hislop, "in place of paying them properly! It's identifiably 'This is you' – you're not being submerged in the mass of others." Others just sink into the morass with the rest of us.

This bothers some hacks. "I would like a byline now. If everything I wrote had my name on it I feel I would be like a *god*," chuckles Solomon Hughes, who has been contributing to the "In the Back" pages for sixteen years while trying to convince commissioning editors on other papers that he really exists. Others

welcome the anonymity. "There's too much 'LOOK WHAT I DID!' going on in journalism," says Jane Mackenzie. "I like the absence of all that ego-driven 'exclusive!!!' and showing-your-workings, 'we did this' journalism. It's just 'Here are some facts we found out.' I'd prefer to see fewer bylines anywhere else than have one myself."

"I've occasionally heard people complain that it's cowardice that people aren't prepared to put their names to stuff, but it means that although it's a disparate group of people there is a collective voice," says Francis Wheen, probably the best-known name on the current team of office-based hacks. "One of the strengths I think is that there is a discernible *Eye* tone of voice, with the slang and the catchphrases and the stylistic tics and things. So in a sense it means that the thing can carry on regardless of who happens to be writing for it at any one time. Some of the happiest times I've had have been writing pseudonymously."

Speaking for myself, I have occasional moments of being bothered that, of the hundreds of thousands of words of journalism I have churned out since arriving at the *Eye* on work experience in 1997, very few of them turn up on a cuttings search of my byline. But then I reflect on all the cross phonecalls and punches I have avoided as a result, the freedom it gives me in the telling, and the way that I can just smile modestly when people mention how much they enjoyed something by one of my colleagues. And if that makes me a bad person, then hey, that last sentence wasn't one of mine. I think one of the jokes team probably wrote it.
☞ CUNTS, stupid bloody irresponsible; MURDOCH, Campbell

ANYONE FOR DENIS?
Like "Mrs Wilson's Diary" before it (☞ LORD CHAMBERLAIN), "Dear Bill" (☞) ended up on the stage too. But there was an important difference – whereas Richard Ingrams and John Wells co-operated on the former, Ingrams declined to be involved in the latter, on the pre-emptive grounds that it would be "piss-poor".

"I still don't understand his reasons," says Ian Hislop, who, unlike Ingrams himself, went along to the Whitehall Theatre in 1981 to watch

Angela Thorne as
Margaret Thatcher
and John Wells as
a "scratching and
farting" Denis

Angela Thorne as Margaret Thatcher and Wells himself as Denis. "I said to him then, 'If you'd done it with him, it wouldn't have been piss-poor.' And it wasn't piss-poor. It was just too broad, too farcical." Deprived of the elements that Ingrams brought to the "Dear Bill" table – plot and politics – *Anyone for Denis?* overdosed on Wells's specialities, caricature and farce. "His portrayal of Thatcher, which was very funny, was just too wide," says Hislop. "Too much scratching and farting. I don't say it just because it was Richard, but it would have been better if he had done it." Barry Fantoni, who loyally didn't go and see the play either, remembers "a

The Thatchers arrive at the Whitehall Theatre for an "embarrassing, teeth-gritting" evening

falling out to some extent". Wells was quite clear about the causes: "Richard does not like his friends writing plays and he does not want them to succeed. It's all a question of what he sees as disloyalty to *Private Eye* … I would like to think that he was my best friend, but his shyness and his pride do make him extremely difficult."[2] The situation was not helped when *Anyone for Denis?* turned out to be an enormous hit and boosted the extra-curricular fame of John Wells no end. "Wells very kindly insisted that I should take a cut in his play and I said I didn't want any," sniffed Ingrams to his biographer.[3]

If relations were strained at the *Eye* office, it was nothing compared to the atmosphere in Downing Street after spin doctor Tim Bell decided that the Thatchers should attend a performance of the play in order to promote the entirely erroneous impression that Margaret was "a good sport". Bell, who to be fair was bongoed on cocaine for much of the early 1980s, admitted many years later that "It was a serious error. Denis was horrified by the whole thing. He was disinclined to forgive me at first."[4]

The producers made sure the prime minister and her husband were surrounded in their stalls seats by people who had a financial interest in the production's success, and could be guaranteed to laugh loudly and embarrass the first couple into doing the same. Press secretary Bernard Ingham sat next to Margaret. "It was one of the most embarrassing, teeth-gritting things I ever had to do," he admitted. "My mother

loathed it," recalled Carol Thatcher. "She was acutely offended. It was, not surprisingly, highly offensive to Denis, particularly one scene where he was portrayed as a man unable to tell a urine sample from a glass of whisky."[5]

The prime minister did managed to tell the television cameras waiting outside that it was a "marvellous farce", but the entire nation could see her gritted teeth. Worse, she had agreed to host a reception for the cast and crew at Downing Street afterwards. Denis at least managed to play up to his character at this, keeping everyone's glasses topped up and talking about "fuzzy-wuzzies going on the rampage in Brixton" and "closet pinkoes at the BBC". "It confirmed everything," declared a delighted Wells.

Denis proved a nice little earner for Wells, who went on to reprise the role in a televised version of the play, the James Bond film *For Your Eyes Only*, an Alistair Beaton farce, a Maureen Lipman series and a topical panto on ITV. Filming for the last clashed with Ingrams's retirement lunch in 1986, and meant Wells could not attend. You can imagine how well that went down.

APOLOGIES, real meaning of

"The apologies are drafted by counsel. They are not necessarily what we believe. The fact that they are published in our magazine does not mean that is what we believe." So said *Eye* hack Christopher Silvester in the witness box at the High Court during the case of Maxwell v. Pressdram in 1986 (☞ MAXWELL, ROBERT, full list of complaints against *Private Eye*). That wouldn't surprise anyone who has ever worked in journalism, but it drew gasps from Mr Justice Simon Brown and the assembled lawyers who spent so much of their well-remunerated time negotiating such fictions. (The judge should maybe have got out a bit more, since he also seemed shocked by the idea that the *Eye* might have a mole in Robert Maxwell's employ.)

It was clearly not the done thing to admit in court. So of course, when he followed Silvester into the witness box the next day, Richard Ingrams cheerfully did just that. "There could be circumstances where one was forced – through lack of evidence or some such – to print such a statement, but it would not necessarily follow from that that I believed that article to be untrue," he cheerfully confirmed. "It is quite conceivable that *Private Eye* would say 'We unreservedly withdraw this story' and for me, personally, as editor, to believe, or even to know, that the story was true."

With this statement – which the unimpressed judge referred to in his summing-up as "highhandedly putting question marks over a number of other libel victims who thought that they had been entirely vindicated" – Ingrams demonstrated the tightrope the *Eye* had been walking for years under his editorship. As he pointed out himself, "Any paper depends for its survival on the confidence of its readers, and if it printed lies week after week, and if the word got around, no one would buy it." The *Eye*, though, kept settling, kept apologising, and yet its readers continued to believe in its essential honesty, presumably on the no-smoke-without-fire principle. "I think *Private Eye* made people grow up about the media in that readers realised that having to apologise or correct something didn't mean you'd got it wrong, it just meant that powerful people weren't prepared to have their affairs written about and they would absolutely clobber you at every turn," says Peter McKay, a hack of that era.

Ian Hislop does not share this glass-half-full viewpoint. "The thing I still hate most is being wrong," he says. "I can't brush it over. I think the whole tone of the *Eye* demands that you're a bit better than the people you write about." He's managed to reduce massively the number of apologies the *Eye* prints. Partly that's because the changes in the law make the odds in the libel lottery less attractive for the potential writ-slinger, but it's also largely down to the fact that Hislop has employed journalists who were a bit more conscientious about checking their facts. "I was never in any doubt that that was what I needed fairly quickly," he says. "I got Francis Wheen, and you could give him stories that were difficult or controversial or tough without him thinking 'Ooh, well, I can't really make the phonecall.' It was a huge relief to me because it meant I didn't have to worry about the authority of everything all the time."

He is still assailed by such worries on occasion. "When you get a letter in, and it says 'Grr, this story was wrong,' Ian has a little bit of a tendency to immediately ask you to explain why you got it wrong, rather than why the letter

"I think Private Eye *made people grow up about the media in that readers realised that having to apologise or correct something didn't mean you'd got it wrong, it just meant that powerful people weren't prepared to have their affairs written about and they would absolutely clobber you at every turn"* Peter McKay

writer is wrong," says Jane Mackenzie. "And you have to remind him that people writing in from outside are not necessarily unbiased. But once you have convinced him, he will go all guns to say 'No, the magazine was right.'"

Overall, he gets the balance correct. "Ian has brought a curious concept to the *Eye*, which didn't prevail prior to his era, which is that the stories should be true," confirms Tim Minogue, who joined in the 1990s. "There's nothing that upsets Ian more than if he has to put a retraction in because one of us has fucked up because we haven't checked something out properly. And great! You have no authority to write about things the way we write about things – in an aggressive, scathing sort of way – if what we're writing is bollocks."

APPALLING, it really is

Catchphrase of Charles, Prince of Wales, a far-fetched comedy character created by the *Eye*. Close friend of Dr Barkworth (☞).

APPARENTLY

☞ STRIPS, longest-running

ARCHER, Jeffrey, *Eye* doesn't get prostitute story (or subsequent libel case)

When Aziz Kurtha, a client of prostitute Monica Coghlan, spotted the vice-chairman of the Conservative party also apparently availing himself of her services in September 1986, the first publication he contacted about the story was *Private Eye*.

"I remember that extremely clearly," says

Ian Hislop, who had yet to take over as editor. "Kurtha came in with [*Eye* hack] Paul Halloran, who was a friend of his. And Richard just wouldn't put the story in."

He was right to be cautious. Halloran passed Kurtha on to a friend at the *News of the World* who, recognising the weakness of their evidence, set up an elaborate sting operation involving taped phonecalls and clandestine meetings at Victoria station before they would consider writing a word about it. Even after all that, the best they could print was that Archer had asked a friend to pay Coghlan £2,000 to leave the country. It was the *Daily Star* that rushed into print with the follow-up claim that they had had sex – and was hit with a £1.2 million bill for libel damages and costs as a result – double the Sonia Sutcliffe damages that so nearly put the *Eye* out of business two years later (☞ BANANA, I'm a).

During the 1987 libel trial a sceptical *Eye* questioned Archer's alibi for the night in question and gleefully documented the attempts by the *News of the World* to speak to his former PA Andrina Colquhoun (whom they had named as his mistress way back in 1982). It would be another twelve years before it would officially emerge that he'd lied about the alibi and been having a long-term affair with the PA, and thirteen before he'd be sent to prison for perjury, making good on the *Eye*'s prediction at the time of the Anglia share scandal (when he purchased 50,000 shares in the TV company directly before a takeover bid and maintained that his wife's position on the board was entirely coincidental) that "Sooner or later for sure, Archer is going to blow himself up again, perhaps for good."
☞ YOUNG PRODIGIES

ARDINGLY

Ardingly College – it's pronounced Arding-LIE, just so that they can laugh at oiks who get it wrong – recently celebrated its Sesquicentenary, and if you know what that means, you probably went there, or somewhere like it.

"People ask 'Why do people like you go on about St Cake's? (☞)' Because I was *at* St Cake's," protests Ian Hislop, pointing out a seventeen-year-old version of himself on a school photograph from the 1970s.

He arrived at Ardingly at the age of eight, and boarded there right through to his A-levels as his parents roamed around the world following his father David's contracts as a civil engineer. It was here that he met Nick Newman, who has been his partner in comedy ever since. They were both in a production of *The Massacre of Peterloo* directed by the English master, who was so upset by the first-night audience's failure to take his "earnest, leftie" production seriously that he stormed on stage and harangued them as "arrogant public school bastards". At the party afterwards, Newman asked Ian if he would like to help write and perform in the school revue. He was a couple of years older. "Ian was always very precocious in that way," says Newman. "There weren't that many people around who could do jokes. It was all sub-*Python*. We thought we were so hysterically funny – we weren't."[6]

Some of their material was satirical, or at least as close to satire as teenage boys get. There was a sketch about the bursar stealing all the school's money, which they got away with because the headmaster liked the joke more than he liked the bursar. "We were endlessly trying to do things to upset the applecart," chortles Nick. He managed this quite spectacularly when he wired up the school chapel's PA system to play heavy metal during a service. He was asked to leave that very afternoon. He also succeeded in spectacularly spoiling one of his friend's gags: "Ian and his friends were taking the chapel service and he did it as an Alan Bennett vicar thing. I thought, 'They're going to get into trouble for this, because it's quite funny' – and then in came this burst of music! I suppose it kind of deflected attention away from what they were doing."

Hislop was, if nothing else, note-perfect on his Bennett impersonation. One of his most precious possessions was an LP of *Beyond the Fringe*, the legendary revue in which Bennett had starred with Peter Cook, Dudley Moore and Jonathan Miller, which he had purloined from his parents' record collection. "If ever I decided comedy was what I was interested in, it was then. Eventually working with Cookie was bizarre, he having been a hero of mine since the age of seven." One thing he knew nothing about, however, having spent his formative years in Nigeria, Kuwait and Singapore, was Peter Cook's other project, *Private Eye*. "I think I probably introduced him

A young Ian Hislop in a school revue: Nick Newman is on his left, pointing

Hislop with a surprising amount of hair. "I was told to cut it when this photo appeared!"

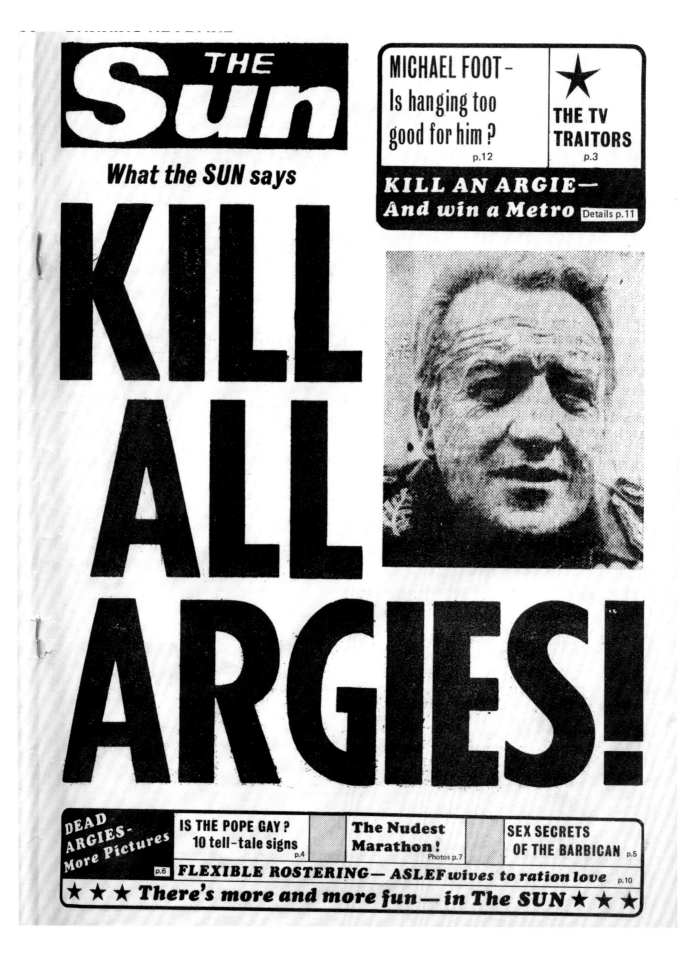

THE Sun

What the SUN says

KILL ALL ARGIES!

MICHAEL FOOT –
Is hanging too
good for him?
p.12

★
THE TV
TRAITORS
p.3

**KILL AN ARGIE—
And win a Metro** Details p.11

to it," says Newman. "I bought the mag from an early age – about fourteen, I suppose. I didn't get any of the stories. But I got the covers, and I loved the cartoons more than anything."

So much did Newman love them that he attempted his own homage: a magazine called *Passing Wind* (☞) which he set up with his friend Simon Park, and took with him to Oxford when he left school. Two years later, Ian Hislop followed him. "Part of the reason I wanted to go was because Nick was there."

Besides, all the other options looked grim. Before leaving Ardingly Hislop had taken the aptitude test in the school careers office. It informed him he was perfectly suited to being a quantity surveyor.
☞ SHREWSBURY

ARGIE, Kill an, and win a Metro

In May 1982, as British forces stormed ashore to retake the Falkland Islands from the Argentinians and with the country still reeling from both the sinking of the *General Belgrano* and its biggest-selling newspaper's reaction to the event – "GOTCHA" – the *Eye* drew up its own *Sun* front page.

Peter Chippindale and Chris Horrie take up the story in their history of the *Sun* under editor Kelvin MacKenzie, *Stick It Up Your Punter*: "When MacKenzie saw it pinned up on the office wall he was lost in admiration. 'Fucking brilliant!' he smiled rapturously. 'Why couldn't we have thought of that, eh?' The hacks found out later that there had been a different reaction to the *Private Eye* spoof on HMS *Invincible*. Many of the sailors on the ship genuinely believed that the page was part of a genuine copy of the *Sun*."[7]

ARKELL v. Pressdram

In April 1971, the *Eye* carried the story of how James Arkell, a retail credit manager, had dispensed with the services of two bailiffs who were on bail on charges of conspiracy to create a public mischief – despite the fact that he had for the previous year been in receipt of a monthly kickback of £20 from their company, Tracing Services Ltd, for putting debt-collecting work their way.

It was not an especially spectacular story, but the subsequent letter from Mr Arkell's solicitors Goodman Derrick (☞ GOODMAN, Lord) and the *Eye*'s response set an important legal precedent which is still often cited as Arkell v. Pressdram (see letters below)

The oft-cited punchline is that Mr Arkell was never heard from again, but in fact a libel writ arrived by return of post, complete with a "curt note" from Goodman Derrick. A year later came the news that Mr Arkell had resigned

Dear Sir,

We act for Mr Arkell who is Retail Credit Manager of Granada TV Rental Ltd. His attention has been drawn to an article appearing in the issue of Private Eye dated 9th April 1971 on page 4. The statements made about Mr Arkell are entirely untrue and clearly highly defamatory. We are therefore instructed to require from you immediately your proposals for dealing with the matter.

Mr Arkell's first concern is that there should be a full retraction at the earliest possible date in Private Eye and he will also want his costs paid. His attitude to damages will be governed by the nature of your reply.

Yours etc.

This letter has now been replied to as follows:

Dear Sirs,

We acknowledge your letter of 29th April referring to Mr. J. Arkell

We note that Mr Arkell's attitude to damages will be governed by the nature of our reply and would therefore be grateful if you could inform us what his attitude to damages would be, were he to learn that the nature of our reply is as follows: fuck off.

Yours etc.

Readers will be kept abreast of any further developments.

from his job with Granada and gone back to "his former business of debt collecting". In August 1972 Goodman Derrick offered to drop the case and pay the *Eye*'s costs in return for an agreed statement – only for their humiliated client to refuse any wording that involved his name appearing again in the magazine. The case fell apart and the action was dismissed "with costs to be taxed and paid to the Defendants by the Plaintiffs". "In view of the above," noted the *Eye*, "Mr Arkell has now, albeit belatedly, complied with the suggestion made to him at an earlier stage in the proceedings."

History repeated itself the following January, when the *Eye* received a letter from Withers solicitors on behalf of an eminent merchant banker: "We act for Sir Kenneth Keith who has seen the article on page 3 of issue no. 262 ... On this occasion Sir Kenneth proposes to treat this article with the contempt it deserves, but should there be any further publication of anything defamatory of Sir Kenneth, he will be forced to take legal action."

The *Eye* published its response directly beneath: "Sir Kenneth Keith is a pompous idiot." Wisely, he fucked off.

BALLSOFF memorandum

In 1971 Nora Beloff was the political correspondent of the *Observer* and a respectable spinster. She was also a fan of the home secretary, Reginald Maudling, and was not pleased by the *Eye*'s insistence on continually reiterating the fact that he was corrupt (☞ POULSON, scandal brings down home secretary). She proposed to her editor that she should write a "study of Maudling putting the evidence accumulated by the *Private Eye* people into the wider context of his political personality and morality". Unfortunately her memo was promptly leaked to the *Eye*.

It was too much for the magazine's then political correspondent to resist. Auberon Waugh penned an accompanying fantasy describing "delicious 78-year-old Nora Ballsoff, frequently to be seen in bed with Mr Harold Wilson and senior members of the previous administration, although it is thought that nothing improper occurred". Just in case anyone failed to clock that this was not meant to be taken seriously, he also described her as the "sister of the late Alec Douglas-Home", who was neither dead nor related.

Beloff didn't see the joke. She sued, not once but twice – firstly for the supposed libel in Waugh's column, and secondly over the reproduced memo. Since the latter was self-evidently true, she was forced to claim breach of copyright rather than libel, and demand exemplary damages. Since she didn't actually own the copyright of the memo herself, she had to persuade the *Observer* to sign it over to her.

The weakness of that particular case was obvious, and it was laughed out of court – literally, when the judge guffawed at the nickname "Ballsoff". The *Eye* was able to argue – with the help of witnesses from the *Observer* itself – that the disclosure of leaked documents was not just the right but the duty of a free press. The *Eye* won, with costs of £10,000 awarded against Miss Beloff. She signed those over to the *Observer* in return.

The *Eye* was not so lucky with the libel case. Beloff was awarded £3,000 damages and £2,000 costs. But it was a pyrrhic victory. Although the magazine admitted it was perfectly capable of raising the money "from our own coffers", it immediately launched "a special fund to be called the Ballsoff Fund so that readers may have a chance to help *Private Eye* pay the money and register a public protest against the litigation". For months every edition of the *Eye* featured a photograph of Beloff next to the very unflattering nickname and the names of dozens of people registering their dislike for her. Potential suers were forced thereafter to consider if ongoing humiliation was a price worth paying.

☞ EVANS, Dame Harold, attitude to press freedom; OFFENSIVE, most, items published in *Private Eye*

BANANA, I'm A

In 1987 the *Eye* was hit with record damages after Sonia Sutcliffe, whose husband Peter had murdered thirteen women and become known as the Yorkshire Ripper, sued for libel. "We were just in shock," remembers Sheila Molnar, then the company accountant. "We had to go back to the office and go through the books and check that we weren't actually trading insolvently, it was that bad."

Ian Hislop famously announced, "If that is justice, I'm a banana." The numbers involved

Previously unpublished cartoon presented to the editor by Ken Pyne

demonstrate just how extraordinary the award was.

NUMBER CRUNCHING

£250,000 = deal *Private Eye* claimed Sonia Sutcliffe had made with *Daily Mail* to sell them her exclusive story

£25,000 = cash she actually received from *Mail on Sunday* for her exclusive story, despite swearing on oath that 'I was not willing to sell my story to a newspaper at all.'

NUMBER CRUNCHING

6 = years in which Sonia Sutcliffe did not complain about or demand correction to *Eye*'s story of January 1981

£600,000 = damages a libel jury awarded her for it

£60,000 = damages this was reduced to at appeal, which meant *Eye* did not go out of business

NUMBER CRUNCHING

£7,000 = average compensation offered to surviving victims of Peter Sutcliffe's hammer and knife attacks

£600,000 = compensation jury felt his wife deserved for being victim of libel in *Private Eye*

NUMBER CRUNCHING

£102,000 = cash gathered from readers through *Private Eye*'s Bananaballs fund
100% = proportion of that cash distributed to the 7 surviving victims and families of the 13 women killed by the Yorkshire Ripper

---

☞ CONTEMPT OF COURT; COOK, Peter, role in later years

BARKWORTH, Dr

Somerset-dwelling expert on architecture, Jungian psychology and the undeniable flatness of the earth who makes regular appearances in the jokes pages of the *Eye*. Is entirely unrelated to Christopher Booker (☞).

BERNARD, Jeffrey

☞ MAD, Colonel

BETJEMAN, John

☞ JOBS, unlikely subsequent ones of *Eye* contributors; NOOKS AND CORNERS of the New Barbarism

BIRDSALL, Timothy

☞ Overleaf

BLAKE, Quentin

Quentin Blake, best known for illustrating Roald Dahl's children's books, provided logos for several of the new columns introduced by the *Eye*'s new editor – "Eye TV", "O.B.N" and "Music and Musicians". "I must have asked him to do some little drawings," reminisces Hislop. "It's a bit of a nerve! I think I'd assume he's too expensive now."

BIRDSALL,
Timothy

Timothy Birdsall, an old Cambridge friend of Christopher Booker's, started cartooning for *Private Eye* in 1962, and was soon providing vast and intricate double-page spreads for the magazine.

He died of leukaemia at the age of just 27, cutting tragically short what would almost certainly have been a long career on the magazine.

BIRTSPEAK
☞ DALEKS, invasion of BBC

BLIGHT, Rose

If the idea of the *Eye* carrying a gardening column seems unlikely in retrospect, the identity of the woman chosen to write it seems even odder, but from 1977 to 1979, under the nom de bloom Rose Blight, that is exactly what Germaine Greer did.

"I met her on the *News Quiz* (☞)," recalls Richard Ingrams. "We got quite pally. She was quite different from what I thought she would be like. She was very jokey, flirty, and she volunteered to do it." Barry Fantoni sums up the editorial arrangement succinctly: "She had a crush on him and he had a crush on her."

Blight took an unconventional approach to horticulture from the outset, urging readers to "pave the whole thing over and park the Cortina on it". But her column was short lived. Having declared war on her fellow feminist Erin Pizzey (☞ HAPPY SHIP, Not a), Ingrams decided it would be amusing to wind up Greer too, and began appending her column each week with the promise that it would, as of the next issue, change from "The Revolting Garden" to "The Nauseating Kitchen". Two months of such promises ("Next week: The Kitchen – a woman's best place") went by before Blight noted that "this is supposed to have become a cookery column. Why I, a gardening writer, should be expected to turn into a cookery writer just like that I cannot imagine, unless it be because my olde worlde editor thinks that my being a woman is sufficient to justify such giddy versatility." She devoted her slot to gardening one final time – specifically, slagging off one Germaine Greer for her horticultural jottings in the *Sunday Telegraph* – and then departed the *Eye*'s pages, never to be seen again. "She picked a quarrel with me over that and stormed out in a huff," says Ingrams disingenuously. "But she was good."

BLIND, *Eye* for the

For most of the past two decades, the RNIB's National Talking Newspapers and Magazines service has been recording selected highlights from every issue of the *Eye* for subscribers to enjoy. "We have two volunteer readers on each one – maybe three for the Christmas edition," says George Beddow, who oversees each recording session in his *Listen with Mother* guise as "Uncle George". "They alternate on pieces, and it's very quick moving. We try to do all the voices and accents – they're all actors of the amateur-dramatics level, and some of them are very gifted indeed. We've got one very good impressionist, his Prince Charles is better than anyone I've ever heard. He was on television once with Barrymore." The readers just take a valiant stab at less well-known names too, and their Glenda Slagg and E. J. Thribb are unsurpassed.

Each edition – available in a number of formats, some complete with the Bonzo Dog Doo-Dah Band's "Cool Britannia" as a theme tune – is sent out every fortnight to more than 300 subscribers.

BLUNT, Anthony, extremely displeased to be outed as spy

Anthony Blunt was recruited as a Russian spy by Guy Burgess at Cambridge in the 1930s. During World War Two he worked for MI5. In 1945 he became surveyor of the king's pictures, an important post in the royal household. He was knighted in 1956. In 1964 he was outed as a Soviet agent, but MI5 granted him immunity from prosecution in return for a thorough debriefing. And this would have remained a secret, had *Private Eye* not spilled the beans in the autumn of 1979.

A new book about the Cambridge spy ring, *The Climate of Treason* by Andrew Boyle, was due to be published that October. Richard Ingrams got an advance copy courtesy of his friend Malcolm Muggeridge, and read with interest what Boyle had to say about the so-called "fourth man" (after Burgess and his fellow Soviet agents Donald Maclean and Kim Philby), whom he code-named "Maurice". Then Ingrams heard that someone else was trying to get hold of an advance copy – Sir Anthony Blunt. The implications were obvious, as was the libel risk. "Everybody in the office said, 'This is it, you're going to finish the *Eye*,'" remembered Sheila Molnar. "But he said 'No, it has the ring of truth.' He really had the courage of his convictions, and we ran with it."

The story of Blunt's lawyer's phonecall to the book's publishers appeared on 28 September 1979. Three issues later, the *Eye* went much further. "As far as Andrew Boyle and Fleet Street are concerned, the Blunt truth is that 'Maurice' = Sir Anthony Blunt."

It was, Blunt complained in the handwritten draft of an unpublished autobiography finally released by the British Library in 2009, "an appalling shock. I believed, naively, that the Security Service would see to it that the story would never become public ... The issue of *Private Eye* appeared on November 8th, the day that I was giving the Zaharoff lecture at Oxford, but fortunately copies did not reach the city till the next day. This did not prevent the press from harassing my unfortunate host, Professor Francis Haskell, when the news finally broke."

For once with an *Eye* story, official confirmation arrived swiftly. Margaret Thatcher announced in the Commons on 16 November that Blunt had indeed been a Russian spy, and confirmed that the Security Service had known for fifteen years. Minutes later, Buckingham Palace annulled his knighthood. Worst of all, dreadful little men from Fleet Street started asking Blunt impertinent questions, which he seems to have regarded as an infinitely worse offence than treason. "The press and 'media' – not unexpectedly – started a campaign of vilification," he huffed. "One of the interviewers put to me a number of questions about my private life which seemed to me totally irrelevant. When the interview was repeated on Television it was accompanied, I am given to understand (I did not myself see it) by the most unfriendly comments. The violence of the attacks on me in the press did not surprise me, but I was, I must admit, astonished by their cavalier attitude towards factual accuracy ... I do not say 'the gutter press' because that would imply that some parts of the press were not of the gutter."

In this case, it appears the *Eye* had got the tone of the bubble on their next cover precisely right.

☞ PRIVATE SPY

BOOKER, Christopher, Editorship of, 1961-63

"Originally I was editor," Booker assures me. "I've still got bits of writing paper with 'Editor: Christopher Booker, Art Editor: Willie Rushton'."

So what was his vision for the embryonic magazine? "My idea at that time was that *Private Eye* should stand for, its basic role was to question all the orthodoxies, all the conventional wisdoms, didn't matter whether they were left, right, smart or trendy," says Booker. At the time, he was, he admits, "very much part of the swinging London scene as it were". Here he is outlining his dream future to the BBC in 1962: "I'd like a really sort of modern house with glass walls and things on Lake Como in Italy, and an aeroplane to fly to and from London … One does see young writers who are very talented and are doing a fabulous job of work and never getting paid enough. But you also see

Booker: "Now, where did I leave that foundation stone?"

> *"Private Eye's basic role was to question all the orthodoxies, all the conventional wisdoms"* Christopher Booker

people who have made a reputation when young getting to the age of forty or fifty and doing very bad work, getting lousy articles in newspapers and getting enormous sums for them."[8] Booker now lives in a Georgian old rectory in Somerset, and has been writing a weekly column for the *Sunday Telegraph* since he was fifty-three.

No one, however, who has read his dispatches there and elsewhere on the "myths" of man-made global warming, passive smoking and Darwin's theory of natural selection could doubt that he has stuck true to what he claims were his guiding principles on the *Eye*: "The job was to be totally contrarian and to see the contradictions and absurdities of whatever's fashionable, whether it's high philosophy or low fashion."

He had specific models for the magazine, too: "If there's one thing more than anything else which turned me on to the idea of doing *Private Eye*, it was Peter Sellers's LP *Songs for Swinging Sellers*. Malcolm Muggeridge's *Punch* was a bit of an influence too, which was totally different to what *Punch* became later [Muggeridge left the magazine in 1957 after giving the management an overdose of precisely the iconoclastic views they had hired him to provide]. The other thing which influenced me, which is totally impossible to reconstruct now, was the impact of Bernard Levin in the *Spectator* writing a political column under the name of Taper. It was totally different to everything else in that rather deferential atmosphere of the early 1950s, when everyone was in their place, and suddenly here was a little Jewish boy from the East End writing this brilliant column with funny names and sending it all up."

The first three editions of *Private Eye* in the autumn of 1961 were pretty much entirely the work of Booker and Rushton. Then in February 1962 the theatre company Tomorrow's Audience (☞) collapsed, taking Richard Ingrams's inheritance and acting career with it, and he rejoined his old schoolfriends to see what they were up to: "*Private Eye* was my complete focus from then on." The staff list for issue 7 in March 1962 lists Ingrams and John Wells as "Twelfth Men". Issue 8 lists an "Editorial Board: Christopher Booker, William Rushton & Richard Ingrams". Booker reasserts his dominance in issue 9, slapping Rushton down to "Artist" and Ingrams to mere "Contributor", but by the summer of 1962 and issue 13 Ingrams has the slightly peculiar title of "Contributions

The triumvirate: Ingrams, Rushton and Booker pictured outside the High Court, 1963

Editor" beneath Booker's superlative "Editor". The staff list was finally dispensed with in early 1967, possibly to stop over-zealous historians reading too much into it in the future.

"When Richard came in on a more regular basis, it wasn't a structured hierarchy, and gradually it all loosened up so we were all in it together," says Booker. "But we were still not really doing it collaboratively." Part of the reason for that was that the other two members of the editorial team were finding their leader increasingly difficult to work with. "The trouble with working with Booker was that he couldn't complete things," says Ingrams. "He was a perfectionist. He would keep changing his mind. There were a lot of late evenings. There were rows."

"You've probably heard stories about how I behaved badly and shouted and threw telephones and things," sighs Booker. "I'm not saying I came out of it perfectly, but I did feel more of a commitment to the magazine in terms of getting it right. The thing that really pissed me off was I thought here we've got a serious magazine to write, and Willie and Richard when they were together were great ones for going off to the pub. And I'd say 'Look, we've got two pages to fill, no, you've got to stay. We need to rewrite that, it's terrible, we can't publish that.' So there were quite a lot of rifts."

"I just remember the feeling that you wanted to go home, and he'd still be at it," groans Ingrams. He claims it was Rushton, who of course is no longer around to answer for himself, who had the biggest problem with the triumvirate. "Willie was a very well-organised person. He was very methodical. Very professional about everything he did. And he couldn't work with Booker at all, because Booker was absolutely the opposite."

Booker's style of working impacted on the other staff, too. Co-founder Andrew Osmond remembered him being "an inspirational writer who was quite prepared to keep people waiting till four in the morning in order to drive his copy down to the printers".[9] Since this task usually fell to Mary Morgan, one of the secretaries who was by that point well on her way to becoming Mrs Ingrams, this didn't exactly endear the editor to Richard either.

There were moments of calm between the storms. Booker recalls "one Sunday afternoon in the summer of '62 when we went to Jimmy's, a Cypriot restaurant in Frith Street, and I said 'Richard, what are you thinking of doing with your life?' Because of the way he'd come into it and was sloping around, I didn't feel he was totally committed to the mag at that point. And he said 'The one thing I'd really like to be is the editor of a magazine.'"

Booker ruefully concludes: "Only a year later did I realise which magazine he had in mind."

☞ OZ AND UZ, founding fathers of *Private Eye*

BOOKER, Christopher, sacking of, 1963

"In '63 I made this disastrous marriage,[10] and I resolved that, since I hadn't had a holiday in a long time, I would go off at the end of June on a prolonged honeymoon to Scotland," remembers Booker. "I was meant to come back to London in September because *TW3* was starting again [☞ THAT WAS THE WEEK THAT spoiled everything]. I must have written a note to the lads saying 'I'll be back next week for the next issue.' And then I got this letter from Rushton. And it was very blunt. Basically it said we have talked about this and we don't want you to come back."

No copy of this letter exists any more. Rushton always said that, although he signed it, it was written by Ingrams – offering as proof the fact that it featured the word "obdurate", which he had never come across before. New recruit Barry Fantoni (☞) claims he signed it too – "I didn't actually know what it was, I thought it was a card, 'Happy Marriage Booker', I didn't know what a round robin was." Ingrams, as we have seen, is still trying to pass the blame on to Rushton, although it is noticeable that when questioned about this he is even more taciturn than usual, which is saying something. He pauses a full eighteen seconds before admitting that "I remember coming to the view that the magazine couldn't survive if Booker continued to be the editor, because we would quit. It couldn't go on."

"I could see that Richard was gradually getting more and more in control of the magazine only by default, because Booker was very seldom there," remembers Barry Fantoni. "Booker threw a typewriter out of the window at one point in a fit of rage! I don't think it hit anybody, but I distinctly remember it." Nonsense, says Booker: "I don't remember even a typewriter falling off a desk, although it may have done." "I don't remember it happening," agrees Richard, though he does concede "there were rows".

"To be fair, I think the truth is that deep down in Richard's very murky soul, he probably does feel quite guilty about what happened in '63," sighs Booker. "It was a big shock. I thought, not totally without justification, 'Hang on, this is my baby, and they've just hijacked it. And I don't think they're going to do it very well.' I was absolutely adamant that I didn't like what they'd done while I was away and I thought we needed to shake the thing up again. And I will say this absolutely without fear or favour, I thought the magazine that was produced for the next few months was *dire*. Circulation went down – it was 90,000 when I left, and it went down to 25,000 – and all I could say watching from afar with a certain amount of Schadenfreude was 'I told you so, and if it goes on like this, it doesn't deserve to stay on.'"

☞ TRIUMVIRATE, joke-writing group formed after return of Christopher Booker

Published by Pressdram Limited, at 22 Greek Street, London, W.1. Tel. GER. 4018/9/10. Subscriptions: 30/-d. per year, or for life £10.

EDITOR: Richard Ingrams.

ADMIN/PRODUCTIONS: Tony Rushton, David Cash, Sir Charles Harness, Gaby Hughes, Rita Shear, Patsy Anderson and Diana Clarke.

CONTRIBUTORS: William Rushton, Claud Cockburn, Peter Cook, Christopher Logue, Gerald Scarfe, Ralph Steadman, John Wells, Bill Tidy, Alan Brien.

Ingrams in dastardly mode: playing his part in controversial film *Masturbani's La Lustre* in issue 21, October 1962

***Right:* Staff list from a post-Booker world**

BORDES, Pamela, not in photograph with Andrew Neill

There is a photo – you've probably never seen it, it's quite obscure – which is not of Andrew Neill and the girlfriend he shared with *Observer* editor Donald Trelford, Pamella Bordes. The *Eye* has never claimed it is of Pamella Bordes (it's actually of a make-up artist going by the name of Sajata, who boasts on her personal website of being "very popular among New York's elite, the television industry and in Europe"[11]), although plenty of other people – including the ginger whinger himself – are convinced they have. "The one thing that they get completely wrong is the picture of me and 'Pamella Bordes'. Except it's not Miss Bordes," Neill told *Total Politics* magazine in 2010. "That was a picture of a woman from New York that I was going out with in 1995. She worked at Fox and she is an Afro-American. She's not Asian, she's not Indian, she's not British. The picture was taken as we came off the beach in Barbados by Terry O'Neill. It's been presented now as if a) it's Miss Bordes and b) that we were in some kind of nightclub and I'm there in this stupid shirt in a nightclub. It was a beach we'd come off hence the baseball cap and the beachwear. And this woman, this lovely, lovely ... I've not seen or heard from her for 15 years – she's no idea she's the most famous face in *Private Eye*. But it's not Miss Bordes. Anyone slightly looking at her would see these are the features of an Afro-Caribbean lady. But sometimes these public schoolboys are not very good."[12]

He sounds rather touchy for someone who has claimed to "rather like"[13] the repeated use of the photo, doesn't he? The *Eye* has never claimed it was taken in a nightclub either (although it has claimed it illustrated, among other activities, bungee jumping, a three-legged race, charity work by Help the Aged, a superglue accident, the separation of Siamese Twins and the work of the Society for the Protection of Old Jokes Long After They Have Ceased to Be Funny. It was actually taken – as the *Eye* made clear in a series of lengthy reports during 1996 – at a villa in Sandy Bay belonging to the TV producer Beryl Vertue, with a camera belonging to Terry O'Neill, although there was some dispute over whether it was taken by the snapper himself or by a fellow guest, newspaper editor Sir Nick Lloyd.

It would be gratuitous to print the photo in question here. So instead here is a picture of Andrew Neill with Pamella Bordes.

L-R: Pamella Bordes, Andrew Neill

BOURN, Sir John, resigns as auditor-general following *Eye* revelations

Sir John Bourn stepped down as head of the National Audit Office – the body charged with getting value for money for taxpayers – after six months' worth of articles in *Private Eye* pointing out the eye-watering amounts of taxpayers' cash he had himself spent on overseas trips (£365,000 in three years) and meals in expensive restaurants (£27,000 in the same period).

"He'd been there nineteen years, and he had built this empire, and one of the founding principles of his job was that there were no rules – he set his own rules, he was so independent from everybody that nobody could tell him what to do," says Richard Brooks, who winkled out the necessary information with the help of a series of Freedom of Information requests. Brooks had himself been entertained by Sir John, after the *Eye* brought some scandalous Whitehall spending on management consultants to the NAO's attention. "And all I got was a cup of tea and that was it! Just as well really. Imagine if I had taken a lunch …"

☞ TAXMAN

BOXWALLAHS

"We were all boxwallahs, which was a colonial word for Indian chaps who slaved away at figures and didn't actually run anything," says the *Eye*'s first business manager Peter Usborne, who still hasn't quite forgiven Richard Ingrams for saddling him with this nickname. "Richard was very actively anti-anything to do with numbers or business or anything like that. The general atmosphere was that all that business stuff is boring and pretty contemptible." Usborne got fed up after just a few years, departed the *Eye* for Fontainebleau Business School and has since proved his business acumen in a rather more receptive atmosphere by setting up Usborne Publishing and turning it into one of the most successful children's book publishers in the world. He retains 2,160 shares in Pressdram, and is "still the happy recipient of a few thousand quid of dividends every year and that, for me, is emotional. That says I Did It. And I love that."

"It's a terribly odd job," says Ian Hislop of the managing director's role currently filled by Sheila Molnar, who joined the *Eye* as an accountant in the 1970s and shares the mischief-making gene common to all long-term employees. "What

Far left: Peter Usborne, the *Eye*'s first business manager

Left: The appropriately-named Dave Cash, who oversaw the business for 26 years

Below: Early accounts book

Week Ending 15th November 1963   33

	Gross	N H I	Tax	Grand Pen	Nett	EMPLOYER. N H I.		
Brooke G	26 -	– 19 4	3 2 –	– 7 –	21 11 8	– 16 8		
Ingrams R	60	–	–	–	60 – –	–	4 e 18/-	3 12 –
Brown D	26 –	– 10	– – –	– 7 –	25 12 2	16 8	2 e 8/-.	17 6
Cash D	30 –	1 3 4	1 8 –	10 4	26 18 4	19 4	6 e 2/4	6 8 –
Rushton A	60 –	1 3 4	13 7 –	15 4	44 14 4	19 4		
Rushton W	60	–	–	–	60 – –	–		
Usborne P	60 –	1 3 4	13 7 –	15 4	44 14 4	19 4		
Wedderspoon J	26 –	– 19 4	3 2 –	– 7 –	21 11 8	16 8		
Fantoni B	30	–	–	–	30 – –	58 –		
	378 –	5 9 6	34 6 –	3 2 –	335 2 6	5 9 6		10 17 6
						10 17 6		

you have to do is be good enough at running a business to make it continue, but also accept that there are quite ridiculous decisions that are made about money that aren't your business. And you have to support them. And that's the brilliant thing about Sheila – you say 'There's this person you haven't heard of who had a case in Hong Kong and it's related to this man who's president of the Law Society and it'll probably wipe out a lot of the budget for the entire year, particularly if we lose [☞ INJUNCTION]. How's that then?' And she says 'Yes, absolutely, bastards, yeah, let's do it.' It's a bizarre job."

Hislop was equally fond of Dave Cash, who performed the role with aplomb for twenty-six years before Molnar (there was a chap called Chris Haslam for two years in between them, but he went off to work for Richard Desmond and was one of the *Express* executives who goose-stepped round an office singing "Deutschland über alles" on Desmond's orders, so we don't talk about him much). "Dave loved a legal fight. Even if it meant the figures were completely bonkers." Cash grins when asked if he ever tried to rein back the risk-taking. "No. That was just part of the make-up of *Private Eye*. If you start pruning it back too much, it loses its edge."
☞ RUSHTON, Tony sacking of (failed)

Below and right: Sheila Molnar as accounts assistant in the mid-1970s and, between colleagues Hilary Lowinger and Bridget Tisdall, as managing director in 2001

BREEZE, Hector

Hector Breeze started contributing to the *Eye* in 1963. His cartoons often feature a downtrodden everyman battling against the world – with tramps and monks a particular speciality.

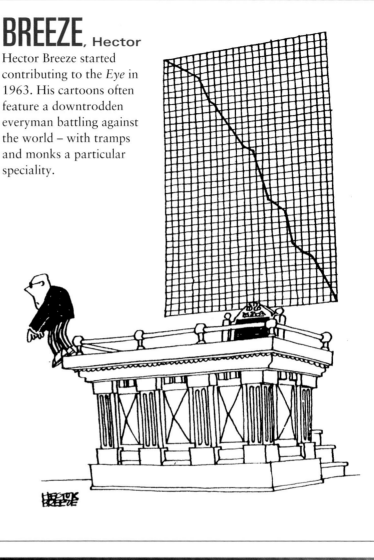

BRENDA and family

In July 1971 the "Grovel" column revealed that the Queen was "known as Brenda to her immediate staff". The *Eye* inserted itself uninvited into that intimate circle and has been calling the monarch by the nickname ever since.

Four years later "Grovel" added that "Margaret's new nickname in her circle is 'Yvonne' while Prince Charles is called 'Brian'." And in 1982 Princess Diana was welcomed into the family: "She is known as 'Cheryl' in royal circles."

BRISTOL heart scandal

Dr Phil Hammond – aka M.D. (☞) – claims in his two decades on the *Eye* to have "exposed enough medical scandals to make your head explode". The biggest, however, remains what became known as the Bristol Heart Scandal. When a public inquiry finally reported on the work of the paediatric cardiac surgery unit of the United Bristol Healthcare Trust in 2001 – a mere nine years after Hammond had first reported on

the problems there – it concluded that a third of the children who underwent open-heart surgery had received "less than adequate care", that the unit was "not up to task" and "not safe", and that between thirty and thirty-five babies had died unnecessarily.

"The NHS at that time was full of Bristols," admits Hammond. "Staff with inadequate resources and expertise getting bad results but struggling on regardless because there was no mechanism to help or stop them."[14] His role with the *Eye* is as a kind of whistleblower-in-chief. "He has a great network of people he knows through the system," says Hislop. "Every pissed-off doctor thinks 'Oh, I'll ring up Phil,' and so you get stuff early." Their efforts are rarely appreciated by the NHS. One of Hammond's sources on the Bristol story, anaesthetist Stephen Bolsin, admitted to the public inquiry that he passed on information to Hammond after attempting to raise his concerns about high death rates with the Trust's chief executive and the Department of Health. He paid with his job and is now practising – "very successfully" says Hammond – in Australia. Hammond himself is always aware of the effect his journalism can have on already over-stressed and dysfunctional medical teams. "I doubt my *Private Eye* articles helped teamwork or morale, not least because they spread mistrust: 'Which of you bastards has been speaking to the press?'"

It all kicked off with a story in May 1992, in which M.D. revealed that the paediatric cardiac surgery unit in Bristol was known as "The Killing Fields" because its mortality rates were so high. "Despite a long crisis of morale among intensive-care staff, the surgeons persistently refuse to publish their mortality rates in a manner comparable to other units. And although the chief executive and the Department of Health are well aware of the problems, they won't recognise them officially."

"It had a slightly sort of scary factor about it," admits Hislop, who had been employing Hammond as a columnist for only four months. "When someone knows they're right, and you think 'Oh, God, you'd better be.' But I always trusted Phil, I thought he was terrifically good. I thought it was genuine, felt it was a great story." Plus, as a local – Hammond is a GP in Bristol – he had a personal interest in the matter. "His kids could have been in there."

Almost immediately, nothing happened. "It followed that pattern of *Eye* stories where you have to keep on telling it and eventually it comes good," says Hislop. Hammond returned to the topic in July, October and November of that year, noting that the mortality rates were running at ten times those on a comparative unit in Birmingham and that James Wisheart, the associate director of cardiac surgery, had failed to notify the local Trust of the alarming results of an internal audit. When concerned *Eye* readers wrote to health secretary Virginia Bottomley asking her to investigate, she referred the matter to the very managers in Bristol who were busy covering things up. Internal letters which emerged years later showed that plenty of people knew the Bristol unit was not fit for purpose, but allowed it to carry on operating anyway for fear of creating a scandal. The retired surgeon tasked with overseeing such units by the Department of Health wrote to his old friend Wisheart to tell him that the *Eye* reports had merely caused him to "acquire an even deeper hatred of the behaviour of the press".

It was only in 1995 after the high-profile death of an eighteen-month-old boy during an

"I doubt my Private Eye *articles helped teamwork or morale, not least because they spread mistrust: 'which of you bastards has been speaking to the press?'"* Phil Hammond

operation which the unit had been instructed not to attempt that, in Hammond's words, "the shit hit the fan and the rest of the media finally cottoned on".

Hammond himself gave evidence to the public inquiry, which opened in 1999. Despite the fact that the General Medical Council had already admitted that there was a problem and had struck off Wisheart, one of his colleagues and the hospital's chief executive ("one of the biggest arse-covering operations in the history of medicine", according to Hammond), he was not about to be thanked. "I was vaguely threatened with a custodial sentence for not revealing my sources," he remembers. "I realised then that I should probably have brought a lawyer along." He was clear that the blame didn't lie with any of the individuals who had already been punished: "I said that the Bristol surgeons were fall-guys for a much wider problem in the NHS – a complete lack of accountability."

Does he think things have got better? Not much. "It finally forced the NHS to at least think about quality and safety, although this momentum was lost when they disappeared up the arse of Labour's competitive and secretive NHS market." He points out that the government ignored a 2003 review of child heart surgery which "recommended the concentration of scarce expertise and equipment in fewer centres … for fear of the political ramifications. Had they acted, the Oxford heart scandal of 2010 [when paediatric heart surgery at the Radcliffe Infirmary was suspended after it was revealed that death rates were about five times what would be expected] would never have happened."

There are, however, some encouraging signs. When Hammond wrote about allegations of errors in histopathology reporting at the Bristol Royal Infirmary in June 2009 – patients who didn't have cancer were told they did, and were treated for it, while ones who did were given the all-clear – an external inquiry into the matter was announced within seven days, as opposed to seven years. At time of writing, it is still ongoing.

BROWN, Craig

Craig Brown pictured in 2006

CRAIG BROWN
(the real one)

For the past twenty-two years I have been writing a fortnightly celebrity diary for *Private Eye*. This has been the fulfilment of all, or almost all, my ambitions.[15]

YOKO ONO
(as told to Craig Brown)

Peel an apricot. Place it between your toes. Put on a sock and walk to work. When you arrive, your foot will be very messy, but the sky will still be blue. Yoko Loves You.

IAN HISLOP
(the real one)

The great thing about Craig is he doesn't tend to do the big figures from the week's news – you want to read Craig doing Paul Johnson, or Simon Heffer, you don't necessarily want him on the main subject, as it were. Though he'd probably do it better than us. Which is why I won't let him.

SHIRLEY MACLAINE
(as told to Craig Brown)

I am sitting on a vehicle on Boulevard 909, travelling east on my way to the set of *Postcards from the Edge*, overachieving as usual. My vehicle runs over someone, not a star at all, but an ordinary person, probably a woman. I love my fellow human beings on the most profound level, so I take the trouble to place my head out of the vehicle window. Caringly, I look down to the place where the woman is lying under the wheel. Total strangers, yet connected for one short moment in time by a car.

CRAIG BROWN
(the real one)

Before I write a parody, I pedantically underline and then copy out four or five pages of my target's most telling phrases. I then take a deep breath and recopy them, with a tweak here and a tweak there, rather in the manner of a drunken court stenographer. Over the years, my parodies that have attracted most praise have been those that have most faithfully reproduced the original. On occasion, it has even proved necessary to tone down an original to make it less overtly ridiculous before it can pass muster as parody. Tony Benn's real-life diary entry for Sunday December 26 1976 reads: "Caroline gave each of us a copy of the *Communist Manifesto* in our stockings, published in English in Russia, and she gave Josh a book called *Marx for Beginners* and gave Hilary Isaac Deutscher's three-volume biography of Trotsky." This would have been far too unsubtle to publish as parody: one would have to think up something far less flat-footed than a stocking filled with the *Communist Mani-festo* before anyone would even half-believe it.[16]

MARTIN AMIS
(as told to Craig Brown)

The possibility that Iraq will soon have nuclear weapons could have chilling consequences for the world. It is up to writers who have the power to articulate the unimaginable to stress the urgency of the situation, to pick words of sufficient terror to show that nuclear weapons are the exploding turds of our age, that a nuke-turd is like a liquefied-biro in the top pocket of a beige suit, probably three-piece, that the aftermath of nuclear collar-hoist will be more serious than anything we have so far encountered, like a gob of snot-phlegm – phlot? snegm? – on a shiny kitchen surface, or an ear-glob in a plate of vichyssoise.

DAME BARBARA CARTLAND
(as told to Craig Brown)

Others may have found him tiresome, but Captain Hook was always frightfully sweet to me.

It was a moonlit night. A piano was gently tinkling somewhere far away.

"You are so very lovely, my dear," he said, "and I do so want to place my arm around you."

With that, he placed his right arm around my shoulder.

Alas, his prominent hook, never his strong point, caught the strap of my brassiere and then with a resounding snap unloosed my ballgown.

I stood naked on the dancefloor.

Among the assembled onlookers were the Governor of the Bank of England, Lord Beaverbrook, the Duke of Devonshire and the Admiral of the Fleet, all of them interesting people.

Before the tune had drawn to an end, all four of them had requested my hand in marriage.

CRAIG BROWN
(the real one)

"Have you ever seen a tot in tears, a poorly tot of three or four years of age – in tears?" asks my Max Clifford. "Well, I have. It cuts me up. It really does. And whenever I see a poorly tot with great big tears rolling down her tender little cheeks, I say to myself, 'Never will I allow a tot to suffer like this.' With that, I lift the phone, call a top editor and provide him with an exclusive scoop concerning an MP's three-in-a-bed kinky love-romp for 120k up front." Each of these phrases has been used by Max Clifford, although not necessarily in that order. I like the way in which my particular combination reduces his great undertow of self-righteousness to a nonsense. But has Clifford changed his tune since this piece first appeared? Not a bit. Vanity gorges on all publicity, good and bad. I wouldn't even be surprised if he had it pinned to his wall.[17]

NORMAN TEBBIT
(as told to Craig Brown)

I see a film about Oscar Wilde is playing at my local Odeon. Would it not be more worthwhile to honour a true British hero, such as Douglas Bader or Margaret Thatcher?

It's yet another example, I fear, of the limp-wristed brigade hosing us from the rooftops with their unsavoury message.

Sodomy. Not a nice word, is it? Sounds foreign to me.

And its meaning's not all that nice, either.

Let me put it in words of one syllable. It means two blokes removing their suits and ties and touching one another all over, even getting into bed together and going the whole hog – tongues, knees, fingers and heaven knows what else – before wriggling and rolling and yelping with pleasure, and begging and panting for more at the top of their voices.

That's not my cup of tea. Never has been, never will be.

JORDAN
(as told to Craig Brown)

David Starkey was talking about the Second World War.

"That's terrible news," I said, just to show I had brains as well as boobs. "No one even told me about the first." He proceeded to tell me about the Western Front and the Battle of the Bulge. I felt he oozed sex appeal and judging by the bulge on his western front David felt the same way about me.

Before I saw Dave again I had my boobs enlarged specially but as I took off my bra I told him no touching as they was still a bit sore.

But no way, he wouldn't play ball. I didn't see him for dust. I can never forgive him for running away on me like that. Yes, Dr David Starkey let me down badly. He had showed me his nasty side. I should have realised he was only after a quick shag with Jordan the glamour model, and he was never interested in getting to know Katie.

THE CHAPMAN BROTHERS
(as told to Craig Brown)

Jake Chapman: For the past seven years we have been trajectorising the downsize of the paradigm shift in our culture in a work in progress called–

Dinos Chapman: Fuckface. It's called Fuckface. It's basically like a kind of pubescent face with two penises where the eyes should be.

Jake: Essentially it represents and attempt to recuperate the issue back to the reclassication of its own symptoms vis-à-vis the recuperation of an attempt at representation.

THE CHAPMAN BROTHERS
(the real ones)

We felt compelled to respond to the Craig Brown diary piece 'Chapman Brothers'. We have to say it's the best interview we've ever not given – it really is very, very funny and frighteningly close . . .

Best

Jake and Dinos Chapman

December 2003

CRAIG BROWN
(the real one)

In the New Year edition of *Private Eye* in 2003 I wrote a parody of Roy Jenkins, who was then still very much alive. It was a rejigging of his new book *Twelve Cities*. In my version, he was writing about his favourite tube stations instead. After he had died at the beginning of January, Jenkins's family found a letter on his desk, addressed to me. They forwarded it. It is strange to open a letter from someone who is dead. In it, he says he found my parody "very funny, unwounding and even affectionate".

HAROLD PINTER
(as told to Craig Brown)

Who killed Cock Robin?
I, said the sparrow.
Because I'm a fucking Yankee imperialist
And I sodomise anything that moves.

CRAIG BROWN
(the real one)

Seven or eight years ago, I was at a large party consisting of perhaps a couple of hundred people. At one point I glanced across the sea of heads to the other side of the room, only to be confronted by the terrifying sight of Harold Pinter staring back at me, his face set in a gargoylish grimace, each thumb stuck to the side of his head while his fingers waggled about in the traditional schoolboy gesture of derision. It was a scary sight, at one and the same time daft and threatening, not to mention weirdly psychic. How did he know that I would glance over at that moment, or had he been pulling faces for some time on the off-chance?[18]

BUBBLE COVERS

The speech bubble covers were the first of a great many defining contributions to *Private Eye* from Peter Cook, who claimed to have been "very annoyed" when his friend from Cambridge Christopher Booker showed him some sample issues: "I'd wanted to start a practically identical magazine, then bloody *Private Eye* came out and I was really pissed off."[19] Cook did, however, show him in return a copy of an American magazine he had picked up which used speech bubbles on its cover and suggested they did the same.

The appropriation did not go unnoticed in New York. "The whole front cover of *Private Eye* with the speech balloons was taken from *Help!* magazine. *Help!* did it first," protested staffer and subsequent member of *Monty Python* Terry Gilliam. He wouldn't have minded so much if it wasn't for his reception in Greek Street (☞ OFFICES) a few years later: "I remember coming to London and going up to the *Private Eye* offices with my cartoons and nobody was interested."[20]
☞ COVERS, top ten most frequent stars

Far left: Issue 5, the first to feature the traditional speech bubble in February 1962
Left: The stencil used to draw almost every speech bubble on every cover until the mid-1990s

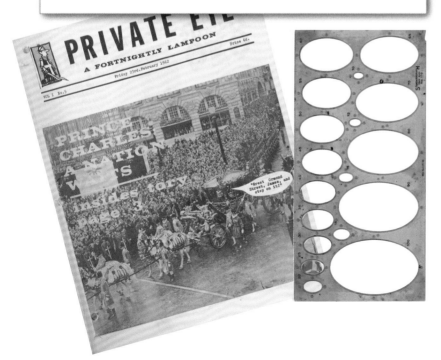

"Will you please take your feet off my best chair!"

chatto

I must admit that lately I'd been having my doubts about the Market . . .

. . . talks not going too well . . .
. . Heath having a difficult time getting the right conditions . . .

. . . But when that bloody Frog de Gaulle says he'll do anything to keep us out . . .

. . . I think the time has come for us to get in AT ANY PRICE!

PRIVATE EYE

6 CARLISLE STREET, LONDON W1V 5RG 071-437 4017, FAX 071-437

Revenue *Pellingay Phipps* . . . . Nick
P G Wodehouse

Bertram Wooster . . . . Ian Hislop
Richard Ingr

Jeeves
Dahlia . . . H. Tone

TWIN PEAKS
(Cast in Full)

Laura Palmer	Liz Eliot
Leland Palmer	Richard Ingrams
Bob	Barry Fantoni
Ben Horne	Peter Cook
Leo Johnson	Ian Hislop
Lucy	Alice Pitman
Andy	Tone
Norma Jennings	Hilary Lowinger
Jerry Horne	Steve Mann
Big Ed	Ed Glinert
Dr Jacoby	Dr Booker
	Willie Rushton

PETER CARTER-RUCK AND PARTNEI

SOLICITORS
PRIVY COUNCIL AGENTS

INCORPORATING
CHRISTOPHER SMITH & CO

Our Ref: AS/MPH

NOT FOR PUBLICATION

The Editor
Private Eye
6 Carlisle Street
LONDON
W1V 5RG

. . . later delivering a . . . he clear suggestion made in the article is that our client must have known in each case that the original estimate was false at the time he gave it.

KEEP IT UP, LADS AND WE'RE HOME AND DRY !

CAKES, St

St Cakes, the public school long celebrated in the pages of *Private Eye*, bears an astonishing resemblance to the alma maters of the magazine's editors, Shrewsbury and Ardingly.

	ST CAKES	SHREWSBURY	ARDINGLY
Founded	1442 (re-founded 1973)	1552	1858
Location	The pages of *Private Eye*	Shropshire	West Sussex
Motto	*Quis Paget Entrat* 'Who pays gets in'	*Intus Si Recte Ne Labora* 'If right within, trouble not'	*Beati Mundo Corde* 'Blessed are the pure in heart'
Terms	Quantock, Maastricht, Legover	Lent, Michaelmas, Summer	Separated by Long Leaves according to school 'Kalendar'
Staff	R.R. Kipling, A.L.B. Handin-Trouser, Gerald Gerund, The Rev. Upton Nogood	Anthony Chenevix-Trench, Frank McEachran, Laurence LeQuesne, Alex Binney	Headmaster Christopher Bulteel (first non-clergyman to head school after his predecessor made a Bishop), Colin Temblett-Wood
School Song	'When our locks are old and hoary/ Our thoughts will turn to former glory' (performed with a traditional punch to the head of the boy in front)	*'Rex Edwarde / Te Canamus / Pium Fundatorem'* (performed with a traditional foot stamp between the repeated refrain)	'We didn't have one. But we sang Jerusalem a lot. Often for no apparent reason.'
Slang	'The pavver' – Cricket pavilion where Ark of Covenant was discovered being used as an ashtray 'Hands' – run over Founder's Bottom in April 'Sock Race' – traditional St Cake's game where teams from two houses try to kill each other in a sea of mud using only their socks as weapons 'Trimfittering Exhibition' – scholarship awarded to weedy boys from broken stately homes	'New scum' – first years 'Tea Boy' – pretty younger pupil 'Capping' – ear touching gesture obligatory when greeting a master outside class 'Spells' – poetry to be learned by heart	'Shell' – year nine 'Fifth' – year eleven 'Wagga Bagga' – waste paper basket 'Deputy Sacristan' – second holiest prefect 'Gobbos' – domestic staff 'Congers' – held at 8.30 sharp on Tuesdays 'CCF Pelican Stalk' – departed on same day as Remove Parent's Consultations (Under)
Famous Old Boys	*Cakeians:* M.V.Q. Onanugu, coup leader and Supreme Life President of Rumbabwe William Squirt, promoted straight from 6th form to Conservative cabinet	*Salopians:* Charles Darwin Sir Philip Sidney	*Ardinians:* Terry-Thomas Victor Silvester Charles Cruft (founder of dog show)

CARTER-FUCK, Peter

Libel lawyer Peter Carter-Fuck established the law firm which still bears his name after the solicitors he had worked for four decades begged him to retire at the age of sixty-seven: his new colleagues eventually got sick of him and ejected him too (though they retained his name and astronomic bills).

"Often he tempted us to settle by offering to take far less than the going rate of damages for his client in return for agreeing not to question his own inflated fee," remembered one-time *Eye* lawyer Geoffrey Bindman. Bindman hit on a novel method of negotiation: "We kept them down only by encouraging the belief – by no means unjustified – that if he pushed too hard the *Eye* would cheat him of his fees by closing down."

In 1989 Carter-Ruck asked Bindman's successor Oscar Beuselinck if he could stop the magazine from referring to him as Carter-Fuck. Beuselinck passed the request on, and issue 727 announced that "in deference to the sensitivities of this old age pensioner, we will never refer to him again as Mr Peter Carter-Fuck. We trust that Mr Peter Farter-Fuck is happy with this new arrangement."
☞ CHURCHILL, Randolph; GOODMAN, Lord; MILLION-POUND WIN; PARKINSON, Cecil, his part in Nigel Dempster's downfall; TAKE THAT v. *PRIVATE EYE*; TRAFIGURA

CARTOONS, choosing

"Every time you go through the pile there might be someone new who's good," says Ian Hislop of his trawl through the hundreds of cartoons submitted to the *Eye* each fortnight. Between fifteen and twenty spot cartoons make it in to each issue, alongside all the regular strips. New cartoonists are joining the *Eye*'s roster all the time. "I always think it's one of the best bits of being editor, choosing the cartoons," says Hislop. "And I wouldn't give it away."

CESSPOOL, Lord Liver of

A case brought by Lord Russell of Liverpool, a legal adviser at the Nuremberg trials, centring on whether or not his book *Scourge of the Swastika* was pornographic, was the first accusation of libel against *Private Eye* actually to make it to court, in 1965.

The success of the *Eye*'s defence can perhaps be best summed up by this exchange in the courtroom.

David Turner-Samuels (for the *Eye*): With your permission, my lord, I will read an extract from *The Times Literary Review* – 'Lord Russell's works could be said to be pornographic.'
David Hirst, QC (for the plaintiff): Read the rest of the sentence.
Turner-Samuels: Very well, I will. 'But they are not.'[21]

The *Eye* lost. Lord Russell – who had managed to produce what Peter Cook described as "lots of war heroes with no legs in court, which swayed the jury to some extent" – was awarded £5,000 damages and costs of £3,000, a sum the magazine could not possibly pay. A begging note was inserted into issue 110, and raised £1,325 from the generosity of readers. There was a raffle of drawings by artists including David Hockney and Bridget Riley. And in May a benefit concert, the Rustle of Spring, was held at the Prince of Wales Theatre with tickets at ten guineas. It was enough to clear the £8,000 debt entirely by June.

It would be not be the last court defeat, nor the last time the magazine threw itself on the mercy of its readers.

CHURCHILL, Randolph
☞ WRITS, first of many

CIRCULATION

Do bad times for the country mean good times for the *Eye*?

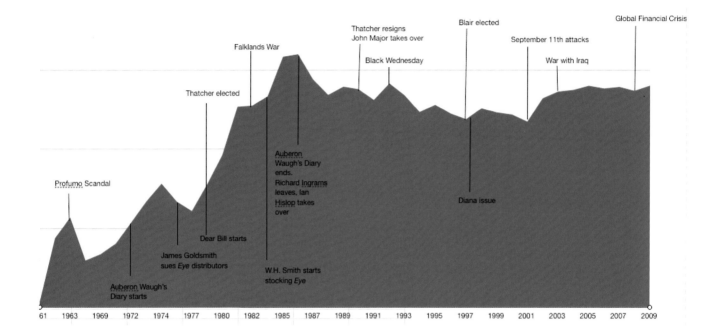

- Profumo Scandal
- Auberon Waugh's Diary starts
- James Goldsmith sues *Eye* distributors
- Dear Bill starts
- Thatcher elected
- Falklands War
- W.H. Smith starts stocking *Eye*
- Auberon Waugh's Diary ends. Richard Ingrams leaves, Ian Hislop takes over
- Thatcher resigns John Major takes over
- Black Wednesday
- Diana issue
- Blair elected
- September 11th attacks
- War with Iraq
- Global Financial Crisis

61 1963 1969 1972 1974 1977 1980 1982 1985 1987 1989 1991 1993 1995 1997 1999 2001 2003 2005 2007 2009

THE CLOGGIES by BILL TIDY
An everyday saga in the life of Clog Dancing Folk

CLOGGIES

By September 1967 *Private Eye* had established a permanent jokes team and a distinctive journalistic voice and was on a reasonably sound financial footing. Clearly all that was missing was a fortnightly half-page about clog-dancing.

Thankfully, cartoonist Bill Tidy was on hand. "The Cloggies – An Everyday Saga in the Life of Clog-Dancing Folk", ran for fourteen years.

Richard Ingrams remembers, "I once met Graham Greene at a lunch the *Spectator* put on, and he was sat next to this Italian journalist, engaged in a very serious conversation, and you could see Graham Greene was a bit bored by this man, and it went on and on. And eventually he stopped, and Graham Greene looked across at me – he hadn't said anything to me before that – and he just said, 'Hands up all those who don't think the Cloggies are funny.' And he put his hand up."

"The Cloggies" finally danced off to pastures new (the *Listener*) in 1981.

CLUFF

Cartoonist John Longstaff has been contributing since 1982. While he provides a daily political cartoon for his local paper the *Northern Echo*, for the *Eye* he specialises in outright, unadulterated silliness.

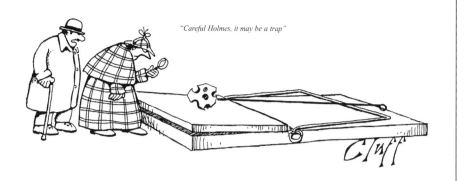

"Careful Holmes, it may be a trap"

COACH AND HORSES

☞ LUNCH

COCKBURN, Claud

Claud Cockburn was a man from another generation. He had covered the 1929 stock-market crash for the *Times*, interviewed Al Capone, reported first-hand from Berlin on the excesses of Hitler's stormtroopers, joined the Jarrow marchers on the road and abandoned reporting on the Spanish civil war in favour of fighting for the republicans instead. He had been a keen Communist party member since the 1930s. He was nearing sixty and living in rural Ireland when, in 1963, he received an invitation that "baffled" him, to guest-edit an edition of a magazine he had never seen, *Private Eye*.

"Just for a start, I was approximately twice the average age of the men who had conceived the paper, were running it, and were giving it its unique character," he recalled. "A person of my generation would probably, I thought, even in a single issue, seriously damage its 'image'."[22]

Richard Ingrams had other ideas. He had just finished Cockburn's three-volume autobiography, which dealt with his founding of the fiercely independent subscription paper the *Week* in the 1930s, designed to drag out into the daylight stories such as the abdication crisis which the British press refused to touch. So effective had it proved that the government banned it during World War Two. In Cockburn's words, it "reported extensively on what was really being said *sotto voce* by informed observers … All sorts of people, for

motives sometimes noble and quite often vile, would approach the *Week* to draw its attention to the most extraordinary pieces of more or less confidential information. Sometimes it came from frustrated newspapermen who could not get what they considered vital news into their own papers. More often such confidences were the outcome of obscure financial or diplomatic duels. They would come, for instance, from the Counsellor of an embassy who was convinced of the wrong-headed policy of the Foreign Office and the Ambassador, and wished, without exposing himself, to put a spoke in their wheel."

This was music to the ears of Ingrams, who was still determined to make good on the original plan to include serious journalism in *Private Eye*'s mix, but kept running into an obvious problem: "We didn't have any contacts! It's all very well saying you want inside information, but it doesn't grow on trees."

Cockburn agreed to Ingrams' invitation to come over to the metropolis to helm an issue of the *Eye* in Booker's absence on honeymoon. It was, however, with the stipulation that he must have three weeks' preparation "in order to inform myself of the state of affairs: to see some men who knew some men". "He was a friend of [Roger] Hollis, the head of MI5, who was later on suspected of being a Russian spy, though I don't think he was, and he knew a lot of old lefties, like [Richard] Crossman and [Tom] Driberg [☞]," remembers Ingrams. By "an amazing fluke" Cockburn arrived at the height

Willie Rushton provided a picture byline for Claud Cockburn's contributions

of the Profumo scandal, with Stephen Ward (q.v) on trial at the Old Bailey and the prime minister Harold Macmillan fighting for his political life. The febrile atmosphere rendered Cockburn's old friends, and some new ones, vocal: "Under certain stimuli the normally taciturn or discreet members of the British Establishment can become quite astonishingly talkative," he noted. "The reek of the political mess of that year provided such a stimulus for many. A surprising number seemed to feel that the best way for all good men and true to come to the aid of the country was to spill whatever beans they might have to an uninhibited satirical magazine."

And spill that magazine certainly did, in an issue that the weight of public expectation pushed up to record-selling levels. Cockburn revealed in issue 43 that the prime minister's wife Lady Dorothy Macmillan was having an affair with his fellow Tory MP Bob Boothby, called Lord Astor "a lying sonofabitch", shattered all protocol by naming the head of MI6 and claimed that a cabinet minister had paid £2,375 to have his head removed from the infamous "headless man" photograph which was presented in court as evidence of the Duchess of Argyll's adultery.

The naming of Sir Dick White as chief spook prompted panic in Whitehall. Documents revealed by the Public Record Office over thirty years later revealed that prosecution had been discussed at a specially convened meeting chaired by the cabinet secretary. It was regretfully concluded that Cockburn, the proud subject of an MI5 file running to twenty-six volumes, could not be charged because White's name was so well known in Fleet Street that it would be impossible to prove that his source had broken the Official Secrets Act.[23] Cockburn, tipped off by "a source I had good reason to consider well informed who arranged to meet me in an agreeably open space without microphones", thought it wise to retreat to Ireland anyway, which meant that when the head of the government's D-Notice Committee responsible for keeping the nation's secrets, Colonel Sammy Lohan, paid a personal visit to the *Eye* office he found only "a pack of obviously terrified overgrown schoolboys". Ingrams and his pals were "asked round to the Ministry of Defence where Lohan read us a long lecture on the Red Peril".

Cockurn's biggest scoop, however, was the story of artist Hal Woolf, who had died of extensive injuries after being detained by police. The story had been rejected by every newspaper in Fleet Street before Woolf's wife brought it to Cockburn, who in turn brought it to the attention of the MP Stephen Swingler, who raised it in the House of Commons, leading to interest from the daily papers and, eventually, a Home Office inquiry. Lest readers be in any doubt about the nature of this grim little story, Cockburn prefaced it with a stern intro:

August 1963: The birth of serious journalism in *Private Eye*

Come to lovely London and find **HOW TO BECOME DEAD** Without anyone knowing how

There are some sad little old sacks about who still try to miss their round in the bar while they hold the customers enthralled with the tale that a lot of the stories that appear in Private Eye are "merely" jokes - things that couldn't, ha-ha-heil, happen here. Just for the record, the following event was no joke, and it did happen here.

(Before everyone gets depressed, let's state that this is at least one bit of you-know-what which is not going to be swept under the carpet. Stephen Swingler M.P. has assured Private Eye that he is going to question and cross-question the Home Secretary - in the House and out of it - until some explanation of the bloody death of Harold Woolf emerges from the normal miasma of lies.)

This man Woolf (60 when he passed on) was in his day a good and fairly widely [...] his later [...]

Mrs. Woolf then got in touch with a Mr. Cotton, a mutual friend of hers and Mr. Woolf, an antique dealer. He telephoned the Harrow Road Police Station and he was asked to go over and declare Mr. Woolf missing, this Mr. Cotton did and was told by the police that they would telephone him immediately if they had any news.

On Novemebr 17th Mr. Cotton and Mrs. Woolf again visited Harrow Road Police Station and were told that there was no news of their friend.

On the following day Mr. Cotton went to Mr. Woolf's rooms and found his passport. With this he went to Harrow Road Police Station and gave them a copy of the passport photograph which might help to trace him. The police said that his photograph and description would be transmitted to all London Police Divisions and [...] Cotton went to P [...]

and abrasions on his legs and shoulders". He was X-rayed and found to have no fractures.

As soon as he was discharged, the police picked him up at the hospital. On the following day he was brought back to the hospital in a condition which caused the hospital doctor to have him sent to the [...]

Cockburn would go on to write a column for the magazine until his death in 1981, but his most important contribution was to kick off the second central element of *Private Eye* – investigative journalism.
☞ FOOT, Paul, gives thumbs-up to job at *Private Eye*

COLEMANBALLS

The Colemanballs column, devoted to things that sports commentators didn't quite mean to say, has literally been running since 1977. Much to the displeasure of the man who gave his name to it.

"I definitely never said, 'Juantorena opens his legs and shows his class' – it was Ron Pickering. Ron laughed his head off about it."
DAVID COLEMAN, *Daily Mail,* 1992

"It wasn't good for the kids. There used to be a regular Colemanballs Christmas Book. The children would see it in the shops and they would ask what was going on. What's Dad doing in there? I think I have risen above that."
DAVID COLEMAN, *Daily Mail,* 1998

"I've been quoted in that column for making remarks at events I've never been at. One was about what I said at a snooker competition. I've never covered snooker in my life. What really annoys me is when newspapers pick up these things and turn fiction into fact. People now make up quotes for a living. It doesn't worry me now. People don't take it seriously because they've sussed it out."
DAVID COLEMAN, *Daily Mail,* 2000

"Coleman has always refused to accept responsibility for the gaffes he has allegedly made and admits to only one: 'If that had gone in, it would have been a goal.'"
Daily Record, 2001

☞ HONDOOTEDLY; UNSUNG HEROES

CONTEMPORARIES,
grouped with Ian Hislop for purposes of restrospectively hilarious lists of movers and shakers in magazines in 1980s

"The whizz-kids", *Harpers and Queen,* 1983
Boy George
Torvill and Dean
Princess Diana

"Bright Young Things", *Elle,* 1988
Charles Moore
Nicholas Coleridge
Ferdinand Mount

CONTEMPT OF COURT

After *Private Eye* had succeeded in getting Sonia Sutcliffe's libel damages reduced by 90 percent (☞ BANANA, I'm a), she and her solicitor Eileen Pembridge reported Ian Hislop for contempt of court. He had published two further articles about Sutcliffe in the run-up to the action, over which the magazine eventually had to pay a further £100,000 in libel damages.

Mr Justice Popplewell threw the contempt case out of court in 1990. But in an extraordinary legal manoeuvre the attorney general, Patrick Mayhew, appealed against this. It came soon after the *Eye* itself had been denied leave to appeal against the libel verdict on the grounds that it had emerged that a £25,000 payment that Sutcliffe had declined to identify while she was testifying that she had not been paid by any journalists actually came from the *Mail on Sunday* via a carefully disguised route. "It was pure 'Let's get the *Eye*,'" says Hislop. The Court of Appeal found him guilty of contempt, fined him £10,000 (the *Eye* itself was fined a further £10,000) and warned him that if he did it again, he would end up in prison. "I was looking at two years in front of three not very sympathetic judges," he remembers. "And my wife was in the front row looking pregnant and worried. And I had my toothbrush with me."[24]

The threat remains. The *Eye*'s lawyer Robin Shaw outlined it in no uncertain terms when Hislop proposed printing a parliamentary question which the oil firm Trafigura (☞) insisted was the subject of an injunction in October 2009. "He said to me 'You do know this is still current?' It's not mentioned casually. Literally that morning with running the injunction there was a definite moment of Robin looking at me thinking 'I have just said this – are you going to do it?' Contempt is still hanging there. I think about it now and then."

He's not scared, though. "Part of me wishes I'd gone in. I'm not making that up. I think I could have edited from the cell, ha ha! It was Leigh Hunt of the *Examiner*, wasn't it, the last British editor to do it from prison, in 1812? I think it would have been terrific."

COOK, Beryl, cover by

In December 1984 artist Beryl Cook provided the Christmas cover for the magazine.
☞ FLUCK AND LAW; XMAS covers by Steve Bell

Peter Cook and Richard Ingrams drumming up publicity for the *Eye*, **1966**

COOK, Peter, begins regular editorial contributions to *Private Eye*

"Our amazing success had been part of the whole satire boom. And then it became a little passé," says business manager Peter Usborne of the situation in early 1964, after the record high sales recorded during the Profumo scandal had plunged to a record low. "We had unquestionably been a fashion object. And then we became an unfashion object." Pressdram was trading at a loss of £4,500 a year.

Things weren't right on the editorial side, either. The blazing rows might be a thing of the past (☞ BOOKER, Christopher, Sacking of), but only because there was hardly anyone left in the office for Richard Ingrams to argue with following the departures of Christopher Booker and Willie Rushton. "He'd made himself effectively editor of the magazine," recalled Usborne, "and he was very nervous, sitting there alone with a little notebook, ringing people up trying to find stories."[25] John Wells was appointed as a nominal co-editor in 1964, but his parallel career as a performer, playwright and director was already taking off

and he never quite gelled as a part of the general joke-writing team: "More often than not my little decorations for the comedic Christmas tree were ostentatiously removed, spat on and ground into the carpet," he complained.[26] Certainly there are fewer jokes in the post-Booker editions of late 1963 and early 1964: in fact there is less of everything, except white space. "I think it was a sixteen-page issue at that time, and the jokes were very large on a page," says Barry Fantoni. "And if Richard could get someone to do a big drawing, that meant he could get home on the 4.30 train rather than the 5.30, which kind of governed his life to some extent." The reduced team even seemed to have lost confidence in their own trademark innovations: the majority of covers in this period carry not photo-bubbles but cartoons by Scarfe, Rushton or Trog. One such cover – a particularly weak one – was the only comment the magazine dared make on the assassination of JFK in November 1963, which was otherwise respectfully (and shamefully) ignored.

Their problem soon became apparent: they had too

'The turning point': Cook provides a legendary cover in June 1964

few Cooks. Their proprietor (☞RICH OWNER, Search for a) walked back into the office in June 1964, having completed his run on Broadway with a transferred *Beyond the Fringe*. It was the first time any of them had seen him in two years. And he was there to stay. "Peter was wonderful. Suddenly this amazing atmosphere of glamour had hit this poverty-stricken office," says Usborne. "He conjured up money out of nothing and took over the magazine and that was that."

The cash injection came partly from Cook's own pockets – his then wife Wendy recalls selling "a pair of rather pretty diamond brooches, a legacy of my grandmother, for the price of a couple of brand-new Minis" and dutifully handing the cash over[27] – and partly from those of a number of his equally glamorous acquaintances. "I remember him sitting in the office in Greek Street ringing up all his famous friends and saying 'I've got this magazine needs some money: would you like to put some money in?'" says Usborne. If you need an illustration of the sort of level of celebrity Cook was at in the mid-1960s, both John

Lennon and Paul McCartney were regular dinner guests at his house and several people, including Wendy, think he had an affair with Jackie Kennedy. "As soon as you got a phonecall from Peter Cook you sat up and said yes, basically," concludes Usborne (☞ FAMOUS FRIENDS).

Not that it was ever about the cash as far as Cook was concerned. "The purpose of the magazine is to keep going, rather than to make money," he maintained. For decades, even after their loans had been converted into significant shareholdings in the magazine, his celebrity friends received only a crate of wine in lieu of a dividend. Until very late in his life, Cook never asked for any payment in return for his own contributions.

And these were huge. From the moment he joined the team, Cook threw himself whole-heartedly into the jokes. He immediately reinstated the bubble covers, with a new twist: Théodore Géricault's 1819 painting *The Raft of the Medusa* was adapted so its cannibalistic survivors paid tribute to a recently collapsed holiday company: "This is the last time I go on a John Bloom holiday." "That cover absolutely marked the turning point," says Usborne. "*Private Eye* might have been heading for extinction but he added that extra genius touch of brilliant, brilliant and fresh humour. He just crippled us with laughter." John Wells recalled that Cook "almost always did the cover bubble. He used to come in on Sunday mornings, and he'd have a cigarette on the go, and he'd think about it and just go slightly out of focus and then come up with some colossally good joke."[28]

Cook settled into the tiny Greek Street office and began to dictate inspired streams of consciousness to his appreciative audience. "A lot of Peter's things were improvised, the sort of things he would come up with sitting in the pub," recalled Ingrams. "The awful thing is, like with a lot of very funny people, you fall about laughing, and afterwards, when people say 'Well, what were the jokes?', you can't remember anything about it."[29]

The trio soon found that the key to working together lay in judicious use of the biro. "I would write things down and he would just recite them," says Ingrams. "Cook only ever wrote out one joke, which was the introduction to the Turds [☞ TOPES, Spiggy]. 'I want you to meet four very young, very exciting Turds.' And as far as I remember, that was the only thing he ever wrote down. He would stalk about the room, walk up and down dictating." His colleagues quickly discovered the method that got the best material out of Cook: "We'd often go into an interview and I would be a sort of straight man asking him questions. Wells was brilliant at that too."

TO THE EDITOR OF THE TIMES

Chairman: Universal Products Ltd.
Sir Herbert Gusset   LONDON E.C.3
Secretary:
Fred Harbottle

THE PULSE OF BRITAIN

Dear Sir,   From Sir Herbert Gusset

Your correspondent is quite right. The recent
abstention of so many Conservatives at by-elections
is proof that the country is suffering from a
serious malaise.

However, there can be no doubt in my mind
that great opportunities are beckoning ahead, if
only we have the faith and courage to seize
them firmly. The Common Market opens up a
vast new horizon, a great vista. We are going
ahead. Our native scientific genius, that produced radar, penicillin and the steam engine in
response to the great challenges of the past has
once again reasserted itself in the Hovercraft,
this splendid symbol of Britain's resurgence
into the Sixties.
   Only the other day, indeed, I observed two
workmen on a building site. They were not, as
you might have expected, merely drinking tea.
They were getting on with the job. I have no
time for people who denigrate the British wor-
kingman, who when given proper leadership
from those he can respect is the finest in the
world.

Thus was Sir Herbert Gussett born, firing off letters to
the *Daily Telegraph* about "my lady wife, whose name
for a moment escapes me". Giant snakes, "many of them
millions of miles long", slithered through the pages. Spotty
Muldoon offered advice to anxious correspondents.
Rhandi Phurr dispensed Eastern wisdom to the masses two
years ahead of the Maharishi doing much the same, more
profitably and for real.

Cook also came up with "The Seductive Brethren", a
defiantly non-satirical sect devoted to nothing but silliness
and, of course, "the bodily seizing of young women". Chief
Rammer Sir Basil Nardly-Stoads introduced his followers
(Sir Arthur Stargborgling – "the exact number of the
Brethren at any given time is always hard to calculate but
it can be safely said that a figure of two would be exact")
in issue 68, and their adventures played out thereafter in
fortnightly instalments. "It became a hit," says Fantoni.
"And in a way Cookie saved the magazine in that first crisis,
by inventing something that everybody could identify with
and want to buy it every fortnight."

Cook worked pretty much full-time on the magazine
until *Not Only But Also*, his TV series with Dudley
Moore, took off in 1965 and his contributions became
less regular, though no less vital. He was the creator of
a host of other long-lasting characters and serial features
that made their first appearances as the circulation inched
inexorably upwards over the next few months. His celebrity

SEDUCTIVE BRETHREN

Sir Basil Nardly-Stoads explains

As chief **Rammer** of the Seductive
Brethren, (writes Sir Basil Nardly-Stoad
it is often my pleasure and privilege to
seize hold of young women and clamber
hotly all over their bodies.

I am often asked, by those who want t
know (continues Sir Basil Nardly-Stoads)
what exactly the Seductive Brethren do
and what they believe in: to this there
is no simple answer but to say that the
BODILY SEIZING OF YOUNG WOMEN is
at least part and parcel of our belief
would be no exageration.

THE FUNCTION OF THE RAMMER

In my position, or rather in my
numerous positions as Chief Rammer,
(Sir Basil Nardly-Stoads writes) it is my
solemn duty to uphold the traditions of
the sect and deal with the thousand and
one contingencies that need must occur ir
an organisation of this kind; in this I am
assisted by the Holy Dragger (elected
annually), Sir Arthur Starborgling.   Sir
Arthur saw service and, indeed, a numbe
of other things in Dieppe.   Between them
the Rammer and the Dragger control the
discipline of the Brethren.

was shamelessly used to sell the magazine, with personal appearances on records, posters and adverts, and even a promotional tour of the country to drum up sales. But Ingrams pays tribute to an aspect of Cook that has often been overlooked: his editorial judgement. He was a fierce supporter of the journalistic side of the *Eye* and a shrewd judge of the political scene. "Cook had a very good instinct about who to go for. He was very, very good at being able to identify political humbug. There was a starry-eyed feeling about Harold Wilson rather like there was with Blair, and, funnily enough, Cook never succumbed to that." "He added a wonderful kind of rage," Wells recalled. "He did get incredibly angry about bad politicians."

The *Eye* team photographed in front of the mural on the wall of their 22 Greek Street office in 1966: Back row L-R – Christopher Logue, Peter Cook, Christopher Booker. Middle: John Wells, Claud Cockburn, Richard Ingrams. Front: Gerald Scarfe, Tony Rushton

LORD GNOME SAYS: THESE QUINTIN HOGG CUSHION KITS, IN THREE VIVID COLOURS, ON STRONG IRISH CLOTH, ARE ABSOLUTELY GENUINE, LIKE MY WELL-KNOWN CONSERVATIVE POSTERS AND CAR-STICKERS. THEY ARE AVAILABLE FROM:- "IT'S HERE" CARD SHOPS — PRESENTS OF DOVER STREET — PRESENTS OF SLOANE STREET — INGRAMS INTERNATIONAL DESIGNS, AND ALL OTHER GOOD GIFT SHOPS. OR DIRECT FROM ME AT PRIVATE EYE PRODUCTIONS, LTD., 22 GREEK STREET, LONDON, W.1. THEY ARE CHEAP AT 12/6 EACH, AND THEY WORK. INDEED, I HAVE STUFFED ONE MYSELF. I FIND IT VERY SATISFYING, AND I KEEP IT BY ME ALL THE TIME. TRY ONE YOURSELF.

Cook becomes the face of *Eye* merchandise, 1964. Hogg sued, which took care of most of the profits from this particular item

COOK, Peter, role in later years

There is an accepted narrative of Peter Cook's life, in which early promise gave way to indolence, alcohol and obscurity according to the Aristotelian rules of tragedy and newspaper profiles. It makes for a nice rounded obituary, or TV drama. There's just one problem with it – it's nonsense. Having achieved his youthful potential when you're meant to, in his youth, he settled down to spending the rest of his life doing exactly what he felt like doing. Some of that was playing golf, some was watching telly, some was calling up late-night radio shows, a lot of it was drinking vodka, but an enormous amount – an amount that the absence of bylines never really made clear – was *Private Eye*.

"I should have a year's financial security to do what I really enjoy and that is writing for *Private Eye*," he told the *Times* in 1974. His second wife Judy recalled that in the early to mid-1970s "his day to day life" involved spending "a lot of time at *Private Eye*'s offices in Soho … Sometimes he will go every day for days or even weeks on end. He loves immersing himself in *Private Eye*. So much of his life is transient, but *Private Eye* is always there."[30] His involvement became less regular towards the end of the decade, but in 1980 he told a student Ian Hislop that he was turning down other work if "it conflicted with my writing for *Private Eye* which I really do enjoy. I do three afternoons on a working week. I co-write the humorous stuff with Richard and whoever else is in."[31] Four years later he claimed in the *Sunday Times* that "I don't bother much with *Private Eye*, haven't been there for ages, in fact I hardly ever leave Hampstead these days," but since he claimed in the same article to be farming jojoba and to have a family of twelve Soviet dissidents living in his bathroom, this may not have been strictly accurate. In 1988 he told a chat-show audience that "I go into *Private Eye* about two days a fortnight – what with the change in altitude and the timezones between Hampstead and the West End, you're about one millisecond behind the rest of the world, and I find that very fatiguing."[32]

"He would come in after maybe five or six months' or a year's absence. You never knew when he was going to come in," says Richard Ingrams. "Towards the end he came in a lot more. Because he didn't have very much else to do. He would never ring up to say he was coming in or anything, he would just turn up. He was great." Ian Hislop remembers him dropping by at random times, to "see if I fancied 'doing a few jokes'. I always did." "I used to work with Cookie just me and him which was really good fun. The thing was when he came in you just tended to listen, because Cookie would monologue, that was more his way of doing it. Whereas with the others it's more sort of orchestral, or whatever the word is. Cookie was more of a soloist, I think." Sometimes, if they happened to coincide

Cook leads the celebrations at the *Eye*'s 30th anniversay party . . .

. . . and in the office, at the slightest excuse

with his visits, he would join in the regular joke-writing sessions. "When Cook came in it was the biggest blast of all – just to sit in the room with the world's funniest man was quite something," says Nick Newman. "But he was incredibly generous – if you came up with a joke he would laugh and develop it, take it up. I remember one of the first ideas I got in in those sessions was about the revelations of the fourth man in the spy thing [☞ BLUNT, Anthony]. And I sort of said something about the 'third fourth man' and Cook just came up with a half-hour of stuff about the fifth fourth man and the fourth third man, and all we had to do was sit back and laugh while Ian wrote it all down."

"He wasn't around much, but when he came in he made a huge difference," says Barry Fantoni. "His laughter and his presence were particularly uplifting. He became obsessed with this picture he'd found in a porn magazine of a man who vaguely looked like Edward Heath hitting a girl with a walking stick. And he carried this around in his briefcase with his flat bottle of whisky and his cigarettes, hundreds of them, and he'd bring it out every time as if it was something new: 'Should we do something with this?' We all used to wait for the thing to be opened, and for it to be presented. Even after Heath had gone years and years beforehand."

Even when he didn't attend, Fantoni feels he was there in spirit. "Cookie was sort of omnipresent. I think all of us in our deepest hearts when it came to reflect on what we'd done at the end of the session would probably say to ourselves 'Would Cookie like this?' There was no doubt that he was the master of it."

Plus, of course, he was still the magazine's owner – even if he wasn't always sure of the fact himself. "I think I'm still the proprietor. I own the same number of shares, so I must be, mustn't I?" he declared in 1982.[33] A decade later he wrote to his own magazine: "Sir – It has been brought to my attention that in issue 793 Mr Mike Molloy asserts that I am the proprietor of *Private Eye*. It is hard to imagine a more damaging libel. Yours, Peter Cook, Hampstead."

"He was the proprietor, but his powers were never fully explained, possibly never understood, certainly never exercised," remembered Auberon Waugh.[34] Judy said her husband was not "remotely interested in turning up to board meetings or getting involved in the financial side of things". But that didn't stop him being the ideal top man for the *Eye*. "Cookie was the best," says Hislop with feeling. "I wouldn't see him for six months or so, and then he'd suddenly turn up, he'd appear and wave magic about. And then if there was a court case, that's what he really liked. Cookie loved the trouble. It was brilliant, it

"Cookie was the best. I wouldn't see him for six months or so, and then he'd suddenly turn up and wave magic about"
Ian Hislop

Celebrating the Sutcliffe appeal outside the Royal Courts of Justice

was like thinking 'Well, we haven't got a PR firm but we've got Peter Cook.' In sunglasses, having had a few, being very silly, whatever the case. And in pure morale terms, it was invaluable." When Robert Maxwell (☞) turned up to give evidence in his libel case against the *Eye*, Cook sat in the gallery and waved his chequebook at him (☞ CZECH, fat, Fat cheque given to). When the *Eye* lost, he led his troops on an audacious sortie into the beast's own lair (☞ MIRROR BUILDING, Peter Cook leads *Eye* raid on). When Sonia Sutcliffe nearly put the magazine out of business in another libel case (☞ BANANA, I'm a) he threw himself fully into the appeal. "He was great," Dave

Cash recalled. "He made a rather sombre occasion rather jolly. He came to all the meetings we had with lawyers, he spent a great deal of time in court and he phoned me several times a day." Up until very late in his life, when his cash from other sources was starting to run out, Cook never took a salary. "He wasn't being paid for it, he just enjoyed coming in," says Cash.

Christopher Silvester remembers Cook as a regular visitor to the office during the Maxwell and Sutcliffe actions. "He was drinking very heavily, but he never seemed to be drunk in the sense that most people might seem to be drunk. I think because he was permanently sozzled. I remember a very, very powerful impression he formed on me once which was that I could smell vodka coming out of the pores on his skin. Not his breath, but his whole aura was smelling

Hislop, Cook and Cash discuss legal tactics in the *Eye* office at the height of the Sutcliffe case

Above and right: Cook reduces his audience to hysterics at the *Eye*'s 30th anniversary celebrations and a staff Christmas party

of vodka. And vodka doesn't normally have a scent. You need to have a lot of vodka in your system to be exuding vodka fumes. He obviously had a sort of level, and he never really went below that level. And occasionally he'd just top it up."

He also maintained his keen interest in the journalistic side of the magazine. "As I was effectively one of his employees he took it that he could ring me at all hours of the night, because he didn't sleep very much," remembers Francis Wheen, who joined in 1987. "So the phone would ring at two in the morning and it would be Peter saying 'Have you seen this thing, have you read this?' in sometimes quite obscure magazines. I think Ian got a fair bit of that too."

Editorially, however, Cook never tried to interfere with anything. "I never believed there could be such a person. He was the essence of the non-interfering proprietor," said Paul Foot, who joined the staff in 1967. "Even when his best friends were attacked, or people he thought well of, never once, I am absolutely certain of this, never once did he seek to intervene."[35] The admiration was mutual. "He loved Paul Foot," says Hislop. "It's the only speech that Peter ever made in his entire life where the audience were bored. At one of the *Eye* parties, he went on and on and on about how brilliant Paul Foot was – 'Ashashabsholutely brilliant' – and there were no jokes at all. He just loved it. It was part of what he wanted the mag to do really. Get into trouble."

Other party speeches are fondly remembered by staff years later, although they have difficulty recalling exactly what it was that reduced them to hysterics at the time. Cook tended to ignore the occasion in favour of focussing on some small and irrelevant point and building an elaborate fantasy on it: once it was a bottle of aftershave called 'Mandate' which he had found in the *Eye* office and accused Christopher Booker of dousing himself with for extra masculinity; another riffed on the sautéed potatoes which had featured on the lunch menu. "Twenty minutes on sautéed potatoes. It was just brilliant," remembered Hislop. "Absolute genius. Every single line was totally inspired. And I can't remember a word of it," recalled Auberon Waugh. It was at an *Eye* Christmas party, held around the photocopier and layout table in the office, that Cook fell into conversation with Clive Anderson: from this arose the 1993 episode of *Clive Anderson Talks Back* in which he played four different guests, and which was to be his last public triumph. It echoed the question-and-answer sessions he and Ingrams had indulged in in the *Eye*'s early days.

Peter Cook died in January 1995. He was just fifty-seven. "It was press day, and Michael Heath [☞] came in and said 'Cook's dead,'" remembered Ian Hislop. "And someone said 'Fuck.' I mean it was absolute disbelief. I don't know why – no reason Cookie should have been immortal, you just assumed he was, really."

He penned his own poignant tribute to his hero, mentor and proprietor in the edition which went to press that afternoon. "That's not enough Cook – Ed."

☞ HONEYMOON, presence of Dave Cash on Peter Cook's; WILL, Peter Cook's

Cook and wife Lin enjoying an *Eye* party

No. 863
Friday
13 Jan. '95

PRIVATE EYE

So. Farewell then...

PETER COOK
17.11.37 – 9.1.95

CONDLIFFE v. *Eye*
 MILLION-POUND WIN

COVERS, top ten most frequent stars (correct as of June 2010)
Bubbling under: Cherie Blair (18 covers), Princess Di (17), Michael Foot (15).

1. Margaret Thatcher 94 covers

PRIVATE EYE

BLAIR'S FRESH START

From now on it's no more spin...

I think that'll play really well

INSIDE: 50 GLORIOUS SMEARS!

2. Tony Blair 91

PRIVATE EYE

Well Marcia I've made a Lady of you at last!

Cheeky!

IT'S LADY SLAGHEAP!

WILSON'S SHOCKER

3. Harold Wilson 69

PRIVATE EYE

QUEEN OPENS PARLIAMENT

and I hope you realise I didn't write this crap

HOW MANY POOVES ARE THERE IN WILSON'S GOVERNMENT? see page 3.

4. Queen Elizabeth II 62

PRIVATE EYE

I said Let go of the tramp paper you deaf old bat!

A Gnome Advertisement

CONSERVATIVES CARE !

5. Ted Heath 55

PRIVATE EYE

MAJOR'S SUPPORT LOWEST EVER

Come back, Norma! Please!

6. John Major 47

PRIVATE EYE

BROWN'S BID FOR POWER

Please God – make him resign

Your prayer is being held in a queue and will be answered shortly

Christianity, progressive politics and

7. Gordon Brown 43

PRIVATE EYE

CHARLES IN SECURITY REVIEW

Feel lucky, punk?

8. Prince Charles 32

PRIVATE EYE

THAT TV DEBATE WAS BUSH WIRED?

Say "Hello" George

Hello George

9. George W. Bush 28

PRIVATE EYE

Plaice in our time

Cod War **Callaghan speaks**

10. Jim Callaghan 20

CREW, we happy

The Eye team as seen by Willie Rushton, 1988. L-R: Paul Halloran, Willie Rushton, Ian Hislop, Christopher Silvester, Richard Ingrams, Christopher Booker, Peter Cook, Barry Fantoni, Tony Rushton, sheep, Dave Cash. The picture was a tribute for Cash's quarter of a century's service: it includes a bucket of sick to his left. "I was once sick in a bin," admits a shame-faced Cash, although he continues to deny that he then moved the brimming receptacle from his office into the ladies' loo for others to deal with.

☞ MURAL

THE HOUNDING OF THE POOVES

AN INVESTIGATION

BY DR J Miller

"Pouves, pouves! Que pouvez-vous dire? Sont-ils ils ou elles?" Not even Montaigne himself, the balding sage of old Dordogne, could fathom the ways of the crafty poove.

Doctors have realised, in recent years, that there are many more pooves in society than meet the eye at a glance, many of them running the country, as intellectuals, politicians, artists and even masquerading as women. More than four out of every twenty men you meet on the top of a bus are pooves. While we all know of the married poove, with several children, who has married simply as a vile disguise - to conceal his poovish practises from his wife.

After intensive research, both in this country and in America, we know that your average poove is a sick man. He should be treated as such by society - with aspirin or whatever comes to hand. It is simply ridiculous to say that he is abnormal. Your normal poove is in no way unnatural. Indeed, as pooves come, he is probably considerably more normal than your average so-called heterosexual.

There has been considerable agitation in recent years by irresponsible left-wing elements, pooves etc., for a reform of the so-called Labouchere Amendment which makes the filthy and depraved practices of the poove a criminal offence. It must be remembered, however, that this trivial Amendment was merely the after-dinner caprice of a well-known Commons eccentric, passed well over seventy years ago. To drag this dusty issue up again would be to deprive the celebrated Poove Squad, the most successful Division of the Yard, of its last vestiges of official power. The ever-watchful Poove Hounds would no longer roam the streets and conveniences of London on their ghastly mission. While our women and children could no longer sleep soundly in their beds.

Female practice which could drive a young man to poovery.

Men of the Poove Squad in plain clothes prepare for a raid.

Pooves, or 'queers', at their filthy practices.

Drag Queen avoiding publicity.

Pooves receiving occupational therapy at Poove rehabilitation centre.

Columnist John Gordon reproving young poove.

CUNTS, stupid bloody irresponsible

Peter Cook's *Beyond the Fringe* colleague Jonathan Miller was persuaded to write for *Private Eye* in September 1962, contributing an "investigation into the ways of the crafty poove". It was accompanied by a large and flattering portrait of its author, complete with his medical title.

Miller, who regarded his sojourn in satire as a "fiercely regretted distraction" from his job at University College Hospital, was furious, and fired off an explosive note which has pride of place on the wall of the editorial office to this day.

You stupid, bloody, irresponsible <u>cunts</u> !! You had no permission and therefore no right to use my medical title as a heading to the article. Are you all so completely frivolous and insensitive as not to be able to understand that such a fucking stupid blunder could well mean my being struck off the register? God rot the lot of you!

Jonathan Miller

He never wrote for the magazine again – although as his career was further distracted by opera-directing, film-making and TV pseudery he made regular appearances in the jokes pages. Having declared of the satire boom in 1961 that "one can only hope that blood will be drawn", Miller pronounced himself badly scratched. "*Private Eye* began dumping on me, about which Peter didn't object at all, as an old friend," he whimpered. "Week in and week out I was Dr Jonathan. I just thought, 'Oh, god, I can't really be friends with him any more.'"[36]

KNIFESMITH'S KORNER

when I wear pretty frilly knickers I feel as if I am carrying an exciting secret.

CUTLER, Ivor

Poet, performance artist, songwriter and schoolteacher Ivor Cutler was the man behind a series of whimsical cartoons which appeared in 1962 under the name "Knifesmith's Corner".

CZECH, fat, fat cheque paid to

Ian Hislop's statement after paying £55,000 damages and nearly a quarter of a million in legal costs to the publisher of the *Daily Mirror* (☞ MAXWELL, Robert, full list of complaints against *Private Eye*) was scripted on the back of an envelope on which he and Peter Cook (capitals) were passing each other notes while Maxwell was giving evidence.

"The new manager is quite a 'go-getter', isn't he?"

DRY CLEANERS

OPEN

PRIVATE EYE

No. 1113
20 August –
03 Sept. 2004
£1.30

BLUNKETT IN LOV

Watch out – he's on heat at the moment

E SAY

GO HOME
IRTY
IGGER

THUR NEASDEN

Australian. He owns a number of highly disreputable periodicals in his home country. They specialise in sex and sensation.

Gutter

Earlier this year, Mr Murdoch came to England and bought with his ill-gotten gains the ailing *News of the World*.

Now Mr Murdoch boasts he has in-

NAE FASH GORDON
SCUNNER CAMERON CAN GAB WITH NAE NOTES OR AUTOCUE?

PUFF
PUFF

JOCKSHIRE POST

CAMERON GIVES BROON A DOSE O' LALDY

BROON ALE

CAN BE JUST SPONTANEOUS S THAT WEE BAMPOT!

AYE!

Down the Hatch
By the authors of 'Dear Bill'

One for the Road
Authors of 'Dear Bill'

Just the One
By the authors of 'Dear Bill'
Further letters of Denis Thatcher

D

DAIQUIRI RUM, too
respectable for *Eye*

"On any company board there is bound to be at least one person who at the mere mention of *Private Eye* goes purple in the face," wrote Richard Ingrams in 1964, taking a rare interest in the business side of things. "Not so long ago, owing to a last-minute cancellation we inserted a free advertisement for Daiquiri Rum. Following publication there came a letter from Daiquiri's agent, 'despite the fact that the space was offered free of charge we take the most serious view of the situation'. We were on no account to do it again. The incident was wholly typical."[37]

DALEKS, invasion of BBC

Private Eye began soliciting examples of what it called "Birtspeak" in April 1994, when director general John Birt was busy dismantling the BBC via the medium of his "virtual internal market" and "producer choice" initiatives. It was illustrated with a Ken Pyne cartoon of a Dalek with Birt's face in tribute to playwright Dennis Potter's description of the director general as a "croak-voiced Dalek dressed up in an Armani suit".

It prompted an outraged letter. "Sir – I write in response to the illustration of Mr John Birt as a Dalek. I speak for a number of my colleagues in saying that I find this a very upsetting image. How are we to remain the superior beings in the universe with this sort of slander continually resurfacing? Love and kisses, the Dalek Supreme, Skaro."

The metaphor is, however, much appreciated among the crew of *Doctor Who* itself. "Birt had no ability to understand comedy or drama or imagination whatsoever," says Rob Shearman, the writer who brought the Daleks back to life in 2005. "The Daleks are a good metaphor to use for saying that someone's really rubbish at their very responsible job," says Nick Briggs, who provides the metallic monstrosities' voices (and obligingly read out some of the *Eye*'s "Birtspeak" columns in character for a recent documentary). "The Daleks don't bother communicating with the people they invade, they just kill them, or tell them what to do or starve them, or make them work."[38]

DEAR BILL

Like "Mrs Wilson's Diary" (☞) before it, "Dear Bill", the fortnightly dispatch by Margaret Thatcher's other half, was a co-production by Richard Ingrams and John Wells. It elevated Denis Thatcher, a very successful but fairly obscure former businessman, to national-treasure status, in the process subsuming his own personality almost entirely in one of the satirists' invention – so much so that when the real Denis died in 2003, the *Daily Mail* decided the best tribute was to reprint several of the fictional one's letters.

Wells first realised the comic possibilities offered by Denis while watching the Tory-leadership election results on television in 1975. "I remember it very vividly. There at the back was Denis grinning very widely – obviously he'd had a few – the television lights reflected off his glasses. He immediately seemed to me to be a very attractive comic character; a really charming saloon bar figure, like the person who you see in a pub saying 'I'm in the chair, have another drink.' Straight away, I thought he was a well-drawn, possibly Wodehousian figure."[39]

"No one really knew anything at all about Denis Thatcher when he arrived in Downing Street," says Richard Ingrams (Slicker [☞] tried, with a very good piece on his past dealings as a director of Burmah Oil in May 1979, but that wasn't nearly as much fun). Weirdly, Wells and Ingrams seemed to get him bang to rights from the very first episode, which saw him regretfully missing a round of golf at Sandwich in favour of getting togged up in "the full kit from Moss Bros. for some kind of State Opening of Parliament or other", which he spent enjoying several tinctures with George Brown and declaring he "didn't like the cut of that fellow Stevas's jib". "On a whole range of subjects, the creators managed to give, in somewhat exaggerated prose, a sample of Denis's views," writes his daughter Carol Thatcher, who felt the *Eye* particularly captured her father's attitude to the "reptiles" of Fleet Street and the "pinkoes" at the BBC. "It used to horrify me sometimes, the detail they had," recalled Downing Street aide Charles Powell.[40] "On one occasion when security had been tightened up we wrote an entirely imaginary account of Denis's chagrin at being trailed round the golf course by his fictional bodyguard, Eric, wearing a gabardine raincoat and with his socks hanging down," remembered Wells. "Within hours of the edition going to press we were told that the real Denis had gone off under similar conditions for a game of golf with Willie Whitelaw and had refused to set foot on the course, complaining that the detective in attendance was 'improperly accoutred'."[41]

"Bill", by contrast, started out as an entirely imaginary creation – "a fictional Bill with a nymphomaniac wife called Daphne, a chequered past in overseas commerce and two fictional friends called the Major and Maurice Picarda," said Wells. But real-life friend and golfing partner of the First Husband Bill Deedes quickly became irredeemably identified with the addressee (even despite a reference to "that nice old boy Deedes, funny way of talking as if he's sloshed, which he is most of the time" in a 1986 letter to the Bill in question). It was a habit: over forty years earlier Deedes had been widely reputed to be the model for the hapless reporter William Boot in Evelyn Waugh's novel *Scoop*. "I was a humdrum journalist and humdrummer politician before Denis began his letter," the former *Telegraph* editor reminisced. "Now we are both famous. My wife and I get invited to functions far above our social status. The chairman says: 'Here's Deedes who I think was in some former Liberal administration and once editor of the *Daily Express* but we welcome him tonight as Bill in *Private Eye*! They lose their glazed look and clap like crazy. The fact that I am not the Bill who Denis wrote to, and keep saying so, excites them even more."[42]

In fact, it was the opposite way round. "We just wrote the letters as we imagined Bill Deedes would have written them," says Ingrams, who knew Deedes well.[43] If that failed, they could rely on his family – Ingrams claims to have taken most of the fictional Denis's favourite terms for drinks – tinctures, sharpeners, snorts – from the real-life conversation of Deedes's son Jeremy.

Deedes (senior) shrewdly pointed out what a propaganda coup the *Eye* had inadvertently achieved on Denis's behalf, particularly given the way that the press could have interpreted the unprecedented situation of having a woman in Number 10: "His friends knew how astute he was, with a considerable knowledge of human kind and a very good judge of character. But *Private Eye* established him as a completely

different figure, which meant that it would look ridiculous if a tabloid accused him of inspiring any piece of legislation or any idea. Once that image was indelibly imprinted on the voting public, how could you pretend that he was a serious figure? It was therefore very difficult to paint Denis as an eminence grise."

Denis eventually grew to love the character so

George Adamson provided the illustrations for Denis's early years in Downing Street

much that his family had his eightieth-birthday cake made up in the form of a mock *Private Eye* cover. Carol Thatcher says he regretted only one thing: "He became annoyed when they were published in paperback and fans began sending books to Number 10 for his autograph; they even expected *him* to fork out for the return postage."

☞ *ANYONE FOR DENIS?*; PRIME MINISTERIAL PARODIES, moments they become reality

DEEDES, Sally

Sally Deedes was the pseudonymn for Liz Elliott, who took over the consumer column from Penny Junor in 1982. Penny was the daughter of John Junor, editor of the *Sunday Express*, and Bill Deedes was the editor of the *Daily Telegraph*, so he might have had a daughter called Sally – do you see? No, no one else did either.

Occasionally young thrusting hack Ian Hislop would stand in on the column, when the accompanying picture would be changed to that of a man and the byline to Solly Deedes.

☞ THE MILLION-POUND WIN

DENIALS

"Letters to *Private Eye* always come out wrong," former "Barry McKenzie" (☞) cartoonist Nick Garland advised his boss Max Hastings after the then *Telegraph* editor admitted he was thinking of writing to correct a tale about himself.[44]

Some people understand this. Colin MacInnes, author of the novel *Absolute Beginners*, got it when he wrote in 1969 to say that he didn't mind that the *Eye* had "had a go at me … when it comes to writers believing they are libelled, defamed or otherwise mocked, it seems to me that the nature of their own activity dictates their own lines of conduct".

Some do not. Brian Basham adopted an unusual tone for a PR man in 1996: "Look here, shit-head – how do you manage to get so many things wrong in one fucking article?" Others adopt an air of pomposity from the

outset, as reader Mark Hearne noted in 2001: "My attention has been drawn to the fact that anyone who addresses an editor with the phrase 'my attention has been drawn …' is a pompous prat. If the implication is supposed to be that the writer is far too grand to bother with said editor's lowly rag himself, the effect is one of ludicrous self-importance."

Far better to fight fire with fire, as impresario and author of the *Henry Root Letters* Willie Donaldson did in 1970:

"The story could perhaps have been improved upon. You did point out that I am middle-aged, balding, dishonest and unsuccessful, but you failed to mention that I masturbate, suffer from haemorrhoids, take drugs and can't satisfy my wife or anyone else."

Either that, or adopt the tactic of L. E. Dale, a civil servant at the Ministry of Transport who was accused of wrongdoing the same year.

"Sir,
You publish (page four, column two)
A tale which can scarcely be true.
For Mandarin Dale
(About whom your tale)
Was not even there. Nor were you!
L.E. Dale."

DESMOND, Dirty

Pornographer Richard Desmond has been a *Private Eye* fixture since way back in the days when he was doing business with the New York Mafia and before the proprietorship of Express Newspapers and Channel 5 was even a glint in his eye. And he claims to love it.

"I think it's good that they call me Dirty Desmond," he told Radio 4's *Today* programme in June 2010. "They call Peter Hill, the editor of the *Daily Express*, Peter 'Mentally' Hill, that's very funny. I've never actually bought a copy, I won't give them the satisfaction. I just go to the newsstand and have a quick flick."

You could have fooled his staff, who have witnessed him ranting about the *Eye*'s coverage of his business empire on many an occasion.

DIANA, Princess, death of, and subsequent lunacy

Princess Diana's death came at a bad time for many people, not least herself. It was the early hours of a Sunday morning, when a set of newspapers full of very unflattering coverage of her romance with Dodi Fayed were on their way to newsagents. And it was the day before *Private Eye* itself went to press, giving the team very little time to react. "I had until four the next afternoon to produce a humorous magazine," remembered Ian Hislop. "It was about as hard as it's got for me."[45]

The blanket rolling-news coverage made it easier. "It was one of those cases where I knew exactly what I wanted to do by the end of Sunday," he says now. "And I had the cover joke in my head which I then put on the cover when I came in."

While the rest of the media unilaterally decided to declare the late princess a saint and themselves amnesiac, the *Eye* went in a different direction. "In recent weeks (not to mention the last 10 years) we at the *Daily Gnome*, in common with all other newspapers, may have inadvertently conveyed the impression that the late Princess of Wales was in some way a neurotic, irresponsible and manipulative troublemaker," declared the Gnome editorial. "We would like to express our sincere and deepest hypocrisy to all our readers on this tragic day and hope and pray that they will carry on buying our paper notwithstanding." The "Street of Shame" pages offered "The Mourning Papers", a compendium of the reverential coverage from Monday's press compared with what the same hacks had been saying about Diana mere days before. "Francis [Wheen] can turn around four columns of what other people have said that contradicts themselves in his sleep. It was particularly sharp – a brilliant piece," says Hislop. "And it defined, I thought, the way we reacted for the rest of the mounting hysteria. I think the *Eye*'s stance over that confirmed for a lot of people that we can call it right, it wasn't stories or even jokes particularly, it was just attitude." Unfortunately, that attitude was out of kilter with the only one anyone was permitted to express in the week after the death of the newly appointed People's Princess.

The magazine appeared on newsstands on

The offending cover, and an extract from Francis Wheen's Mourning Papers inside

HUMBUG ...

"The sight of a paunchy playboy groping a scantily-dressed Diana must appal and humiliate Prince William... As the mother of two young sons she ought to have more decorum and sense. She has for many years criticised Prince Charles for being a distant, undemonstrative father. In the long run he's been the more responsible parent and certainly inflicted less damage, anguish and hurt."
— Lynda Lee-Potter, *Daily Mail*, 27 Aug.

"Throughout their childhood she gave her sons endless loving cuddles... She adored her children."
— Lynda Lee-Potter, *Daily Mail*, 1 Sep.

Don't Miss the Daily Gnome's 94-Page Diana Tribute Special. Including

A particularly prescient piece by the jokes team, published the day after Diana's death

Wednesday 3 September, and disappeared just as swiftly from many of them. It had briefly found itself next to an edition of the *Express* with a front page demanding "SHOW US YOU CARE, MA'AM" and a *Sun* which screamed "WHERE IS OUR QUEEN? WHERE IS HER FLAG?" Her Majesty would be shoved in front of the cameras by the end of the week, propelled by the same "intense public pressure" which had apparently forced the cancellation of football matches on the day of Diana's funeral and made the sort of newspapers which usually moan about the cost of bank holidays to the British economy demand all shops be closed and their staff given the day off to grieve as publicly as possible. According to

the *Mirror*, "the people of Britain" – all of them? – were "expected to line the route of Diana's last journey on Saturday to say a final farewell". This was no time for dissenting voices. This was a time for blind, unquestioning lunacy.

"All that freedom of speech stuff just fell out of the window really," noted Hislop.[46] *Private Eye* was banned outright in Alldays, Gibbs, Paperchain and Dillons for containing "material we felt inappropriate". Another newsagents' chain, Martins, demanded to know "if the cover had been cleared beforehand with Buckingham Palace". "We also had complaints from various Menzies shops as well, and they refused to handle it," says managing director Dave Cash. "And I got a phone call from quite a high-up figure at W. H. Smiths saying she was going to remove it and Smiths weren't going to sell that issue." Apparently she particularly objected to mention of "the car" in one of the speech bubbles, despite the fact that it was satirising the ghoulishness of those who wanted to buy publications which carried details of the accident. "I then phoned up someone else at Smiths and the long and the short of it was that was reversed very quickly indeed," says Cash. "They realized they could be in serious trouble. It disappeared from the shelves temporarily – I think for a morning in certain shops." That, however, was enough to deprive the mag of tens of thousands of sales. At Reading station, the newsagents refused to sell Richard Ingrams a copy of the mag he had helped put together. "I was told that the magazine had

The mob as seen by John Kent in issue 933 a fortnight later

been 'taken off the shelves'. Thus the only paper to preserve some sense of proportion was the only one you couldn't buy."[47]

The magazine lost about a third of its usual sales on the Diana edition. As Hislop noted in the next issue, "The *Eye* will be the only publication in the country not to have put on a large increase in sales and not to have made a large amount of money out of Diana's death. There is, you may note, a certain irony here."

There wasn't much of that on the letters page, which carried a series of scathing missives beneath the heading "Anti": "Shitbag ... keep your gob shut for once in your life ... grossly offensive ... total and complete tastelessness ... I never want to read your publication or hear of you ever again. You are the foulest bunch of cretins of whom I have ever known. You are what creeps out, covered in green slime, from beneath large flat stones. You offend the nostrils. You are beneath contempt ... 'Jokes' of this nature, and at this time of national grieving especially, will NOT be tolerated." Fortunately, the "Pro" letters outnumbered these by a factor of ten. The "Media News" page revealed that the BBC had received an even higher proportion of complaints from those who could not empathise with what the corporation had declared the national mood – but had decided to delay an edition of Radio 4's *Feedback* programme saying so until after the funeral "out of respect". The jokes pages demanded "Did the Press Overkill Diana?", and E. J. Thribb offered his own apology (right).

The same edition also punctured the bubble of Diana's brother Earl Spencer, who had temporarily inherited her saintliness following his oration at her funeral, by pointing out that he had attempted to set up a photospread of his house and family in *Hello!* even though he was campaigning for a privacy law. He objected violently, telling the *Daily Mail* that his "lawyers were considering his position", so the *Eye* printed extracts from his correspondence which proved he had literally been prepared to sell his mother to the magazine.

Meanwhile, as the sanctification of the late princess went on, and the press continued to take the increasingly bizarre fantasies of Dodi's father Mohamed Fayed at face value, the *Eye* took steps to ensure that it could not be cut off from its readers so easily again. New subscribers were offered a free copy of the "banned" issue

"while *very* limited stocks last": the number of subscriptions doubled. Hislop republished all the Diana jokes in the *Eye*'s 1997 annual which came out in October, too. When, after the 2005 terrorist bombs, newsagents again expressed discomfort about a cover which showed London mayor Ken Livingstone proposing to invite the perpetrators "round for tea" as he had previously done with suicide-bomb fan Sheikh Yusuf Al-Qaradawi, the editor was furious. "It's none of their bloody business! I got very angry and said 'You're not allowed to pick and choose, you sell what we give you or we don't give it to you.'"

Looking back fourteen years on, it's very hard to see what all the fuss around issue 932 was about. "It was an extraordinary period," muses Hislop now. "I thought 'This is historic,' not in the sense that it's being portrayed as historic, but in the sense that something is happening in this country that I don't recognise and I don't feel part of." Thankfully – even if they were a bit wary of saying so at the time – plenty of people turned out to feel the same.

☞ OFFENSIVE, most, items published in *Private Eye*

POETRY CORNER

In Memoriam Sir Georg Solti, Jeffrey Bernard, Mother Teresa, General Sir John Hackett, President Mobutu, Hans Eysenck, Burgess Meredith

So. Farewell
Then.
All of the
Above.

Unfortunately there
Is not sufficient
Space

To write a
Poem about
You.

E.J. Thribb (17½)

SPENCER vs WINDSOR

The young Princes should not be brought up by a man who was unfaithful to his wife while she was suffering from an eating disorder... Still, I'll have a go

DIARY, Auberon Waugh's

"Auberon Waugh's Diary" ran from 1972 to 1986. It started, at Richard Ingrams's suggestion, as a parody of former *Eye* contributor Alan Brien's weekly diary in the *Sunday Times*, complete with byline photo of Waugh in an atrocious false beard, but had evolved into something completely different by the time Brien lost both beard and column a few years later. It kicked off with a warning that "all characters and incidents are fictitious. No resemblance is intended to real persons or events whatever," but for the next fourteen years some readers – usually those least qualified to enjoy a humorous magazine – insisted on taking its contents entirely at face value. One can only assume that those who thought Waugh honestly believed the entire working class was "pig-like" and cancelled their subscriptions accordingly also believed that Princess Anne had genuinely given birth to a centaur, and that Waugh really had assassinated both Kennedys.

These extracts, which give Waugh's own account of life at *Private Eye*, are hopefully slightly less accurate than the material surrounding them.

OCTOBER 1972

To get into the Women of the Year lunch at the Savoy Hotel I was forced to dress up in drag and give my name as Glenda Slag, first lady of Greek Street. I disliked doing this, as it seems to cheapen everything the Women's Freedom Movement stands for. I also thought my beard might excite ribald comment, but in this it seems I underestimated the sisterhood. As Jill Tweedie of the *Grauniad* (who happened to be with me) points out, it is time people realised that women have the fundamental right to grow beards if they want to. Men have taken it for granted for too long that theirs is the only sex capable of an act which is, fundamentally, as natural as going to the lavatory.

DECEMBER 1972

The traditional *Private Eye* lunch. After Grace has been said by The Blessed Arnold [Goodman (☞)] we have to listen to poor Max Aitken moaning on about all the Australians, New Zealanders and Indonesians who laid down their lives in seven world wars. He really is becoming the most dreadful bore and his tip-offs about Vere Harmsworth are becoming less and less reliable. Soon, I fear, we will have to stop asking him.

On the other hand, the food is so filthy at these lunches I can never ask any of my smart friends like Roy Jenkins.

NOVEMBER 1975

All 25 members of *Private Eye*'s editorial staff are former presidents of the Oxford Union, and so are most of the 73 barristers who call every week to read the magazine for attempted libel. Looking around my colleagues I cannot help feeling that without this millstone around our necks, we might have been able to find more gainful and socially desirable occupations elsewhere, whether in cancer research or showing Arab gentlemen around London.

Nicolas Bentley provided the illustrations for Waugh's diary until his death. "In six years collaboration we never had a cross word or sticky moment," recalled Waugh

JANUARY 1982

In the late morning, the Prince of Wales drops in, hoping for a glass of cherry brandy. He tells me his wife is pregnant. What should he call it, and will I agree to be Godfather?

As the child will be nearly half English, this seems a reasonable request. I tell him that of course the child should be called Auberon, if it is a boy. If it is a girl he can call it anything he likes except Shirley.

A group called Lesbians in Publishing has awarded me a prize for my journalism this year. It takes the form of a marzipan pig covered in pink icing sugar. It is perfectly delicious. Whoever cooked it would probably make a lovely little wife for some lucky man.

OCTOBER 1982

A summons from my beloved proprietor to attend on him at Gnome Towers without fail at 10.45am. This is a bad sign, as it is exactly the hour at which His Lordship generally goes to the lavatory.

Intensely shy, he can talk to his subordinates only when he is seated on the lavatory. He seldom looks at them and never refers to them by name.

Willie Rushton illustrated the diary from 1978. Waugh was equally delighted with this collaboration: "I find political and world events now register only to the extent that they might provide material for a Rushton cartoon."

'Kneel down,' he says kindly as I am ushered in. A long silence follows. Plop.

Marmaduke wishes to talk about herpes, the exciting new venereal disease being promoted by the *Sunday Times*. He has personal knowledge of the disease, having contracted it many years ago in Algeciras, apparently from his step-mother.

He tells me that far from having any deleterious effects, it is entirely beneficial, promoting an active sex life, vigorous hair growth and a lively interest in the affairs of young people. Indeed it is to herpes that His Lordship attributes much of his success in life. Unsightly symptoms may be kept at bay by eating Lymeswold.

JANUARY 1984

Arriving early in the office I find it has been broken into and the whole place turned over by criminals – no doubt victims of Mrs Shirley Williams's comprehensive education policy. Being totally uneducated, they missed all my Fabergé bibelots, my picture of Diana the Huntress by Boucher and a delightful *fête champêtre* attributed to Fragonard, stealing only a Sony Walkman which belongs to the boy who sticks my articles on pieces of cardboard. I spend the whole morning trying to comfort the sobbing lad.

APRIL 1984

Back from an extended cruise in the South China Seas I find that in my absence they have moved *Private Eye*'s offices to Carlisle Street, just off Soho Square. My own penthouse suite now includes a double bath as well as sauna and Jacuzzi, in case I should ever wish to take a bath with my masseuse.

JUNE 1984

In Gnome House to sort out my correspondence I hear a secretary scream and fear the worst: someone has accepted my challenge to debag Tony Blackburn and is claiming the £100 prize. A photograph of the scene is much too horrible to show here. I lock it away in my safe beside photographs of Prince Andrew and Koo Stark, Vicki Hodge, Ted Heath, Harold Wilson in Moscow and other filth too appalling to mention.

SEPTEMBER 1984

The Queen's hatred of Margaret Thatcher is becoming so obsessive that I look forward to the times when the Royal Family are at Balmoral. She keeps urging me to attack Mrs Thatcher mercilessly in *Private Eye*, but I have to tell her it is not that sort of magazine. We on the *Eye* are not interested in politics. If Ma'am has any good stories to tell us about Bishops and actresses, or homosexual clergymen, she will be paid at the usual rates.

DECEMBER 1984

A summons to Lord Gnome's penthouse suite on the 48th floor of Gnome House. All 17,000 employees are gathered together and kneel in respectful silence on the malachite floor of the Green Ballroom waiting for the aged philanthropist to be wheeled in. There is a general fear that he may have chosen the Christmas season to announce one of his occasional 'shakedowns' or mass sackings. Many of the older secretaries are in tears.

In fact he wishes to announce that after 23 years W. H. Smugg [q.v.] has agreed to sell his illustrious organ. This will mean an incalculable increase in his own wealth. As a token of his pleasure he has agreed to give every member of the staff a photograph of himself and two Jaffa oranges.

SEPTEMBER 1985

To Gnome House for the publishing event of the century. Not since Shakespeare's First Folio appeared in 1622 has there been anything like it. All the elegance, beauty and talent in London parade themselves on the floodlit lawns. In silk-walled drawing rooms there are fountains of champagne with lovely topless Quartettes [employees of Quartet Books, noted for their pulchritude] splashing in them (by graceful permission of His Highness Naim Attallah) disguised as mermaids, to the sublime music of the London Symphony Orchestra playing snatches from Gilbert and Sullivan. The party celebrates *A Turbulent Decade: The Diaries of Auberon Waugh 1976–1985* (Deutsch £4.95). Wandering through those familiar rooms, the scene of so many momentous events, where now the indescribably delicious perfumes of Avant l'Amour and Après l'Amour compete tantalizingly with each other, I see Princess Margaret endeavouring to join a group of topless, trembling Quartettes in the Bernini fountain. She is restrained by a Lady in Waiting.

Should she have been prevented from expressing her joy in this natural and healthy way? There are serious doubts about the general sense of direction in Gnome House nowadays.

NOVEMBER 1985

A summons to the executive penthouse suite where Lord Gnome has retired since losing all his money in his foolish libel action against a Welsh solicitor. White robed attendants wear face masks and rubber gloves as they push his Lordship around in a wheel chair whose rubber tyres make no sound on the walnut parquet.

We face each other for a while, the silence broken only by the terrible clicking of his eyes as they roll around in his head. "Waugh," he says – he who used to call me Peregrine and once gave me his Pekingese puppy to play with, "Waugh, you have been attacking me in the press, on radio and television. You have betrayed the great trust which I reposed in you …"

Is it my imagination, or does a slight German accent creep in as his Lordship's voice rises to a scream?

"Unt ferzer more vee haf not zold ein single copy of your *Diaries*. You are secked, fired, dismissed. Get out off mein haus!"

A serene Malaysian nurse gives him an injection in the arm, and two beautiful smiling Filipinos hurry forward to see if his nappy needs changing. It is a sad, sad sight.

☞ HP SAUCE, Auberon Waugh's stewardship of

DIGGER, Dirty

This is Rupert 'Digger' Murdoch the last of the Great Press Barons, escapee, master of disguise, the man who made a fortune out of filth. Read his story in PRIVATE EYE Astonishing!

"Digger" was a slang term used for Anzac troops during World War One. The *Eye*, as street-smart as ever, applied it to Rupert Murdoch when he became proprietor of the *News of the World* half a century later.

DIPLOMACY, *Eye* does its bit for

In 1979 Jack Lundin had reported for the *Eye* from Saudi Arabia on the death of Helen Smith, a British nurse whose body had been found beneath a balcony in Jeddah after a party. Paul Foot then took on the story and, pushed by Helen's determined father, self-described "cantankerous bastard" Ron Smith, continued to uncover mystery after mystery surrounding her death in the face of determined obstruction from the Foreign Office and, eventually, publicly funded legal action by their vice-consul. After three years of fortnightly coverage, Foot and Smith managed to force an inquest to be held on British soil. It noted that Helen's injuries were not consistent with the official account of her death, but recorded an open verdict. Both Foot and Ron Smith always remained convinced she

had been murdered, with British officials co-operating in a cover-up for diplomatic reasons.

The magazine opened up hostilities with the Foreign Office on another front in October 1980 when it revealed that the recently retired deputy under-secretary of state and high commissioner to Canada Sir Peter Hayman had been arrested for sending 'correspondence of an obscene nature' to fellow members of the Paedophile Information Exchange, but that the director of public prosecutions had declined to bring any charges against him and the whole affair had been quietly glossed over. It was not until the following year that Hayman was named in the House of Commons, which, his *Times* obituary mildly noted, "sadly tarnished the lustre of his achievements".
☞ PERSIA, Shit of

DIRECTORS
☞ STRIPS, longest-running

DITTO MAN, the

"A Mr Norman Scott has sent me some very curious material concerning his close friend, the Liberal leader Jeremy Thorpe," announced the "Grovel" column in November 1975. "If Mr Thorpe would send me my usual fee I will send him the dossier and say no more." This was something of an in-joke, given that Norman Scott had been doing the rounds of newspaper offices and pubs for years by that point. No one – not even the *Eye* – was willing to print his claims. He was a classic example of one of Claud Cockburn's loons (☞), a man who had spent time in psychiatric institutions, so obsessed with and damaged by his own story that he was unable to tell it clearly, waffling on at such length about the supposed theft of his national insurance card that the other part of his story – that he had had a lengthy affair with Thorpe during the 1960s, when homosexuality was still illegal – did not get taken seriously. By this point, however, he had become enough of a nuisance for someone to try and kill him.

Famously, they failed. The fact that the assassin chosen for the job, an airline pilot called Andrew Newton, managed only to

Those present in the magistrates' court certainly did learn more – Scott blurted out his belief that he had been targeted because of his affair with the politician – but hardly anyone else did, thanks to the best efforts of Thorpe, who, the *Eye* noted, had spent a great deal of time "on the phone to the editors of one or two national papers asking them not to mention him in their court reports". Several were happy to comply. "The *Daily Mirror* had an enormous file on the case which never looked remotely like getting past the libel lawyers," remembered *Eye* hack Patrick Marnham. "Nevertheless, two *Mirror* reporters continued day by day to collect the most detailed information purely for purposes of 'background' ... They considered this to be standard Fleet Street practice." The *Sunday Times*, in a bizarre bit of mixed-up thinking, claimed that the *Eye*'s willingness to consider that a homosexual might have been targeted for assassination demonstrated that they were anti-gay. Harold Evans (☞) even printed affectionate letters from Thorpe to Scott in which he promised him that "bunnies can (and will) go to France" and insisted these were evidence of the staunch heterosexuality and businesslike behaviour of the Liberal leader.

Paul Foot, then editing *Socialist Worker*, had started coming in to the *Eye* again for regular sessions attempting to get to the bottom of Harold Wilson's resignation in March 1976, and the paranoia the PM had begun to air about plots against him. One such fantasy was that Jeremy Thorpe had been targeted by the South African security service, BOSS, for "destabilising". As Foot dug further, it became obvious that this claim was nonsense – but that the story behind it was even more astonishing. Throughout Newton's prison sentence for his "attempt to endanger life", Thorpe continued to insist that he had had nothing to do with the curious incident of the dog on Exmoor. But the police were increasingly convinced that he had.

Foot learned this from the officer in charge of the investigation into the attempt on Scott's life, who had become frustrated by the reluctance of the director of public prosecutions to press charges against Thorpe for conspiracy to murder despite the mass of evidence he had built up against the politician. Foot had not been prepared to rely on Scott's word alone – he had actually thrown him out of the office when

shoot Scott's dog, a Great Dane called Rinka, added to the sense of farcical unreality which surrounded the entire affair. It was well suited to "Auberon Waugh's Diary", where it featured that December: "West Somerset is buzzing with rumours of a most unsavoury description. Information about this puzzling incident has since been restricted on Home Office orders, but a man arrested at London Airport on a firearms charge will be appearing before Minehead Magistrates, when we may learn more. My only hope is that sorrow over his friend's dog will not cause Mr Thorpe's premature retirement from public life." Newton was sent to prison in March 1976.

he visited, objecting to a sexist comment Scott made about his colleague Liz Elliott – or that of Newton, who emerged from prison in April 1977 to claim that he had been paid £5,000 by "a prominent Liberal" to shoot Scott. But with the information he received from Detective Chief Superintendent Michael Challes through an intermediary, he was finally ready in July 1978 to go into print with what he called "a scandal the like of which British politics hasn't known for half a century".

"I remember Paul taking me out of the office for a walk in Covent Garden to tell me he was going to predict Thorpe's imminent arrest in the next issue," says Ingrams. "It is not every day that the leader of one of our political parties is accused of murder, so any news to this effect was sensational and obviously risky. I had such faith in Paul's judgement that I had no qualms about publishing."

Jeremy Thorpe certainly did have qualms. As soon as the article – headlined "The Ditto Man" after the repeated reply Thorpe had offered to police following his refusal to comment on their first question – appeared, he issued a libel writ, and referred the article to the DPP and attorney general claiming contempt of court. At which point the Curse of Gnome (☞ WRITS, First of many) kicked in, and the Liberal leader was at last arrested and charged with conspiracy to murder. He was found not guilty the following June.

There was one other pleasing discovery along the way. It turned out that Norman Scott had been an *Eye* cover model, his naked bottom lifted from a perfume ad in 1971, giving readers a chance to appreciate what Thorpe might have seen in him.

☞ VOTE *PRIVATE EYE*

DRIBERG, Tom

Tom Driberg, politician, gossip columnist, gourmet, Security Service asset, champagne socialist and celebrity hanger-on of everyone from Edith Sitwell to Mick Jagger, compiled the legendarily filthy *Private Eye* crossword from 1969 until his death in 1976. From 1972 onwards he used the pseudonym Tiresias.

Though he was perfectly capable of sending in his clues in a legible form, he would always insist on visiting the office on Wednesdays to dictate them. This was because it gave him the chance to ogle the *Eye*'s two "pin-up boys", hack Patrick Marnham and typesetter Steve Mann.

"He was just this sweet elderly gentleman who'd sit there, look at me and sigh," Mann fondly recalls. "Which I found quite flattering. He was also always trying to lure me back to his flat in the Barbican, but never succeeded."

Driberg liked to boast that he could seduce any man, gay or straight, in the time it took the lift at 22 Greek Street to ascend to the third floor. Ingrams installed a notice on the ground floor: "No male member of staff will take the lift on Wednesdays."

☞ LUNCH, tales from the Coach and Horses; POOVES, Richard Ingrams' peculiar attitude to; PRIVATE SPY

E

U-phemisms

THE AUSTERITY MEASURES WILL BE PAINFUL, BUT WILL ENABLE THE E.U. TO SURVIVE

R.G.J

E.U. FINANCE MINISTER

I'm introducing policies which mean you lose your job so I can keep mine

ALL GIRL STRIP REVUE CLUB

Gerald Scarfe.

THE ESTABLISHMENT

LENNY CENSORED BRUCE

ll's well at ends Elwes

est incident in the continuing
f Lord Lucan's disappearance
on November 25 after the
service for his close friend,
Elwes. Elwes committed
September and at the service a
as read by John Aspinall. As
left the church he was punched
ow mourner (and cousin to Elwes)
e Rodd. Mr Rodd said "That's
think of your bloody speech,
", and then retired to the bar of
Club.

e events will have been closely
d by Det. Chief Supt. Roy
of Scotland Yard, who remains
by the Lucan case and whose
to trace the murderer of Sandra
the Lucan nanny, have not been
d by Lord Lucan's beautiful friends.
om the beginning the police have
bstruction and silence from the
of gamblers and boneheads with
n Lord Lucan and Dominic Elwes
iated. On the morning after the
der John Aspinall held a lunch to
h he invited the Lucan circle so that
could decide "what to do if Lucan
ed up". Aspinall received several
s of money to help the fugitive
telephoned and

Lucan had spoken of his intention to
murder his wife. When the inquest into
Sandra Rivett's death was held, Greville
Howard was in bed with backache, pillow-
ing his head on a sackful of certificates
from the fashionable doctors who were
of the opinion that he could not be moved
an inch.

When he is feeling stronger, Greville
Howard works for Goldsmith at Slater
Walker, which the latter has taken over
following the early retirement of Jim
Slater. Before this, Goldsmith made his
fortune with Cavenham Foods and Anglo-
Continental Investment. He is a cousin to
the French Rothschilds, and in the City is

fact the
politics i
was a ke
The poli
John As
in his pr
conclude
by genet
address ,
blood",
genetics
remindi
Chaplin'
however
lumberin
Elwes
had caus

The
the end
number
rather u
armies,
military
case) thi
to Carti
needed

For s
Lucan c.
relations
circle. A
had app
Magazin
between
closest f
Birley, I
Birley, a
Goldsmi
responsi
snaps of

WOO!

YEH!

LB

Reeve...

"More 'E', Vicar?"

EDITORS, astonishing
similarities between

● Richard Ingrams's and Ian Hislop's fathers were both international travellers who died when their sons were very young. Ingrams lost his father at fifteen. "I didn't have a father breathing down my neck saying 'When are you going to get a proper job?', luckily. My mother was very easy-going as far as all that was concerned. He wouldn't have approved of *Private Eye* at all. Had he been alive, things would have been very different."[48]

Hislop's father died when he was just twelve. For a long time, he felt duty-bound to follow in his footsteps: "I started off doing the wrong A-levels, because I thought I should be my dad, because I'd lost him and I thought 'Well, obviously I've got to be a civil engineer, proper job, scientist.' And then about halfway through the first term in sixth form I thought 'I actually want to do English

Richard Ingrams camps it up at Oxford in the company of Johannes Brahms and Paul Foot . . .

and French,' so I changed. And then again I applied to Oxford to read PPE, because I thought I should do Economics, and then while I was in my year off I thought 'I don't want to do this – I want to do English.' So I kept being diverted by the thoughts of doing something properly."

Thankfully, his mother was as supportive as Mrs Ingrams had been. "I said 'I don't have a job, but what I'm going to do is go to London with some friends and share a flat. That's it. You'll be really surprised because it will go very well.' And that's what I did."

● Despite being from different generations, they both went to ridiculously traditional public schools (☞ CAKE'S, ST), where they became close friends with cartoonists with whom they would still be making jokes many decades later (Willie Rushton, Nick Newman).

● They both went to Oxford University. Richard was there from 1958 to 1961, when

... while Ian Hislop (far left) does the same two decades later. Marcus Berkmann, who now compliles the Dumb Britain column for the *Eye*, is third from right

he was reunited with an old schoolfriend, Paul Foot, and proceeded to "fart around, put on plays and write magazines" (☞ *PARSON'S PLEASURE, MESOPOTAMIA*).

Ian was there from 1978 to 1981, when he was reunited with an old schoolfriend, Nick Newman, and put on plays and wrote magazines (s☞ *PASSING WIND*).

● They both arrived at *Private Eye* not long after graduating and rapidly took over the editorship (*That's enough Eds*) ...

☞ HISLOP, Ian, Ten things you never knew about; INGRAMS, Facts about family that may help you towards an understanding of Richard's personality

EDITORS, fundamental differences between

"The thing about Richard is his instincts are fantastic," says Ian Hislop of Richard Ingrams. "Not only for a joke, but for what's going to turn into a story. I mean they are *really* good. He has his quite mystical ring-of-truth thing (☞). But I don't have that. So I analyse. I read. And I try and work it out."

Having had his eyes well and truly opened by the Profumo affair (☞WARD, Stephen), Ingrams devoted himself to pointing the finger at those figures in positions of power who were behaving in less than admirable ways. And, in many cases, at people he merely suspected might be. "I remember Claud Cockburn [☞] saying 'Who's the person who nobody's got a bad thing to say about?' and Willie saying 'Albert Schweitzer' and Claud said 'Right, we'll have a go at Schweitzer' – that was his attitude," says Ingrams admiringly. Later investigations into the Alsatian medical missionary suggested that some of his activities in Africa were in fact dubious – "He could have helped all these lepers if he'd used the latest scientific advances, but he was relying on Victorian methods," says Ingrams – but you get the feeling that it was simply the naughtiness of having a pop at such a revered figure that so attracted the editor. Later regular targets – Esther Rantzen, Robert Maxwell, Harold Evans – tended to have fairly inflated opinions of their own saintliness. Show Ingrams a halo and he'll start looking round for rocks with which to try to knock it off.

"I never had a campaigning feel," he told his biographer. "We exposed shits for fun."[49] He certainly doesn't offer any overarching mission statement for his editorship. Here's what he had to say on the topic in November 2009:

Richard Ingrams: I would call myself an anarchist more than a leftie, and Cook was like that, and so was Bron, I think. There was always a conflict between that attitude with Booker and I suppose with Ian to a certain extent too. That kind of slightly reckless attitude.

Adam Macqueen: Is it the difference between wanting to finish it all off, or wanting it to work better?

Ingrams: Um – no. I don't think it's either of those really. More of a – just create a bit of a stir, I suppose.

AM: Just mischief-making?

Ingrams: You could put it like that.

AM: So it's not really politics at all – it's just poking everyone with a stick.

Ingrams: Yes.

When Ingrams retired as editor, he was presented with a Gerald Scarfe portrait of himself in the costume of a mediaeval jester, the figure who was licensed to tell the truth – as rudely and amusingly as possible – to the monarch and serve as a vital safety-valve for the stiflingly hierarchical system which surrounded them. He hated it, and left it behind at his leaving do (it leaned against the wall in the lunch room at the Coach and Horses for decades afterwards). But it might not be such an inaccurate depiction.

Ian Hislop, by contrast, is usually depicted by profile writers and cartoonists as a churchman – the trendy curate in a leather jacket when he first took over the editorship, but these days more usually a bishop. His attitude to his work is much closer to the "savage indignation" that fellow satirist Jonathan Swift claimed for himself. (He's also much more willing to describe himself as a satirist than Ingrams, who would feel himself edging uncomfortably close to "Pseuds Corner"). "I'm not an anarchist, not a revolutionary, I think this is a gross misconception of what satire is and what it can do," he said in 1993. "What satirist ever toppled the government? I think Swift managed to get one small tax changed in the whole of his career. You're not there to end regimes. In a democracy, people vote, but the satirist condenses the argument and I think we're still doing that."[50] In 2009 he reckoned that "the job is to question whoever is in power. It is meant to be considered, and you are meant to be going for the areas which you think are wrong, criminal, foolish."[51]

The essential difference between the two of them is that while Ingrams aimed to kick up a fuss for the sake of it, Hislop is more determined to ferret out the things that are really worth kicking up a fuss over. "Fifty years of the *Eye*, just the fact that it's survived means people take it more seriously," he says. "And I would hope to say that its record now suggests that it gets a lot of things right. That was always what I wanted people to say about the *Eye*, not that they read it and thought 'Well, that must be untrue,' I want them to read it and say 'That's true!' That seems to me real influence."

EVANS, Dame Harold, attitude to press freedom

Former *Sunday Times* editor Dame Harold Evans holds the British Press Awards' Gold Award for Lifetime Achievement of Journalists, an International Press Institute Hero of World Press Freedom Award, has been "overwhelmingly voted" the All-Time Greatest British Newspaper Editor and received a knighthood for Services to Journalism. All these achievements he boasts about on his official website. But he holds another equally impressive title: he is the only man who has ever, through repeated legal actions, forced *Private Eye* to guarantee that it won't write anything nasty about him.

"He just kept suing!" wails Richard Ingrams. "The slightest derogatory statement was enough to provoke a letter from his lawyers threatening litigation and demanding an apology. In the end, I lost track of the number of writs he issued."[52] Eventually Ingrams gave up. In October 1977 he signed a memo to staff which the *Sunday Times* editor had drafted for him: "No reference, direct or indirect, to Mr Evans is to be made in anything printed by *Private Eye* unless it is true, unambiguous and not malicious … Contibutors should realise that if *Private Eye* publishes references to Mr Evans in disregard of the undertaking both I myself and Pressdram Ltd will be liable to proceedings for breach of the undertaking, and there will be the possibility of actions for libel. This will place *Private Eye* in serious trouble which could endanger its future."

Since this book is published by *Private Eye*, this means I am unable to tell you about 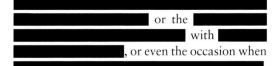 or the █████████ with █████████, or even the occasion when ███████████████. Instead, let us enjoy some inspirational words from the man himself, from his article accepting the title of Greatest Newspaper Editor of All Time from the British Journalism Review in 2002:

"At *The Sunday Times*, we fought injunction after injunction, through trial after trial. We set a precedent by challenging suppression all the way from the House of Lords to the European Court, where our triumph imposed on government a reforming Act of Parliament . . . Editors have been at their most effective, I think, when opinion takes a ride on such risk-charged reporting – and they don't give up at the first call from Sue, Grabbit and Run."[51]

Oh, and that nickname? Ingrams adopted the "Dame" title (a reference to actress Dame Edith Evans) from Lord Arran, a columnist who used it in the *Evening News*. Arran had to stop using it after – you've guessed it – Evans sent a lawyer's letter threatening action because of the "suggestion of effeminacy" in his client.

EXPENSES, MPs

JUST FANCY THAT!

July 2003: HP Sauce points out that "Speaker Martin's almost complete silence over the use he, his wife and daughter make of his parliamentary allowances and perks is not unusual. The Commons is always uneasy about investigations into the financial affairs of its senior members. One reason for the near silence may be what is known as 'the Dagenham defence', aka 'they all do it'. There is nothing to stop MPs employing their families at the taxpayer's expense and many do."

May 2009: Michael Martin resigns as Commons speaker following the exposure of widespread abuse of parliamentary expenses and allowances by MPs and a long battle to keep them secret.

EYE TV

There have been several small-screen spin-offs from *Private Eye*:

The Saturday Special: Mrs Wilson's Diary

Filmed version of the stage musical (☞ LORD CHAMBERLAIN) broadcast in ITV's theatrical slot in 1969.

Eye TV

1971 celebration of the 10th anniversary, produced for BBC2 by Barry Took. Featured Willie Rushton, Richard Ingrams, Barry Fantoni, John Wells and others acting out various cartoons and jokes from the *Eye*'s pages in costume, and adding little in the process.

Anyone for Denis?

TV adaptation of John Wells's stage version of "Dear Bill" (☞), filmed on location for ITV in 1982.

Bore of the Year Awards

Presented by Angus Deayton and featuring Peter Cook as Lord Gnome, this BBC2 version of the long-running end-of-year round-up from the

Irrelevant but amusing collage that was pinned to a noticeboard in the *Eye* office for many years

magazine was co-produced by Harry Thompson and Victor Lewis-Smith in 1993. "It was one of the strangest programmes ever," remembers Ian Hislop, who still retains a BOFTY award in his office. It ended with a lengthy performance from Mike Oldfield with Smashie and Nicey.

Sermon from St Albion's

1998 version of "St Albion Parish News" brought to life for ITV by Harry Enfield as Reverend Blair (and everyone else) and written by the *Eye* jokes team. "I said to Fantoni and Booker 'I'm not having you saying the telly's no bloody good, here's a contract, you are going to write it with me and Nick, so that we are doing it as a piece,'" says Ian Hislop. "I was against

that. I didn't like it. I thought Harry was piss-poor actually," says Barry Fantoni.

Celeb

2002 critically lambasted live-action version of Peattie and Warren's strip (☞ STRIPS, Longest-running) starring Harry Enfield as Gary Bloke and Amanda Holden as Deb. Highlight came off-screen in form of angry letter from Ozzy Osbourne's lawyers who were convinced it had been based on Osbourne's own, admittedly cartoonish, family.

☞ *HAVE I GOT NEWS FOR YOU; NEWS QUIZ*

FAMOUS FRIENDS

"There are no practical prospects of distributable profits in the foreseeable future," ran the briefing note put together by business manager Peter Usborne in 1964, which Peter Cook used to persuade several celebrity acquaintances to donate their cash to the magazine (☞ COOK, Peter, begins regular editorial contributions). "It is quite obviously not going to attract speculative capital, nor would it particularly wish to. We hope, however, that there are enough people who consider *Private Eye* to be worth a good deal more than £15,000 by the unique function it performs."

There were. And these are they:

JANE ASHER

She of cake fame. Then the girlfriend of Beatle Paul McCartney, she later met cartoonist Gerald Scarfe at a *Private Eye* party – and reader, she married him. Her investment was converted into 102 shares in the *Eye*'s publisher Pressdram, which she still holds. For decades, the only return shareholders saw was a crate of wine each Christmas in lieu of a dividend.

DIRK BOGARDE

The matinee idol may have forgotten that he owned 103 shares in the magazine by 1981, when he wrote to comfort a friend who had been unflatteringly depicted in its pages: "I suppose some other poor person is being readied for the knives next time around … What a perfectly filthy world we seem to inhabit now, when all grace, all decency, all honour is sacrificed for a tuppeny bit of paper. What amazes me, and always will, is that there are people who actually read the damn thing."[54] His shares were passed on to a nephew when he died.

PETER SELLERS

Former Goon and future Clouseau, Sellers declined to become a shareholder and had his loan repaid instead.

HUGH HEFNER

The *Playboy* boss declined the chance to throw some of his millions in the *Eye*'s direction, despite Cook offering his rather more glamorous magazine first dibs on "a very different kind of humorous photo-cartoon documentary" by himself and "Willie Rushton our fat cartoonist". "He told me to piss off," Cook recalled.[55]

ANTHONY BLOND

The publisher put the most cash into the *Eye* in 1964 and received a large holding – 2,400 shares – in return. He was a long-time friend to the magazine until he made the mistake of venturing some opinions as to how it should be run when it was going through a particularly difficult financial time in the late 1980s. This was unacceptable behaviour for an *Eye* shareholder and Peter Cook promptly bought back all his shares.

BRYAN FORBES

Fresh from directing *Whistle Down the Wind* and *The L-Shaped Room*, the filmmaker purchased a number shares but had disposed of them by the 1980s.

BERNARD BRADEN

Actor and presenter of consumer programme *On the Braden Beat*, he received 103 shares in return for his investment and returned the favour by recruiting Cook to his show to deliver a weekly monologue as E. L. Wisty. Richard Ingrams insists that the fact the BBC sacked Braden in favour of Esther Rantzen played no part in the magazine's subsequent antipathy towards her. The shares were sold to other shareholders after his death.

OSCAR LEWENSTEIN

Lewenstein invested some of the cash he had made as producer of *A Taste of Honey*, *The Loneliness of the Long Distance Runner* and *Tom Jones*, and received 103 shares in return. He later sold them to other shareholders.

LORD FARINGDON

The only (known) homosexual Communist peer to have taken his seat in the House of Lords. Most famous for addressing his speeches to 'My Dears' instead of 'My Lords'. His 102 shares are now held by his estate.

FANTONI, Barry

Barry Fantoni did not go to Shrewsbury. He didn't go to public school at all. "I came from a working-class Italian Jewish family. I had no academic qualifications because I'd gone to art school when I was fourteen." Nevertheless, he managed to work his way into the Greek Street clique, and make himself an essential ingredient of the magazine.

"I had an exhibition of paintings at the Woodstock Gallery in 1963," he remembers, "and I took some photographs to *Private Eye*, and I met Richard [Ingrams], who was then the contributions editor, and he liked them and he said would you do something like this for us?" The exhibition included a Prince Philip as a cut-out-and-dress-up doll, *Portrait of the Duke of Edinburgh in his Underpants*, which got the newspapers excited but also impressed Ingrams: even better, the new boy was keen to collaborate. Ingrams had tried his own hand at cartooning in the *Eye*'s early days with a series of whimsical little pockets signed "Ingo"; one of the aspects he went on to enjoy the most was working on strips and panels with more talented artists like John Kent, Nick Newman and Fantoni himself.

"We agreed that we would do something called the Hall of Fame. We would discuss between us what the essence of the drawing would be, and from the essence I would then add

my own particular detail," says Fantoni. The pair quickly produced striking portraits of the royal family at Princess Alexandra and Angus Ogilvy's wedding, a disintegrating Maurice Chevalier, a sickly Harold Macmillan and a Terry-Thomas unflattering enough to prompt a writ for portraying him as "a dissipated, drunken, dissolute character" rather than the "highly respected actor and clean figure of fun" his manager insisted he was. All were large-scale projects,

rendered in oil or gouache and then photographed for inclusion in the magazine, but Fantoni is modest about the work involved: "I work quickly: I suppose one of them would take me a couple of days to do. But bearing in mind it was fortnightly, I had that off-week to get it done in. And if we had a couple of ideas, I would do another one as well, so we had one in stock."

As almost everyone else hurtled off into the orbit of *TW3* (☞ THAT WAS THE WEEK THAT spoiled everything), Ingrams quickly tethered this new talent and put him on a retainer. He provided many of the illustrations for regular features, some of which, like the heading on the 'In the City' page, still appear to this day. "The 'Police 5', the little drawing that used to appear on the 'Grovel' column, with the monocle, they're all mine. That was part of my job to do things like that."

Even better, it turned out he could write as well. And he had areas of expertise lacking in Ingrams, who had surveyed swinging London, sighed in disapproval and retreated to a cottage in Berkshire. "What I recognised, and you can probably see it from my very first contribution, was that where they were weak was in their understanding of popular culture, and popular culture at that time was what people were really interested in," says Fantoni. "The Beatles. The summer of '66, and *Sergeant Pepper*, and Woodstock, the whole world became this kind of pandemic of pop. The weight of Cookie and myself on to Richard forced him to recognise that there was a world of popular music."

Fantoni was so very, very groovy that he has been

". . . and a little man from the village delivers our vegetables"

known to declare to impressionable youths that "I *was* the Sixties." He even had his own TV pop show *A Whole Scene Going*, a title that might have been rejected as a bit much if he'd suggested it for a parody in the *Eye*. Fantoni's time as a wannabe Jimmy Savile was short lived, however: he is a man who changes careers like others change their trousers. "His friends recall Fantoni the pop singer, Fantoni the cricketer and footballer, Fantoni the jazz band leader, Fantoni the straight actor and Fantoni the music critic," wrote his colleague Patrick Marnham in 1982. "At one point it was thought that he might found 'The First Church of Christ Sensualist'. Then he seemed to branch off into vegetarianism and Jungian philosophy. Next he published

SCENES YOU SELDOM SEE

"This is all very personal, Andrew. I have no intention of discussing it on my mobile in public."

a slim volume of poems … he is currently establishing a reputation as a writer of detective stories, but only a rash man would suggest that he has at last found his true vocation."[56] Since then, Fantoni has thrown himself whole-heartedly into Chinese horoscopes, been the pocket cartoonist for the *Times*, given up cartooning, taken it up again, become a professor of media studies at the University of Salerno, written a harrowing song cycle about the Holocaust, a play about Modigliani performed in French and "a satire about footballers' wives based on the plot of *Lady Windermere's Fan*", and at time of interview (summer 2009) was claiming that "My only ambition is to write a successful piece of theatre that would incorporate all the things that I really care about, which is my Italian heritage, my Jewish mother and the Italian *commedia dell'arte*." By the time this book is published he may well be perfecting his shot-put skills for the 2012 Olympics or reading the *News at Ten*. He may or may not still be at *Private Eye*, having announced in December 2010 his intention to retire to France and achieve some of the "so much else I've still got left to do".

The one constant in his professional life has been *Private Eye*, where he has been an integral part of the joke-writing team ever since he first turned up. He comes to the writing sessions with a definite mission statement: "I hate those psychopaths who run things so much. I can't do anything to stop the way the world's going, I can't do anything else with my life to show how much I hate them but by attacking them and hoping that some of them feel some kind of pain. My reason for being on the planet very largely, whether I like it or not, has been to spend nearly fifty years at *Private Eye* wilfully wishing people to be hurt from what I write. I can't get a gun and shoot Blair, much as I'd love to – but the best way I feel is that sometimes these guys might go to bed at night and feel a little bit injured by the fact they've been ridiculed."

At heart, though, he's a lover, not a fighter. Like Ingrams and Nicholas Luard (☞) before him, Fantoni found a wife, Tessa Reidy, among what he calls the "*Eye* Birds", but not before running through enough conquests to fill the "Grovel" column for several years running. "The worst one was when I was having intercourse with a girl in the office, on a shitty old armchair upstairs," he reminisces, "and the others shut all the doors and went home. We were stuck. We had to climb out the back window and all the way out down Greek Street, falling over skylights trying to find a way out in the pitch black. Bless her, she was a good sort." If his attentions were less welcomed by the women in the office as he grew older – and the record should show that more than one past colleague has described what Fantoni

'I hate those psychopaths who run things. The best way I feel is that sometimes these guys might go to bed at night and feel a little bit injured by the fact they've been ridiculed' Barry Fantoni

A bearded Barry, snapped in the 70s

calls his "tendency to embrace people physically" as making him "a total pest, really gross" – he now claims to be "reformed thoroughly" in the company of his partner Katie. "If you find somebody that you really really love, at seventy years old, what would be the point? Why buy a bottle of wine when I've got one open?"

This did, however, come too late for a couple of incidents that have become legendary: the first when Ingrams politely stepped over Fantoni and a young admirer as they rolled around on the floor of his office, made his way to his desk and continued working, and the time Fantoni clasped a pair of bejeaned buttocks bending over the photocopier only to discover they were attached to art director Tony Rushton rather than the similarly clad secretary he was aiming for. Although several people swear blind to have witnessed this, the record should probably also show that Barry claims to have "no recollection of that. That's not true."

FIRST ISSUE

Co-founder Peter Usborne had had the idea of making the magazine stand out by printing it on yellow paper, and proposed the name the *Yellow Press* (☞ NAMES, rejected for magazine). No one else liked it. Nevertheless, he says, "I stuck with the yellow paper. It's worth about five thousand quid now, if you've got an original."

Willie Rushton did all the illustrations for the early issues, and all the layout as well.

"I would have written that," says Christopher Booker. "At this very early stage it was less collaborative in that one sat at a typewriter and punched it out. Whereas quite soon we got on to more collaboration."

"The idea was to find out whether we were any good, and whether anybody else thought we were any good, and then whether anybody would actually buy it," says Usborne. Feedback was good, says Booker: "The first one sold pretty well, particularly in the Troubadour in Earl's Court. And then they said 'Are we going to get another one of those?' So we did, a few weeks later. And then we had a third one before Christmas with our friend Danae Brook as Santa Claus on the front cover. And they'd all gone so well that the feeling was that in the new year we should start the thing on a regular basis."

"Rushton's bedroom," recalls Booker fondly. "Me sitting at a battered old typewriter, and then we'd stick down the pages." Rushton recalled that "It was chaos. It looked like the floor of a betting shop."[58] His mother kept them regularly topped up with "little trays of tomato soup and beer", for which she finally got credit in issue 5: "Thanks for help are also due to Mrs Rushton."

This, presumably, is the private eye in question. Being not as attractive as Gnittie (☞), he only survived for the first three issues.

Price 6d

NEXT

contents

Harold Throbson
interviews Sir
John Feelgood
       (see Arts)
Arts (see Belmondo)
Film Man Dead
       (see Press)

Mainly for Children
  (Part IV:Fallout)
And – revealing
new serial starting
this week – The
Memoirs of an
    Ordinary Man

(see inside)

BORE
f the
WEEK
ack page)

"We decided to try it out in Kensington," says Usborne. "It was mainly Andrew [Osmond] who was very energetic in shipping it out. He took 500 copies to pubs and persuaded them to put them in places where customers could see them." Osmond remembered, "I would put a stack out in some likely spot with an honesty box. When I came back, the copies were always gone and the box was always empty."[57]

"The John Feelgood interview was Wells," says Booker. "He was very much around." This was despite the fact that Wells had secured himself an extraordinarily incompatible day job (☞ MURDOCH, Campbell).

"*Last week, you'll remember, we told you how to make a simple old-fashioned atom bomb out of a few old TV sets, some Sellotape, and an ordinary lump of household uranium.*" Booker's lecture on nuclear fall-out for the under-tens is the funniest thing in a not very funny debut. It got better.

A box on page 2 of the six-page magazine promises "the true story behind the Cunarder Scandal ... Read the FACTS exclusively in 'The Vote Buyers' – a *Private Eye* Enquiry, two weeks' time." "One of the things we had in mind right from the start was not just to be a jokes magazine but to do factual reporting exposing scandals," says Booker. But not this one – there was no mention of the subject in issue 2, or ever again. "I knew a little bit about it. But I didn't know enough," admits Booker ruefully.

"I can't remember who thought of the idea," says Booker of the longest-surviving feature from issue 1. "There are times when you remember you've had an idea and there are times when you're all sitting around, and everyone's chipping in inspired by what came before and adding the next sentence. So you can't say that anything is written by one person. The first three regular issues were basically me and Willie."

The inaugural bore was Mr Punch. "People say 'What was the purpose of *Private Eye*?' Well, Willie used to say 'We've got to knock *Punch* off its perch,'" points out Ingrams. "And in a way, that was it. There wasn't any grand ideas about bringing down the government, or anything like that. *Punch* had a massive circulation when the *Eye* started."

FAWKES, Wally

 Trog

FIRST SUBSCRIPTION CANCELLATION

This honour went to no less a personage than the Marquess of Abergavenny, in May 1964.

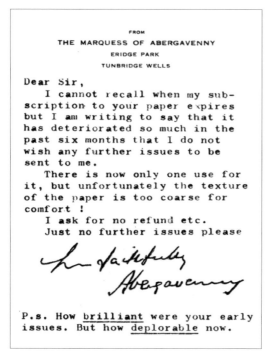

FROM

THE MARQUESS OF ABERGAVENNY

ERIDGE PARK

TUNBRIDGE WELLS

Dear Sir,

I cannot recall when my subscription to your paper expires but I am writing to say that it has deteriorated so much in the past six months that I do not wish any further issues to be sent to me.

There is now only one use for it, but unfortunately the texture of the paper is too coarse for comfort !

I ask for no refund etc.

Just no further issues please

Abergavenny

P.s. How <u>brilliant</u> were your early issues. But how <u>deplorable</u> now.

FLEET STREET, changing relationship with *Private Eye*

"It's always been the rubbish dump for those stories that Fleet Street can't use, for one reason or another," sniffed former tabloid editor Derek 'Sid Yobbo' Jameson of *Private Eye* two decades ago. "We all know as editors in Fleet Street that the moment you say 'Sorry cock I can't use that, my goodness you must be joking, highly dangerous,' we know with total certainty that within a matter of days it will be in *Private Eye*."[59]

In the past four years, journalists from the newsrooms of both the *Times* and *Independent* have requested I punt any stories *Private Eye* rejects in their direction.

FLEXIDISCOGRAPHY

FLEXIDISCS:

These were given away free with the magazine. All material was performed by Richard Ingrams, Peter Cook, Willie Rushton, John Wells and (from 1987 onwards) Ian Hislop, plus special guests including Larry Adler, Chris Barrie, John Bird, Eleanor Bron, Sally Grace, Barry Humphries, Spike Milligan, Dudley Moore, John Sessions and Pamela Stephenson.

His Master's Vass – October 1964
I Saw Daddy Kissing Santa Claus – December 1964
The Rites of Spring – April 1965
BBC Gnome Service – December 1966
Abominable Radio Gnome – December 1967
The Loneliness of the Long Playing Record – February 1969
Dear Sir, Is This a Record? – December 1969
Just For The Record – December 1970
Hullo Sailor – December 1972
Farginson – March 1975
The Sound of Talbot – December 1980
Record Damages – December 1987
Skeye Flexi-Dish – April 1989

SINGLES:

Private Eye Sings! – Artists and Repertoire Presents,1962
The Neasden Song – Willie Rushton with the Ron Watford Sound (B Side *The Trout* by John Wells) – Spark, 1972

LPs:

Private Eye's Blue Record – feat. John Bird, Eleanor Bron, Barry Fantoni, Barry Humphries, Dudley Moore. 1965
Private Eye's Golden Years of Sound (collected Flexidiscs, 1964- 1970, Lyntone 1973)
Ho-Ho! Very Satirical (recorded in 1971 but not released until 1998, as a cassette by MCI Spoken Word)
Private Eye's Golden Satiricals (best of the Flexidiscs, Springtime Records 1981)

CDs:

40 Glorious Minutes: Private Eye's CD-Romp, featuring Eleanor Bron, Jon Culshaw, Harry Enfield, Barry Humphries, Lewis MacLeod, Kate Robbins and John Sessions. Given away free with 40th anniversary issue, October 2001

☞ *EYE TV*

FLUCK AND LAW

As well as special Christmas covers featuring Michael Foot and Robert Maxwell in 1981 and 1986 respectively and an election special in 1992, the puppetmakers Peter Fluck and Roger Law produced a series of posters featuring regular *Eye* characters and a Toby Jug of Richard Ingrams for the magazine's twenty-first anniversary in 1982.

Two years later producer John Lloyd recruited Ian Hislop and Nick Newman as chief scriptwriters for Fluck and Law's new ITV show *Spitting Image*.

FOOT, Paul, gives thumbs-down to job at *Private Eye*

After Christopher Booker's sacking as editor in 1963 (☞), Richard Ingrams, fired up with editorial zeal and a new thirst for serious journalism wrote to offer a place on the editorial board to his old friend Paul Foot, now working on the *Daily Record* in Glasgow: "I had been sent up there by Hugh Cudlipp, and was patronized everywhere as another toffee-nosed careerist sent up to pretend to get his fingers dirty before going back to London to sidle his way to the top."[60] Unlike most toffee-nosed careerists, he was spending his weekends on a soapbox at the shipyards addressing young apprentices about revolutionary socialism.

In his letter Ingrams stressed that the magazine needed to be edited "from left of centre". Foot declined, deliciously: "You see, Ditch, I'm part of a movement now."[61]

FOOT, Paul, gives thumbs-up to job at *Private Eye*

He couldn't hold out for long. Foot left Glasgow in 1964 to work for the *Sun*. Shurely shome mishtake? This was the pre-Murdoch, broadsheet *Sun*, cobbled together from the reclaimed fixtures and fittings of the TUC-affiliated *Daily Herald*, contractually committed to the Labour movement, headed by Hugh Cudlipp and actually a fine fit for Footy. Unfortunately, it was also a disastrous white elephant, and he swiftly jumped ship – to the *Sunday Telegraph*. Definitely shome mishtake. Within weeks he had started to drift into the *Private Eye* office on his days off – the magazine went to press on Sunday in those days – and bash out pieces for the investigative page Claud Cockburn (☞) had inaugurated at the back of the magazine, the "Illustrated London News". While the two enormously admired each other's journalism, they were separated politically by the length of an icepick: Paul was a Trotskyist while Claud remained a resolute Stalin fan. "Inspired by near-Communist sources", was the verdict of Harold Wilson's sidekick George Wigg on a 1966 story by Foot about the prime minister's attempts to spin that year's Seamen's Strike – a sign of the mag's resolutely left-wing position at the time, but also of how seriously it was beginning to be taken by those in power. In the same year Foot revealed that the Porton Down military research facility was hard at work developing new and terrifying methods of germ warfare, and *Private Eye* received a "stern phone call"

"I was drawn to it like a bee to a honeypot, it's independent publishing. It's independent of any kind of profit motive or shareholders' interference or advertising pressure. That's very important." Paul Foot

Foot, as seen by Fantoni

from the Home Office requesting that it back off the story "in the interests of security".

"I was drawn to it like a bee to a honeypot," Foot admitted. "It's independent publishing. It's independent of any kind of profit motive or shareholders' interference or advertising pressure. That's very important."[62] Finally he could resist no more, and joined the staff full-time in 1967. "I still recall the almost overwhelming sense of liberation," he wrote three decades later. "Off my back were the cloying hierarchies, the silly office intrigues and petty censorships which stifled so much writing in the official press."[63]

He liked it so much he put his name on it. The first "Footnotes" pages appeared in issue 138 on 31 March 1967. They carried lengthy stories on the Highland Development Board's siting of a petrochemical complex in Invergordon, the anti-Vietnamese propaganda that publisher Cecil King had inserted into children's comics, Welsh nationalist firebombers and the infiltration of the local media by National Front candidates in west London.

1967: the first Footnote

It was a masterclass in the sort of off-diary, passionate, non-metropolitan and questioning journalism that the *Eye* would make its trademark. And while the man himself may have come and gone during the following thirty-seven years, it was Paul Foot who more than anyone else was responsible for that formula.

He brought a journalistic thoroughness to the magazine, battering the reader with a barrage of scrupulously researched facts, often in article after article over a period of months or years, until someone in power sat up and took notice. "As journalists, we want things to be true," was his simple rejoinder to those who persisted in claiming that the *Eye* didn't check its facts. "On the other hand, there is a defeatist and pusillanimous view that nothing can possibly be published unless it's proved to the hilt. Richard's great contribution is that *Private Eye*'s been much more ready to publish." Between them, he and Ingrams usually picked the right causes to take risks on. Foot relentlessly explored the reasons for the partial collapse of the east London tower block Ronan Point in 1968, undeterred by legal threats from construction giant Taylor Woodrow Anglian, and was the first to point out that forty other newly completed blocks across the UK were also "quite literally more likely to fall down than stay up". The home secretary was forced to resign in 1972 as a result of a long-running Foot campaign (☞ POULSON, scandal brings down home secretary). He wrote his first stories casting doubt on the guilt of those convicted in 1979 of the murder of Staffordshire paperboy Carl Bridgewater within a year of their convictions, and returned to the topic regularly during the eighteen years it took to get them pardoned and released from prison.

One thing that delighted Foot was the way that the *Eye* swiftly became self-sustaining, as a rich seam of correspondence from readers opened up. "Each postbag bulged with marvellous stories," he recalled. "Disaffected and disorientated middle class and professional people mischievously, usually anonymously, provided inside information about their employers, their competitors, their jilted lovers or their heroes."[64] Foot quickly built up a network of sources, tending to work closely with one key mole or informant on each long-running campaign. He would build up a relationship of mutual trust that meant not only that they would pass on incriminating evidence without fear of exposure, but also that he was able to tell them what did or didn't constitute a story when, inevitably, they were too close to be able to judge.

Foot in the office he shared with Auberon Waugh, and on the road reporting . . .

. . . and still firm friends with his erstwhile editor decades later

He had the same relationship of mutual trust with Ingrams, his closest friend as well as his editor. While Ingrams remained bemused by his friend's lifelong commitment to the cause of International Socialism, he never felt it got in the way of his other passion, journalism. "He wouldn't propagandize, it was always stories. We very seldom disagreed about political issues, the only tension arising from Paul's belief that whenever there was a strike he had to support the union, regardless of any rights and wrongs."[65] He even got on well with Auberon Waugh, with whom for a while he shared an office and absolutely no political convictions at all. "He became a good friend," said Waugh. "He was the moral justification for all our confusion of unharmonious responses to the modern world. We all sought his approval, as if he had been a beautiful girl."[66]

It helped that the big difference between Foot and many of his comrades on the far left was that he had a sense of humour. He enjoyed a gossip and a giggle along with the rest of the office – only Fantoni's laughter has ever echoed louder around the building. He also recognised that jokes were a more effective tool than outrage: "Nothing hurts important humbugs more than the sound, the huge roar of the people laughing at their absurdities."

He also refused to take his own skills too seriously. "It's a complete fraud, the idea that there is a race apart called investigative journalists," he warned. "It leads to hierarchical notions of grand journalists as opposed to less good ones." For the whole of his career he remained as happy to work with, and listen to, a rookie reporter as the biggest names in law or politics. Claud Cockburn's son Patrick, now a distinguished foreign correspondent, did a stint helping out in the office as "my first job out of school, at the age of eighteen. I found Paul's presumption that I knew what was going on in the world – even if the details had momentarily slipped my memory – extremely encouraging." Thirty years and innumerable awards later Paul was doing exactly the same thing for an even dumber me – although I never revealed my inexperience in quite as spectacular a way as Patrick: "I was always too nervous to admit that I didn't know these nicknames that were being bandied about the office, and I once phoned up Whitehall and asked to speak to Sir Havid Cunt, to gales of laughter from Paul."

Foot remained modest to the end of his life. "I never learned a skill, I never even learned shorthand. I was never very good with a tape recorder. There are certain skills that you learn from experience, but the main point is to be curious and sceptical. Anyone who can ask a question is qualified to be a journalist."

☞ ANONYMITY, reasons for; READERS, mutually-beneficial relationship with; WHISTLEBLOWERS

FOOT, Paul, leaves *Private Eye* to start revolution

1972 was a very odd year. Prime minister Edward Heath declared the third state of emergency of his premiership, in reaction to a national miners' strike. He had introduced internment without trial in Northern Ireland, where troops shot dead thirteen protesters on Bloody Sunday in January. The Vietnam War raged on, despite the leaked Pentagon Papers having proved that the US government had been lying to the public for years about the scope and tactics of the conflict. And everyone, no matter where they sat on the political spectrum, seemed to think the state was about to be overthrown.

"It was a strange period altogether," says Richard Ingrams. "Part of the reason Paul left was that he thought like a lot of lefties at the time that there was going to be a revolution, so the *Socialist Worker* seemed to be where he should be at."

And so he threw his lot in fully with the publishers of that sixteen-page weekly, the International Socialists (not to be confused with the International Marxist Group, the Young Socialists, the Independent Young Socialists, the Socialist Labour League, the Revolutionary Communist League, the People's Front of Judea or the Judean People's Front). So, in turn, did a lot of other people. "Our little organisation had grown from zero to perhaps two thousand members by 1972," wrote a delirious Foot. "Many of us started to believe that instead of it being a hobby, which it was, there was a possibility of a real revolutionary party."[67]

His departure was not just down to external politics, however. There had been increasing tensions at the *Eye*, which did not afford figures from the left the respect he did – or rather, insisted on treating those of every political persuasion with the lack of respect they deserve. "Sometimes, the *Eye* selects the wrong targets in a desperate attempt to show that it has no favourites," grumbled Foot in 1974. He singled out in particular the magazine's treatment of Black Panther Angela Davis, who was spoofed as one of a number of "Loonie Ladies" in April 1972: "god, Angela Davis was on trial for her life!"[68] As Ingrams's best friend, Foot tended to blame others for such excesses: "Booker was responsible for it," he insisted many years later. "Richard and I had a terrible row. It was one of the things that made up my mind I should leave."[69]

He also objected vocally to the treatment meted out to one of Davis's fellow "Loonie Ladies" from the same issue: the Ulster MP Bernadette Devlin. When she became pregnant in 1971, enraging her Catholic supporters because she was not married, Ingrams proposed to publish the cover on the left.

Foot threatened to withdraw his pages from the magazine if the cover was used. "Richard couldn't believe it. We had this terrific row. Ultimately, he said 'Well, if you feel that strongly, we'll change the front page.'" Ingrams confirms this, but insists that "It was very minor, everyone forgot all about that. He accepted that we didn't see eye to eye on everything. He justified his leaving later on by saying that he'd had differences with me, but I never really had any differences with him."

"It was terrible to leave," Foot said later. "Their laughter was so infectious. In many ways it was the most uncomfortable decision I've ever made in my life. I felt I was abandoning Richard."

He didn't go all that far. "I find it hard to recall the dates of his various comings and goings because there was never any animosity on either side and he never stopped contributing," says Ingrams. In 1976 Foot started to come in for regular sessions in an attempt to get to the bottom of Harold Wilson's resignation; out of this came the coverage of the Jeremy Thorpe case (☞ DITTO MAN,

DROPPING THE REVOLUTIONARY.

John Kent's vision of Foot's departure, prompted in part by the cover that never was (*left*). Fantoni, Ingrams and Booker are in the pulpit.

The) which he spearheaded. In 1978, having left *Socialist Worker*, "much downhearted that the revolution had not materialized", he "drifted back to the *Eye*" full-time, but only briefly: the following year he was recruited to the *Daily Mirror* where he had his own investigative page for the next fourteen years. Even then he continued to be a major part of any number of the magazine's most high-profile stories (☞ DIPLOMACY, *Eye* does its bit for; FOOT, Paul, The second coming of).

There is, however, no doubt that the back pages of the *Eye*, where the investigative stuff has always resided, were considerably weaker for lack of Foot's day-to-day involvement – and that's not just because they were retitled "Business News" despite often having very little to do with business and sometimes not a lot to do with news either. "There was a problem in the 1970s caused by Footy leaving," admits Ingrams.

FOOT, Paul, the second coming of

"I spent my entire time – well, not my entire time, but rather a lot of my time – trying to get Paul to come back," says Ian Hislop of his early years as editor. Then contentedly ensconced at the *Mirror*, despite what he described as proprietor Robert Maxwell's "brooding, toad-like presence squatting at the top of the building",[70] Foot was happy to bung the odd piece in the *Eye*'s direction. Hislop wanted more. "If he'd write two pieces I'd say 'These are great, we need three next time.' Or 'This is very much an *Eye* story, you won't get this in anywhere else …'"

The pair had established a relationship of mutual support two years before Hislop took over. In 1984, having fomented revolt among his in-house hacks for his own amusement (☞ HAPPY SHIP, Not a), Richard Ingrams decided to go on holiday – he never went on holiday – and leave the twenty-four-year-old in charge. "I think he partly did it to take the piss really, and annoy everybody," says Hislop. It certainly did the latter. Hackette Jane Ellison announced that she "didn't work for the second eleven" and walked out of the office. The other hacks refused to file copy either. "No one would do anything apart from the comedy people, who all thought it was hysterical," recalled Hislop. "So I called up Foot and said that I hadn't got anything for that issue. Did he want to write loads? Footy was absolutely brilliant, and essentially he just filled the whole magazine. All his stuff was better than theirs anyway."[71]

So when Hislop took over full-time in 1986 (☞ INGRAMS, Richard, decision to retire as editor), Foot was one of the first people he called. "He was so *obviously* what it needed, and what it lacked. I said to him 'You can have two pages, you can call it "Footnotes", you can do whatever you like, just come back.'" Part of the reason Foot was unwilling to leave the *Mirror* was that he had built up a unique method of working there: a personalised page on which he could "openly solicit information from whistleblowers, grasses and finks, providing a name (and a photograph) with which they could communicate".[72] Hislop offered to replicate it all in the *Eye*: "I always wanted him to be first port of call so that people would come here rather than the *Mirror*. I wanted him on site."

Why didn't he agree? "He felt the *Eye* had gone very right wing," says Hislop. "The *Mirror* was a left-wing paper. Never underestimate Footy's commitment to the old goals. There was a feeling on the left that the *Eye* wasn't for them; it had got too identified with the right at a particular time, which is curious given its history, but I think there was a period where that was true."

Foot in the *Eye* office, late 1990s

Foot found the young Hislop far more to his own ideological taste. He was not the only one. "Since the departure of [Richard Ingrams] I find it increasingly difficult to distinguish any difference between the slant of your publication and *Marxism Today*," wrote a reader in November 1986. For the record, Hislop was voting SDP–Liberal Alliance at the time.

The latter half of the 1980s saw a much heavier Footfall at the *Eye*. Moonlighting from the *Mirror*, he was responsible for most of the *Eye*'s best investigative work – coverage of the SAS shooting of an IRA team in Gibraltar, the fire on the oil rig Piper Alpha, Lockerbie (☞), the sinking of the *Marchioness* pleasure boat in the Thames and many many more, all of it printed anonymously. "Anything you identify as looking 'headline', that'll be Footy," says Hislop. "It was sort of 'When are the stories going to come back – oh, here they are!'" He even helped the *Eye* out by running new and vital information about Sonia Sutcliffe in his *Mirror* column when the attorney general insisted the magazine could not (☞ CONTEMPT OF COURT). But he still wouldn't accept a job there. Not, that is, until Maxwell fell off his yacht in 1991, and – unbelievably – someone even worse took over at the *Daily Mirror*.

"David Montgomery rampaged through the *Mirror* sacking everyone even marginally associated with the union and what he called 'the old *Mirror* culture'," recalled Foot. "To prove a little point about freedom of the press, I submitted a column cataloguing the revolting bullying of the Montgomery management, his share dealings and his colleagues' association with Maxwell. The column was passed by the lawyers, but for the first time in fourteen years

it was censored by the editor." Foot printed the column up at his own expense and handed it out to passers-by (and to several press photographers and TV crews) outside the paper's office on the morning it should have appeared. The editor, David Banks, promptly announced that he was offering his star columnist sick leave to take "a period of rest … We sincerely hope he seeks professional help during this time." Since Foot was no madder than he had ever been, the paper eventually had to stump up a large amount of cash to avoid an employment tribunal – despite the fact that, as Foot liked to point out, "I actually resigned!" For good measure, they dismissed a load of other *Mirror* hacks too, including Tim Minogue, who would later also join the *Eye*: "I was surrounded by security guards and marched out of the building for 'gross misconduct'. And the gross misconduct turned out to be that I'd been seen shaking hands with Paul Foot while he was doing this picket."

Less than two months later Foot was back where he belonged. His colleagues welcomed him with their very own version of the banned *Mirror* page (right).

His own double-page spread at the back of the magazine looked rather familiar, too, carrying over both the picture byline and the plea for information from the *Mirror* column. "We got a more tabloid design into the back pages of the *Eye*, which I was perfectly happy with while it was him, because there was this personality-feel about it," says Hislop. It certainly worked. Those of us who worked the lonely off-week shifts in the late 1990s were kept company by the sound of Paul's personal answerphone rumbling away upstairs as reader after reader accepted the invitation at the bottom of every edition of "Footnotes": "You can write to Paul Foot at 6 Carlisle Street, or leave a message for him on 0171 287 3183." He would spend the next decade in terrier-like pursuit of a number of high-profile victims: the ministers who had overseen the sale of arms to Iraq, Jonathan Aitken (☞), the police investigating the murder of Stephen Lawrence, governments of both stripes who pushed through the Private Finance Initiative and the Inland Revenue for their sale of their properties to a company based in a tax haven (☞ TAXMAN). He followed the Bridgewater Four and Colin Wallace (☞ PRIVATE SPY) cases through to the appeals that cleared them, and helped get a judicial inquiry into the *Marchioness* disaster after a decade. All these, and hundreds of other lower-profile stories, he pursued with what his friend Francis Wheen described as "the triumphant enthusiasm of a cub reporter turning in his first scoop: 'We've really got the bastards this time!'"

And in between all this he found the time to fire up a

THE DAVE SPART PAGE THAT LORD GNOME WOULD NOT PRINT

DAVE SPART reporting

The never-before published tribute to Foot's defection, created by his friends at the *Eye*

One in the Eye

Fair Shares

ER... basically this column will not appear due to the totally sickening attitudes of the capitalist management i.e. Lord Gnome and his henchmen who have turned the paper of working people everywhere *viz* Private Eye into an utterly bankrupt tool of the Tory party thus denying the labouring classes a genuine voice in their struggle against a system that is er morally and totally anyway that is the sole and sickening reason why censorship

by er the new so-called Press Barons has er basically occurred.

EDITOR STROBES: What a bastard!

E. Strobes owns 1,278 preferred shares in GnomeCo, Grand Cayman. GnomeCo is a subsidiary of the Gnome Trading Group, Jersey. Lord Gnome owns 54% of the ordinary shares in GTC, leased through the Panamanian clearing house of Amazinc, SA. Strobes himself therefore stands to gain 7½p per share at the standard rate of issue on any future takeover of GTC via GnomeCo *whether or not sanctioned by the Trustees which Strobes himself appoints via his directorship of Amazinc!* They will never print this.

PRIVATE SHAME

Slagg was out of a job. There was no warning and no reason given. She was simply handed a huge cheque and the telephone number of the editor of Today.

Comrades, this is the sort of

serving Private Eye journalist who covered all the world's great stories from his seat in El Vino's.

● E.I. Addio. Fleet Street's premier football correspondent whose in-depth knowledge of clubs like Neasden FC and Dollis Hill made the Eye's back pages legendary.

● E.J. Thribb. The country's most popular poet and Eye Literary Editor. Penned his own valediction, "So. Farewell Then E.J. Thribb", which Gnome's hench-

men typically refused to print.

● Silvie Krin. Court Correspondent since the paper's inception, Silvie broke some of the biggest Royal stories ever in the pages of the Eye, such as "Princess Margaret Takes Up Smoking" and "Is Prince Charles Bald?" Said one colleague: "You cannot replace staff like Silvie."

And there will be many more in the weeks to come.

Watch this space in the column that they will not print.

At 2.43pm last Tuesday Glenda

---

new generation of reporters with the same zeal. "It was just incredibly instructive," says Sarah Shannon, who joined the *Eye* straight out of journalism school in 1994. "I'd sit with him and write stories, and do them together side by side. He was so generous, praising everyone else's work and underplaying his own." Jane Mackenzie arrived in 2002, and was quickly put at ease when she spotted that Foot, forty years her senior, fretted just as much as she did: "He was always saying 'Ooh, I've got no stories, I'm going to get sacked.'" Tim Laxton, who co-wrote with Foot the *Eye*'s take on the arms-to-Iraq affair, *Not the Scott Report*, says that "Above all, Paul taught me that journalism could be fun. Working with him always made me laugh." Heather Mills, one of the group of hacks who keep up his legacy in the "In the Back" section, describes him as "a mentor figure, really. It was such a great thing to work with him."

He set – or rather reset – the tone for the *Eye*'s investigative work, an achievement which was recognised with the *What*

the Papers Say Campaigning Journalist of the Decade award in 2000. "I felt I'd inherited a particular way of doing the back and I didn't want it," says Hislop. "Footy's thing was questioning the official verdict, so whatever is said to you you think 'Well, that might not be true.' We established fairly early on that I thought he was a great journalist but I wasn't really interested in the Socialist Workers' Party and its particular world view. That sounds haughty, because it gave him the passion and the commitment to the ordinary story that made it work, but you don't want to read that, you just want to read the story. The great thing about Paul was he had a very good sense of humour. I had a tape recorder which was bust, and I used to get his copy when he was there, and I'd say 'Now this is the Spartometer,' and I'd run it over the copy and say 'Hmm, very Sparty about here.' And he'd laugh, and take it out."

Hislop is totally clear: "Getting Footy in was probably the single best move of my life."[73]

FOOT AND MOUTH
disease

"To date, the best investigations available to the public are those produced by Devon County Council and, surprisingly, *Private Eye*," declared *Country Life* magazine after more than a million farm animals had been slaughtered on government orders following an epidemic of Foot and Mouth disease in 2001. The *Daily Telegraph*, still at that point the favoured sheet of the shires, was equally surprised: "*Private Eye*, in a remarkably thorough investigation, is scathing. It accuses the government of slaughtering millions of animals unnecessarily, of acting outside the law, and of setting its policy to suit Labour's election timetable."

The special report to which both publications referred was *Not the Foot and Mouth Report: A Special Investigation from Private Eye*, written by Christopher Booker and Dr Richard North, both former custodians of the "Muckspreader" column which had originally been kicked off by the Conservative MP and chair of the parliamentary agricultural select committee Richard Body. "That column had quite a following, and it was a useful place to say things about farming," says Booker. "Richard did it for four years, and I did it for ten." Together they worked their way through the evidence and crunched numbers to identify how around 7.7 million animals, or one-eighth of all the farm animals in Britain, had been slaughtered, most of them unnecessarily, in "a case of maladministration for which it is hard to recall a precedent".

Nearly a year after the *Eye*'s special report, and following three separate inquiries into the government's handling of the epidemic, each held in private, rural affairs secretary Margaret Beckett accepted that "mistakes" had been made, and that vaccination – as Booker and North had urged – would be part of the strategy for dealing with any future outbreak.

FORKBENDER, Lady

Harold Wilson's political secretary Marcia Williams, aka Lady Falkender, hated many things. Being stood up by the prime minister – she once stormed into a speech-writing session and called him a "little cunt" in front of colleagues for abandoning her at a party. Tax bills, which she regarded as "persecution" and demanded Wilson's help with. State schools, at least when it came to the education of her own children (she demanded the Labour leader's help with that, too). Handing over papers when she didn't feel like it (the prime minister once had to break into her garage to retrieve some documents). Not having constant access to the tranquillisers that she carried in a locket around her neck at all times.

But most of all she hated *Private Eye*. "She wrote that there had been an occasion when she had been so outraged by something that we had written about her that she had to be restrained from coming round to Greek Street and punching me in the face," recalled Richard Ingrams.[74]

Why so? The *Eye* was the one publication that insisted on reporting that the prime minister's right-hand woman had been in a relationship with, and had two children by, the political editor of the *Daily Express*, Walter Terry. Terry even took delivery of strictly restricted material in ministerial red boxes when they were driven round to Williams's home. This was, by anyone's reckoning, a significant story. Thirty years later, when people were considerably less bothered about the extramarital aspect, Blair aide Anji Hunter still felt duty-bound to leave Downing Street after becoming romantically involved with the political editor of Sky News, Adam Boulton. But in the early 1970s no one but the *Eye* would breathe a word about it. This was partly down to the extraordinary lengths Harold Wilson and his associates went to to cover it up – his fixer Lord Goodman (☞) leaned heavily on any publication that showed an interest, and the prime minister personally signed a document waiving Williams's security clearance after she refused to answer any questions about her family, leading to the conviction among certain elements in the security services that they were both up to no good (☞ PRIVATE SPY).

The *Eye* first started hinting at the relationship in 1970, when Wilson was in opposition: "In future she wishes to be known as Mrs Marcia Terry-Williams – that at any rate is how she signs her cheques." But it was not until Wilson returned to Downing Street in 1974 that the magazine told the full story of how the widow of a civil servant called Michael Halls was demanding compensation from the Treasury, claiming that he had been driven to a fatal heart attack by the stress of working with Williams. The magazine also noted that a number of other staff lived in fear of Williams's demanding behaviour and constant tantrums, but if anything it was guilty of *under*exaggerating: her colleague Joe Haines later claimed there were serious discussions within Number 10 of whether it would be easier to murder her to "take the weight of Marcia off the Prime Minister".[75]

From then on it was war. "Mr Walter Terry wishes to go on being known as Mr Walter Terry," the *Eye* scathingly noted after Wilson raised Williams to the peerage as Lady Falkender, despite her dragging him into the sleazy family scandal that became known as the Slagheap Affair. It mercilessly picked over her various business deals and her friendships with dodgy businessmen – the "Marfia", as the magazine dubbed them – who invariably seemed to end up being recommended for honours by her boss.

In Downing Street, where Falkender was feeding Wilson's increasing paranoia as a way of maintaining her control over him, a bunker mentality soon set in. "I went up to see the PM in his study," confided aide Bernard Donoughue in his diary in October 1975. "He was particularly interested in my reports of the allegations of John Allen's *Private Eye* smear campaign ... He said that Allen is sad and they only kept him employed in Number 10 to prevent him leaking stories if they kicked him out." If that was the plan, it didn't work. "John Allen, who's dead now," says Ingrams, when asked who his biggest source for anti-Marcia stories was. Another source was the late Will Camp, who had spin-doctored for Wilson in the 1970 election campaign: bizarrely, Donoughue claims that Falkender included Camp on the infamous "Lavender List" (☞ GOLDENBALLS), only for him to be struck off by Harold Wilson for the crime of being "too close to *Private Eye*". Just months after his resignation in 1976, the former prime minister was gleefully touting what he claimed was "a *Private Eye* address book" around his contacts on Fleet Street.

It had been acquired via the magazine's dustbins, courtesy of another man named on the Lavender List. He was the secret weapon Falkender and Wilson used to take revenge on *Private Eye* for its many provocations.

Ironically, the magazine's "Grovel" column had noted their first meeting, in July 1975: "David Frost recently entertained to dinner the dazzling trio of Jimmy Goldsmith, Harold Wilson and Lady Forkbender."

"That was some time before the libel thing started, when I'd probably never heard of Goldsmith," reflects Ingrams ruefully
☞ GOLDENBALLS; SEMITISM, alleged anti-

FORTNIGHTLY APPEARANCE

One of the key decisions which everyone agrees has been central to the lasting success of *Private Eye* was taken in November 1961. Co-founders "Usborne and Osmond were pressing us, pinning us down and saying you've got to go regular," recalls Christopher Booker. "I remember Willie [Rushton] and I sat on the Embankment, and we said 'Look, this is going to be bloody tricky because [Richard] Ingrams is elsewhere, and [John] Wells wasn't around, so basically it's you and me have got to do it.' And we didn't think we could do it once a week. So we sat there and said 'Well, what about fortnightly?' And by the end of our conversation we were convinced. And I thought 'Well, there must be magazines which come out fortnightly,' and of course there aren't any."

"The magic thing was to hit on this fortnightly gap, quite by chance," says Ingrams, who firmly believes that this is the reason the joke-writing team at the *Eye* has remained so constant for so long. "People weren't in constant day-to-day contact with one another. You didn't live on each other's backs."

An announcement duly appeared in issue 3, published on 30 November 1961: the magazine "was to appear in this experimental format every fortnight from now on".

The next issue was published precisely ten weeks later, on 7 February 1962.
☞ JOKE-WRITING TEAMS, Extraordinary longevity of

FOUNTAIN, Nev
☞ MUTT AND JEFF

A paparazzo, pictured in as flattering a light as possible

FRASER, Jason

Jason Fraser is a paparazzo. Sorry, no, he insists he is employed in "just taking pictures of people in as flattering a light as possible" – although not always successfully, as the *Eye* pointed out in a catalogue of his more intrusive and uncomplimentary snaps of celebrities in the early 2000s. Fraser was so furious to be accused of invading people's privacy that he invaded the editor's privacy to tell him so. "He got obsessed. He always had my phone number," says Ian Hislop. "When I moved house he phoned me up, I think it was on New Year's morning, to say 'I've got your number, I know where you live' – literally, that's what it was about."

Hislop found out how the photographer had got hold of his ex-directory number only when he was visited by staff from the Information Commissioner's Office who had been involved in a police raid on a private detective's premises in 2003. "They had the detective's bank book, and it said 'Hislop: Friends and family, bank manager', whatever, and he had all my numbers. And 'client paid: Jason Fraser'. He'd shelled out to get all my private numbers, hoping to turn me over."

In July 2000, while Fraser was busy training his long lens on the celeb-packed beaches of the Mediterranean, the *Eye* printed an unauthorised but flattering picture of Fraser himself. He complained to colleagues that he thought this was "unethical".

FROM THE MESSAGEBOARDS

The *Eye*'s fortnightly dispatch from the more rabid reaches of cyberspace is written by Ed Barrett, features editor on satirical website Anorak.co.uk. "It's brilliant, and the readers love it," says Ian Hislop. "I couldn't do that, but I recognize it, so let's get someone else to do it. ☺"

G

The Curse of Gnome

Shopping Centre

Church

Greetings from Neasden

Station

Pub

Lookalike

Dancer

Editor

GOING LIVE

Gardening Notes

No. 500

GAMBOLLARDS

In 1991 Eve Pollard, editrix of the *Sunday Express* and a long-term fixture of "Street of Shame", accepted £5,000 which *Private Eye* had offered to pay into court in settlement of a libel action.

Shortly afterwards she wrote to Ian Hislop to congratulate him on the *Eye*'s new cartoon strip "The Gambollards", about her and her husband, *Daily Express* editor Nick Lloyd. "Can we please buy the originals to the first three offerings?"

Hislop wrote straight back. "Of course ... The price is £5,001 plus costs (approx £5,000) making a total of £10,001. I am sure you agree that this is a bargain."

GARLAND, Nick
☞ Mackenzie, Barry

GELDOF, Bob, comes to the rescue of *Eye* hack

In June 2010 *Eye* hack Richard Brooks (☞ TAXMAN) was banned from the launch of CDC's annual report after writing a string of articles criticising the way in which the body formerly known as the Commonwealth Development Corporation was concentrating on enriching the management of its part-privatised wing Actis rather than poor people around the world. His attempt to hand out copies of his stories to the arriving guests outside the reception was greeted by a CDC press officer with an invitation to "Fuck off, you little piece of shit."

At which point Bob Geldof intervened, secured Brooks's entry to the event and used his own speech to pronounce "enormous admiration" for the *Eye*.

Which made it slightly ironic that the magazine had called Geldof "bonkers" and accused him of giving "a world-class demonstration in how not to handle media criticism" over his reaction to a BBC documentary three months earlier.

GENERATIONS, employed by *Eye*

NUMBER CRUNCHING

23 – age of youngest regular contributor in *Eye* office

74 – age of oldest regular contributor in *Eye* office

☞ YOUTH, voices of

GILLARD, Michael, International Man of Mystery
☞ SLICKER

GLASHAN, John

John Glashan contributed to the *Eye* from 1962 until his death in 1999. He specialised in simply-sketched figures, baroque and intricately-detailed backgrounds, and beards.

GILES, response to *Eye* cartoon

In February 1967, Ralph Steadman spoofed the work of Giles, the *Daily Express* cartoonist.

Poor Old Grandma. She's got to do something seeing as how Mr. Giles hasn't come up with a good joke since 1952.

Giles's response arrived in the post, addressed to Richard Ingrams, not long afterwards.

GNITTIE, Little

Gnittie was the star of a special issue of *Mesopotamia* (☞) devoted to the story of his progress around Oxford.

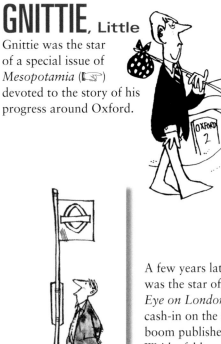

A few years later, he was the star of *Private Eye on London*, a hasty cash-in on the satire boom published by Weidenfeld and Nicolson in 1962.

Rushton based him on the young John Wells.

He appeared on the cover of the November 1960 edition of *Mesopotamia* in the garb of the *Daily Express*'s crusader with a flaccid sword.

A year later he made his first appearance on the masthead of *Private Eye*, and he has been there for almost every single issue since.

GNOME, Lord, life and times of

1863: Birth of Klaus Anatoli Koch in Serbo-Croatia on 24th March (reputed). Details of early life disputed due to tendency to sue anyone who writes about him, but officially claims to be heir to Baronetcy of Gnome and seventh son of Mr and Mrs Luigi Schwartz of Brooklyn, New York.

1912: Attempt to reach the South Pole by camel ends in failure. Gnome is only survivor of expedition, his companions perishing of frostbite and bite injuries.

1945: Adopting the name Captain Gnome, goes into business looting antiques and defrauding the inland revenue.

1961: As Aristides P. Gnome, makes his first appearance as proprietor in second edition of *Private Eye* in November, offering "Terylene-bound copies of a new treasure for every family library, *Private Eye Looks Back Over Two Weeks*".

1962: Receives peerage as Lord Gnome of Zurich in the County of Flint.

1964: Buys Aldermaston March, plans to sever political links on grounds that "these were not really appreciated or understood by the majority of marchers".

1965: Recruits E.Strobes as amanuensis. He has served him loyally ever since.

1967: Publicly reveals that Kim Philby was one of the co-founders of *Private Eye*, but sacked "earlier this year as Moscow correspondent for writing such boring copy".

1968: Throwing weight behind *I'm Backing Britain* campaign, orders "typists, waiters, chefs, chauffeurs, cigar cutters and game keepers employed at Gnome House" to work extra hours on voluntary basis. Half hour tea-breaks are cut by half an hour.

1969: Young starlet Rita Chevrolet sells story of her "wonderful life with the man who has been described as the Croesus of the 20th Century." Lord Gnome sues *News of the World* for libel.

1972: Celebrates 78th birthday. Rita Chevrolet badly mauled by tiger in Lord Gnome's private zoo.

1975: Tragically disappears, presumed drowned off coast of Miami. Lady Gnome announces he is "definitely dead, and any further search for him is in vain." He is discovered four weeks later in Australia in company of Ms Chevrolet.

1976: Queen makes Royal visit to Gnome House. Lord Gnome shows her round the writ department where she watches "trained writ-sorters sorting through the latest batch of writs and throwing them into the wastepaper basket".

– Denied peerage in Harold Wilson's resignation honours list on grounds that he is already a Lord.

1977: Instructs his record label GNOMEMI to tear up contract with "The Horrible Yobs" after the band misbehave during a TV interview with Mr William Pissartist.

1978: Launches *Daily Smut*, a new tabloid "concentrating on pictures of naked women. It will appeal quite blatantly to illiterate morons".

1980: Stands in Labour party leadership election, loses to Worzel Gummidge.

1981: Denies he was not invited to wedding of Prince Charles and Lady Diana, claims not attending for health reasons as "I will be 87 in the autumn". Manages to attend own wedding to Rita Chevrolet in Las Vegas. Emmanuel Strobes is best man.

Sorry, I never give away less than £100,000

1983: Appointed by Mrs Thatcher as "Overall Supreme of the National Coal Board".

1984: Celebrates 70th birthday.

– Launches £1million bingo game. First winner is a Miss R.C. who donates winnings to the Lord Gnome Fund for the Families of Distressed Miners (cheques payable to Lord Gnome).

1985: Attempt to roller-blade across Atlantic to gain title of World's Greatest Bearded Idiot ends in failure.

– Gnomevision satellite TV service launched with advertising campaign "Puts the Broad back into Broadcasting!! Get a Saucier Saucer now!!" Defends US import *Rapeman* as suitable for daytime viewing.

1987: Denies accusations of illegal share dealing during Gnomess takeover of Dishonest PLC, and "welcomes the inspectors from the DTI with open arms".

1988: Publishes authorised biography by E. Strobes. Sues E. Strobes for libel.

1989: Celebrates 90th birthday with vast party for celebrity friends in Timbuktu. Rita Chevrolet (73) released from Dr Bernardo's Clinic for Famous Alcoholics specially to attend.

1990: After successfully overseeing privatisation of the National Pork Barrel Corporation as government minister, accepts appointment as Chief Executive of British Troughs Plc.

– Gnome International Scientific, Technical and Electronic But Definitely Not Military Supplies Plc under investigation for exporting 700 foot-long threaded metal biros "with computer launch system for the blue ink" to Iraq.

1991: Apologises after his newspaper *The Peephole* censured by PCC for running front page photograph of Queen naked beneath headline "Bare to the Throne". Editors confirm he is "hands-off proprietor – it's hands off his dictator friends".

1992: Leads calls for Queen to pay income tax; declines to pay any himself as he is resident of Grand Cayman and beneficiary of the American Anglo-Australian Filth Holding Trust.

1993: Following the death of Lady "Bubbles" Gnome, announces engagement to Ms Ree Ta Toyota (nee Chevrolet).

LORD GNOME WANTS **YOU**

SEMPER·MISER

Gnome

1994: Company Gnomelot wins contract to run National Lottery. Slogan: "It Could Be You (But Actually It Will Be Us)".

1995: Voted "Man of the Year" by listeners to Radio 4's *Today* programme, all of whom, it emerges, used the same phone in his office to cast their votes.

1996: Lady Gnome receives surcharge of £300billion for gerrymandering as leader of Neasden Council.

1997: Offers heartfelt tribute to close friend Princess Diana; also offers chance to buy *Daily Gnome* Souvenir Candles with special hairdryer "Wind" attachment for just £799.99.

1999: Successfully applies to retain seat in revised House of Lords on grounds of "my record as a distinguished legislator, and the fact that I have a number of compromising photographs of senior cabinet ministers".

2000: Son the Hon. James Gnome promoted to take charge of satellite business Dirty Digital TV. Daughter Gnomella launches self as TV cook, with signature dish "fish fingers a la ketchup".

2002: Cancels long-running *Bores of the Year Awards* citing danger of members of the paedophile community with camcorders attending, likelihood of Al Qaeda attack and fears ceremony would breach Human Rights Act. Denies any connection to financial difficulties following recent collapse of companies Gnomeron and eGnome.com.

2004: Lord Gnome and Lady Sharona Gnome deposed by "petty-minded Lilliputian" share-holders of Bollinger Group objecting to excess remuneration. Exiled to Elba.

2008: Royal Bank of Gnome taken over by government. Lord Fred Gnomewin leaves as condition of deal, and walks straight into job as financial adviser to HM Treasury.

"Of course, I always wanted to be an artist" said Lord Gnome yesterday, as he flew out for a Nassau, Bahamas, holiday.

GOLDENBALLS

In September 1975 a playboy gambler, Dominic Elwes, committed suicide, leaving a note which read "I curse Mark and Jimmy from beyond the grave. I hope they are happy now." Mark Birley and tycoon Jimmy Goldsmith were two of the richest and most powerful figures in the "Clermont Set", an exclusive group of gamblers who attended the Clermont Club in Berkeley Square, and who had blackballed Elwes after he displeased them.

Richard Ingrams: I was intrigued. I knew it was all in some way linked with the famous murder case of the previous year, when Lord Lucan broke into his wife's house and killed his children's nanny under the misapprehension that she was his wife Veronica, before disappearing. I thought: "Something is going on here that may make an interesting article for *Private Eye*." What it was, I had at that time no clear idea. I asked Patrick Marnham to write a long piece which appeared on 12 December 1975.[76]

Patrick Marnham: *Private Eye* published an account of the aftermath of the murder of Sandra Rivett and the tensions which had grown up within the circle of Lord Lucan's friends. The paper unwittingly libelled Goldsmith by repeating an error which had previously been made in both the *Sunday Times* and *Daily Express* and stating that he had been present at the lunch that John Aspinall gave on the day after Lucan's disappearance.[77]

Ingrams: In the next issue of *Private Eye*, Michael Gillard [☞ SLICKER] examined a statement that Goldsmith had made to the *Financial Times* on taking over at the bank Slater Walker, which implied that he had no links with the past. But this was far from being the case. Goldsmith and the resigned chairman Jim Slater were not only close friends, their companies were also linked in a variety of ways, as Gillard detailed. "It is legitimate to query", he wrote, "whether Goldsmith is the most independent chairman."

Michael Gillard: The Department of Trade was pressing for a full, open inquiry, which was opposed by the Bank of England on the grounds that it would damage confidence in the City. [Prime minister] Wilson was persuaded to overrule the DoT request to go further. This suited Slater and Goldsmith as it meant that little about their interlocking share dealings and bank loans

would be revealed. It was this position that was also threatened by the *Eye*'s disclosures and its questioning of his suitability.[78]

Ingrams: At no time during this period was I conscious that we were doing anything special or taking any particular risk. It therefore came as something of a surprise when on 12 January [1976] Goldsmith issued sixty-three writs, against *Private Eye* and thirty-seven of our distributors, and applied to the High Court to bring proceedings for Criminal Libel in respect of the Elwes article.

Marnham: You can spend years stirring up as much trouble as possible and get no more than a couple of letters marked "not for publication". Then one day the roof falls in. Over the course of the following 12 months, Goldsmith would bring a total of nine separate actions, involving the issue of more than 100 writs.

Ingrams: David Cash, the *Eye*'s Business Manager, called a meeting to try to reassure the distributors. Few of them had seen a libel writ before. The victims were evidently chosen hurriedly and at random, for they included three firms that did not sell *Private Eye* at all, and one that had recently been taken over by Goldsmith's own company, Cavenham.

Dave Cash: He sued them and he said "If you stop handling the *Eye*, I'll drop the action against you." I was always confident that *Private Eye* would survive any libel action, because it was so popular. I thought the only thing that will put the *Eye* down is people not buying it.

Ingrams: With the help of our solicitor Geoffrey Bindman, we tried to convince [the distributors] that there was nothing to worry about. *Private Eye* would indemnify them against any damages. Seventeen decided to fight the action. Sixteen agreed not to sell *Private Eye*.

We lost 12,000 copies out of a circulation standing at that time at about 100,000.

I remember saying that as far as I was concerned, it was just another libel action. At the time I meant it.

Far from it. By applying to bring a private prosecution for criminal libel – the first since 1923 – Goldsmith aimed to have both Ingrams and Marnham thrown into prison. He was given judicial leave to use the law in April 1976, and in May the director of public prosecutions refused to intervene to stop the prosecution, despite requests from sympathetic MPs.

Ingrams: The whole thing seemed rather absurd. The offence of Criminal Libel dates back to the days of the sixteenth century. Offenders were liable to the severest penalties. The Puritan agitator William Prynne had his ear cut off and was branded on both cheeks. John Wilkes and William Cobbett were prosecuted for the offence. The most famous case was that of Oscar Wilde, who in 1895 brought a prosecution against the

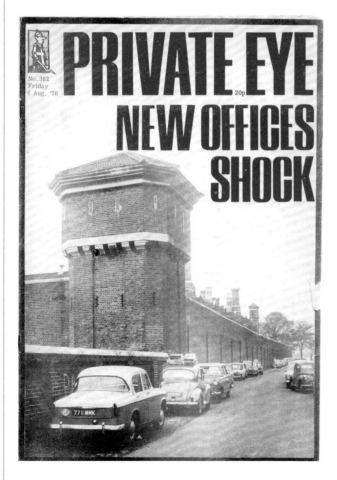

Marquess of Queensberry who had accused him of "posing as a Sodomite", which led to his own downfall. Though English laws fall into desuetude, they are seldom repealed until they prove an embarrassment. They remain on the statute book like rusting old weapons in an armoury.

Nigel Dempster: He was frightened. I remember going to Bow Street for the committal proceedings – Richard had had a haircut and bought a new corduroy jacket – and we went to Bow Street that day in the sure knowledge that Richard and Patrick were going to prison. No doubt about it.[79]

Ingrams: In his sworn affidavit setting out what he considered to be the Criminal Libel Goldsmith complained only of the introductory paragraphs dealing with the Lucan murder. These, he claimed, suggested "a conspiracy amongst a group of his friends to obstruct the course of justice" and "that I played a leading and dominant part". Our QC took a rather gloomy view of the defence. He thought it possible for Goldsmith to substantiate the conspiracy charge. There was, for example, our use of the word 'obstruction', an interesting example of the way in which a single word can alter the libellous connotations of an article. "From the beginning," Marnham had written, "the police have met obstruction and silence from the circle of gamblers and boneheads." Of course, "obstructing the police in their enquiries" is a criminal offence; yet we had not intended to suggest any criminality. A few days before the case was due to be heard, Geoffrey Bindman sent a letter to Goldsmith's solicitor. "Our clients are satisfied that there could be no truth in the suggestion that Mr Goldsmith was a party to an attempt to obstruct the police … we accept that in our client's honestly held belief that your client was present at a lunch given by John Aspinall they were mistaken." The letter received no reply.

Marnham: Then Goldsmith sought an injunction against the magazine, its editor and five independent contributors with wide access to other papers from "writing, speaking, printing, publishing, distributing or circulating any words or any pictures or visual images of any matters whatsoever" referring to him. This injunction was denied him on the grounds, not surprising, that it was too wide. Then Goldsmith sought to commit the editor to prison for contempt of court. Then he sought to sequester the paper's assets, which would have closed it down.

Ingrams: At long last on 5 July we had our first opportunity to observe Goldsmith at close quarters

No. 377
Friday
28 May '76
15p

This cover is sub judice

when he attended a court hearing. A tall, restless, nail-biting man, expensively dressed, he looked at least ten years older than forty-three. His face was tanned, his eyes a steely blue. In repose, his expression was peculiarly dead. But his face would frequently crinkle into a smile and – which was disconcerting – from time to time he looked across at me, nodding and grinning, as if trying to convey a message of some kind.

The case, as it wore on, involved some extraordinary behaviour by two witnesses, PR man John Addey and lawyer Leslie Paisner, who both volunteered to help the Eye *before going over to Goldsmith's side. Addey even lied that the magazine had been blackmailing him. Despite summonses, neither man turned up in court. But what drove Goldsmith's fierce determination to destroy* Private Eye?

Ingrams: Goldsmith was a confirmed gambler, and had been ever since his prep school days. Every endeavour was a game which could be won or lost.

Cash: He was such a baddie figure – he was barmy really, a megalomaniac.

Ingrams: Goldsmith got it into his head that *Private Eye* was in the forefront of this revolutionary conspiracy in the media. He often referred to this "cancer" in the media, which was Marxist, and Footy was part of this and Gillard too. Completely mad.

James Goldsmith: *Private Eye* is in fact a club of journalists, who are not only working in *Private Eye* but also working throughout the press. And when you start looking, and investigating these people, you find these sort of revolutionary views, people who want to destroy Parliament. That's where this nation for so many years has been fed pus. Unfortunately, small subversive groups have been allowed to infiltrate all sorts of the activities of the nation. Vital parts of the nation. Tolerance of extremists who are trying to destroy our society is not a virtue. I believe that it is cowardice and treason.[80]

Ingrams: He was a manic depressive who was prone to go off the deep end from time to time. When cast in gloom Goldsmith liked to restore his morale by spending a week or two in a fascist country. The problem was that they were getting more and more difficult to find, what with the overthrow of the Greek colonels and the death of General Franco.

Anthony Blond:, *Eye* **shareholder who acted as go-between in attempt to negotiate a settlement:** Jimmy became wilder and wilder whenever I suggested he stop persecuting *Private Eye*. "They have attacked my son," he said. "I will throw them into prison. I will hound their wives, even in their widows' weeds." Then he gripped my arm. It was quite anxious-making.

Ingrams: There were times during that wonderful summer of 1976 when we seemed to be in court almost every week.

Marnham: Goldsmith's application for a blanket injunction protecting him from being mentioned in *Private Eye* was heard on the Tuesday. On the Wednesday the *Daily Express* led its front page with the headline "IT'S LORD GOLDSMITH". In his resignation honours list Harold Wilson had recommended Goldsmith for a life peerage. Goldsmith was known to be bitterly hostile to socialism, to be a supporter of the Tory Party and to have no outstanding record of public service. Many suspected the list had been drawn up not by Wilson but by Lady Falkender [☞ FORKBENDER, Lady]. She was a friend of Goldsmith.

Lady Falkender: It wasn't my list, it was his list. Of course it was. He was the Prime Minister.[81]

Harold Wilson: The list was drawn up by me from some names suggested by Transport House at my request and written down by Lady Falkender. The other names were written by me on a card in a notecase I always carry with me.[82]

Ingrams: Peter Jay, who had heard it himself from David Frost, told me that at their very first meeting at Frost's house in July 1975, Goldsmith had offered to rid Wilson and Falkender of "this turbulent magazine".

Bernard Donoughue, Downing Street adviser, in his diary for 29 January 1976: [Cabinet minister] Harold Lever said that Jimmy Goldsmith is prepared to put up £250,000 to destroy *Private Eye*.[83]

Ingrams: An old friend of Goldsmith's told me in 1978 that the honour was intended as a reward for his legal action. The citation was a private joke between Goldsmith, Wilson and Falkender. The "services to ecology", he said, consisted of ridding the country of the pollution of *Private Eye*.

Marnham: By the end of 1976 even the rich variety of English adversarial procedures was almost exhausted. Goldsmith's writs and summonses had engaged the attention of two magistrates, one High Court master and seventeen judges. Seven more judges would be needed before he was done.

Ingrams: In the meantime Goldsmith was busy with a new interest. He had developed ambitions of being a press lord. Beaverbrook Newspapers planned to sell parts of the Express Group, including the *Evening Standard*. Goldsmith stepped forward with an offer.

Eleven days before the Criminal Libel case was due to begin at the Old Bailey, I had arranged to have lunch with the paper's newly appointed young editor, Simon Jenkins. He

Chatto

I hold no brief for *Private Eye*. . .

. . . I've always thought it was a disgraceful little rag, full of nothing but schoolboy abuse and childish lies. . .

. . . but if this frightful little jumped-up squit from Slater Walker, Goldthorpe or whatever his name is, thinks he can close it down. . .

. . . then I say the whole of our British way of life is threatened!

wanted to know was whether I was prepared to settle with Goldsmith. He had already spoken to him, and said he was willing to deploy what he called "maximum flexibility". He had discovered that his continuing litigation against *Private Eye* was considered a black mark against him, and the prospect of having to sit in court for up to two weeks was very inconvenient.

That same afternoon, following a meeting with Goldsmith, Jenkins met me in a Soho coffee bar to tell me the terms: an apology to be published as a full-page advertisement in the *Evening Standard* – Jenkins assured me I would get the bargain rate – and a contribution towards Goldsmith's costs of £30,000, payable over ten years. The *Eye*'s distributors would be released from their undertakings. Without waiting to consult my lawyers, I agreed.

Cash: It was tremendous publicity, old Jimmy Goldsmith. He was one of the best things that happened to the *Eye* in my view.

Peter McKay: I always think Goldsmith saved *Private Eye*. He came along at just the right moment. The dynamic of *Private Eye* was such that if you did get a very big character like Goldsmith or Maxwell, although you might have lost money to them in legal costs, it put on sales. And it gave everyone a – we were all pulling together somehow. There were all these parties helping get money up, it was marvellous.

Ingrams: The readers sent in money spontaneously for what we christened 'The Goldenballs Fund'.

Tony Rushton: We had John Peel on side who was organizing gigs, and we had a very successful auction at Bonhams, and there were lots of things going on to raise money. And as you can see from the lists of donors, it touched a nerve with the readers. They liked to see their name in the mag. But they also knew that this was an institution that shouldn't be allowed to go under because of the whims of one unpleasant gentleman.

McKay: It was this fantastic cheek – I've worked on all the papers in Fleet Street, and newspapers no matter how dastardly would never ask their readers to pay their libel costs! Ingrams was perfectly happy with this, thought it was quite appropriate. He has a kind of patrician view of the readers. That they're there basically to congratulate the magazine, and if it gets into difficulty to bail it out. To pick up the bill!

Ingrams: The readers had by now contributed over £40,000 to the defence fund and we could hardly go on indefinitely asking them to subsidise what some of them, with justification, might interpret as an obsession.

It still meant, however, that on the appointed day, 16 May 1977, Marnham and myself had to enter the dock at the Old Bailey's famous Number One Court and plead "Not Guilty" to the charge of Criminal Libel. Our lawyer then rose and explained to the judge that *Private Eye* had apologised to Sir James. We were pronounced "Not Guilty".

- *James Goldsmith died in 1997. "I was quite relieved" commented Richard Ingrams. "I always had the feeling about him that he was lurking." Private Eye continued to write about him until the very end.*

- *The law of Criminal Libel was finally abolished in January 2010.*

- *Lord Lucan is still missing.*

☞ HAPPY SHIP, Not a; MAXWELL, Robert, full list of complaints against *Private Eye*; TALBOT!

GOODMAN, Lord

Graham Sutherland's portrait of Lord Goodman, with additions by *Private Eye*

There were many reasons for the *Eye* to hate Lord Goodman, and vice versa. He was a solicitor who never failed to encourage his many influential clients to go to law to protect their good names, and vied with Peter Carter-Fuck (☞) for the title of most libel writs served on the *Eye*. He was a trusted confidant of Harold Wilson. As chair of the Newspaper Proprietors' Association he was notorious for keeping embarrassing stories out of the papers. He had a hand in the glossing over of just about every establishment scandal from Profumo to Jeremy Thorpe.

No one at the *Eye*, however, expected the shitstorm which erupted as a result of a September 1971 report that a bank account in his name was "overdrawn by nearly £20,000 ... an internal Barclays note earlier this month commented: 'The time must be fast approaching when we will have to consider making a formal demand.'"

Goodman, who had just returned from Rhodesia where he had been negotiating with the government on behalf of prime minister Edward Heath (he was nothing if not well connected) instantly demanded a meeting with Richard Ingrams, Paul Foot, who had written the story, and their lawyer Geoffrey Bindman. "We sat in a large room while Goodman rampaged around us yelling," remembered Foot. "Our article, he screamed, was an outrage, a monstrous invasion of personal liberty. We were a menace to the public and a disgrace to journalism."[84] He didn't just want an apology or retraction: they had committed theft and he wanted the entire magazine closed down. Bindman pointed out that the *Eye* hadn't stolen anything: it was a matter for Barclays if his confidence had been breached but they had received the leaked documents in good faith. "He was incredibly pompous, spoke in this amazingly Victorian lawyer-style," recalled Bindman. "He was absolutely furious,

probably partly because he realised there was nothing he could do about it."[85]

His bluster was, nevertheless, enough to secure an apology from the *Eye* in the following issue: "it was a nominee account held in Lord Goodman's name … he had no direct or indirect personal interest in it". It would be twenty-five years before anyone discovered why he was so cross. The account belonged to a trust fund Goodman had set up on behalf of the Portman family, aristocrats who owned most of Dorset and significant chunks of London too. And for years he had been pilfering from it. An investigation in 1993 revealed that an amount which would have matured to be worth £10 million was missing from the trust. Much of the missing cash "had been lent or given to leading figures in the Labour party". Characteristically, Goodman, then in his eighties, settled things with the Portman family in secret. "We accept unreservedly that Lord Badman was nothing more than a thief, swindler, crook and conman," wrote a gleeful *Eye* when the scandal finally emerged.

"Sometimes I wonder if these kids really live in the catchment area"

GRIZELDA

Grizelda Grizlingham got her first cartoon into *Private Eye* when she was just sixteen, after "my sister and her boyfriend nagged me every day for weeks to draw it up. I thought it was a complete waste of time though – until it got printed". She has been contributing regularly since the late 1990s, specialising in barbed observations on the latest social trends.

GOVERNMENT READING LISTS, *Eye* joins (and leaves)

JUST FANCY THAT!

"There is little doubt that our system of regulation has become extraordinarily complex and remarkably ineffective. When I was a junior minister at the Department of Trade I did discover that I read more newspapers, and *Private Eye*, which revealed prima facie evidence of wrong-doing. I did give instructions that *Private Eye* should be read more effectively."[83]
Stanley Clinton-Davis, government minister 1974-79 and 1997-98

"Some of us have other things to do than read *Private Eye* all the time."
Culture Secretary Ben Bradshaw, speaking on Question Time, October 2009. Seven months later his party were swept out of power.

GRAUNIAD

So resigned were staff on the *Guardian* to the *Eye*'s persistent misspelling of their title that in May 1999 – three years after the paper's website was first launched – they registered www.grauniad.co.uk as the property of the Guardian Media Group. It redirects to the paper's own (mostly) properly spelt website.

GREER, Germaine

☞ BLIGHT, Rose

GROCER, The

Edward Heath, the chippiest man ever to become prime minister, hated being called "the Grocer" almost as much as he hated being deposed by Mrs Thatcher. He was convinced he had earned the nickname because "*Private Eye* could never forgive me for the fact I didn't go to a public school."[87] He was wrong, as Richard Ingrams explains: "He was called Grocer because much of his career was involved with groceries – all those early Common Market negotiations when the whole thing seemed to revolve around what we would have to pay for cat food and that kind of thing."

He made his debut – apron and all – long before he reached Number 10, during his abortive attempt to get Britain into the Common Market in 1962.
☞ HEATHCO

GROVEL and the rise of gossip

The "Grovel" column debuted in November 1970, with tales of scandalous doings by Richard Branson (he'd bought a big house), historian Arnold Toynbee's granddaughter Clare (she was working as a stripper) and *Oz* editor Richard Neville (he'd been filmed having sex). It was named after the "Charles Greville" column in the *Daily Mail*. Greville, like William Hickey or Ephraim Hardcastle, was a fictional character, and "Grovel" himself swiftly adopted the same first-person style as his pseudonymous Fleet Street counterparts, writing of "my good friend" and claiming that its subjects had personally volunteered the most damaging revelations about themselves.

The column was the brainchild of Patrick Marnham, who had joined the *Eye* as an editorial assistant from law school four years previously. It started off as a kind of spoof. "It was intended as a way of telling amusing stories about complete nonentities," he recalled. "It was criticised for being more amusing than factual."[88]

To address one of these issues – it's not entirely clear which – he recruited Nigel Dempster and Peter McKay, then junior gossip columnists on the *Daily* and *Sunday Express* respectively. "Dempster was, in his day, a really excellent radical journalist and very good at attacking all the shits and exposing people like Aspinall and Goldsmith (☞ GOLDENBALLS)," according to Richard Ingrams.[89] He brought the magic ingredient that Ingrams had always wanted for the *Eye*, insider knowledge. And what's more, unlike a lot of Fleet Street insiders (☞ LOBBY

Patrick Marnham

'Dempster was, in his day, a really excellent radical journalist and very good at attacking all the shits and exposing people like Aspinall and Goldsmith'

Richard Ingrams

Nigel Dempster . . .

SYSTEM, The problem with), he was willing to use it. "He was very good at having it both ways. He knew that he had to keep in with people in order to get the information that he wanted, but at the same time he had to, in order to be effective, put the boot in. He was very good at it. Gradually over the years he turned into a sort of glorified PR man. It happens to journalists quite a lot. Temptations of freebies. He wasn't that at all to begin with."

During the 1970s Dempster became a celebrity in his own right. "When he revealed in the *Mail* that Harold Pinter had run off with Antonia Fraser suddenly Dempster was the focus of attention and became immensely famous, rather as Andrew Gilligan did during the Iraq war or Matt Drudge did during the Monica Lewinsky business," recalls *Eye* hack Francis Wheen. "And professionally he became quite insufferable." At some point during this period the *Eye* started calling Dempster the Greatest Living Englishman. If it was meant to be ironic, its subject did not take it that way.

"Grovel" swiftly moved on from amusing stories about nonentities to the sort of stories about well-known celebrities you definitely wouldn't read in the *Mail*. In May 1975 the column revealed that Michael Foot was suffering from haemorrhoids and Denis Healey had had an operation to remove a cyst from his right testicle. "Richard loved that kind of completely unjustifiable story, it was his favourite thing, especially if they were very, very famous and very powerful, no matter how wildly unsourced they were, or whatever," chortles Dempster's partner in crime Peter McKay.

How did it work in practice? "We'd come in on the Monday, on publication day, it was always at the last minute. And there'd be stuff that was sent in by readers, which we were supposed to check and write up, so it was mixture of sources. Dempster would tend to do his own thing, and I would spend more time in the office and sift through what readers had sent in. It wasn't a big thing – it was just chucked off, no one spent much time on it at all, it was just something we knocked off every second Monday morning."

McKay continues to hone this method on the *Mail*'s "Ephraim Hardcastle" column to this day. He is known in the trade for finding a way to publish any fact he comes across without fear or favour (and quite often things he just feels ought to be facts as well). Auberon Waugh believed "he would cut your throat and destroy all chance of friendship for two lines in the *Daily Express*". Friends testify to the accuracy of Marnham's 1982 description of the "Grovel" pair: "Dempster has a cold eye, like a fish on a slab, but he has a warm heart. He has been known to take a story out in order to save someone's feeling. McKay has a merry twinkling eye, he is the life and soul of any party, he singles you out on a winter's night and beckons you across the bar to his cigars and double scotch. It is only months later you may find that for most people he has no heart at all."

Their scattershot approach did, however, manage to hit a few impressive targets. "Married ladies who have caught the eye and fancy of the Heir to the throne include Camilla Parker-Bowles, wife of cavalry officer Andrew," "Grovel" noted in November 1977. A year earlier it had asked, "Why did Jonathan King keep on disappearing into his white Rolls Corniche with darkened windows at the Knebworth Festival? Through

. . . **and Peter McKay**

the smokescreen windscreen I could just make out that he had two chauffeurs inside, both male, and – in my view – somewhat under the driving age." It would be a quarter of a century before the record producer was jailed for sex offences against teenage boys. Irish Taoiseach Charles Haughey's extra-marital affair was revealed twenty years before the mistress herself spilled the beans. The column also gleefully chronicled the breakdown of Princess Margaret and Lord Snowdon's marriage and her relationship with Roddy Llewellyn, pointing out that her royal highness had "a so-called drink problem" and repeatedly referring to "the most important fact about the royal romantic crisis, ignored by Fleet Street: Roddy Llewellyn is a poove".

The increasing emphasis on scuttlebutt in the *Eye* of the 1970s did not find favour with some of the old faces of the 1960s. "It has been far too ready to accept the sort of gossip which we all exchange about our friends in whatever circles we move, which is based on exaggeration, and perhaps malicious fabrication from time to time," complained Christopher Booker in 1976. "It's reprinted in black and white, often at great damage to the people who are being gossiped about." Fantoni complained that "the hacks who fill Grovel cannot write a sentence unless

it carries a sneer calculated to offend".[90] John Wells, who was ascending through the social stratosphere at a rate of knots by this point, was even more distressed. "Wells strongly disapproved of the Dempster side of *Private Eye*, partly because he was a bit of a snob," chuckles Ingrams. "A lot of the people written about were his friends. There was a story in Grovel about Hugh Fraser, a Tory MP who was married to Antonia Fraser before she went off with Harold Pinter, and Fraser ended up living in a flat in a house in Kensington which belonged to Wells. And when Fraser died, this was the story, Antonia had come round to the house and removed all the valuable furniture. And that got into *Private Eye*, and he then wrote me a letter for publication saying he wanted to make it clear that he had nothing to do with it. Amazing thing to do." The pompous missive accused the *Eye*

Grovel himself, as seen by Fluck and Law in 1982

of "a less than admirable exercise in trampling a newly dug grave and beating up the mourners".

Ingrams was having none of it. On privacy he likes to quote his hero William Cobbett: "when [a man] once comes forward as a candidate for public admiration, esteem or compassion his opinions, his principles, his motives, every action of his life, public or private, become the fair subject of public discussion". He has claimed that he has often been asked "by indignant members of the public" whether he took the possible distress of the stories' subjects and their families into account. "But my answer, which only seemed to make them more indignant, was that I never gave a thought to the question for the reason that in most cases one had no means of knowing how people might respond to what others considered an embarrassing or damaging revelation."[91] One of his good friends, A. N. Wilson, pointed out in 1992 that "Richard is a solipsist who lives entirely within his own world. He's almost like an autistic child in that respect. He just doesn't realise the effect his words and actions will have on other people."[92]

And to be fair, Ingrams never once complained when his own personal life exploded rather spectacularly in the 1990s and was gleefully chronicled by Dempster and his Fleet Street rivals, eager to give the former *Eye* boss a taste of his own medicine. By then, however, Dempster was psychotically opposed to the *Eye* and everything it stood for (☞ PARKINSON, Cecil, his part in Nigel Dempster's downfall), and the "Grovel" column itself was about to become history (see MARQUESA).
☞ BRENDA and family; UGANDA, Talking about

EXCLUSIVE 48 PAGE INTERVIEW WITH SADDAM HUSSEIN: FAMILY MAN, DOG LOVER AND GOLFER

"Mum, Dad... I'm a homo sapiens"

— Tony Husband

PRIVATE EYE

No. 1099
6 February –
19 Feb 2004
£1.30

HUTTON REPORT IN FULL

...and in conclusion, I find Dr Shipman innocent of all charges

Your sinner is in the oven

— McLACHLAN

That Interview in full

(continued from page 49)
and although only 27, the new editor of *Private Eye* ... blah blah ... disturbed the old guard ... blah

blah ... Dempster . MacKay ... Dempst... Waugh ... blah blah glasses ... balding . diminutive ... blah ... blah blah ... pu... school ... blouson j... ... blah blah ... ho... only 25 ... blah bla... MacKay ... Dempst... blah blah blah ... a... 26 ... blah blah ... of lager ...

(continued on page 94)

...agson. Chill out, du... awesome contest for my Bi... excitable columnist amoun... to a Vanilla Ice concert. "Yo... miss out on this one." Mean... Minogue "is baring all" in h... which Piers dutifully plugs... And so gormlessly on...

PRIVATE EYE 1961–1982 SORT OF AN EXHIBITION

HAMILTONS 13 Carlos Place London W1

NEW TECHNOLOGY BAFFLES PISSED OLD HACK

DAILY PAPER
STREET OF SHAME
Lunchtime O'Booze
EXCLUSIVE!

HACKWATCH

The "Hackwatch" column, which forensically dismantles the work of a particularly dreadful journalist, began in June 1991. At first, the editor took some persuading. "The first ever 'Hackwatch' was about Dempster, and the second one was about Peter McKay," remembers Francis Wheen. "I thought if I do them then it'll go down awfully well and be fine forever after, I can do whoever I like."

In two decades, only one Hack has publicly objected to being Watched. "Minette Marin cut up rough," says Wheen. "Years later I met her at a party and she said 'It was *so* upsetting,' and she went on and on about how distressing it was. And I had to go and look it up, because to be honest it hadn't really made much of an impact on me."

The endless Goldsmith litigation, as seen by Michael Heath and the *Eye* team

HAMILTON, Neil

The MP for Tatton wrote to the *Eye* in February 1984, following a lengthy piece linking him to the lobbyists Ian Greer Associates. It was, he told the magazine, "an excellent firm offering an excellent service to the client companies lucky enough to retain it. I have never received a penny piece from the company."

Twelve years later his libel case against the *Guardian* spectacularly collapsed after it was proved he had taken £10,000 in commission payments from Ian Greer Associates and lied about them.

HAPPY SHIP, Not A:
Private Eye post-Goldsmith

"The strain of an apparently unending stream of cases was beginning to tell," admitted Richard Ingrams of the latter stages of the Goldsmith battle (☞ GOLDENBALLS). "I could talk or think of little but Goldsmith. At night I dreamed about him. The obsession was plainly turning me into a bore as far as my immediate circle was concerned, and meanwhile *Private Eye* was suffering from neglect."[93]

It was hardly surprising. Not sooner had James Goldsmith abandoned his attempt to have Ingrams sent to prison than Jeremy Thorpe (☞ DITTO MAN, The) joined in too. "At one point Thorpe was going to sue for criminal libel, and I think Goldsmith put him up to that. Goldsmith even paid Thorpe's legal expenses."

Home life was no respite. In 1976 Ingrams's elder brother PJ disappeared on a climbing trip in the Andes; in 1977 his younger son Arthur, born with brain-damage, died at the age of seven. His wife Mary was a manic depressive, and her condition steadily worsened.

At the office, everyone's salary had been halved to help pay the legal costs of the fight. As hackette Jane Ellison put it, "everyone just soldiered on penniless out of loyalty to this great man Ingrams".[94] Admirable, but the mixture of gratefulness and guilt can hardly have helped the editor's mood. "During the Goldsmith case he seemed to seek an unnecessary degree of isolation, becoming more and more difficult to talk to as the pressure increased," remembered Ingrams's co-defendant on the criminal libel charge Patrick Marnham. Paul Foot remembered visiting his friend at home during this period, taking Ingrams out for a "great walk across the Berkshire Downs" and discussing the possibility of him losing his house

Great Bores of Today. 50.

". . . and I now ask your Lordships to turn for a moment if you will to the cartoon on page 4 of *Private Eye* Issue 389 that's exhibit JMG 586 in your Lordships' bundle and there can be no doubt in our submission that this cartoon constitutes a clear and undoubted reference to myself in the light of which I crave leave to refer your Lordships for a moment to *Rex v Aspinall Steam Laundry* where it was stated by Mr Justice Cocklecarrot Times Law Report 1936 that to hold up the Learned Counsel of a party to litigation to obloquy thereby subjecting him to public contumely and opprobrium constitutes and this is our submission in this case my lord a clear case of *scandalum magnatum* for which the defendant should be imprisoned. . ."

"and everything" as a result of the Goldsmith case.

And looking back at the issues of late 1976 and early 1977, the tail-off in quality is noticeable. (So is the fact that the cartoonists were cashing in by submitting lots of jokes about judges and juries, all of which an obsessed Ingrams put straight in.) Stupid mistakes crept in. A production cock-up meant that issue 388 went out with no speech bubble on the cover. More and more space was given over to long, pointless letters from mouth organist Larry Adler which served no purpose but to drive readers mad.

The other thing that is noticeable about the years following the Goldsmith case is an increasing nastiness about the *Eye*. While the magazine had – admirably – never spared anyone's feelings, it now seemed more and more often to be crossing the road especially to offend. In 1977, as the National Front reached their zenith, a "Letter from Lahore" was bylined "A. Paki". "Grovel" described Bianca Jagger as "the Nicaraguan slag funded by a poove New York frock maker" and complained about how London was full of "disgustingly fat Arabs and their English tarts making the place smell like a sewer". Erin Pizzey, founder of the first refuge for victims of domestic violence, was derided as "a lard mountain and vast pudding" whose ex-husband was paying "generous settlements for their children (and bastard grandchildren)".

The jokes were subject to the usual complaints about taste, but in 1979 a reader eschewed knee-jerk outrage to muse thought-provokingly on the "bland lack of concern displayed by your making [victim of police brutality] Blair Peach's murder a subject of humour. The possibility that policemen are going to demonstrations armed with lead-filled coshes and ready to use them does not seem to worry you in the slightest." That would certainly not have been the case when Paul Foot had been penning "Police 5" a decade before. His investigative zeal was missed. "The paper still seems to be living in the shadow of the excitement of the Goldsmith case," wrote Patrick Marnham, who was in the process of falling out rather spectacularly with the magazine, in 1982. "Its investigative side has declined, and there have been more personal attacks on relatively trivial figures." In the same year Julian Barnes pointed out in the *London Review of Books* that "anyone studying the magazine over the last few

"There was something incredibly malicious, malevolent and twisted about it. And that's pretty well gone now." Christopher Booker

Gathering shadows: Ingrams at work in the late 70s

years and recalling the *Eye*'s successive attitudes to Macmillan, Home, Wilson and Heath might be astonished at how lightly Mrs Thatcher and her cabinet of yes-men have got off".[95]

Foot, who had continued to help out behind the scenes, actually made a brief bylined return in 1978, but was soon tempted away by the *Daily Mirror*. "I can't bear [Ingrams's] prejudices, which get worse as he gets older," he said two years later. "*Private Eye* is a weathervane of middle-class opinion, and as far as I am concerned this is a criticism … If you're going to be a powerful satirical magazine your targets would be different from the rest of the media. You should attack the strong, not the weak. Under Booker's influence there is a tendency just to add a satirical gloss to the *Daily Telegraph*."[96] Actually, Christopher Booker deplored much of the content during this period too. "Ian [Hislop] has done a lot of good things for *Private Eye*, and one of them is to take away that – it was very much influenced by [Nigel] Dempster and Bron [Waugh]: 'Let's *really* put the boot in,'" he says. "There was something incredibly malicious, malevolent and twisted about it. And that's pretty well gone now."

Hislop reckons "Bron's viciousness was redeemed by a wit, so that was forgivable, but that rather clumsy tone elsewhere – the Dumpster thuggery – it was actually rather tabloid, it was physical characteristics, everyone's a shit and a

Paul Halloran

man's friends and colleagues rushed to testify to his blamelessness. "A calumny … not fair game … mendacious and malicious … a grotesque and malicious fabrication," protested letters printed in the following edition, which crowed that "our story seems to have created considerable interest". Unfortunately, years of entanglement with Goldsmith had conditioned Ingrams to regard vociferous denials as verification. Besides, he had evidence – not from De'Ath, who had vanished without trace – but from a burly New Zealander who turned up in the office to tell Ingrams that "You don't have to worry at all – this bloke's a piss-artist and a shirt-lifter." Ingrams liked him so much he gave him a job.

"Martin Tomkinson introduced me to Paul Halloran," says Ingrams. "I always liked Halloran. Footy and [Michael] Gillard particularly were very anti-him. He's a strange man. The extraordinary thing about him was that he had a huge range of contacts, all over the place. And what I remember is that if stuff came in anonymously I could wave it in front of Halloran and in an awful lot of the cases he could somehow check it out. He seemed to know a huge amount of people."

"He liked to give the impression that he knew everything and he knew everyone," snorts Francis Wheen. "He had one or two contacts, arms dealers, the odd one in the Middle East, but he was parlaying that into that there wasn't a country in the world where he didn't have a top-level contact. Whatever subject came up – if I mentioned to him something I was writing about, it would be 'Yeah, but do you know the story behind that?' 'What's that, Paul?' 'That's for you to find out.' And I'd say, 'Well, if you know it, Paul, we're colleagues, you could tell me.' He always liked to give the impression that he knew more than he was letting on."

He certainly didn't in this particular case. Despite relocating – uninvited – to the offices of the Oxford student paper *Cherwell* for some time, he dug up precisely no dirt whatsoever on the hapless chaplain. Three months after the original article, the *Eye* carried a cringing "Apology and Retraction … We thought our information to be reliable. It turns out to have been totally false … The trouble is that our readers are apt to think that 'there is no smoke without fire'. If that is the rule, this is the total exception to it. Publication of this piece was a disastrous mistake."

fuck and a wank and you just – eurgh! Do we have to do that? It seemed to be an aberration, that."

But if people thought Dempster was bad, they hadn't seen anything yet. In January 1980 Wilfred De'Ath, a homeless former BBC producer who had lost all his money in a libel action, and who would go on to spend time in jail for fraud offences, offered the magazine a stonkingly scurrilous story about the chaplain at an Oxford college. Ingrams gave it prime spot in the magazine, with full details of how the clergyman was not only "a homosexual whose activities caused grave embarrassment to the college authorities" but "an atheist and a drunkard", and had "managed to lose the college £30,000 per annum as Domestic Bursar". There was just one problem. It wasn't true. Scores of the

At this point, many editors might have dispensed with the services of everyone concerned and tried to pretend it had never happened. Ingrams, with his usual impressive bloody-mindedness, did the exact opposite. An entirely unrepentant Wilfred De'Ath is comfortably installed as a columnist on Ingrams' *Oldie* to this day. And Halloran was retained at the *Eye*, and given the specific task of compiling a new column called "Church Times" dedicated to exposing "homosexualists in the Church of England and the frightful Gay Christian movement". The same reasoning lay behind both decisions. "Halloran was taken on because he annoyed everyone," says Hislop. "He was badly behaved, and drunk, and would abuse people, and Richard liked that. Which had a certain logic to it." And "Church Times" was instigated precisely because it went against the spirit of the new tolerance being pushed through by figures like Ken Livingstone, and annoyed and upset so many readers. And, come to that, many of Ingrams's own staff and friends (☞ POOVES, Richard Ingrams's peculiar attitude to).

Auberon Waugh thoroughly approved of "Church Times", but thoroughly disapproved of the other editorial innovation. "The atmosphere was beginning to deteriorate," he recalled of the early 1980s. "Ingrams seemed to be taking less interest in the magazine. A new employee, O'Hanrahan [it was a favourite Waugh put-down to pretend not to know people's names, as Ian Hislop, aka Hinton, aka Driscoll, would soon discover] made rude noises and insolent faces

The illustration for *Church Times*, one of the most controversial regular features ever to appear in the *Eye*

every time any of the public school-educated contributors walked in or walked out."[97] "He gave everyone the heebie-jeebies," remembered Christopher Silvester. "No one could believe this creature was sitting there in the office," said Jane Ellison, who shared a room with the new boy. "One of the things Richard used to do, which gave him great amusement, was to mimic people's disgust at Halloran. At the *Eye* lunches, Halloran used to get drunk and abusive, and Richard just sat there spectating."

"Nobody knew why he was there really," says Francis Wheen. "Whenever you asked Richard about him he would just quote that Peter Sellers line, 'One must have such a man.' Anyone who's ever seen a bit of raw Halloran copy, it was quite extraordinary, like an early draft of *Finnegans Wake*. It was incomprehensible. Just random collections of words."

That, of course, was not what he was there for. Although records show he did produce his fair share of stories for the magazine, Halloran was primarily there to amuse Ingrams, who needed to shake things up to stave off the feelings of boredom and fatigue that had settled over him. "There was nothing Ingrams liked more than an atmosphere of fear and loathing around him," reckoned Jane Ellison. "'Not a happy ship,' he would murmur, as hacks bickered and accused each other. 'Not a happy ship.'"[98]

They didn't need much encouragement. "Almost everybody who works for the magazine hates everyone else," Ellison claimed. "John Wells hates Auberon Waugh; Waugh hates Barry Fantoni; Fantoni hates Peter McKay. And so on."[99] "The hackery in the old days was horribly competitive and sneery," says Nick Newman, another new boy during this period. "Halloran was a real work of art. He was always rumbling away in the background, 'Oh, you're Hislop's bum chum.' Jeffrey Bernard could be incredibly rude too. Dempster. People delighted in basically telling you you were no good."

Ian Hislop plunged into this piranha tank in 1981. "I remember Ian when he arrived, he was this shy young boy," chortles McKay. "I thought God no, it would be too cruel and ghastly for him. Ha ha! Little did we know." Little indeed. "Jane Ellison and so on – none of them liked me very much. Or at all," laughs Hislop now. "Which is fine. They made a bit of an effort – McKay once took me to El Vino's – but it wasn't

A young recruit downstairs . . .

' " The Private Eye Story ", sir? On the shelf next to " Great Bores of Today ".'

Fantoni's view of the last 'official' Eye book, as published in the *Times*

my world, I didn't like it and I couldn't pretend I liked them. And I thought all of that was just sort of pointless. I came in, did my stuff and then left."

Occasionally blood would spill on to the carpet. When Patrick Marnham, an *Eye* contributor of sixteen years' standing, wrote his official history of the magazine's first twenty-one years in 1982, the fall-out was so violent he had to leave. "Tired and inaccurate malice", was Christopher Booker's review in the *Spectator*, while Ingrams told the *Daily Express* it was "a bloody awful book" (it isn't). In a very Ingramsesque manoeuvre, he then used both quotes in an advert for the book in *Private Eye*. He had already chosen the month the book's co-publishers André Deutsch were distributing copies to bookshops to print an attack on them in the *Eye*'s "World's Greatest Publishers" column which Deutsch himself, described as a "Hungarian dwarf-like philistine wheeler-dealer", said "hurt me deeply".[100]

As the *Eye* lurched madly on from libel case to libel case – "The 1980s were extraordinary: some years we had up to a dozen actions or so. We used to get hammered," remembers then managing director Dave Cash – many suspected that the editor was on a deliberate kamikaze course. "A favourite theory we discussed at the time was that in a wild fit of self-destruction, Ingrams would deliberately perpetrate the most damaging libel of all time, the 'big one' against,

say, the Queen or Mother Teresa, bringing £1,000,000 damages down on his head and go out, all guns firing." recalled Ellison.[101]

In fact, he had a totally different plan – one that none of them had seen coming.

☞ INGRAMS, Richard, decision to retire as editor and appoint Ian Hislop as his successor

. . . and a 'self-destructive' editor upstairs

HAVE I GOT NEWS FOR YOU

Nine years on from the defenestration of Angus Deayton and fifteen years on from Paul Merton's one-series sabbatical, Ian Hislop remains the only participant to have taken part in every episode of the BBC panel show *Have I Got News for You*. His involvement is enthusiastically supported by his staff at *Private Eye*, partly because, as he says, "I hope it drives people towards the magazine" but mostly because when it is being broadcast a car comes on recording day at 5.30pm to take him to the studio and we can all go home early.

Contrary to a widespread belief among profile writers, the recording sessions are pretty much the sum of his commitment to the programme: "It is a journalistic idea that 'He's just swanning about on the telly all the time' and that therefore someone else must be running the mag. But on an alternate Thursday for a few issues a year I miss half an hour when I would usually be in the office. Which I don't think constitutes not being at the day job."

Equally, any other celebrity commitments – Hislop has in recent years fronted documentaries on the war dead, the railway system and the scout movement and co-written sitcoms, radio dramas and a feature film with Nick Newman – are slotted in around the *Eye*'s fortnightly schedule: "I do say three days' filming, and I do it from Tuesday–Wednesday–Thursday after we've gone to press, which are pretty *Marie Céleste* days here, there's not a great deal happening."

And all of them, hopefully, funnel potential readers in the *Eye*'s direction. "I think *Have I Got News* probably does help the mag. It's twenty years of being on telly. But I suspect for a lot of people they would have no idea that I have a day job nor any interest in it."

☞ FORTNIGHTLY APPEARANCE; *NEWS QUIZ*

"WELL YOU WILL JUST HAVE TO STOP GROWING WON'T YOU."

HEATH
on
Fallout
Shelters

"YES, IT MUST BE VERY FRUSTRATING FOR YOU."

"IT MUST BE NICE TO HAVE A HOBBY."

"THERE'S SOMETHING AT THE DOOR DEAR."

HEATH, Michael

Michael Heath's first contribution came in issue 12 in June 1962. His characteristic spiky style and preoccupation with the vulgarity and awfulness of much of modern life has been a feature of the magazine ever since. "I guess all cartoonists are right-wing, they're all pretty down on pop music and young people, they're three-piece-suit men, really," he says.

As well as his own cartoon strips – "The Regulars", "The Gays", "Numero Uno", "Heath's Private View" – and spot cartoons, Heath worked on collaborative features such as "Great Bores of Today" with the magazine's jokes team, and even had a stint contributing to the speech bubble covers. "The reason I'm prolific is because, on the whole, it pays very badly," he grumps.[102]

Great Bores Of Today.

". . . I used to read the *Eye* when it first came out in the seventies when it had some kind of bite that was when David Frost was connected with it along with all the TW3 people it seemed to have some purpose then but nowadays quite frankly a lot of it is just schoolboy smut and if you want my opinion there's no excuse for attacking people in their private lives I knew someone they went for and it's not funny he had to go and live in the Channel Islands and all this stuff about Goldsmith week after week why don't they leave him alone I prefer *Punch* myself that Alan Coren have you heard him on the radio? bloody brilliant he's much funnier than the bloke from *Private Eye* no I don't see it any more the kids sometimes bring it home and I glance at it now and again did you see the cover last week? I couldn't understand it. . . "

HEATHCO

"Heathco", the prime ministerial parody during Ted Heath's period in Number 10 from 1970 to 1974, has been unjustly neglected. A series of company newsletters issued to the staff of a multi-national supermarket chain, it captures Heath's grumpy petulance and the prevailing atmosphere of industrial unrest perfectly. "We never did a book of it, and it never got famous like all the other pieces, and it's a real shame," says Barry Fantoni, who co-wrote the series with Ingrams. "It was such a funny country then. It was the plastic beaker disposal unit that got the unions and all that absolutely right."

This device, the bane of the managing director's life, was the product of the Phuwatascorcha Corporation of Japan and was constantly misused by his ungrateful staff. "I counted no less than 326 plastic cups jammed tight with cigarette ends," he complained after the staff New Year party in 1972. "Mrs Thatcher spent all morning clearing up and tidying to make the place look shipshape again before lunch." The following year the company was forced to bring in a new wage-restraint policy: "you brought this Phase 3 on yourselves and all the other bloody phases", he told his staff. "Until you can learn to behave yourselves and stop bellyaching on every hour of the day and night, then you'll just have to be told what to do."

Heath finally surrendered his space in the company car park in February 1974, as his real-life counterpart called a general election asking "Who governs Britain?", only to find out that it wasn't him. "All these people want is trouble. You could offer them the moon and they still wouldn't be satisfied," he grumbled in his valedictory letter to the workers on the shop floor. "I've done all that's humanly possible to sort this one out. Now it's your turn for a change."

The very first Heathco, November 1970

A message from the Managing Director

Hullo everyone!

On behalf of us all I would like to extend a very warm welcome to our two new managers, Mr Davies and Mr Walker.

John Davies comes to us after a long and distinguished career in many fields of business. He worked for some time in the accounting department of British Petroleum where he certainly made his mark. In 1960 he became a Vice Chairman and Managing Director of Shell Mex — the oil company.

In 1965 he was appointed Director General of the Confederation of British Industry — no mean feat for a man of 49!

John now takes over as head of our brand new Trading and Export department — a task to which I am sure he will bring all his experience and energy to bear on.

John Davies is married and has two children. I am sure all of us will wish him the very best of luck.

Our other new recruit Peter Walker comes to us from the world of high finance. He is a well known figure in the City of London where he has gained a wide knowledge of every aspect of the commercial scene. Many of you may be surprised to know that he is only 38!

Like John Davies, Peter is a married man and has an eight month old son, Jonathan.

Whilst on the subject of new recruits I would like to put in a word about our Mr Rayner who is working with me in the back room helping to run down a few lines which haven't been quite as profitable as we had hoped.

Derek Rayner is a brilliant young accountant, who comes to us from Marks and Spencers. Starting in the cake department he quickly made his mark and rose to the top of the tree. Derek knows more about cakes than anyone I know and I am sure he will bring a welcome breath of fresh cakes to our accounting department!

You will all have the opportunity of meeting our new men (and I hope, their wives) in a social capacity at our Grand Annual Fancy Dress Gala Evening to be held in the canteen on December 5th.

I am sure there will be a good turn out as usual. There will be many attractions — including Tombola, a Beauty Contest, and of course special Fancy Cakes provided by our own Mr Rayner!

Tickets are on sale now. Apply Mr Barber, Room 11.

Mr Davies   Mr Walker

HISLOP, Ian, Ten things you never knew about

1 He's Welsh. David Hislop was a civil engineer who worked on projects around the world, taking his family with him and raising his children in such exotic locations as Nigeria, Saudi Arabia and Hong Kong. In July 1960, however, he and his wife Helen happened to be based slightly closer to home, in Mumbles, South Wales, which is where their son Ian was born and spent the first six months of his life before departing for Africa.

2 He appears in 1980 studio-busting mega-flop *Heaven's Gate*. Look carefully at the extras in the Oxford-filmed graduation scenes that open the film and you may spot him. "I'm standing behind Kris Kristofferson."

3 He once attempted stand-up comedy as support for a band called Chuck Farley and the Headbangers. "Fifteen minutes of

Hislop as seen by his Spitting Image colleagues

Brideshead jokes, didn't gain one laugh. It was a ghastly experience."[100]

4 He got his big break in comedy when he sold half the Edinburgh Fringe revue he had written (and appeared in) to the BBC. It had shared a venue with a production of Cabaret directed by a young Jeanette Winterson.

5 When he left *Spitting Image*, on which he and Nick Newman had been chief scriptwriters, in 1989, they made a puppet of him specially.

6 He invented Tim Nice-But-Dim. "Harry Enfield came to me and Nick and said 'all my characters are yobs. Can you do someone who's quiet and isn't working class?'"[101]

7 He once failed to make the video recorder in his office work and solved the problem by hurling it down the stairs. "It came thumping down – thump, thump, thump," remembers Sue Roccelli, who was working on the ground floor at the time. "He told me to stop doing whatever I was doing and go out and get him a new one. I was so scared I went up to Oxford Street and managed to persuade one of the guys from Dixons to come all the way back to the office with me and set it up so it would definitely work."

8 He owns a fullset of Teletubbies, purchased at a charity auction for £1,000 in 1997.

9 Ricky Gervais once phoned him up and asked his permission to call him a 'stupid bald cunt' in his stage show. "I told him that it was kind of him to ask, but it was not really up to me to give permission for jokes about myself to be performed on stage. 'I do not want to be offensive,' he said."[102]

10 He despises articles with titles like "10 Things You Never Knew About . . ."

HISLOP, Ian, arrival at *Private Eye*

In 1980, Helen Hislop noticed an interview with Richard Ingrams in which he mentioned that *Private Eye* could do with some new blood, and pointed it out to her son, who had interviewed him the previous term (☞ QUESTIONS, asked by Ian Hislop of Richard Ingrams at their first meeting). "I sent him a letter saying 'Time you employed me,'" chuckles Ian. Wisely, he also included some copies of his student magazine *Passing Wind* (☞) – including a spoof of James Burke's BBC science series *Connections*. He got a swift reply (below).

"He wanted me to come in and join a writing session and I couldn't do it while I was a student," says Hislop. He did submit jokes from outside

Private Eye
34 Greek Street
London W1
Nov 27 '80

Dear Ian,

I've been through the <u>Winds</u> which are full of good things. My favourites are the Punch take-off and the Burke special. If you wanted to do another Burke for us when he does another series I'm sure I could use it. But as I said I think you should try any parodies, TV or newspaper. Please have a go. Best to keep them short I would think. You can always use the p.94 cut-off.

If you wanted to work on something with me we could fix an afternoon date perhaps during an on-week.

Please encourage Newman to submit some jokes.

Don't forget to write to John Lloyd at *Not the Nine O'Clock News.*

Richard Ingrams

though. His first one was published in March 1981: a cash-in on the cash-ins on a recently deceased Beatle. "It was a piece about top ten books where they were all about John Lennon. He put this in and I got this cheque, I remember it was for thirty quid and I was thinking 'This is fantastic, I'm going to have a great summer' – unbelievable sums."

Spring Books

The John Lennon I didn't know
by Tony Palmer
(Snipcock and Tweed £46)

John Lennon, the case for Canonisation
by Rev David Shepherd, Bishop of Liverpool
(Runcieballs and Gay £47)

Lennon's influence on Shakespeare
by Clive Jaws
(Longford Books £89)

Lennon: Poet of the People
by Dave Spart
(Spartacus Press 46p)

The John Lennon Book of the Countryside
(Logburner & Vole £703)

The James Herriot Book of John Lennon's Yorkshire
(Ripoff Press £68)

Further pieces followed, including his notorious version of the *Sunday Times*'s "A Room of My Own" feature by IRA dirty protester Bobby Sands ("he has chosen a simple pastel brown to decorate all four walls"). "Then I sort of started turning up that September, October, just writing with Richard."

Was it terrifying? "Yeah, it was," Hislop grins. "Richard's technique of dead silence is very worrying. Someone has to fill it, and it's going to be you. So that's quite daunting. Part of Richard's thing is, 'I'm bored: amuse me.' And I always took that as a challenge. And I enjoyed that."

Finding that thirty quid doesn't actually stretch that far when you're living in London, he took on a day job as well – "I worked for a private tutoring college in Earl's Court, teaching English A-level retakes to boys who'd been thrown out for smoking." There are a host of forty-eight-year-old former reprobates out there completely unaware of the identity of the keen young chap that got them into university. The rest of the time he was writing comedy sketches for anyone that would take them – "I got in on *Carrott's Lib*, which was Jasper Carrott trying to reinvent himself with younger comedians." His most concerted efforts, however, went into the fortnightly sessions with Richard Ingrams, which were providing more and more material for the magazine.

It didn't take the old guard long to notice that there was a cuckoo in the nest. "[Christopher] Booker and I used to spot 'There's a piece here, we didn't write this!'" says Barry Fantoni. "And finally Richard said 'Well, there's a lad coming in called Ian Hislop. And we have an afternoon together and we do a little piece.' And it was fine. And then one day we were all there together. And it was good. He seemed to get all the jokes. And I thought, 'This is terrific – we've managed to find someone new.'"

"They were extremely tolerant and friendly and very generous," says Hislop of his infiltration of what had at that point been a closed shop for two decades. "Barry being a musician always says it was time to be a quartet, the trio had had enough. I think because Richard had been editor for a long time and therefore chose what happened in a very broad sense, they quite liked the idea that – whoops! – it was a bit more up for grabs." The new boy was in.
☞ HAPPY SHIP, Not A

HONDOOTEDLY

"Hondootedly Mossis Thotcher …" The broad Ulster brogue of the BBC's political editor, as phonetically rendered in the pages of the *Eye*, remains one of the most fondly remembered features from the 1980s.

Except by one man. "It annoyed me," a furious John Cole told an interviewer in 2001. "I don't like *Private Eye*. I just don't like it. They're minor public school boys who've never grown up. I regard myself as a pretty serious journalist. I was successful in broadcasting. I didn't want to turn into a buffoon … As a newspaper editor I'd mixed with leading politicians for 20 years or more. And none of them were ever ill-mannered enough to say I had an accent. And that's the way I expect to be treated: as a gentleman, by other gentlemen and ladies."[106]

☞ COLEMANBALLS

HONEYMOON, Presence of
Dave Cash on Peter Cook's

When Peter Cook married his third wife Lin in 1989 and went on honeymoon to Paris, he took the managing director of *Private Eye*, Dave Cash, with him. They were combining a business trip – to buy out a France-dwelling *Eye* shareholder, Anthony Blond (☞ FAMOUS FRIENDS) – with pleasure.

"I flew over with them and we stayed at the Ritz Hotel," reminisces Cash. "It was great fun. We went to a very upmarket sleazy club and we were drinking lots of champagne, and these girls were dancing around half-naked, and a fellow came over with the bill and it was absolutely

The newlyweds snapped at the airport. "The press spotted Peter and I hid so I couldn't be seen", remembers Cash

huge, hundreds, and we just didn't have the money between us to pay. And this heavy came over, a very large gentleman with big shoulders,

HONEYSETT, Martin

Martin Honeysett began contributing to the *Eye* in 1970. He specialises in fleshy, grotesque visions of life in suburbia – despite which his cartoons are so appreciated in Japan that he was made a visiting professor at the Kyoto Seika University.

and I thought 'Oh God, this will make the papers.' And I remember Peter, whose French was actually quite good, charming this fellow and we sort of eased ourselves out."

In the midst of all this, the new Mrs Cook decided to bring up the subject of money too. "We went in this rather wonderful café in Montmartre where a woman was playing the accordion and singing Edith Piaf songs, and it was all very jolly," says Cash. "And Lin was very serious, and she was suddenly questioning me, why wasn't Peter getting more money out of the magazine? And I remember thinking 'Oh, fucking hell, Lin – we're having a jolly.' And I always remember Peter saying to her, 'You don't understand, Lin, what the *Eye* is about.'"

The upshot of the conversation was that Peter, having never asked before, suddenly started being paid a £20,000 salary by the *Eye*. "He was very pleased about having that, not just because the money was useful to him at that point, but I think he appreciated the recognition," says his sister Elizabeth. But the negotiations also set the tone for the difficult relationship between the magazine and the woman who would become its largest shareholder just six years later.
☞ WILL, Peter Cook's

HOT POTATOES, as
recommended by editor of French satirical magazine

"I remember when we were first doing *Private Eye* I was a huge admirer of *Le Canard Enchaîné*, and I went over to Paris and interviewed the editor," says co-founder Peter Usborne. "And he said, 'Well, I don't think you're going to make it because you're far too young. *Canard Enchaîné* gets its hot potatoes' – as he called them, in English – 'from our friends who are in government, and your friends won't be in government for twenty years so if I were you I'd take a twenty-year break and come back when you're forty-five.' And that probably slowed down our ambitions."

Whether Usborne and Ingrams mentioned this to their young friends from Oxford Peter Jay, Margaret Callaghan or Robin Butler is not known.

HP SAUCE, Name of column

The political page launched in March 1970 was named after the vinegar-based condiment in which Mary Wilson (☞) claimed the then prime-minister liked to 'drown everything' she cooked for him.

"I was very pleased with the title of HP Sauce," grins Ingrams. "That's survived, hasn't it."

HP SAUCE, stewardship by
Auberon Waugh

Auberon Waugh was sacked from the *Spectator* in January 1970, for the crime of altering the list of contributors on the magazine's contents page so that the notoriously bibulous hack George Gale became Lunchtime O'Gale. Since it was an *Eye* joke that had got him in trouble he went straight round to the *Eye* to offer his services. It involved a pay cut, but it came with other perks. "He had this tiny little grotty office and he insisted, which I organized, that he had to have William Morris wallpaper," remembers Dave Cash.

For his first two and a half years he was "the first political correspondent of *Private Eye*".[107] Not that this actually meant much in the traditional sense of the term. "As a relatively new magazine, and because it had never had one before, *Private Eye* had no automatic right to a Press Gallery ticket in the House of Commons," explained Waugh. "The Lobby [journalists] decided, perhaps not surprisingly, that they did not wish to have *Private Eye* on their patch."

Waugh did not take this lying down. His exclusion, he declared in the first helping of "HP Sauce", was "the greatest affront to democracy since the burning of the Reichstag by Hitler's power-crazed hooligans in similar circumstances 37 years ago". The tone was set. The "HP Sauce" page sketched out a parallel Westminster where the leader of the House of Commons, Richard Crossman, was "a former Nazi sympathiser of German extraction who had almost certainly been parachuted into this country disguised as a nun". The environment secretary Peter Walker proposed an expansion of Britain's sewage works merely to deal with the threat to the nation posed by his seven-month-old son Jonathan who "drinks 17 buckets of liquid and requires 200 clean nappies an hour". Edward Heath was downed by a tranquillizer dart accidentally fired at the cabinet table by Lord Balniel.

At the centre of it all was the essential thing that Waugh's critics, particularly those on the left, never recognised: "the material is entirely jocular; it contains no serious allegations whatever and everything in it is untrue".[108] The explicit untruthfulness of the copy made it easier to secrete a deeper truth within it: the fact that those in charge of us are often incompetent, easily corrupted and interested in power only for its own ends, as well as being, in Waugh's oft-repeated phrase, "social and emotional cripples". His colleague Patrick Marnham summed it up as "cutting out the balls-aching business of gathering 'facts' and going straight to the underlying suspicion ... By use of this technique Waugh established a kind of 'existential' or 'Waugh' fact, a fact of an alternative nature."[109] Given that this was the decade when the former postmaster general faked his own death, the prime minister was going round telling journalists to kick blind men in the hope they would reveal details of the conspiracy against him and the Liberal leader was put on trial for conspiracy to murder after a dog got shot, it's not surprising some people couldn't spot the difference.

In September 1973 Waugh bequeathed the "HP Sauce" page to more factually fixated authors and began what he described as "the series of which I am most proud of all the hundreds of thousands of words I have written in a life's scribbling" (☞ DIARY, Auberon Waugh's).

Private Eye has never been given a Commons press pass.
☞ BALLSOFF MEMORANDUM

HUMPHRIES, Barry
☞ McKENZIE, Barry

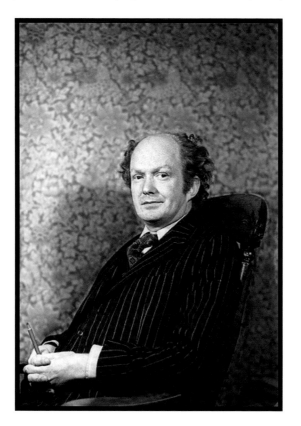

HUSBAND, Tony

"I sent a batch of cartoons to the *Eye*, and they came back with no note inside so I presumed they had been rejected," remembers Tony Husband. "A week later a friend rang to congratulate me on having two cartoons in *Private Eye*. Puzzled, I dashed to Stockport to get a copy (there was nowhere in Hyde, where I lived, that sold it) and there they were. Still one of the highlights of my professional career."

☞ STRIPS, longest-running

**m the Milan Opera House, La
da, Berlusconi's comic operetta
n Nostra**

The curtain rises to show
Silvio, the Robber Baron,
in his palazzo, surrounded
by a chorus of beautiful
teenage nymphs who sing
about how they are shortly
to be elected as members
of the European

ent *('We're All Going To Brussels On A
Holiday')*.

e is a loud noise from the courtyard
The chief of the local carabinieri has
arrest Silvio again on charges of
mbezzlement, tax-evasion and
rigging (not to mention making
s to young women who are not his

laughs scornfully and sings that he
ady bribed his English lawyer, Signor
take the blame *('Tre Millione Euros')*.
chief of police apologises for
ng the Robber Baron on such a trivial
Silvio laughs and invites
eri to join him in a celebratory
. *'Sono Immuno'* he sings in a
g aria, in which he describes how he
sed a retrospective law giving him
y from any crime he may have
ed, or is currently committing even
peak.

retires to a nearby secluded gazebo
ss the European Union's policy on
with one of his future MEPs,
a Rumpi di Pumpi.

"The lack of tourists has driven him to it"

IMRAN/GOLDSMITH WEDDING SHOCK

May I have your daughter's hand?

Why? Has she been shoplifting?

THE EDITOR OF PRIVATE EYE

Mr. Richard Ingrams, after long and
sober reflection, has accepted the
Government's offer to become Assistant
Vice-Commissioner to the 2nd Secretary
to the Governor of the Windward Islands,
and has severed all connection with this
paper.

Mr. John Wells has been appointed
Acting -Editor during his absence.

JOHN WELLS WRITES:

It has been my privilege to work with
Richard Ingrams for almost five years.
During that time I have never kn

MAGGIE SEES NNER CITIES

This is quite close enough thank you

There are some ugly stories about us going around

INGO

"That's the man!".

Ulster Latest

NO ONE KILLED FOR FIVE MINUTES

by Our Northern Ireland Correspondent **Sir Patrick Mayhem**

THERE was renewed tension in the province yesterday when
dered for a space of five minutes. Spokesmen
both sides condemned the non-violence as
aramilitaries from both the Republican and
quick to deny responsibility

NEW-LOOK ULSTER

Claim No HQ09X04132

**HIGH COURT OF JUSTICE
B BENCH DIVISION**

the Honourable Mr Justice Tugendhat on 13 October 2009

EEN:

(1) RJW
(2) SJW

- and -

(1) GUARDIAN NEWS AND MEDIA LIMITED
(2) THE PERSON OR PERSONS UNKNOWN

or about September 2009 offered or supplied to the publishers of *The Guardian*
/or to David Leigh a copy of, or information contained in or derived from, the
ument described in the Confidential Schedule C to this Order relating to the
operations or affairs of the First Applicant and/or the Second Applicant

Defendants

ORDER

rned judge having read correspondence betwe
dant on 13 October 2009 agreeing to a variation of t
ptember 2009 which extended the Order of Mr Ju

RDERED BY CONSENT that

Nothing in the Order of Maddison J of 11 Septem
of 18 September 2009 shall prevent the First Def
reporting or publishing information relating to:

i.   any proceedings of the United Kingd
      information or matter published on the we

ii.   any proceedings of the Scottish Parliame
      matter published on the website www.scot

iii. any proceedings of the National Asse
      information or matter published on the we
      or

iv.   any proceedings of the Northern Ireland A
      or matter published on the website www.ni

Bunny says we were right to

Fancy a kneecap... I mean 'nightcap'?

FRIK. 72

INGRAMS FAMILY, Ten facts about them which may help you towards an understanding of Richard's personality

1 His maternal grandfather, Sir James Reid, was Queen Victoria's personal physician. The elderly monarch was "very much annoyed" by his marriage to her Maid of Honour Susan and spoiled their honeymoon by interrupting it with regular updates on her bowel movements.[110]

2 His father Leonard was a financier nicknamed "the flying banker" for his habit of travelling round Europe by private plane.

3 Leonard spent World War Two working for the British secret services producing black propaganda against the Nazis. His secret service work may or may not explain the photographs that emerged of him at a meeting of the Anglo-German Fellowship before the war broke out – but Hitler certainly disliked him enough for his name to appear on a blacklist of British people he wanted assassinated. Richard only found out years later that Leonard had been sent to interrogate all the leading Nazis, including Goering, at Nuremberg. "It's the sort of thing that when I was a small boy, if I'd known that about my father, I'd have been so proud of him, but he never said anything about it. He was quite a distant figure."[108]

4 Leonard was the son of an Anglican vicar and "very fiercely anti-Catholic." His second wife, Richard's mother Victoria, was such a fervent Roman that she converted the garage of her family home into a chapel. They decided to compromise by dividing up their four sons: the eldest, PJ, would be baptised as a Catholic, Richard, born in 1937, would be Protestant, Rupert Catholic and the youngest, Leonard, Protestant. His father, who didn't like having Catholics in the house, promptly suggested PJ should be sent away to boarding school overseas. Victoria got her own back by having Richard and Leonard junior pledged to Rome when he was out – something else Richard only found out about decades later.

5 He did not learn to speak until he was three. He continues to avoid doing so wherever possible.

6 The Ingrams shared their home in Cheyne Walk with a Kikuyu boy called Thieri Njine, who PJ had adopted from Kenya. He was dangerously mentally ill, and if left unattended attempted to flood the house, put hot coals in the piano, break into the neighbours' houses or try to kill cats. "It was very difficult," recalled Victoria. "Luckily I had an awfully nice daily, Mrs Livett, who'd keep hold of him while I went out and did whatever I had to do."

7 All four brothers were sent to West Downs prep school, the sort of place where you were taught Latin but not anything useful, like what it actually was. Richard can remember "thinking, aged about nine, what was this language we were all learning? I looked up this atlas and saw a country called Latvia, and I decided it must be from there." It was here that at 12 Ingrams launched his first publication. Rupert wrote home: "Dich has inventer [sic] a newspaper for his form called the S.D.II Weekly Newspaper."

8 During a visit to a friend of their mother's who lived at Hampton Court, all four Ingrams boys had to be brought down from the roof of the Palace, where PJ had led them in a mountaineering expedition. In 1976 PJ, now a teacher, led a different group of boys up Mount Antisana in Ecuador. He climbed ahead of the group in bad conditions and disappeared. His body was never found.

9 Victoria Ingrams once discovered that Princess Margaret had been rude to her nephew Sandy at a banquet. She promptly wrote "a scorching letter" to Kensington Palace scolding the Queen's sister for her impertinence.

10 He is a distant relative of both Sir Alec Douglas-Home and Princess Diana. When Earl Spencer found this out, he was horrified.

INGRAMS, Richard, decision to retire as editor and appoint Ian Hislop as his successor

"I'd wanted to retire for a long time," admits Ingrams. "I was getting very lax, and not bothered any more." Why? "Boredom. Just boredom. I just found that on press day I couldn't keep up with it all. Come lunchtime I would be totally knackered. And you can't be like that. To avoid being in court you have to be on the ball all the time."

Ingrams had begun to respond ostrich-style to legal threats. "He doesn't like anyone else to organise him, the way he lives his life – it's got to be led at Richard's pace," says Peter McKay. "And to have to have long meetings with lawyers, and explain himself, I think it got Richard down, and that may have persuaded him more than ever that he had to find someone to take over from him."

"I found myself more and more thinking like Reggie Perrin," Ingrams told Radio 4 in 1991. "A sort of strange recklessness creeping in. And feeling 'What does all this matter? What does Robert Maxwell matter?'"[112] The problem was, that if Robert Maxwell is throwing the full weight of the British legal establishment at you (☞ MAXWELL, Robert, full list of

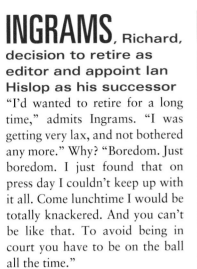

complaints against *Private Eye*) it has to matter very much indeed. Once, Richard might have relished this. But he'd already been through it with Goldsmith. And it wasn't fun any more.

"It was partly due to the change in the way the *Eye* operated," he says. "When we were down at the old offices everyone was kind of on top of one other, and everybody used to go to the pub at lunchtime. We had a separate table there that was permanently reserved. So that everybody

in the *Eye* knew what was going on because there was so much contact between everybody. And once we moved into that bigger office on Carlisle Street [in 1984], that stopped. There was no communal lunch or anything. And everyone became much more ... separate boxes."

Even in their separate boxes, the staff had noticed something was afoot. "Out of the editor's presence, the future of his organ was always a subject of intense speculation," recalled Jane Ellison of her time as an *Eye*

> *"I remember saying can I think about it for a couple of days. Then he said 'so would you like to do it?' and I said yes immediately"*

Ian Hislop

hack. "Who would take over when Ingrams went, as he sometimes hinted he might do? There was talk of asking Paul Foot to come back, of begging Peter Cook to do the jokes. No one of the present generation somehow seemed up to the job."[113]

For some time, Ingrams had privately thought the same. "I was hampered by the thought that there wasn't anyone that I could appoint," he admits. Asked in 1981 who he would appoint as editor if Ingrams went mad, Cook had replied that "He did that years ago. But [Christopher] Booker would be the number-one choice as replacement." Ingrams, however, says that "You couldn't put someone like Booker in charge because he'd have annoyed everyone, and also he had no interest – he still doesn't – in the factual side of *Private Eye*. He didn't really approve of it." Fortunately, five years on there was a glaringly obvious candidate – even if no one else seemed to have noticed.

"Ian was the only person who had a foot in both camps," says Ingrams. "He had done quite a lot of stories in *Private Eye*, about the BBC. He certainly took an interest in that side. He had very definite ideas about it."

"I did some journalism," Ian concedes, "not terribly well I don't think. I had to do some consumer stuff and I did a thing called 'London Calling' for I can't remember how long," detailing the excesses of Ken Livingstone's first stint running the capital. And that BBC stuff? History should recall that the man who famously banned smutty gossip from the pages of *Private Eye* got his big journalistic break with … a sex story. Richard Somerset-Ward was a BBC executive with a penchant for flagellation. When the *Eye* reported that he had offered a secretary a spanking as an alternative to having a disciplinary offence recorded on her permanent record, he sued – and the Curse of Gnome (☞ WRITS, First of many) descended upon his head. "Harry Thompson started the story off, which then Richard said I had to do. It was essentially my first 'Here's a big shitstorm of libel, you sort it out.' That was my first experience of talking to witnesses, getting statements. It was my early demonstration of a sort of caution. But I thought, if you've got it cold, *then* you can go wild. You can put 'Spanks for

the Memory' as a heading, *this* big, because you've got the story right." And they had. Somerset-Ward resigned from the BBC, and dropped his libel action after eighteen months, news recorded in a gleeful editorial: "The *Eye* says: Sod Off Spanker!"

Hislop had gelled on the joke side as well. "Ian was very funny, and he liked everybody, and he was likeable," recalls Barry Fantoni. His youthfulness was no deterrent. Ingrams had been exactly the same age himself, twenty-six, when he wrestled the editorial chair from Booker's bottom.

And Ian had already had a trial run. "When I was away having an operation on my spine Ian took over for three or four issues, I guess, and there was quite a lot of muttering from the hacks, but it worked all right from my point of view. I realised that he could do it. I also realised that if I started consulting people like [Dave] Cash and Sheila [Molnar], they would all object," says Richard. "And I was right, because afterwards they did make a terrific fuss." So the first person to find out that Richard was retiring was his twenty-six-year-old protégé, when he asked him to stay behind at the end of a joke-writing session.

"It was in the office, in here," recalls Hislop, sitting in the room he inherited on the first floor at 6 Carlisle Street. "He said he was fed up and he didn't want to do it any more, he didn't want to do the legal stuff. He'd sat through a lawyers' meeting and he said 'I realised I wasn't listening to any of it, I was looking out of the window thinking "I just don't care," and I realised I shouldn't be doing this any more.' What he wanted to do was make jokes. I don't think he had or has lost that. But the mechanics of it, and everything about it, he just didn't want to do."

"I remember saying can I think about it for a couple of days, over the weekend or something. Then he said 'So would you like to do it?' and I said yes immediately."

Did it come as a complete surprise? "I'd stood in for him and I'd done it and I'd sort of felt … I mean the timing of it was a surprise. I think I probably thought he might go in five years' time. I certainly didn't think he would go then. Nobody did. I think it was partly Bron going." Auberon Waugh had decided to leave the *Eye* after being offered the editorship of the *Literary Review* at the end of 1985. "Something like a couple of weeks passed. I told Victoria [his then girlfriend, now wife], but I didn't tell anyone here. And then I bought dinner for ten close friends, we had a celebration at a Chinese just up the road here with Nick, Bob Bathurst and all my old mates. That was pre-announcement."

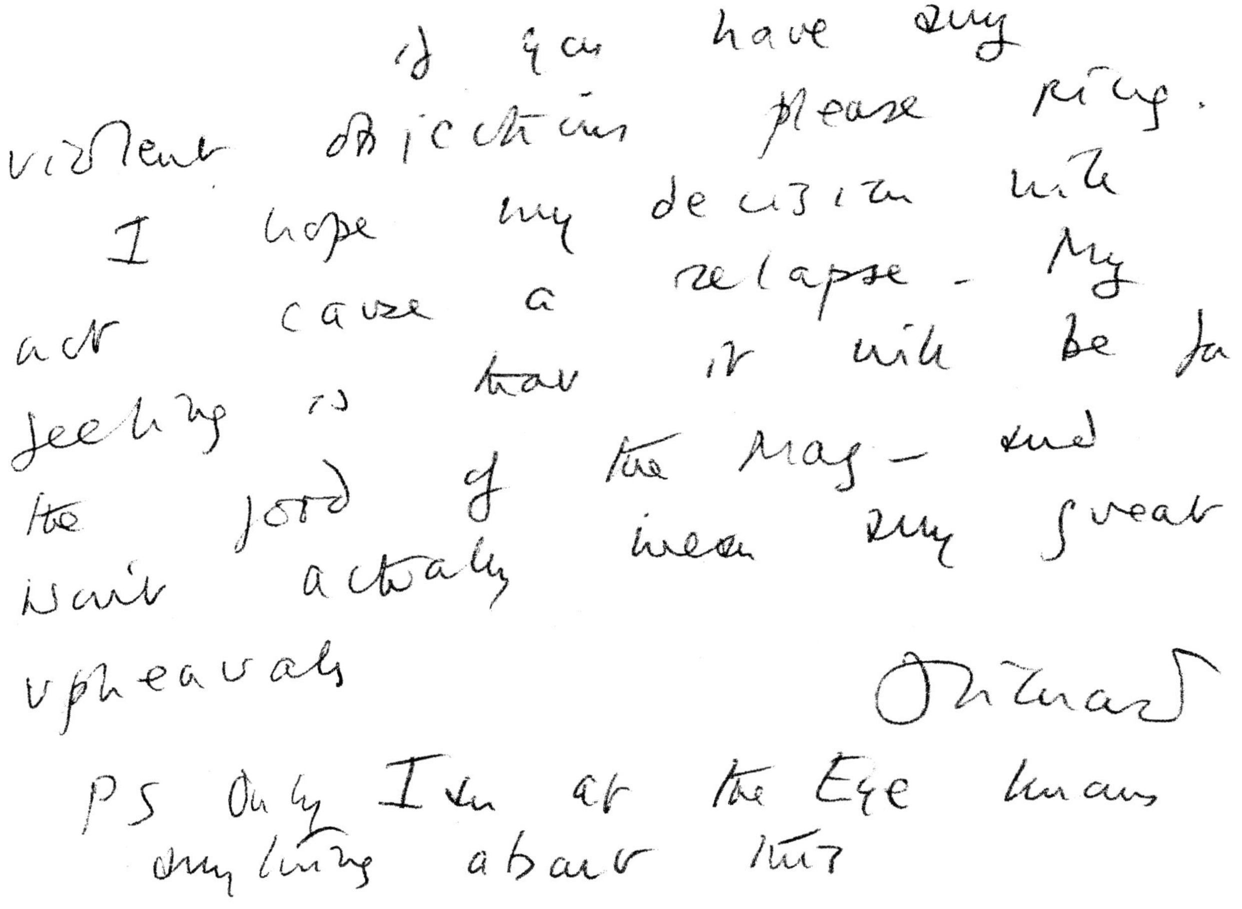

[handwritten letter:]

if you have any violent objections please ring. I hope my decision will not cause a relapse – My feeling is that it will be for the good of the mag – and won't actually mean any great upheavals

Richard

PS Only Ian at the Eye knows anything about this

"It was completely out of the blue," says Nick Newman. "I can remember Ian ringing me up in great excitement and saying he was having a drink with a group of us, and he made this announcement."

The only other person who was told anything was the chief boxwallah, laid up at home with a bad back. "Richard actually wrote me a letter, which was very generous of him, because I think I was possibly the only person he told that he was going to give Ian the editorship," recalls Dave Cash. "This letter said he was going to stand down and

he was going to nominate Ian as editor, and if I had any views, to let him know."

It might not have been all that generous. "I actually received it after the announcement was made. I don't know if that was deliberate."

Now all that remained was to break the news to the staff, and the outside world. And, of course, for Ingrams to find the worst possible circumstances in which to do so.

☞ RESIGNATION, Ingrams's, as recalled by those who were there

INJUNCTION, proves money spinner for lawyers, money loser for one particular lawyer

One of the criticisms often thrown at the *Eye* over the years is that its hacks do not "check their stories", by which the critics – inevitably people who have been written about – mean not that they don't gather credible information, but that they don't phone the subjects ahead of publication and give them the chance to put their own spin on that information.

Here is an example of what happened on an occasion in 2009 when hackette Heather Mills did exactly that. She had established that solicitor Michael Napier had had a conflict of interest in a case he handled, that the Law Society had upheld a complaint about it, and that an ombudsman had been highly critical of the way that that complaint had been handled and of the failure to reprimand Napier adequately.

"I don't always phone up everybody who's going to be mentioned if I think there's enough information that's proof so that I don't have to ring them," says Mills. "And it was pretty well ready to go – I had an ombudsman's report and the Law Society thing. But in this case I phoned Napier to say 'What have you got to say about the fact the ombudsman says you might have got off a bit lightly here because of who you were?' He said he would call me back, and then the next minute there's a call from Carter-Ruck, saying 'We think this is confidential material.' And I said, jokingly, 'Well, I don't, so I'll see you in court.' And I did!"

The resulting emergency injunction, lengthy discussions with lawyers, days in court and then an appeal lasted five months and cost the best part of half a million pounds. "It was amazing how this simple point of law could just become this *huge* money-spinner for lawyers," says Mills. "I was staggered how something simple could become these *files* of documents. And the lawyers were all getting for an hour what I was getting for two weeks' work. This is the sucking-up bit, so you shouldn't put this in, but I was really impressed by Ian and his principles. He never for one minute hesitated that we weren't doing the right thing."

Napier lost the case, suffered severe damage to his professional reputation and ensured that the coverage stretched over two double-page spreads beneath the rare headline "*Private Eye* Wins Court Case!" rather than the few paragraphs tucked away in the back that had originally been intended. He had to pay the magazine's costs, too. "It's very funny that he's £350 grand out of pocket," chuckles Hislop. "It's serious money for three days in court. But well worth the gamble I think."

☞ MILLION-POUND WIN; STORIES YOU CAN'T PRINT; TRAFIGURA

INTERNET, *Private Eye's* lack of enthusiasm for

☞ NOT.COM

J

JAGGER, Mick

He may have been the lead singer of the Rolling Stones for almost half a century, but Mick Jagger has another even greater achievement to his name: he was employed to sell early editions of the *Eye* while a student at the London School of Economics.

JAMIESON, Tom

☞ MUTT AND JEFF

JAWN

Princess Margaret once phoned up the *Eye* office and asked to speak to her good friend "Jawn".

It was not an incident Wells was ever allowed to forget, as the bubbles added to the sketch below by Fantoni show.

JOBS, unlikely subsequent ones of *Eye* contributors

1971 – **John Betjeman** becomes architectural correspondent, with Nooks and Corners of the New Barbarism column (☞).
1972 – Becomes Poet Laureate.

1971 – **Brian Sedgemore** starts legal column under pseudonym Justinian Forthemoney.
1974 – Becomes Labour MP for Luton West.

1978 – **Penny Junor** starts writing consumer column.
1987 – Becomes biographer of Prince Charles and, far more impressively, Cliff Richard.

1980 – **Keith Raffan** begins writing "The New Boys'" column, profiling those who have recently entered parliament.
1983 – Becomes Conservative MP for Delyn and features in "New Boys" column just weeks later.

1980 – **Paul Halloran** starts contributing as hack and pet Rottweiler of Richard Ingrams
1988 – *Sunday Times* reveals he has been working as fake arms dealer in Texas-based sting operation.

Early 1980s – **Patricia Scotland** does some libel-reading for the *Eye*.
2007 – Becomes Attorney-General for England, Wales and Northern Ireland.

1984 – **Graham Harvey** starts column "Down On The Farm" under pseudonym Old Muckspreader.
1997 – Becomes Agricultural Story Editor for *The Archers*.

1985 – **David Eady QC** appears for *Private Eye* at Court of Appeal in attempt to prevent Robert Maxwell from serving an injunction on magazine.

2008 – As Mr Justice Eady, gains reputation as judge who can most be relied upon to halt publication of embarrassing information about public figures.

1989 – Solicitor **Keith Schilling** represents *Eye* in legal battle with Sonia Sutcliffe.
2003 – Becomes known as "the injunction king" heading "the pre-eminent claimant law firm in England, specialising in safeguarding the reputations of high profile individuals".

1994 – **Ben Summerskill** becomes regular contributor to *Eye*.
2003 – Becomes chief executive of gay rights lobbying group Stonewall.

JOKE-WRITING TEAMS,
extraordinary longevity of

Rob Newman and David Baddiel – whom older readers will recall were the duo that proved comedy to be the new Rock'n'Roll – managed four years before falling out spectacularly. Rob Grant and Doug Naylor of *Red Dwarf* succeeded in putting up with each other for a decade. The key joke-writing teams at Private Eye, however, are among of the longest-running comedy-writing partnerships *ever*.

Frank Muir and Dennis Norden	1948 – 1960	12 years	
Monty Python	1969 – 1983	14 years	
Punt and Dennis	1985 – present	26 years	
Hislop and Newman	**1984 – present**	**27 years**	
Galton and Simpson	1951 – 1978	28 years	
Marks and Gran	1978 to present	31 years	
Ingrams, Fantoni and Booker	**1965 – 2010**	**45 years**	

Above: **Richard Ingrams, Barry Fantoni and Christopher Booker, photographed by Eric Hands, 1974**

It seems to be working for the next generation, too: Nev Fountain and Tom Jamieson (☞ MUTT AND JEFF), who write their *Eye* material together, have been working together for over 15 years now.

Right: **Ingrams, Fantoni and Booker photographed by Eric Hands, 2006**

JOKE, missed

The following letter was received by *Private Eye* in September 1984:

"Sir – I saw your paper on a newspaper stand with the picture of Mr Robert Maxwell and I said to myself, I would like to read what you have to say about him. Therefore I spent 40 pence. On the front page it reads quite clearly that full details are on page 94. There is no page 94 in your paper. It goes from page 1 to 28. Therefore you've misinformed the public. I'm sure there is a law against this.

I phoned your office and was told by your telephone operator that the whole thing was a joke. I asked her what kind of a joke and she said that I should find it out for myself and she hung up.

T Wenger, London"

 NINETY-FOUR, page

JOLLEY, Richard

 RGJ

JUNOR, Jonah, confusion caused to Victor Matthews by

The "Jonah Junor" column was a spoof of the bilious *Sunday Express* column written by its monstrous editor, Sir John "pass the sick bag, Alice" Junor. It was written by Richard Ingrams and Peter McKay, both of whom were personal friends of Sir John. And it caused great confusion to the *Express* proprietor, Lord Matthews. "He called JJ in to see him," recalled Junor's daughter Penny. "'I think you should give up *Private Eye*,' he said. My father assumed he was talking about his lunches with Richard Ingrams. 'He's very well informed,' he protested. 'No, no, not that,' said Matthews, 'the column you write. I know you've changed the name, but I know it's you.'"[114]

KENNEDY, Charles, purchases wedding memento

In July 2002, as controversy raged over Jeremy Paxman's questioning of Charles Kennedy about the drinking habits that would lead to his resignation as leader of the Liberal Democrats four years later, the *Eye*'s cover commemorated his recent wedding.

The original artwork was promptly purchased by ... Charles and Sarah Kennedy.

KRAYS, first named in *Private Eye*

Issue 68 of *Private Eye*, guest-edited by Peter Cook in the absence of Richard Ingrams in July 1964, saw the first ever public naming of the Kray twins.

"If reports in the *Mirror* are true, whole areas of London, east and west, are being terrorized," Cook wrote. "People who resist, ask questions or talk are maimed and liable to be murdered: prominent public figures are blackmailed, but the victims are powerless, the police are powerless, the newspapers are powerless. They, of course, know the names. So, of course, do the police. So, of course, does everyone except the unfortunate 'general public'. The men referred to have for a week been discussed and denounced in every bar in Fleet Street."

> PRIVATE EYE considers this situation both farcical and intolerable. Either the charges are true, in which case the newspapers should have the guts to publish them, whatever the risk of libel action. Or they are untrue or grossly exaggerated, in which case they should stop scaring the people with this horror movie of London under terror.
>
> PRIVATE EYE thinks it sensible and proper to print the names.
>
> The two people being written and talked about are the twin brothers, Ronald and Reginald Kray.
>
> For ten years both have been well known figures of London life.
>
> They are rich.
>
> They have criminal records.
>
> They are credited in the underworld with immense power. Criminals have "authoritatively" told researchers that the Krays can whistle up 300 thugs for

So, with a cry of "Publish and be absent," Cook printed the names – and promptly disappeared on holiday to Tenerife, leaving someone else to deal with the consequences.

KENT, John

John Kent drew regular political strips for *Private Eye* from 1970 until his death in 2003, including "Grocer Heath and His Pals", "The Brothers", "Maggie Rules OK", "John Major's Big Top" and "Capt. Bob", all set within their own surreal worlds but anchored to reality by spot-on caricature. "Fellow cartoonists said if you needed to know how to do someone, you simply looked at Kent's version," remembers Ian Hislop.

Most were written in collaboration with members of the regular joke-writing team. "I always thought that political cartoons worked better if you discussed the idea with them," says Richard Ingrams. "We always did that with John Kent, who was very good. He'd come in every fortnight and we'd talk for about half an hour, an hour."
☞ OFFENSIVE, MOST, items published in *Private Eye*

KRIN, Dame Sylvie, collected works of

Love in the Saddle – The Princess Anne and Mark Phillips story
Amoroso – The romantic adventures of Andre Previn
Roddy is my Darling – The Princess Margaret and Roddy Llewellyn story
After The Break – The Anna Ford and Ronnie Beaujolais story
Stassi – The Bernard Levin and Arianna Stassinopoulis story
The Greatest Love Story Ever Told – The Enid Rancid and Desmond Wilcox story
To Err is Human . . . But to Forgive Divine – The Hugh Grant and Liz Hurley story
Love is Blind – The romantic adventures of David Blunkett

The Thanet Airport Experience Harold Pinter and Lady Antonia Fraser Collection
The Bells That Never Chimed – the Harold Pinter and Antonia Fraser story
When Love Beckons – by Lady Antonia Fraser, as told to Dame Sylvie Krin

Duchess of Love

The Departure Lounge Low-Cost Library Rupert Murdoch and Wendi Deng Collection:
Heirs and Graces
Never Too Old

The Ryanair No-Frills Romance Library People's Princess Collection:
Hell Hath No Fury (featuring Will Carling)
The Princess and the Playboy (feat. Dodi Fayed)
The Princess and the Pharaoh (feat. Mohamed Fayed)

The Easyjet Easyread Prince of Wales Collection:
Heir of Sorrows (long-listed 78th for the Booker Prize 1983)
They Sailed Into the Sunset
Love on the Nile
The Prince of Greens
The Duchy of Love
How Green Was My Rally
La Dame Aux Camillas
Forbidden Alliance
End of the Line
It Really Is Nepalling
Monastery of Dreams
A Man of Letters
On Bended Knee
Born Not to be Queen
Born to be Queen Consort
The Wedding Bell Tolls
Duchess of Love
Happy Ever After?
Life Begins At . . .
The Duchess of Hearts
The People's Prince
Put Out More Flags
Duchess of Tears

RIVA[T]

PUBLISHING
HISTORY
MADE

FIRST
LUPIN SCENTED
COVER

Apply nostril here

One Libel Voucher

1. Cut out this FREE Libel Voucher
2. When you have collected 500 Vouchers
   fill in the form below and send to:
   Private
   22, Gre

PLEASE CALL ME A :-

DRUNKARD
POOVE
LIAR
CHEAT
COWARD

1. I enclose 500 LIBEL
   Vouchers

2. I promise to abide by
   the rules of the Lunchtime

NAME..................
ADDRESS..............
....

Clarke

*"h yes, we can change your
s. It's quite an operation, but
can do it"*

A SPECIAL REPORT FROM £1.50
May/June
2001

PRIVATE EYE

LOCKERBIE
THE FLIGHT
FROM JUSTICE

Dawes   Horlick

7.

E. LIBEL ACTIONS.

Some risks a good deal greater than most magazines would allow have been
taken by Private Eye in this field.   In the early days, under Christopher
Booker's editorship, some serious mistakes were make, the most expensive being
the affair with Randolph Churchill, settled for £3,000.   Actions with a
writer, Colin Watson, and playwright, Wolf Mankowitz were settled for about
£1,000 each, and one action dating back to the very early days, with Lord
Russell of Liverpool, is still outstanding.   A few other actions have been
settled for negligible costs.   The average costs per action settled to date,
including the three more expensive ones mentioned, worked out at £1,100 each,
and it is on this basis that provision of £3,300 has been made in the accounts
at 4th April, 1964, for the three actions outstanding at the moment.

Apart from Lord Russell, these could be settled for far less than that sum.
It is probable that Lord Russell might accept less himself.   But we have not ha
any money available to make offers to anyone recently.   Given refinancing, we
wc

Ur
ex

We
ne
go
th
pl
yc

PRIVATE EY[E]
[L]UNATIC
e Eye says: If we are
ong, let him sue us.

"Bloody luger louts!"

RODIN'S
COACH-DRIVER

LORD ARTHUR AND HIS ROUND TABLE

ARTHUR HAS A LOT OF GET-UP-AND-GO

LAMB, K.J.

Kathryn Lamb was an Oxford contemporary of Ian Hislop and Nick Newman, and drew cartoons for their student magazine *Passing Wind*. She beat them both to the *Eye*, kicking off her regular strip "Lord Arthur and His Square Table" in 1979. She now illustrates "Pseuds Corner".

LANGUAGE, Eye phrases
pass into

- In 2003, after Prince Harry had been photographed attacking paparazzi outside a nightclub in London, Clarence House announced that the third in line to the throne had "been drinking and was **tired and emotional**".

- Opposing John Prescott's 2002 plans for English regional assemblies, Conservative spokesman David Davis told the House of Commons that the devolved bodies would "usher in a new layer of politicians, and a new layer of bureaucrats, officers, advisers, secretaries, researchers, spin doctors, budgets, expenses, allowances – and **trebles all round**".

- In 2010 an anonymous "senior Tory" told the *Guardian* that the leaking of a series of emails by Conservative strategy director Steve Hilton was the work of "the **Bufton Tufton** crowd. They feel aggrieved that they are not being listened to by the leadership."

- The same year former Labour minister Chris Mullin spoofed the hoo-hah surrounding the release of Tony Blair's autobiography in a press release about his own book: "The Mullin Foundation (head office, **Neasden**) confirms no plans to produce a 'Bible Edition' of the book to retail at £150."

- In 2008 the *Mirror* assured its readers that Unison general secretary Dave Prentis was "no rabble-rousing **Dave Spart** nutter but a union leader on the sensible left".

- The 2008 sacking of Ed Stourton as a presenter on Radio 4's *Today* programme delighted headline writers on the *Guardian* who could finally use the headline "**That's Enough Ed.**" The 2010 departure from frontline politics of David Miliband after losing the Labour leadership to his brother Ed, rather than the other way round as everyone had expected, did not.

- A 2009 biography of Tory philanderer Alan Clark revealed that he declined lunch invitations on the grounds that "I am usually engaged in **Ugandan discussions** at lunchtime."

- In his 2010 autobiography Keith Richards revealed that his nickname for fellow Rolling Stone Mick Jagger was "Her Majesty, **Brenda**".

- During the first six months of 2010, the phrase "**surely shome mishtake**" was used in the *Scotsman*, *Racing Post*, *Times Educational Supplement*, *Pretoria News Weekend* and *South China Morning Post*.

- What do Jonathan Aitken, Paul Dacre, Max Hastings, Garry Bushell and Harold Evans have in common, apart from being regularly and virulently criticised in *Private Eye*? They have all nicked at least one of its jokes in the past decade, citing in print its fictional law firm **Sue, Grabbit & Runne**.

- In one month alone, September 2010, British newspapers said "**So. Farewell then**" to David Miliband (the *Sun*), Harriet Harman (*Independent on Sunday*), the chief executive of quango Ofqual (*Independent*), the Pakistan cricket team (*Sunday Express*), the president of CNN (*Independent*), TV dramas *Heartbeat* (*Daily Express*) and *The Bill* (*Guardian*), reality show *Big Brother* (*Daily Telegraph*), Peggy Mitchell from *EastEnders* (*Daily Star*), Ringo Starr's former home (*Liverpool Post*), the leader of UKIP (*Wales on Sunday*) and the Audit Commission (*Guardian*).

☞ LUVVIES; McKENZIE, Barry; PRIME MINISTERIAL PARODIES, moments they become reality; PSEUDS, Britain's ten biggest

LEWIS-SMITH, Victor,
Funny Old World of

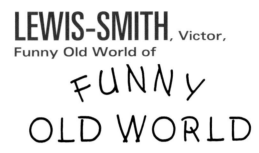

"He is a very peculiar man," editor Ian Hislop told reporters in Soho. "I had worked with him when he was producing *Start the Week* – I was a

LARRY

Cartoonist Larry, aka Terence Parkes, specialised in visual gags – never captioned – in the slapstick tradition of silent film. They often featured an everyman character he called "the bloke", or versions of Rodin's sculpture *The Thinker*.

He was such a prolific contributor that in 1974 an entire book of his cartoons was published as *The Private Eye Cartoon Library Number 3*. That same year, his agent wrote to the magazine: "It occurs to us that you may well be interested in using some of his cartoons in your magazine from time to time."

guest on one of the most fantastically awkward and bad-tempered shows ever where he put me with Dennis Potter and Clive James who both attacked the *Eye*."

Victor Lewis-Smith had been sacked from the programme, posed as a disabled euphonium player demanding to appear on *That's Life* and a Tourette's sufferer demanding to audition as a BBC continuity announcer in calls broadcast on Radio 1, worked as Julie Burchill's holiday relief on two different publications and been described as a vastly overpaid "major irritation" in *Private Eye* before Hislop finally hired him in June 1993 to take over the column compiled from peculiar newspaper cuttings from the retiring Christopher Logue (☞).

Renamed "Funny Old World", it kicked off with the tale of a man in North Devon who cut off his own penis and a farm worker who sprayed his fellow workers with excrement by squeezing a live chicken in their direction, and has kept the tone up rather brilliantly ever since. Lewis-Smith lives in Cumbria, and never, ever comes in to the office.

LITERARY REVIEW, page
added to *Private Eye* specifically to annoy Auberon Waugh

In 1986 Auberon Waugh left the *Eye* to edit the *Literary Review*. It was partly out of chagrin with Ingrams, who had declined to fight a libel case arising from his "Diary": "Bron was pissed

Lookalikes: magazine edited by Auberon Waugh; magazine edited to annoy Auberon Waugh

off, he was looking forward to this great libel action where he would be the star witness, and he thought I'd chickened out."

In retaliation, Ingrams decided the time was right for the magazine to have a special page devoted to books. And it should be called ... "Literary Review".

"Typical Richard," chuckles Ian Hislop. "It wasn't an idea about expanding the range of the magazine, it was just to annoy Bron. But then it turns out to be one of the great bits."

A. N. Wilson was immediately installed as the page's – bylined – author, submitting the latest literary sensations to an acid-bath treatment, but shortly afterwards he decided (temporarily) that criticism was incompatible with his own literary career. Since then a team of around three regular reviewers have shared the slot, with none of them signing their work. Professor John Mullan devoted an entire chapter of his 2007 book *Anonymity: A Secret History of English Literature* to making the hermeneutic case for this, pointing out that "*Private Eye*'s literary pages scorn the complicity between authors and reviewers that sometimes seems to be the rule elsewhere," so it might disappoint him that novelist and biographer D. J. Taylor says "I've got no problem at all about being outed," and lawyer and critic Paul Magrath happily 'fesses up to being "another segment of 'Bookworm'".

The reviews remain almost entirely uncomplimentary. Presented with a critique of Norman Lebrecht's *Why Mahler?* by another of his team in July 2010, Ian Hislop sighed in an editorial meeting that it was "not as rude as I expected, but rude enough to run".

LOBBY SYSTEM, the
problem with

One of the reasons the *Eye* has always been able to turn up stories that no one else will print is that it has always existed outside the lobby system – not just the non-attributable briefing club which officially exists in parliament (☞ HP SAUCE, under Auberon Waugh's stewardship) but in all sorts of other areas too. "Groups of journalists band together and are briefed by the authorities, on condition that they never reveal the source of their information and with the implied threat that if they step out of line they will be blackballed from the club," points out Richard Ingrams. "Such a system operates not only in politics but in other areas as well – notably crime, where the police find it easy to get their version of events into the press." [115]

The *Eye* not only hangs around on the outside of this tent pissing in, it also regularly exposes its inhabitants for their dutiful trotting out of particularly egregious bits of spin.

In the more high-profile cases (think of the misinformation spread after the shooting the IRA suspects in Gibraltar, the Niger uranium "evidence" cited ahead of war with Iraq, or pretty much anything Alastair Campbell

has ever said), the more mainstream papers generally come round to the true version after a few months or years. At which point, of course, the *Eye* gets another story by gleefully pointing out their 180° turnaround.

LOCKERBIE

"The view of many – that Palestinian extremists planted the bomb – may not be too far away from the truth," wrote Paul Foot one month after PanAm Flight 103 was downed over Lockerbie in December 1988. None of the information

---

LOGUE, Christopher, True Stories about

CHRISTOPHER LOGUE'S TRUE STORIES

*C*hristopher Logue's uncle was the attendant at the gentlemen's convenience at Willesden Green station. His name was Constant Logue. He named his only daughter Eric – "we wanted a boy so we called her Eric."

*L*ogue's attempt to produce "a left-wing dirty book", Lust *was published in 1952 under the nom de plume Count Palmiro Vicarion. "I want one full encounter of at least five pages for every ten pages," publisher Maurice Girodias instructed.*

*J*oining Bertrand Russell's Committee of 100, Logue took part in several sit-down demonstrations, and was arrested for obstructing the highway. He was imprisoned for a month alongside Robert Bolt, who was meant to be writing the screenplay for *Lawrence of Arabia* at the time. On emerging from prison, Logue discovered a letter from Andrew Osmond inviting him to come and work for *Private Eye*. It was 'a magazine I had not heard of.'

*H*is column, True Stories, *ran from 1962 until 1993. It consisted of "funny or bizarre newspaper items précised. When my own collection of stories was exhausted, Ingrams invited the* Eye*'s readers to submit stories for me to rewrite. If they*

were used, the senders were paid." It was the beginning of a fruitful and mutually-beneficial relationship between the magazine and its readers which would lead to many other long-running features.

*L*ogue changed the names of people featuring in "hurtful" stories, "as the people involved were not fame seekers. This caused great outrage to professional snail trainer Chris Hudson, who wrote in 1975 to complain that 'inserting your own weak humour and changing names (not just mine but also of my snails) you offer an insulting rendering of an original story . . . Snail-racing should not be treated with such triviality."

*F*rom 1969 onwards, Bert Kitchen, best known for his work on children's books, provided the illustrations to "True Stories".

TRUE STORIES

*L*ogue appears in Terry Gilliam's *Jabberwocky* (1977) as "Spaghetti-eating fanatic."

*O*n retiring from Private Eye *in 1993, Logue decided to cash in on the complete collection of issues of the magazine he had amassed as a pension pot and made discreet inquiries to see if anyone would be interested in buying them. Someone was – David Bowie.*

that has emerged in the two decades since ever convinced Foot or his *Eye* colleagues that the bomb which killed 270 people was planted by the Libyan Ali Mohmed Al-Megrahi, who was convicted of the crime in 2001. That same year, in a special report, *The Flight from Justice*, Foot detailed how a Palestinian terrorist gang were engaged in creating bombs of precisely the type in question for use on aircraft in the weeks before the tragedy, that a suitcase identical to that employed had been added to a baggage container at Heathrow (rather than travelling via Malta and Frankfurt as the prosecution contended), that the initial suspects for funding the atrocity – Iran and Syria – had been discounted after it became necessary for America and Britain to get them onside during the first Gulf War, and that the witness who had identified Al-Megrahi had given an entirely different description of the suspect earlier in the investigation.

"When you work on a national newspaper you write a story, say about Lockerbie or something. And then six months later there will be a development and you'll go to the news desk and they'll say 'Well, we've done this,'" points out Heather Mills, who inherited and advanced the Lockerbie story after Foot's death, including identifying CIA payments to key witnesses at Megrahi's trial. "And the great thing about the *Eye* is that they do keep running with stuff – so they'll keep running with Deepcut [a series of

mysterious deaths at an army barracks where bullying was rife], keep running with Lockerbie, keep running with these guys who are still banged up in jail when they're patently innocent. You can come back to it and revisit it. There are people I've been writing about since I joined that I'm still writing about now."

In the case of Lockerbie, the truth may never officially be told. The release of Al-Megrahi in 2009, supposedly on the grounds of his ill health, put paid to any possibility of appeal, and of evidence of his innocence – and the guilt of others – being aired in court. It will continue to appear in the pages of *Private Eye* as yet more emerges.

LOONS, the importance of listening to

Paul Foot: *Private Eye* attracted all kinds of nutters with an axe to grind. What impressed me most about Claud Cockburn (☞) was the time he would spend with such people, and how, more often than not, they had more stories than had all the Reuters and AP tapes put together. "Listen to the loons," was his first lesson.[116]

Heather Mills: There is a small proportion it actually sounds awful to call nutters because they clearly have mental health problems.

LOOKALIKES

The *Eye*'s "Lookalikes" feature kicked off in 1980. Sadly, lack of space means we can only print the ones that are inserted into the magazine whenever the editor goes on holiday.

Lookalike

Editor   Hung Kaiquan

Sir,
Pardon me for Beijing the question but could there be a family connection between your very own Ian Hislop, and the world's shortest 25-year-old, Huang Kaiquan of China?
I think we should be told.
Yours faithfully,
SIMON HUMPHREYS,
Claremont, South Africa.

Lookalike

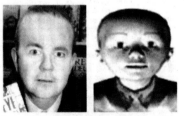

Gnome-like Character   Bloke Off The Telly

Sir,
Have any of your readers noticed the resemblance between that bloke off the telly whose name escapes me, and the cute, gnome-like character who stars in the advertisements for the internet bank, First Direct? Are they fuggin' well related or something?
Yours faithfully,
ENA B. AL-FUGGER,
Knightsbridge.

What's a bit sad in that is that they may have become nutters because at the bottom of it there was a basic injustice but it becomes so overwhelming that they have lost their sense of proportion, become slightly unhinged by it. There's probably a portion that are genuine cases that I miss because they appear to be nutters when they're not.

Jane Mackenzie: I think one of the least investigated things in journalism has to be faults in the mental health care system. Because you never get to talk to anyone bar the "nutters", who have access to that information. I did some pieces on fire safety at mental health wards in Leeds, and when your information comes from people who the officials can say "Well, you know he's been sectioned five times …" you say "Yes, that's why they know – because they were sectioned into the building that wasn't fire safe!" It's so easy for officials to just brush off the nutters.

Sarah Shannon: They put me sometimes in that little tiny office downstairs to talk to the loons, and there was no escape. And they would just go on and on and on. I can remember literally falling asleep as they were talking to me because they were so boring – it didn't really matter whether you were there or not. The whole "CIA are controlling my thoughts through an aluminium filling that a Cuban dentist put in and they're outside now

Carefully catalogued and sensitively-labelled archive in the *Eye* cellar

watching me …" You feel at least you've got to give them the cursory listening-to. And then you spend the next six weeks regretting it as they pursue you and send you other things, and then you start seeing your name added to the list of baddies.

Lookalike

Hislop   **Griffiths**

Sir,
Watching the old Boulting brothers' satire I'm All Right Jack *on Channel 4 recently, I found myself wondering what your editor was doing wearing a bowler hat and calling himself Fred Griffiths. Is this a new career direction?*
Yours faithfully,
JONTY DRIVER,
Northiam, E. Sussex.

Lookalike

Hislop   **Baker**

Sir,
Much has been made of Mr Hislop's resemblance to a certain potato-headed '80s singing star, but as the enclosed photo shows, his link to the world of pop music goes back much further – twice as long, in fact, to California in the early 1960s when his first doppelganger, Bob Baker, played rock 'n' roll piano...
Regards,
DAVE PENNY,
Leyton.

Lookalike

Dyb, dyb, dyb   **Dob, dob, dob**

Sir,
At the Scout Association's centenary jamboree last week, I acquired photos of two lads who attended that first Baden-Powell camp 100 years ago. Identical twins, by the look of them, and clearly keen as mustard – but alas anonymous. Do any of your readers know who these forgotten pioneers might be?
Yours,
ARCHIE WHEEN,
Essex.

Criterion Theatre

10
I love H

Mrs Wilson's Diary

an affectionate lampoon

by Richard Ingrams and John Wells

produced by
JOAN LITTLEWOOD

LORD CHAMBERLAIN,
role as censor of *Mrs Wilson's Diary*

In April 1967, the script of a theatrical version of the "Mrs Wilson's Diary" column, with songs by Jeremy Taylor, that the radical director Joan Littlewood proposed to present at the Theatre Royal, Stratford East, was submitted to the Lord Chamberlain for censorship. Lord Cobbold immediately forwarded a copy to Number 10, with a helpful covering note:

"This is a sniggeringly unfunny romp about the present PM, his wife and other people in the public view with a touch of the paranoia to be found in the plays of Spike Milligan, plus the sudden violent obscenity ... Wild swipes at undergraduate level are taken at various public figures. There is curiously no attempt at political satire. The whole thing is beneath contempt. The thing is so cheap and gratuitously nasty that it is not recommended for a licence."[117]

Cobbold was, however, worried that denying the play a licence would serve only to give it publicity.

In May Harold Wilson's private secretary Michael Halls sent back a copy of the play that had been read not only by the prime minister and his wife – who was "not too keen" to do so – but also by some of the other cabinet ministers who appeared as characters: Jim Callaghan,

LOWRY, Raymond

Dark, dirty, distinctive and slightly deranged, Ray Lowry was the most rock 'n' roll cartoonist ever to contribute to the *Eye* – not least because he worked for the *NME* and designed the sleeve for the classic Clash album *London Calling*. His cartoons appeared from 1969 until his sudden death in 2008.

SYNTHESISERS

"This one can simulate the sounds of guitars, bass, drums and a wildly enthusiastic audience response"

George Brown (who "says he has had just about enough of this sort of thing") and George Wigg. Two-and-a-half pages' worth of lines were marked in red for deletion, including one which the chancellor's wife objected to: "I shall never forget that time Audrey Callaghan was taken short by the tea-place."

Despite the cuts, the play was a great success, transferring to the West End and running for 254 performances.

Later that year home secretary Roy Jenkins (played by a young Nigel Hawthorne on stage) presented the cabinet with his proposal to do away with the Lord Chamberlain's anachronistic role. Cabinet minutes show that a still-disgruntled Harold Wilson demanded "safeguards against the theatre being used deliberately to discredit or create political hostility towards public figures" and insisted "a solution be found to the problem of the portrayal of living persons on stage". Once Jenkins had convinced him that the libel law did that anyway – which took some time – theatre censorship was finally abolished in 1968, leaving the Lord Chamberlain with more time for his other duties, which mostly involve beefeaters or swans.

☞ *ANYONE FOR DENIS?*

LUARD, Nicholas, own opinion of role in *Private Eye*

Nick Luard was a friend of Peter Cook's from Cambridge, who had gone into business with him, and who bought Private Eye *on his behalf in June 1962 (☞ RICH OWNER, Search for a). Or so everyone thought.*

Nick Luard: Peter never liked the business from the start. When I wrote to him to say that Andrew Osmond had offered us his shares, he replied on a postcard: "Nick, this isn't for me," he said. "If you want to go ahead, do it on your own. They'll do nothing but fight, and it'll all end in tears." I ignored his advice, and agreed to buy Osmond's seventy-six percent holding. *Private Eye* was the first venture we hadn't taken on in partnership.

Peter's hostility to *Private Eye* was, I think, due to little more than what's known now as "bad chemistry". He just didn't like what he called the cunning and quarrelsome dead fish he had to deal with. Peter was right, they were always at each other's throats and some of their feuds have lasted to this day.

My effectively sole ownership of the magazine didn't last for very long, although it did span the time when the *Eye* started to become a national institution.[118]

LUARD, Nicholas, others' opinion of role in *Private Eye*

David Cash: I'm afraid that's nonsense. Everyone gets very annoyed when this comes up yet again, that Nick Luard started the *Eye*. It was Peter. Peter's input.

Christopher Booker: It's ridiculous! Absolutely ridiculous! I do remember Cookie saying I'll have to talk to Nick about it, but it wasn't "I'll have to talk to Nick cos I want to fob you off," it was "Yeah, it sounds quite exciting but will the moneybags agree?" I happened to be involved with that so I do remember.

Peter Usborne: Nick managed to give the impression constantly to the press that he *was Private Eye*, and this irritated us beyond belief. Because he absolutely wasn't. But he did, very gratefully, soak up the glamour. And he was "the Emperor of Satire". And we got more and more furious at his posturing.

Richard Ingrams: Luard was very peripheral I think.

In the meantime, the Establishment club was falling apart. It was being incompetently run, had fallen foul of the local protection racketeers, and run up massive legal fees attempting to persuade the Home Office that Lenny Bruce should be allowed to enter the country and bring his "sick jokes and lavatory humour" to its stage.

Usborne: Eventually we constructed plan B, me, Richard and Willie I think it was, which was that unless Luard got out we were leaving and we were going to start "Public Eye". And I went to him with plan B, and he left. I give him a lot of credit for it, he realised his position was untenable, and he would be seen as the man who wrapped up *Private Eye* and this brilliant team had gone off, and I think he rang up Peter in New York that afternoon and Peter sent his lawyer over from New York.

Cook claimed to have been surprised to learn that the shares Osmond had sold were held in the name of Nicholas Luard and not, as he thought, Cook & Luard productions.

Cook: I was very cross indeed. I sent over a famous New York lawyer called Sydney Cohn. I thought if anything should emerge from the shambles, I should like to retain the *Eye*. And somehow or other he did it. The *Eye* never knew how close it got to going down the tubes.[116]

Cook & Luard productions was declared bankrupt in September 1963, and the Establishment Club sold. It became a porn cinema not long afterwards. Luard left the country.

The *Eye* team photographed by Jane Bown, backstage at the Establishment in 1962. Clockwise from left: Booker, Ingrams, Rushton and Luard

LUNCH, tales from the
Coach and Horses

● The *Private Eye* lunch has been taking place in an upstairs room at the Coach and Horses on Greek Street every fortnight since the autumn of 1966. "We started asking people as a way of getting information," says Richard Ingrams.

● "Mine was the nearest pub to the office," replied landlord Norman Balon when asked why his establishment came to host this semi-legendary event. "Richard never thought it had any charm. He just thought we served very good food. Richard has always appreciated a good spotted dick and custard: it probably reminded him of school. The traditional *Private Eye* menu was melon, then steak and chips, and lastly treacle stodge, a sort of suet pudding. If people don't like what is on their plate, that's their bad luck."[120] Ingrams says "I always regarded it as a test of stamina for the guests, whether they could get through this disgusting food." Since Norman retired in 2006, things have gone a bit gastro.

● The only regular guest for whom Balon would make an exception was Labour MP Tom Driberg (☞). "He was a gourmet, and tried to get me to serve him vegetables. I used to bring up a few bits of cabbage on a saucer."

● On one occasion when Ingrams was away in 1983, the entire lunch rebelled and went to L'Escargot instead, sending the editor the bill. "I haven't seen a good story out of it yet," Ingrams grumbled to the *Times*.[121]

● While still reliably boozy affairs – the first bottles of wine are opened at 1pm and it is rare for there not to be a few guests still there by the evening – Richard Ingrams has

Left: **Norman Balon, landlord of The Coach and Horses**

Below: **Ingrams and Waugh head the table**

been on the mineral water since 1967. "I got to feeling very ill, and I was convinced that I was dying, and the doctor said my liver was several sizes too big and I should give up drink."[122] A bereft Balon remembered that "He used to be an amazingly large drinker. He'd put it down by the ton."[123]

● "Almost everyone came," remembers Peter McKay, a regular attendee in the early days. "Quite big names – I suppose they still do now. I don't think we ever had a serving prime minister or a member of the royal family but otherwise nearly anybody would come. Because they were intrigued. And they were all served in the same horrible way by Norman, saying 'Aw, fack off!'"

● The astonishingly pompous journalist Peter Jenkins (aka Mr Polly Toynbee) once arrived at the pub and asked Balon where he should go for the *Eye* lunch. "Who the fuck are you?" asked Norm. Jenkins stormed upstairs and told Ingrams he had "never been so insulted in my life", at which the *Eye* editor laughed uproariously, so he left and never came back. Labour MP Willie Hamilton didn't even make it that far, being so outraged by Norm that he didn't get further than the bar.

● "Paul Foot was sometimes worried that the people he had invited might get offended by me and would hang around downstairs and bring them up himself," Balon admitted. The only guest he ever personally escorted upstairs was the multi-millionaire businessman Arnold Weinstock. "Foot says I fawn to tycoons."

● Certain *Eye* staff still reminisce fondly about the occasion when a young Ian Hislop got very drunk at lunch and came back and fell asleep on the sofa in the office reception. Since he was made editor this has not happened again.

● Harold Wilson's barmy political secretary Marcia Williams (☞ FORKBENDER, Lady) attempted to get Ingrams's Oxford friend Robin Butler sacked from the civil service after she discovered he had once been a lunch guest. She failed, and he went on to become cabinet secretary to five different prime ministers and head of the civil service. Fearing that Number 10 would find out he too was a regular guest, Driberg always demanded that he be introduced as "Mr Richmond", and insisted to the gathered guests that Wilson's head of security George Wigg had spies parked in a car parked outside the pub.

● Hackette Cristina Odone once popped into the *Eye* office early, to find out who else was on the guest list. When she found out that Alan Clark was coming, she changed into a shorter skirt.

● Kitty Kelley acknowledged Ian Hislop as one of her sources for her notorious book *The Royals*, unreleased in Britain because of the libel risk. When he protested that "I told her zip" she clarified that it was merely thanking him for his "hospitality – those rubber steaks you served me at various *Private Eye* luncheons".

● Andrew Neill (☞) and BBC documentary-maker Adam Curtis once attended the same lunch, and had a long and enthusiastic conversation about who was the most deserving winner of *The X-Factor*.

● Germaine Greer and Jeffrey Bernard (☞ BLIGHT, Rose; MAD, Colonel) once had a lengthy discussion on oral sex at an *Eye* lunch, much to the discomfort of newspaper editor Derek Jameson, who was sitting next to them. The conversation concluded with Greer telling Bernard, "Jeffrey, you've just talked yourself out of a fuck."[124]

● At least one lunch guest has had a lengthy conversation with *Eye* hackette Heather Mills while under the impression that she was Paul McCartney's wife.

THE 'PRIVATE EYE' LUNCH

The weekly *Private Eye* luncheon in a London pub—the spirit of Grub Street in the purlieus of Soho. This week's cabal, clockwise from bottom left, are: Jilly Cooper; Frank Muir; Martin Tomkinson; Ned Sherrin; Patrick Marnham; Sally Beauman; Anthony Blond; Anthony Haden-Guest; Ann Chisholm, and editor Richard Ingrams

The *Sunday Times* gains access

● Saudi dissident Muhammad al-Masari came to one lunch (he didn't drink). Later he started calling for the "annihilation of all Jews". He didn't get invited back.

● Former "Barry McKenzie" cartoonist Nick Garland came to lunch in 1986. He did not have a good time. "Separated from the pack, *Private Eye* people are just like anyone else; together, they are weird. They even have a strange noise they all make together; it's a forced cackling laugh."[125]

● Kingsley Amis spent an entire lunch ignoring Auberon Waugh, who was sitting next to him, on the grounds that he "had once had the temerity to criticise one of his books".[126]

● Liberal Democrat MP John Hemming got, in a fellow guest's words, "hogwhimperingly drunk" and confessed to everyone present that he had got his mistress pregnant and was about to be exposed in the *News of the World*. Sadly, most MPs are rather more discreet.

● Rod Liddle was due to come to the lunch when the story of his affair with twenty-two-year-old Alicia Monckton erupted into the papers thanks to a war of words between him and his wife. Far from cancelling, he insisted on bringing Monckton with him to the Coach and Horses. Every other guest present came away thinking "poor girl".

● Piers Morgan brought Max Clifford with him on the one

occasion he attended in 1996. Paul Foot refused to speak to him on the grounds that he was a completely unsuitable editor for the *Mirror*, to which he had just been appointed. "And as always happened with Footy, in no time at all Piers was flattering him and he was saying 'He's a very bright young man, that Piers Morgan, gosh I'm impressed with him,'" remembers Francis Wheen.

● Amanda Platell came to lunch, stayed late into the afternoon, and confessed she was supposed to be writing an pro-Euro speech – so Francis Wheen helped her with it. Shortly afterwards she was appointed spin-doctor to the rabidly anti-Euro William Hague.

● A national newspaper editor – still in post at time of writing – confessed in 2009 that his paper was "all gone to bollocks".

● Alan Yentob came in 1986, and chose a lull in the conversation to announce that "I think you should attack this Tory MP who's just resigned from the Commons to present *Weekend World*." Which was the moment Christopher Silvester chose to introduce him to "the man next to him, who he had ignored throughout the meal" – Matthew Parris, who had just resigned from the Commons to present *Weekend World*.

● George Carman, an old friend of the *Eye*, was quite happy to come to lunch during his period representing Mohamed Fayed in his libel battle against Neil Hamilton (☞) and gossip about what an awful man he thought his client was.

● John Mortimer had a 'funny turn' at the lunch in the late 1990s, but just when everyone thought he had died, recovered enough to have another drink.

● Former Liberal leader Jo Grimond arrived at lunch in the mid-1970s completely unaware of the lurid rumours surrounding his successor Jeremy Thorpe (☞ DITTO MAN, The). Auberon Waugh took great pleasure in filling him in.

● A later Liberal leader, Charles Kennedy, was closely watched at the first lunch he attended after announcing he was a recovering alcoholic. He didn't have a drink.

● Political columnist Peter Oborne arrived at lunch not long after the MPs' expenses scandal was exposed thanks to fellow guest, freedom-of-information campaigner Heather Brooke. He immediately dropped to the floor and kissed her feet.

● John Peel came and was reunited with his old schoolfriends (☞ SHREWSBURY). "I sat next to Paul Foot. He was enchanting, clever, funny and kind. Ingrams I found cold, even hostile."[127]

● Margaret Thatcher came to the lunch twice in 1968, long before she was elected Conservative leader. She flirted outrageously with Paul Foot. "I was not that taken by her," remembered Balon. "I remember Richard Ingrams saying she wouldn't get anywhere."

● Foreign correspondent Kim Sengupta was once negotiating a very tricky army checkpoint in a civil war zone when his mobile went off. The large man in uniform he was talking to motioned with his machine gun that he should answer it. It was *Eye* secretary Hilary Lowinger asking him if he would like steak or salmon when he came to lunch.

● Television presenter Cliff Michelmore once declined an invitation by telegram on the grounds that "I am busy denying some totally inaccurate magazine article." *Observer* editor David Astor wrote that "various commitments and considerations make me unable to accept". Art critic Brian Sewell declined because he was "convinced that his intending host would find the experience disagreeable".

● Richard Ingrams once invited "an old man, a German banker, a friend of my father's, about eighty", to the lunch on a whim, and then worried that he would have nothing to talk to him about. He sat him next to former cabinet minister Richard Crossman. They turned out both to have been married to the same woman (at different times).

● An undergraduate Tina Brown, invited to lunch by a besotted Auberon Waugh, subsequently reported in her student paper that "the watchword of the *Eye* lunches is Flair and Devil-May-Care. If it resembles any social occasion at all, it is probably the Hell Fire Club in the era of John Wilkes – for in every pair of eyes there is a satirical gleam that bodes ill." Ingrams read the piece. "I thought, well, she's not a good journalist," he says. "I never thought she was any good."

● The *South Bank Show* filmed a specially convened *Eye* lunch for a thirtieth- anniversary documentary in 1991, with guests including John Diamond, Tony Banks MP, Tariq Ali and Germaine Greer. Whenever the conversation veered towards topics Ian Hislop did not want broadcast, he made loud rude remarks about Melvyn Bragg's novels to ensure they were edited out.

● Francis Wheen came to his first *Eye* lunch as a youthful guest in 1979. "I was so terrified I just clung to Peter McKay for dear life." He now sits at the head of the table with the most attractive women, at the opposite end to Richard Ingrams (the old bores' end). Ian Hislop sits in the middle.

● This is something of a change from the seating plan of the late 1970s, described by Auberon Waugh thus: "You'll find the Trots at one end of the table and the human beings at the other."[128] Paul Foot then took one end of the long table, and Patrick Marnham the other, with Ingrams in the middle.

LUVVIES

"My friend John Sessions came up with the term Luvvies when he was camping about with Kenneth Branagh. I hadn't heard anyone else using it before. I think it was RADA slang."
Ian Hislop, September 2009

LUVVIES

"The worst thing that ever happened to our profession – and it's only happened in England and it certainly wouldn't happen in America – is the word 'luvvie',

because it's a derogatory word to denote an actor and, as a result of it, the public generally has lost a great respect for the acting profession. The role of an actor in America, Eastern Europe and in Western Europe – everywhere apart from this country – is considered a very serious job and a very necessary function. Here we are just luvvies, which is a great shame."
David Suchet, The Stage, May 2010

"'Luvvie' is as appalling and as abhorrent as any racist word. It's a word that's had a deadly impact. I think it's a word as disgusting as the word 'yid' or 'nigger'. It categorises everyone of a particular grouping as the same, and not only categorises them but patronises them and puts them down. It's a word which says you are hysterical, trivial, under-educated, self-indulgent, absolutely regardless of your background, education, lifestyle or manner."
Trevor Nunn, Vogue, September 1996 (the column was briefly renamed "Trevvies" in his honour)

McCARTNEY, Paul, dons black jacket about being featured in "Pseuds Corner"

In April 2001, a poem by Paul McCartney featured in "Pseuds Corner".

> Sadness isn't sadness,
> It's happiness
> In a black jacket.

The former Beatle was furious (or, as he would probably put it, serene in a red hat). "My God, bastards!" he railed to a *Radio Times* interviewer. "*Private Eye* isn't supposed to turn on me. I'm their friend. That's the last donation I give them."[129]

"His PA turned up in reception and whinged on for ages, wouldn't budge," remembers Sheila Molnar. At the time no-one could find any trace of a donation from McCartney, although it has since emerged that he gave a personal artwork to be auctioned on behalf of the Goldenballs (☞) fund a quarter of a century earlier. But he really should have realised this didn't count as an insurance policy against future mockery. Business mogul Tiny Rowland had instigated the fund with a £5,000 cheque and the instruction "There will be no quid pro quo. You must go on writing about me whenever you want."[130]

"Money can't buy you love, he once sang," noted issue 1029 after McCartney's outburst. "Nor, it seems, can it buy you a sense of humour." All in all, it's lucky no one told Macca when he first appeared in "Pseuds Corner", for describing "Mary Had a Little Lamb" as "a heavy trip … very spiritual", way back in 1972. ☞ PSEUDS, Britain's ten biggest

McKENZIE, Barry

Despite the chilly reception an appearance as Edna Everage had received at the Establishment Club in 1963, Peter Cook was impressed enough by Barry Humphries to suggest that he collaborate with budding cartoonist Nick Garland on a series for the *Eye* – "an Australian *Candide* … Sort of 'An Arsehole Abroad'."[131]

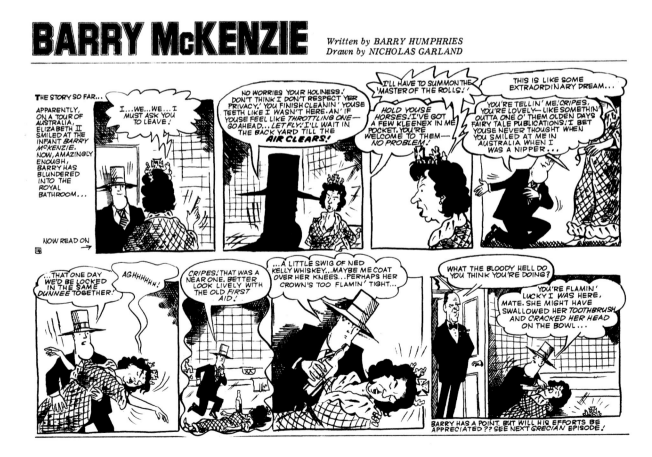

Humphries and Garland quickly settled on a look for their lead character, who they christened Barry McKenzie (or McKensie in his very first appearance). "He was inspired by Chesty Bond, a cartoon figure in an Australian advert for underwear. I felt he should seem rather old-fashioned in a double-breasted suit and tie, like the former Australian prime minister Sir Robert Menzies, and we decided he would always wear a broad-brimmed hat, like the rural Australians sported when they came to town for the Royal Agricultural Show,"[132] remembered Humphries.

If these references were obscure to a British audience, that was nothing as to McKenzie's colourful vocabulary, which was "a synthetic Australian compounded of schoolboy, service, old-fashioned and even made-up slang". Barry would regularly *shake hands with the wife's best friend*, aka *siphon the python*, aka *point Percy at the porcelain*, aka *drain the dragon*, usually as a prelude to *laughing at the ground*, aka *parking the tiger*, aka *calling for Ruth*, aka *a liquid laugh*, aka *enjoying oneself in reverse*, aka *chundering*. These emetic episodes were invariably caused

"That was the first really popular feature that was in Private Eye *– people bought the magazine because of 'Barry McKenzie'"* Richard Ingrams

by an overdose of Foster's, a hitherto obscure Australian lager, to the discomfort of its manufacturers: "They had recently spent a large sum of money with an advertising agency to make commercials in which their product was depicted as a rather sophisticated tipple," recalled Humphries.

"That was the first really popular feature that was in *Private Eye* – people bought the magazine because of 'Barry McKenzie'," says Richard Ingrams. The strip was popular enough to branch out into two feature films (in which McKenzie was played by Barry Crocker who went on to sing the theme tune to *Neighbours*), and it also "very much inspired" Men at Work's 1983 number one "Down Under".

The strip ended in 1974, partly due to the fact it was "becoming increasingly obscene". Patrick Marnham remembers the artwork that

McLACHLAN, Edward

Named "the cartoonists' cartoonist" by Wally Fawkes (☞), Ed McLachlan has been contributing since 1964. His intricately detailed scenes often depict anthropomorphised or enlarged animals running amok. "I've been battling with Ian to accommodate a proper-sized McLachlan for as long as I remember," says art director Tony Rushton. "So much thought goes into them."

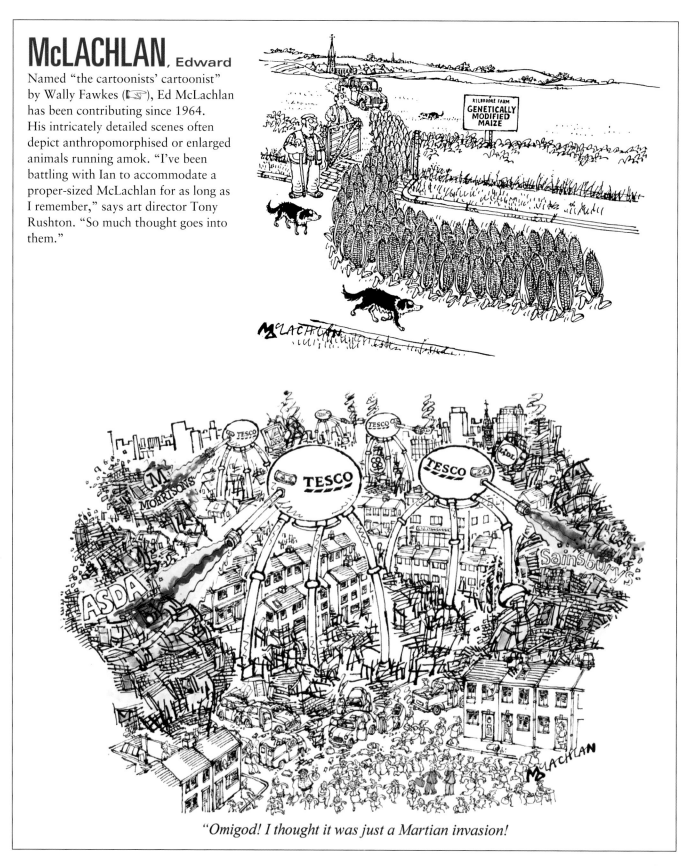

"Omigod! I thought it was just a Martian invasion!"

proved the final straw: "It was a drawing of a woman with her skirt up, a full-frontal – you really could see everything." Ingrams says this was not the whole story. "Humphries was at that stage a *serious* alcoholic. And he kept not delivering the copy. So that Garland would be left with no script at all. You couldn't do a strip cartoon like that. You can't miss an issue. But I think when it lasted, it was brilliant."

Nick Garland went on to be the political cartoonist for the *Daily Telegraph*, where the speech bubbles were rather different. Barry Humphries has long since given up drinking. McKenzie has not. He was last heard of in a compilation of the strips published in Australia in 1988, nursing a war wound from Vietnam and a grudge against Foster's on the grounds that he had not been rewarded for his part in the lager's global success.

MAD, Colonel

Colonel Mad was the pseudonym under which turf fan and celebrity drunk Jeffrey Bernard penned a racing column in the *Eye* between 1977 and 1980. It was popular enough in the racing world for racehorse manager Henry Ponsonby to name one of his syndicated horses Colonel Mad in its honour, and for John McCririck to describe it as "crapulent".

Bernard, however, was too unreliable for the column to live for long. "He was a boozer. I didn't have the patience to deal with that," says Ingrams simply. For many years afterwards, the two men had an uneasy relationship in the bar of the Coach and Horses (when Bernard wasn't barred).

MANDELSON, Peter, outed by *Eye*

One of the most extraordinary political storms of modern times broke in October 1998 when Matthew Parris announced on *Newsnight* that "Peter Mandelson is certainly gay."

It wouldn't have come as news to *Private*

"He says we've both been fired" L-R: Jeffrey Bernard, Martin Tomkinson, Richard Ingrams. The bubble was added after both men had been

Original artwork for "The Regulars" by Michael Heath in which Bernard featured heavily

Eye readers, who had been quietly informed of the fact, along with the identity of his then boyfriend Peter Ashby, over a decade earlier in March 1987.

MANDELSON, Peter,
protests at depiction in *Eye*

In August 2009, Peter Mandelson was working hard on reforming his public image, telling the *Guardian* that "I don't really see myself as a big beast. More as a kindly pussycat."

A week later, the *Sunday Times* reported his reaction to the *Eye*'s depiction of Gordon Brown as the Supreme Leader (☞). "It's so funny. Absolutely hilarious." But he was less impressed by his own depiction in the feature. "I'm far more of a Beria."[133]

Lavrenti Beria headed the People's Commissariat for Internal Affairs or NKVD, Stalin's secret police force, responsible for the execution of millions of "enemies of the people".

MANDELSON, Peter, visits
Eye office as birthday treat for editor

On the morning of Ian Hislop's fiftieth birthday in July 2010, a strange figure appeared outside the window of the *Private Eye* office and started pulling faces. It was the man who until a few months before had rejoiced in the title of First Secretary of State, Secretary of State for Business, Innovation and Skills and Lord President of the Council. And now he was reduced to this.

"It was one of the strangest things that has ever happened," says Ian Hislop. "I invited him in and showed him around."

Mandy, who was recording the audiobook of his memoirs in a nearby studio, came back the next day. This time the staff refused to let him in.

MAPELEY
 TAXMAN

MARQUESA, short-lived
replacement for "Grovel"

"I hated 'Grovel'," admits Ian Hislop. "I couldn't see the point of it. "It wasn't funny, never even entertaining. Telling anecdotes about the Duke of Devonshire and cheese for the eight hundredth time, I mean just beyond boring! Dempster's self-importance always seemed to me to be what we should be attacking, and not celebrating."

Nigel Dempster departed, his self-importance swelling considerably in the process, a year before the new editor took over (☞ PARKINSON, Cecil, his part in Nigel Dempster's downfall). His fellow Groveller, Peter McKay, was working in America at the time, and was soon to follow his partner in crime into permanent exile after speed-writing an uncomplimentary book about Hislop's accession entitled *Inside Private Eye*.

The "Grovel" column remained, but with an important difference: the legover was over. "It's not that I'm asexual or celibate or anything dramatic like that, but just endlessly reading about it was something I felt we could leave to Murdoch, really," Hislop protested.[134] "I suppose I thought endlessly saying somebody's marriage has failed wasn't that interesting. It seems to happen a lot. And unless I could find some way that it was important – that it reflected on their judgement, or some element of hypocrisy, or some connection or relationship that wasn't being declared that affected something else, then I wasn't that keen. The magazine is not entirely without reference to sexual intercourse. But there isn't a dedicated legover column."[135]

Many people contributed to "New Grovel", but one of its main authors was Christopher Silvester, a young hack whom Hislop had introduced to the *Eye* in 1983. "He was very amusing. And Chris knew stuff. He was working at Tory Central Office, he knew all the Thatcherite think-tank people." He rapidly bagged himself both a permanent berth at the magazine and a relationship with Richard Ingrams's daughter Jubby. By the mid-1980s he was largely regarded – outside the office at least – as "Grovel"'s representative on earth. It helped that he pretty much modelled himself on Fantoni's illustration at the top of the column. He may never have quite managed a monocle, but Silvester was rocking a bow tie twenty-five

"Ian got pretty berserk, and closed down 'Grovel' as a punishment . . . purely retaliation because he was so angry with Silvester for expropriating the logo and the name for himself." Francis Wheen

It touched a number of raw nerves. Hislop has always been strongly opposed to any kind of "advertorial" deals that would compromise the integrity of the *Eye*. And the wording was horribly reminiscent of Dempster at his worst: "He wanted to be a figure, and run a column, and *be* 'Grovel'. I didn't want any of that. Why would I exchange one figure who I didn't like, why would I start it again with Christopher?"

An item promptly appeared in "Grovel" itself. "Friends pass me an absurd party invitation purporting to come from myself. Suffice to say, it is no such thing. 'Grovel' is celebrating nothing – except perhaps the imminent departure of one of Lord Gnome's more bow-tied minions. Pip Pip!" Hislop turned up at the party, made what Silvester describes as "a bitchy speech taking the piss which was quite funny", and then dumped the column. When the *Evening Standard* asked if these two things were in any way related he said it was "an appalling suggestion and probably true".

"Ian got pretty berserk, and closed down 'Grovel' as a punishment," confirms Wheen. "Purely retaliation because he was so angry with Silvester for expropriating the logo and the name for himself. Silvester was one of the people who wrote stuff for 'Grovel' in the old days, as did I, as did the odd outside person like Giles Gordon. That was what annoyed Ian, that Silvester was taking personal ownership of this thing when actually it was bigger than him."

"Personally I think it was a mistake to have got rid of it," says Silvester, unsurprisingly. "I always thought the thing about 'Grovel' was that it allowed you to put in stories that weren't obviously categorisable in other sections of the magazine. They weren't all sex stories, they were often just weird stories about eccentricities."

"Grovel" was replaced with a pastiche of Hislop's latest bugbear, *Hello!* magazine. "It represents everything that I've tried not to do in journalism my whole life," he ranted to the BBC programme *Room 101* in 1994. The *Eye* had already run its own glossy full-scale spoof, "Hell!", in 1990, but it laid into the title again

years before *Doctor Who* caught on to it, and had so many pairs of co-respondent shoes he used to store the spares on bookshelves in the office. Francis Wheen remembers him as "a sort of boulevardier nimbly skipping around town in his spats with his silver-topped cane, popping in to the Groucho Club here and this party there and picking up all sorts of titbits which he put into 'Grovel'".

It was a party that killed "Grovel" for good. In November 1993 Silvester organised a launch for the *Penguin Book of Interviews* which he had edited, complete with sponsorship which obliged a rather clumsy invitation:

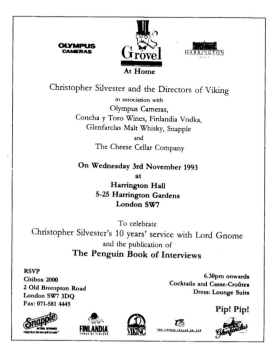

in the year its readership hit half a million. "Hallo!" was subtitled "The Heartwarming Column" and was supposedly the work of the Marquesa, a version of the real *Hello!*'s interview "fixer", absurd Uruguayan aristocrat the Marquesa de Varela. The joke was that it put a heavily ironic gloss on bad behaviour by celebrities, just as the real magazine tended to suck up to jailbirds and multiple-divorcees with questions about their humanitarian works and beauty routines. "I am deeply touched when the movingly sincere David Mellor tells a waiting world that: 'all this publicity is a tragedy for my family.' A tear springs to my eye …"

The problem was, it didn't really work. "It was always a bit of a struggle to write. It had to be cobbled together, really," says Francis Wheen, who along with Silvester, Ben Summerskill and Brian Rostron all had bashes at being the Marquesa until she was killed off in 1997. "I tried to make it post-modern and ironic," admits Hislop. "Rostron nearly made it

work, and then he went home to South Africa. And I thought 'This is my perfect context not to do this column any more.' Basically what I wanted to do was just get rid of it, and it took me a while to twig that."

MAUDLING, Reginald

☞ POULSON, scandal brings down home secretary

MAXWELL, Robert, forecasts inaccurately

"After all these years, I have finally served a writ on *Private Eye*, and shut them up for good. I don't expect them to print any more about me." *October 1975*

MASTHEAD

One innovation introduced by Nick Luard (☞) was a new logo for the magazine. Until issue 11 the lettering for each issue had been the responsibility, and whim, of Willie Rushton.

In May 1962 the magazine's masthead was redrawn by graphic designer Matthew Carter, who had been engaged to work on the menus, programmes and publicity material for Peter Cook's Establishment Club.

His logo has appeared on nearly 1,300 editions, countless sheets of notepaper, books and memorabilia since that day, while Carter himself has gone on to design award-winning and internationally recognisable fonts for Linotype and Microsoft and be hailed by the Design Museum as "the most important typography designer of our time".

Does he get a royalty? Does he heck.

MAXWELL, Robert, full list of complaints against *Private Eye*

● The *Eye* claimed he had borrowed £10,000 from two journalists for a £25,000 deposit necessary to take over the *Scottish Daily News* in 1975, and that the company's accountants and lawyers were unhappy about his involvement.

Capt. Bob says: "It was a tissue of lies and implied that I borrowed money from my employees, which was wholly untrue, or that I had difficulty in meeting my obligations and commitments."

The *Eye* says: Faced with a blizzard of writs from James Goldsmith (☞ GOLDENBALLS) at the same time, the *Eye* had to settle the case, apologised and paid Maxwell damages – despite the fact that two journalists had indeed stumped up £11,000 for the deposit, and the company's accountants and lawyers resigned in protest at Maxwell's behaviour within months.

● One of the magazine's regular "Lookalike" features in 1983 compared his appearance to that of Ronnie Kray.

Capt. Bob says: "Mrs Maxwell and all of our children were utterly shocked to have me, their father, compared to a convicted major gangster."

The *Eye* says: "A deliberately offensive, defamatory and fictitious letter. We profoundly apologise and undertake that we shall not hereafter publish offensive material defamatory to Mr Maxwell." (Apology printed in March 1983. Following this nearly every "Lookalike" which appeared in the magazine was signed "Ena B. Maxwell" with his home address.)

● In 1986 the *Eye* wrote that he was funding foreign trips by Labour leader Neil Kinnock in the hope of getting a peerage.

Capt. Bob says: "That is destructive of the body politic of the government and the country. There was no alternative but to go to court to clear my name of this gross allegation and lie."

The *Eye* says: "Our source was a Labour MP who had been told in a sort of nod and a wink way. Once the complaint was made we got an affidavit from our source, even though we undertook that we would not name him. And that was the problem in a way – not the only problem, because if he had gone to court we would have still lost, because he didn't have enough information really." (Christopher Silvester)

● The *Eye* printed a cartoon of him with "Mr Kinnock as a little lapdog obeying everything that Mr Maxwell says".

Capt. Bob says: "I had no alternative but to take out an application for an injunction to stop the sale of that particular issue of *Private Eye*."

The *Eye* says: "The problem was this: Maxwell tried to injunct the magazine and stop it from being distributed. And simply because Maxwell had tried to use this weapon, we thought, 'We're going to resist this.' And in order to resist it, you have to undertake that you will justify the libel at trial rather than defend it in any other way. So we were committed to pleading justification. Now of course we could have settled it prior to the trial, and perhaps we should have done. But we decided from a mixture of folly and cockiness that we'd take him on." (Christopher Silvester)

● Another "Lookalike" of the Duke of Edinburgh and Adolf Eichmann was signed "Ena B. Maxwell".

Capt. Bob says: [sobbing and raising a handkerchief to his eyes in witness box] "My family was destroyed by Eichmann."

The *Eye* says: "Nobody remembered this thing. The fact it was brought up was extraordinary. We didn't think the jury would fall for it. Richard [Ingrams] and I were sitting together in the front row. It looked very obviously fake to me. I didn't see any tears." (Christopher Silvester)

● The magazine "will publish anything for profit. They do not check their sources, they do not have the guts to apologise or withdraw. They are pedlars of lies and filth."

The *Eye* says: "Bloody hell. Bloody hell" (Dave Cash, in court at the time). Maxwell was awarded just £5,000 for defamation over the Kinnock allegation – but the *Eye* was also hit with £50,000 in "exemplary" damages for the way it had handled the case, failing to attempt to justify the libel in court and admitting that the printing of an apology did not mean a story was not true (☞ APOLOGIES, Real meaning of). Legal costs were around a quarter of a million.

Capt. Bob says: "My first thought was to give the damages to research into finding a cure for AIDS. It comes from a diseased organ, so it is appropriate it should go to AIDS."

During Maxwell's time driving profits at the *Daily Mirror*, incidentally, the paper fought and lost more libel cases than any other title in Fleet Street.

● He was "featured in a strip cartoon called 'Capt. Bob', a reference to Mr Maxwell".

Capt. Bob says: "There are those who praise the *Eye* on the grounds that it has changed the way this generation views its public men, not only by making fun of them, but also by implying that they habitually have their noses in the public trough and act for personal financial or private motives. But is this really a matter for praise? Does it really make a valuable contribution to our society to destroy both in our own eyes, and in those of the world at large, our major national asset of incorruptibility in public life – to replace it by a belief that the instincts of the piggery motivate our public servants and successful entrepreneurs?"

The *Eye* says: "The trouble with people like Rupert Murdoch is he doesn't care. He doesn't sue us. And he doesn't mind the jokes – or as far as we know he doesn't mind the jokes. Maxwell was so thin-skinned. He hated being challenged, he hated being mocked, which made

None of Maxwell's employees were spared the Capt. Bob treatment – not even Paul Foot (left, centre panel)

him very vulnerable. Maxwell *hated* the jokes. Really hated it" (Ian Hislop). The "Capt. Bob" strip by John Kent only started after – and as a direct result of – the Kinnock libel action.

● The magazine insisted, at every opportunity, on bringing up the 1971 Department of Trade and Industry report which had concluded he was "not in our opinion a person who can be relied upon to exercise proper stewardship of a publicly quoted company".

Capt. Bob says: "The bitchiness of British journalists continues. This is a country which hates success."

The *Eye* says: "It was a very good example of how when anything comes to court, what you and I might think are the most important things cannot be mentioned. All the lawyers jumped up and said 'This is most improper, we can't possibly have this referred to.'"[136] (Richard Ingrams)

● The *Eye* wrote that "we owe no apology to Robert Maxwell" over a story involving his company British International Helicopters, having only settled his case over the story in 1990 "rather than face a gruelling and ludicrously expensive trial".

Capt. Bob says: He managed to get an injunction to

halt the distribution of the magazine and force the *Eye* to reprint 100,000 copies without the offending item.

The *Eye* says: The special reprinted edition gave the fat man – and his latest failing newspaper – a starring role on its cover.

● The *Eye* caused "very serious injury to his feelings and reputation" by claiming that he "had ordered the Mirror pensions office to act unlawfully in withholding employer contributions and buying stock in his public company MCC" in August 1991.

Capt. Bob says: Nothing. He fell off his boat a fortnight after issuing a writ and died. He had around a hundred libel writs outstanding against various targets at the time, so determined was he to hush up the truth about what he had been up to. Within weeks it emerged that he had systematically looted the Mirror Group to keep his web of public and private companies afloat, that he had over a billion pounds' worth of debts, and that £440 million was missing from the pension funds of around 30,000 of his staff.

The *Eye* says: "It was incredibly pleasing, the arc of the Maxwell story. We'd had a long campaign – Gillard-led mostly (☞ SLICKER), because he'd covered the inquiry which said Maxwell wasn't fit to run a public company way back in 1971. There was never any worry for me about Maxwell, he really was the genuine crook article. And the other great thing about that story was that no one would do it. For fear of the writs, and also because all the vested interests were lined up. There was a huge amount of legal work, a huge amount of corporate work, mergers and acquisitions – he generated a huge amount of business for a lot of the professionals in the capital. So no one wanted to take him on. And the other proprietors wanted to keep it quite nice and tidy because he was a maverick, and they all did business with him through printing and everything, so it was a huge nexus. And it was terrific to be on the other side." (Ian Hislop)

☞ CZECH, fat, Fat cheque paid to; MIRROR BUILDING, Peter Cook leads *Eye* raid on

MAXWELL, Robert, reader's mea culpa over

Frank Valentine of Caister-on-Sea, mourning the passing of the *Mirror* proprietor, wrote a scathing letter to the *Eye* in November 1991.

> "Sir – Can we now look forward to the *Eye* returning to satire in place of protracted, hate-filled personal vendettas? I refer to one which strangely intensified after the subject took you to court and won. In this you were ably assisted by an army of sycophantic readers quickly realising that they had only to slag off Robert Maxwell to ensure publication of their wearisome letters."

A month later, as more and more evidence of Maxwell's epic larceny spilled out into the light, he wrote again:

> "Sir – In your issue of 22 November you kindly printed a letter from me in which I rebuked the *Eye* for its previous non-stop barrage of abuse directed at Robert Maxwell. Revelations since then, however, have led me to suspect that I may have been wrong. Sorry. Yours sheepishly."

M.D.

Dr Phil Hammond has been the *Eye*'s medical columnist since January 1992. He got the job after attending a BBC Radio Light Entertainment Christmas party in his guise as one half of the medical comedy act Struck Off and Die. "I followed the Beverley Sisters down the stairs and Ian Hislop into the toilet. I offered him a column for *Private Eye* and washed my hands afterwards."[137]

"I said 'That's a good idea. Er ... let's do it!'" remembers Hislop. "There wasn't a huge amount of research or focus grouping."
☞ BRISTOL HEART SCANDAL

MELLOR, David, doesn't lose job over Antonia de Sancha affair – but *Eye* hack does

In July 1992 culture minister David Mellor was revealed to have been having an affair with an actress, Antonia de Sancha. He was kept in the cabinet by his old friend John Major. She was kept in the newspapers by her new friend Max Clifford. The man who had introduced the couple – *Eye* hack Paul Halloran – was not so lucky.

"They used to come into the office!" cackles Francis Wheen. "Mellor used to drop in, turn up at the office and say 'Is Paul in?'" De Sancha was one of a series of "incredibly glamorous women" who would regularly arrive at the office and be hustled into Halloran's room, the door firmly shut behind them. When the story broke, with accompanying details of Chelsea strips and toe-sucking, the *Eye* hack's involvement in their courtship featured heavily in all the tabloids. The *People* called him Mellor's "trustworthy lackey". Ian Hislop did not appreciate it.

"Ian thought this was incredibly unprofessional conduct. Maybe he felt that it somehow compromised *Private Eye* if it was seen to be acting as this pimping agency for ministers," suggests Wheen. "Given that

Ian is not that interested in legover stories anyway, if Halloran had written the story, he would probably not have run it. It was really just a general feeling that Halloran had to go, which was fair enough." Hislop confirms that "Halloran was around far too long."

A show of family unity and an astonishing brass neck ensured Mellor's survival in the cabinet right up until another unconnected scandal broke that September. His friend was not so lucky. "A shocking, damning and incriminating piece of evidence was uncovered which Mr Mellor could not even begin to deny," Lord Gnome solemnly announced after the news of the affair broke in July. "He was a friend of a member of my staff. There can, I am afraid, be no more excuses for Mr Mellor's lack of judgement. He must go – and go quickly."
☞ HAPPY SHIP, not a

MEMOS, Terrifying

Ian Hislop rarely loses his rag, but when he does, it's spectacular. Staff several floors above or below the room where a colleague is receiving a bollocking can generally file an accurate report on every word of the exchange. Sometimes he shouts so loud that those working from home can hear it as well. "Chris Silvester's description of me I think is very good," he admits. "He said something like 'He's capable of being charming but capable of the most outrageous charmless

Card sent by Nick Newman to Ian Hislop on the occasion of his appendectomy

brutality' or something, some very damning phrase which I recognised as being true."

To be fair, he tends to reserve the face-to-face hairdryer treatment for senior and long-serving staff. Others get memos. These are usually dashed out in fury on the sheets of coloured paper Hislop keeps on his desk and then stuffed into pigeonholes to ferment until the addressee is next in the office. Harry Potter fans will recognise them as the owl-delivered Howlers which arrive in smoking envelopes. I got my first one exactly a week after I was given a regular weekly shift on the magazine. It was on yellow paper, and he'd underlined the word "NOT" three times.

It must be recorded that by the time the memos are read, marked and inwardly digested by the addressee, the storm has usually long since passed, the editor is as affable as ever and quite prepared for a calm and reasonable discussion of whatever the problem was in the first place. Former hackette Sarah Shannon remembers getting plenty of scary memos, though she points out that "He also used to send me nice ones, saying good work this time, liked this, liked that. Sort of herograms. I kept those!" Silvester, by contrast, kept all his nasty ones and quoted extensively from them in a speech at his leaving do. Francis Wheen – who is such a goody-goody that he claims "never to have had one" – remembers the office he used to share with Paul Halloran being decorated with many classics of the genre. "There would be piles of these things on his desk, five pages saying 'Paul – this is your last warning.' An awful lot of that sort of thing."

Hislop is also generous with the praise when it's deserved. Quite often hacks get their copy back with a little tick on it, or, if they've been particularly good, two ticks. Sometimes he even writes "V.G." in the corner. Francis Wheen probably gets gold stars.

MESOPOTAMIA

In the autumn of 1959, someone at Labour newspaper *Tribune* noticed the nepotistic deal for a regular advert with which editor Michael Foot had been keeping his nephew Paul's student magazine afloat and cancelled it on the grounds of their own perilous financial status. *Parson's Pleasure* (☞) promptly folded.

Thankfully the cavalry arrived in the form of Peter Usborne, an entrepreneurial Greats student at Balliol known to everyone as Uz. He had recently launched the full-colour glossy *Mesopotamia*, billed as "a new magazine of dedicated lunacy". It was meant to be devoted to comic writing from both Oxford and Cambridge. There were two problems with this. Usborne had hardly anyone from Cambridge to contribute. And everything that came in from Oxford was rubbish.

"It started as an incredibly unfunny magazine," he sighs. "Everybody said 'Well done, Peter,' not quite looking at me. The only person who complimented me wholeheartedly was Richard Ingrams."

Uz returned the compliment by recruiting Ingrams to write for him, roping in his friend Andrew Osmond for good measure. Willie Rushton, then working in a solicitors' office in London (much to everyone's surprise, including his own), volunteered his services too. "In the whole of Oxford, there was nobody who could do cartoons, so we had to import Rushton to draw for us. It boils down to the fact that there are very few people who can make jokes," recalls Ingrams.[138] Uz also unearthed a new talent, whom he unveiled to the team at a meeting in his rooms – John Wells, a third year at St Edmund Hall. "Somebody said there's this absolutely brilliant chap called John Wells, lives in North Oxford, why don't you go and see him, because he's the funniest man ever, ever," says Uz. Wells recalled that "He turned up at my digs in St Giles and told me I was to come round to Balliol. And I met Foot, Ingrams, Osmond, Rushton, the original *Private Eye* lot, all in one morning, just suddenly."[139]

"The chemistry between Richard Ingrams and John Wells was just magic, and when you put them in a room together it was like an explosion," remembered their friend Candida Betjeman. "They could carry on talking in funny voices and being different people infinitely. They never ran out of steam, never ran out of jokes."[140] Richard defined it – and all his subsequent work on *Private Eye* – as "the gang approach to journalism, done by a little gang of people who are all friends".[141]

The magic was in place. "I was very conscious that I had – by default really – assembled a seriously incredible collection of talent," says Usborne. The magazine became a great success. One issue came with a flimsy plastic flexidisc attached to the cover featuring sketches recorded by the team, and the proprietor remembered "just after it came out walking across the quad in Balliol and hearing John Wells' voice coming out of every other window".[142]

The day after their exams finished in 1961, the gang all got together what Usborne remembers as "a sort of *Mesopotamia* party in a field with lots of bottles of red wine". Talk turned to what they might be going to do with the rest of their lives. Osmond, who'd always been a bit more respectable than the rest of them, was making noises about the Foreign Office. Ingrams had got as far as an interview with the BBC. None of the rest of them had a clue. All they knew was that they wanted to avoid Proper Jobs and the outfits that still came with them in the early 1960s. The tale of Gnittie (☞) in *Mesopotamia* had ended with him meeting a fate worse than death: he left Oxford and "fell into a Sea of Bowler Hats, NEVER TO BE SEEN AGAIN".

Willie Rushton joined them from somewhere resembling the real world. He had abandoned the solicitors, and "decided to become a freelance cartoonist. Big decision. Broken-hearted mother. Everybody bursting into tears."[143] He was, however, making a bit of money drawing for *Liberal News*, the official party paper, where to his surprise he had been reunited with his former Shrewsbury contemporary Christopher Booker, now an earnest young journalist.

"My recollection is that people were lying there in the sun chatting about the future, and what the hell they were going to do," says Usborne. "And I think – I can't remember who it was, somebody, I think it was Willie Rushton – said 'We've had an awful lot of fun doing *Mesopotamia*; why don't we go on doing it?' And everyone said 'Shut up, Willie.' And I, the practical one, the publisher sort of person, was lying there half drunk, and I thought, 'Hmm. Not such a bad idea.'"

☞ *PASSING WIND*; OZ AND UZ

This edition came with a hessian cover impregnated with mustard and cress seeds: when watered, the plant "grew"

MI5, possible infiltration of *Private Eye*

☞ PRIVATE SPY

MILLIGAN, Spike

"Spike was always a terrific fan of *Private Eye*," says Richard Ingrams. "He would constantly send things in, cartoons and things. I'd always put them in." He first appeared in issue 10 in 1962, bewailing his statelessness in a letter trailed on the front cover as "the poet Milligan speaks". Issue 11 brought better news: "I have been granted Welsh citizenship, provided I stay on a mountainside and only say 'Baa'."

"This doesn't necessarily mean you'll paint like Toulouse Lautrec."

A Spike Milligan JOKE

MILLION-POUND WIN

How did a brief item in the consumer column in 1992 about overcharging by a Cornish accountant lead to a legal case that rivalled Jarndyce v. Jarndyce for longevity, and Ian Hislop rushing from the courtroom to address the *Eye*'s fortieth-anniversary party nine years later, in all sincerity, with the words "Welcome to the forty-first and final year of *Private Eye*'s existence"?

Two words: Carter-Fuck. The rapacious legal firm agreed to represent John Stuart Condliffe and managed to build up what the *Eye*'s solicitor Robin Shaw describes as "a fairly minor issue of libel" into such a complicated affair that the

Sally Deedes

MANY SMALL businesses in south-east Cornwall are feeling the pinch — not just due to the recession but thanks to the extraordinary behaviour of local accountants Condcliffe Hilton.

Indeed, the Institute of Chartered Accountants has received so many complaints about the fees charged by the firm that it is now "monitoring" the situation — an unheard of occurence as it never interferes in the charges set by its members.

judge before whom it came nearly a decade later pronounced himself "absolutely horrified" by the number of documents with which he was presented. This had swelled from 28 bundles to no fewer than 113. The *Eye*'s counsel, Ronald Thwaites QC, was clear about what was going on: an attempt to "saturate the court with irrelevant material at vast expense – a cynical attempt to obfuscate".

Barely had Condliffe himself – a thoroughly shifty character who sent vastly inflated bills to a series of clients and then bullied and threatened them when they were unable to pay – got into the witness box than he was questioned about the bundles. Why had they been delivered in a jumbled-up, unusable state? Condliffe blamed Carter-Fuck. Carter-Fuck blamed Condliffe. "Is it the case that your solicitors' statements are untrue?" asked Thwaites. "That is correct," replied Condliffe. "Your solicitors were lying?" "Yes," the accountant replied.

You don't have to be a £750-an-hour legal expert to spot that when a plaintiff and his lawyers are accusing each other of lying, the case is not destined to be a success. When the judge also pointed out that another piece of Condliffe's evidence was "diametrically opposite to what you said on Friday afternoon", they gave up the ghost. On 6 November 2001, after the Carter-Fuck team had requested an adjournment to "consider their position", it was announced that Condliffe was dropping his action and would pay £100,000 towards *Private Eye*'s costs. At a bankruptcy hearing the following year he again blamed the whole thing on his solicitors: "I was told by PCR that it had been done to 'make life difficult' for the other side's solicitors so that they would be encouraged to offer settlement terms."

Carter-Fuck denied this. But why might they

"The clear assumption was that the Eye *would get stuffed for all these costs. It was just a fantastically good win"* Ian Hislop

have wished to do so? The firm were representing Condliffe on a Conditional Fee Agreement, aka no-win-no-fee, which allows lawyers to charge up to twice their normal (extortionate) fees to the losing side if they should emerge victorious. Doubles all round, in other words. If the *Eye* had lost, the magazine would have had to pay more than a million pounds, and would almost certainly have been put out of business. "It was *fantastically* expensive, ten years' worth of costs against Carter-Ruck, who had churned all the way," says Hislop. "The clear assumption at every point was that the *Eye* would get stuffed for all these costs. It was just a fantastically good win." It was Carter-Fuck who were left out of pocket and Condliffe who got the enormous bill. The last word went to Robin Shaw, the *Eye*'s solicitor. "As we went to court, a partner at Carter-Ruck was gloating about buying himself a Ferrari when they won. We bought him a Dinky-toy Ferrari instead."[144]

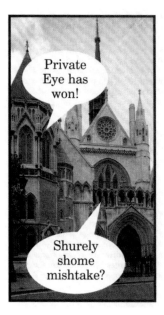

MIRROR BUILDING, Peter Cook leads
Eye raid on
Following Robert Maxwell's 1986 libel victory over the Eye *(☞) he decided to add insult to injury.*

Media Week, 12 December 1986:

This week's issue of *Private Eye* was banned by the country's two largest distributors, WH Smith and John Menzies, on legal advice. The special edition of the magazine, at more than double the usual cover price, was intended to raise funds to defray libel damages. But the distributors were advised that litigation was possible if the publication was distributed. Robert Maxwell's own spoof version of the magazine, *Not Private Eye*, goes on sale later this week, with a print run reported at one million.

Ian Hislop: He'd managed to get *Private Eye* taken off the newsstands, completely. Smiths wouldn't sell us. And he decided he'd print a copy of a magazine called *Not Private Eye* on the Mirror presses.[145]

Christopher Silvester: John Penrose, who was a *Mirror* journalist, had been given the invidious task of producing this spoof. He was one of these Mirror Group executives who obviously didn't have enough to do. So they made him produce this thing. It was basically a piss-take spoof of *Private Eye*, attacking us. It was quite a funny, clever idea actually. Biter bit and all that. But the problem was that the humour and satire was incredibly lame.

Hislop: He printed a full-frontal naked caricature of myself with detailed pubic hair and genitals on display. In its pages I was accused, among other things, of being brainless, drunk, constantly looking up women's skirts, 'fat and perfectly dreadful', eating with my mouth open and of being a midget and a closet homosexual who "smells a bit funny".[146]

Silvester: If it had been brilliant, then of course it would have been very memorable. But it wasn't.

Hislop: Cookie said "Let's send a crate of whisky over to the people who are putting it together, because they won't want to do it, they'll have been ordered to do this." So we sent this crate of whisky over. About two hours later, Cookie said "Let's phone them up and see what's happened." We phoned up, and the four people doing it were completely legless.[147]

Silvester: Cook was saying "Why don't we come over?" Because they'd just finished putting this spoof magazine to bed, and Penrose was pissed, and he basically just invited us over, not quite understanding what this meant. I think he just thought he was inviting Cook over but we all turned up.

Dave Cash: There was Peter, Hislop, Silvester, me and Maggie Lunn. We got a taxi round there and we sort of conned our way in to the Mirror building.

Hislop: It was the first time I realised that if you're very famous you can do anything, because security stopped us and said "Have you got passes?" and we had to say no. Then Cookie appeared and said "We're just going upstairs, lads, is that all right?" And they said, "Oh, it's Peter Cook," and let us in.

Cash: We got up to whatever floor Maxwell's office was on, and these guys were well into the whisky by now. Everyone boozing away, and we saw a dummy of what they were producing. And someone surreptitiously scooped it up, and tucked it away and took it.

Hislop: It was our equivalent of *The Guns of Navarone*. I stole the dummy, and I said, "Let's go, Peter." He said "Oh no, I haven't had half enough fun yet." He then called the *Mirror* catering department and ordered a crate of champagne for us.

Silvester: We went into the chairman's office, and there was Penrose drinking whisky. And we all sat around drinking. There was a lot of banter.

Hislop: So there we were with the champagne. I said "Can we go, Peter?" He said "Why don't we get the *Mirror* picture desk to take a picture of us drinking the champagne?"

Cash: And we got them to take photos of John Penrose pissed and stretched out … it was Peter's booze that did it, and they were so pleased that Peter came. They were meant to be very anti-*Private Eye* but they didn't give a fuck really. It was a very jolly evening, and we all got very pissed.

Hislop: Then we got crayons and wrote "Hello Captain Bob" all over the windows.

Silvester: And I do remember at some stage – because Maxwell was in New York – Cook decided to ring up Maxwell's office there.

Hislop: Peter said "Guess where we are?"

Elizabeth Cook: He rang me from Maxwell's office too. He just said "I'm sitting in Robert Maxwell's chair" or something. He just wanted me to know.

Hislop: And then security burst in and removed us. But we had the dummy.

Cash: So we had the front cover of *Not Private Eye*, and on it they portrayed Ingrams as Himmler or someone, as a Nazi figure. And when I got this I phoned W. H. Smith up to discuss whether they were going to be distributing this publication. I said 'Obviously as far as *Private Eye* is concerned you can do what you wish. But I do know that Richard Ingrams is very sensitive about being called a Nazi.'

Times, 10 December 1986:

Mr Robert Maxwell's tit-for-tat battle with *Private Eye* backfired yesterday when W. H. Smith, the country's largest news wholesaler, announced that it would not be distributing spoof copies of the satirical magazine *Not Private Eye* due to be published by Mirror Group Newspapers today.

Maxwell was forced to intervene.

Guardian, 12 December 1986:

On Wednesday Maxwell got on the blower to Smiths and assured them that he wouldn't be taking action against the Eye, prompting Smiths to say they would handle it after all. But Maxwell also told Smiths that he had been advised by counsel that his derivative organ, *Not*, carried no libel risks. This ran counter to advice Smiths had from their own solicitors, but they went ahead and lifted the ban on *Not* as well.

So which sold better? All was revealed in a photograph in the Eye *two months later.*

Not Private Eye Spy

Submitted by Jonathan Buckmaster. £5 paid for similar submissions. *(SAE required for return of photographs. No transparencies.)*

MMR

Dr Andrew Wakefield first made his claim that the Measles, Mumps and Rubella vaccine might be linked to an increased risk of autism and bowel disorders in February 1998. The *Eye* followed the story up immediately – with a column entitled 'National Bad Science Week' which decried his "showy press conference" and warned that "translating sympathy for the rare victims of adverse reactions to vaccines into approval for Wakefield is to court flapdoodle ... Wakefield hasn't proved the most basic connection using any of the available essays."

The column was the work of Emily Green. "She was a scientist who went off to America, and that was the last time we had a good science column, which the *Eye*'s always been deficient on, there's no two ways about that," says Ian Hislop. "I'm very unsure when you head into those waters, and it seems to me to be something that we have never done very well." It was, however, to be far from the last word that the *Eye* published on the topic of MMR.

The magazine returned to the subject in January 2001 when Wakefield claimed in a further paper that the triple vaccine had been introduced without adequate safety trials, and was publicly slapped down by the Department of Health as a result. "We joined the MMR a few years in, when I thought it had turned into a story about that rather than the science of it," says Hislop. "It seemed to me that there were questions to ask about Wakefield's treatment, about whistleblowing generally, and what if he was right? In those days, it looked as though two other researchers in Ireland and America would replicate his tests, which they didn't. I think I was quite swayed by the parents who said 'He's being portrayed as a lunatic and a megalomaniac but he took our children seriously when they had terrible bowel problems and he was a great clinician.' The picture of him painted as a madman on the make I didn't buy."

Both Hislop and Heather Mills, the *Eye* journalist who led the paper's coverage of the issue from 2001 onwards, still firmly believe there was a story that needed to be reported at the time. "The parents had a class action, and they had legal aid for it, they had to go through various hoops to get legal aid. It's a huge story! An absolute story!" points out Mills. "At the

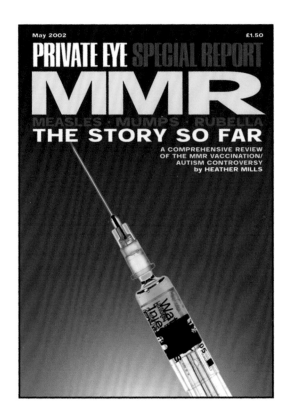

time when all that was being written there was a very senior person – I would never name him – who behind the scenes was saying to me 'There is something behind this.' And now he will not accept my phone calls. And then it became all about Wakefield, a kind of ludicrous polarisation where you were either anti-vaccine or you weren't. It just never occurred to me at the time that it would be perceived to be so partisan."

Hislop recalls the discussions surrounding the stand-alone special report, *MMR: The Story So Far*, which the magazine published in May 2002. "I can remember saying 'We must have a page about how good vaccines are,' which we did. I remember arguing about the cover, because we put an injection on it, thinking 'Is that scaremongering because people don't like injections?'"

"I don't feel there was professional sloppiness or anything," says Hislop. "It isn't as though drugs that are approved by scientific bodies and accepted by scientists then always turn out to be great. There are examples in history where journalists, despite their stupidity and lack of scientific qualifications, point out things that are going wrong. Thalidomide onwards."

Unfortunately, as Dr Phil Hammond, aka M.D. (☞), pointed out in the "peer review" Hislop commissioned for the *Eye* in February 2010, "This could have been one, but it wasn't … *Private Eye* got it wrong on MMR." He concluded, in the wake of the General Medical Council's ruling that Wakefield had acted unethically (he was later struck off), that the magazine should have "conceded the argument" in 2005, after a Cochrane review, "the most rigorous and independent analysis of medical trials in existence", concluded that there was no credible evidence of a link between MMR and autism. The *Eye* had reported the Cochrane review's conclusions at the time.

Ironically, while the *Eye*'s MMR coverage was at its height, Muckspreader – aka Christopher Booker and Richard North – was tearing into the Ministry of Agriculture for its handling of the Foot and Mouth epidemic (☞) as "suicidally ignorant in objecting to vaccination based on their complete failure to grasp modern vaccine science". The same accusation would be thrown at the magazine many times over MMR in subsequent years.

MOHAMMED, Prophet (not pictured)

The *Eye*'s failure to print the twelve cartoons commissioned by the newspaper *Jyllands-Posten* which led to riots around the world in February 2006 was deplored by some readers: "You have been cowed by a bunch of religious bigots … you lost your bottle … pathetic."

Where cartoonists hide

Mike Turner's reaction to the controversy, from *Eye* 1152

Another reader pointed out that the *Eye* had offered something none of the rest of the British media, busy egging the controversy on, had bothered with: "an attempt to analyse the 12 cartoons. So far as I am aware no other publication has tried such a commonsense approach to the issue." The *Eye* was, therefore, the only publication to point out that three of the twelve cartoons were actually critical of the newspaper, calling the attempt to depict Mohammed a "PR stunt" by "a bunch of reactionary provocateurs".

Besides, as Ian Hislop pointed out at the time, "Only one of the cartoons was any good anyway."

MONKHOUSE, Bob, *Eye* supporter

Mahogany-hued funnyman Bob Monkhouse was one of the acts to appear at 1965's "Rustle of Spring", a fund-raising benefit concert which followed the Lord Liver of Cesspool verdict (☞).

Even more surprisingly, so was Arthur Mullard.

MORON, Piers, campaign against Ian Hislop

In 2002 the *Daily Mirror* declared war on Ian Hislop for having the temerity to publish stories about its editor Piers Mogan's dodgy behaviour in precisely the way his own paper recorded that of others.

The "City Slickers" case – in which Moron and other *Mirror* staff bought shares in companies just before they were hyped in the paper's share-tipping column, and then gave contradictory and far-fetched accounts of how and why this came to happen to different official inquiries into the affair – has been well covered, not least in the pages of the *Eye*. Less widely reported was the topic that Hislop believes really sparked the Mirrorman's ire: the fact that in 2000 he walked out on wife Marion and their children for the journalist Marina Hyde, who was sacked from the *Sun* as a result of their affair and had to go and work on the *Guardian* instead. When "Street of Shame" made a further reference to this in May 2002 in an article about newspaper coverage of the sacking of Hislop's *Have I Got News for You* colleague Angus Deayton – "Is Piers Morgan really in a position to dispense advice on marital fidelity?" – war was declared. "Piers, like a lot of journalists, is incredibly thin-skinned," says Hislop. "And he just could not bear the thought that what had been staple fodder for his entire tabloid career could be used on him. There was no one fiercer in the defence of the public's right to know about public figures until it happened to him. And he just went mental."

Two days later the *Mirror*, which had recently announced that it was to "embrace serious journalism and move away from blanket celebrity news and gossip", launched a new campaign. "WANTED!" shrieked page 3 over a vast mugshot of the *Eye* editor. "£50 reward for information leading to the ridicule, embarrassment and humiliation of Ian 'The Gnome' Hislop … He makes a career from humiliating, embarrassing, ridiculing and abusing people. The one major star and hypocritical public figure who obviously escapes this treatment is one Ian Hislop. So it seems only fair to see what ghastly skeletons may fester in his secret cupboards."

So what dirt did they dig? Er … nothing worth printing, even though increasingly desperate pleas to readers for material continued to appear for almost a year. "Someone from the *Mirror* told me they'd looked at the dossier, which was like one of those old cartoons of opening it up and a fly comes out – literally there wasn't anything in there," says its subject. "He had a story once – Man Got Drunk at Oxford Shock – I felt I could cope with that."

It wasn't for want of trying though. "They had a photographer doorstepping me every morning, there when I went to do the school run, which was embarrassing. A phenomenal waste of the *Mirror*'s money. He had a terrible fright because there's an ex-copper who lives near me and he found this bloke just up the lane, sitting in his car, waiting. And he gave him the fright of his life. He said 'Are you a paedophile? I've seen you hanging around. We've got kids in this street. What the fuck are you doing?' It was just wonderful."

Back in Canary Wharf, a crack team was on the case. "They contacted a lot of people I knew from school on Friends Reunited. I got quite a lot of very nice correspondence – a man called Chris Barraclough said 'I got approached by the *Mirror* and asked "Can you tell me anything about Ian Hislop at school?" and I said "Yes, I can tell you to sod off."'"

They also – even Lunchtime O'Booze wouldn't have managed this one – tried to bribe his vicar. "They sent a load of journalists down to the village, and I got a phone call from the vicar. He said 'They wanted to know whether you'd confessed any dirt at Confession.' Which strikes me as two amazing misapprehensions: A, they don't really understand the way the Church of England works, and B, that you would then tell them!"

What made this all rather more awkward was the fact that one of the junior Hislops shared a primary school with a Moron minor (or rather, a Pugh-Morgan minor, his sons having retained the double-barrelled surname Moron dropped to try and fit in on the tabloids). "We had to awkwardly stand on sports day and watch our sons in the races. So that was very embarrassing for a while." Moron, naturally, cited this as yet more evidence of Hislop's hypocrisy. "But as I said to him at the time, that's what we call being polite, being civilised. If I meet you in the classroom I'm not going to say 'You're a thief and you're having an affair with the woman from the *Sun*' in front of a group of seven-year-olds."

The best the *Mirror* ever managed to print was a full-page photo of Hislop looking, in the paper's words, "dishevelled, unshaven and with an arm in a sling". Even their dimmest readers might have been able to work out that the sling (the result of "a fairly major operation on my shoulder") had put his shaving hand out of action, and that, rather than, er, "the investigation that's got all Britain talking" was responsible for his appearance. At Christmas a group of hacks from the paper managed to make themselves very unpopular by raiding a bookshop where the *Eye*'s joke team were signing copies of their *Annual* – "We had a queue 150 people long waiting to get their books signed, who all started saying 'Oh, get lost!' to these incredibly sad people with their 'Gnome Go Home' banners. It was wonderful, we didn't have to do anything because the crowd did it for us. 'I've been waiting ages, can you stop this?'" Eventually, with a last pathetic gasp of defiance in March 2003 – "Our sensational series the Hidden Hislop is just waiting for a quiet spring week to be unleashed" – the whole thing petered out. "I presume at some point someone from the *Mirror* said to him 'What is the point of this?'" says Hislop. A year later they said something similar about the fake photos of soldiers abusing Iraqis Morgan had printed, and sacked him.

"I do think in retrospect it's very good for anybody in our game to have that done to you," says Hislop now. "Because it does make you think about it. Watching the pack in action – that capricious nature of 'I will do this to you because I can' – as an editor I thought it was very good because if you're going to put resources on to a story it had better not be because you don't like the person, it had better be because there's something there."

☞ FRASER, Jason; RUBBISH, stolen and passed to Mohamed Fayed

MOSS, Stirling

So delighted was Stirling Moss with his depiction in the "Aesop Revisited" strip in September 1962 as a "rather a boring little man, introducing TV programmes on subjects about which he knows nothing" that he telephoned the office. When they just laughed at him he was forced to write a letter: "It certainly was me on the telephone and not a mimic." He wanted permission to reproduce the cartoon as his personal Christmas card.

"This sort of thing happens with depressing frequency," sighed Richard Ingrams.

"MOST UNPLEASANT THING IN BRITISH JOURNALISM"

May 1976 was an interesting month for the *Eye*. James Goldsmith had been given leave to bring a prosecution for criminal libel against Richard Ingrams and Patrick Marnham just weeks before (☞ GOLDENBALLS). Takings were well down thanks to his action against the magazine's distributors. Everyone's wages had been halved. Former editor Christopher Booker

"It is hard for me not to feel some paternal sympathy. I still draw part of my wages from Private Eye, *and I suppose that I have probably contributed more words to it over the years than anyone except Richard Ingrams himself"*

Christopher Booker, *Spectator*, 1976

decided that this was the ideal moment to go into print attacking his colleagues.

"It is hard for me not to feel some paternal sympathy. I still draw part of my wages from *Private Eye*, and I suppose that I have probably contributed more words to it over the years than anyone except Richard Ingrams himself," he pondered in the *Spectator*. "On the other hand, it is hard not to view some of the directions the magazine has taken in recent years with distaste, and to feel that it has only too predictably brought some of its present troubles on itself. There has been a streak of petty nastiness about some of the contents, coupled with a carelessness about whether things are true or even probable, that has made *Private Eye* on its day a strong candidate for the most unpleasant thing in British journalism."[148]

With readers rallying round and firing off cheques to the Goldenballs fund and letters supportive of the *Eye* even making their way into the *Times*, it was yet another example of Booker finding a consensus and going against it. But he insists he was not merely being contrary for the sake of it. "Oh gosh, I was really angry," he says now. "Richard liked to lay in to people, and there were three people who I happened to know, Nick Bethell, and Arianna Stassinopoulos, and Bennie Gray. All three of them had been wickedly maligned, and actually all three of them in the end sued *Private Eye* and all of them won. Bennie Gray and I were working together. One of his enemies came to *Private Eye* with this completely fictitious story. Someone said 'We've got this really good story about Booker's friend Bennie Gray.' And in it went, and I was absolutely livid. Bennie was very upset."

Booker has long been convinced that this is all Barry Fantoni's fault. "For some reason he was sitting in the editorial chair. I hope, if I was being really generous to Richard, he wouldn't have allowed it to go in. But he probably wouldn't have checked it. Because Richard's quite a shifty fellow. He would have probably thought 'This is a good mischievous piece so we'll put it in.'" Ingrams gleefully confirmed his editorial policy in a 1991 documentary: "If someone is a friend, they're more than ever likely to be attacked. For example, Christopher Booker is a great friend of Laurens van der Post, but he [van der Post] is attacked every week and ridiculed in Sylvie Krin, partly for that reason, I regret to say!"[149]

What did Richard make of the attack from his predecessor as editor and current right-hand man? "I think I'd kind of got used to Booker being like that, and I probably didn't take too much notice of him. He's always been like that." He even remained unsurprised when, a couple of decades later, Booker joined forces with Goldsmith himself in the Referendum Party: "Booker has a weakness for – he's always looking for gurus, and leaders to follow."

Other colleagues were less indulgent. A photo of Booker was adapted and has had pride of place in the office ever since:

Auberon Waugh wrote to the *Spectator* calling Booker a "shitty little prig". "Not my favourite fellow, Auberon Waugh," mutters Booker now. "He was a total shit. They all thought it was jolly naughty of me to write it while the Goldsmith thing was going on. I can see why they were upset, because they felt defensive. I was never involved in any way in the Goldsmith thing. And after all they did get it wrong."
☞ BOOKER, Christopher, Sacking of, 1963

MRS WILSON'S DIARY

It was Peter Cook who noted the comic potential of a newspaper interview in which Harold Wilson's wife Mary, a keen poet, said she planned to keep a diary of their time at Number 10. "He wanted to send Wilson up as a kind of funny, provincial man in a Gannex mac who didn't really know what he was doing," says Richard Ingrams. But apart from participating in its first instalment – in which Mary bid "Farewell! Hampstead Garden Suburb / With your friendly bustle and hubbub / Oh! To see 'WELCOME' written on the mat again / And have another glass of Sanatogen" – Cook did not write the new feature. That was left to the duo who were in 1964, nominally at least, the magazine's co-editors: Ingrams and John Wells.

Wells, who declared that "editing the magazine with Richard was unbearable. I couldn't get anything past him at all,"[150] had found his metier. He may have had plenty of other achievements to his name, but co-writing surreal farces set behind the door of Number 10 with Richard Ingrams was what he was put on earth to do. Barry Fantoni (☞), who also duetted with Wells on other projects, says his talents were unparalleled "if the piece involved caricature, or character. John was a decorator, a gilder, a gold-leaf merchant, and very, very good at it. Plots weren't his great strength." But with "Mrs Wilson's Diary" he had Ingrams to provide those. "I was naturally involved in what had been going on in a particular week, the political scene, so perhaps I dictated that," reckoned Ingrams when he reflected on their partnership. "John's talent was much more for the sort of word play, fantasy and ludicrous touches that he put in." These were apparent from day one, when the couple arrive at Number 10 only to discover that Mrs Douglas-Home has left them the washing-up and Harold's security man, Inspector Trimfitting, has to sleep between them in the marital bed to ensure the prime minister's safety. Throughout, Mrs Wilson –

Inspector Trimfittering, Harold's personal bodyguard, keeps a close watch

or Gladys, as Harold insists on addressing her – remains a still small voice of calm amid the madness, ever ready to knock up a fork lunch of Spam, a tin of Heinz Italian-Style Ravioli or just a large glass of Wincarnis at a moment's notice and serve them to such guests as General de Gaulle, the Callaghans from next door, or Wedgie Benn in "a stand-up Jimmy Hendrix Experience-style wig and gold-rimmed dark glasses".

"Giles [her son] used to bring it in, and I used to read it," Mary Wilson told the BBC in 1967 when she was asked her opinion of the material which appeared under her byline. "My reaction was that I could have done it so much better myself. I thought it was pretty poor stuff."

She went even further after Harold's departure from Number 10 in 1976, in an interview with *Woman* magazine: "She says that one of the best things about the resignation will be that the satirist John Wells would not be able to write

Ingrams and Wells at work in the office

"I was told by one of Wilson's aides, a civil servant, that he found it very difficult at times to be able to tell if he'd heard of something through being in his job or whether he'd read it in 'Mrs Wilson's Diary'" Richard Ingrams

about her any more in the magazine *Private Eye*. 'If I ever meet that man I shall bite him.'" When they finally did meet, both escaped without a mauling. "I put on a rather regal air, and entertained him in the flat, and we got on like a house on fire. He was a lovely man," she said in 2004. She even insisted she eventually saw the funny side of the "Diary". "I used to get so angry, and then I used to roar with laughter because if they only knew what went on inside Number 10, it was much funnier than that."[151]

Mrs Wilson's image as a Hilda Ogdenesque housewife was not entirely of the *Eye*'s making. After Harold was first elected Labour leader she had given the press a tour of their home, "and Giles, then sixteen, had a mobile of flying storks in his bedroom. Cyril Aynsley [of the *Express*] said that I had flying ducks on the wall. I never got rid of those bloody flying ducks. They came with me everywhere!"[152] And if the "Diary"'s depiction of Harold as a bumbling homebody was not entirely accurate, it was certainly no further from reality than the image he was trying to project of himself – it was left to the *Eye*'s serious pages to point out that he smoked his trademark pipe only in public.

The true extent of his Walter Mittyishness would not however be revealed until his second administration in the 1970s, when some of his fantasies, and the characters he had gathered around him, turned out to be more extraordinary than anything Wells and Ingrams would have dared dream up (☞ FORKBENDER, Lady; PRIVATE SPY). "I was told by one of Wilson's aides, a civil servant, that he found it very difficult at times to be able to tell if he'd heard of something through being in his job or whether he'd read it in 'Mrs Wilson's Diary', that it was so close at times to what had happened," remembered Ingrams. Cook reckoned it was "my first experience of the phenomenon whereby you make something up, and Downing Street begin to think you've got inside information, that people are leaking facts to you. Harold Wilson was quite sure that somebody was informing to us."

☞ DEAR BILL; LORD CHAMBERLAIN, role as censor of *Mrs Wilson's Diary*; NUMBER 10, Richard Ingrams's visits to

MUGS

A selection of the various promotional mugs produced and sold by _Private Eye_ over the years

MURDOCH, Campbell

One name which regularly appeared in the contributors' list during the _Eye_'s first two years was Campbell Murdoch. Who he? None other than John Wells, keen not to rock the boat at Eton College, where he was working as a French master. Wells had been informed on his arrival that his predecessor, David Cornwell, was not thought the right sort for the school due to his having "friends in London" (he did rather better later in life when he adopted the pen name John le Carré). So the headmaster was not best pleased when he discovered that his new French master was appearing in the Room at the Top cabaret in Ilford alongside Ingrams, Willie Rushton and top satirist Barbara Windsor – not least because the news arrived courtesy of a _Daily Mail_ article headlined "ETON MASTER PEDDLES SMUT IN EAST END".

Wells left Eton soon afterwards.

MUTT AND JEFF

Tom Jamieson and Nev Fountain are the vanguard of the third generation of jokewriters to join Private Eye.

Nev: We met on [Radio 4's] _Week Ending_ in about 1996. We worked separately on that,

MURAL

Barry Fantoni (☞) was not impressed by the *Eye*'s HQ at 22 Greek Street, Soho. "It was a shit office. So I painted the big wall upstairs and asked everyone to have a go at it. It must still be there under the emulsion."

L–R: Bust of journalist Alan Brien, an early contributor, by Willie Rushton; portrait of Claud Cockburn (WR); editorial assistant Anne Chisholm (WR); (small trio at front) subscriptions assistants Amanda (WR) and Doris, Dave Cash by Gillian Brooke; (at back) Tony Rushton by Richard Ingrams; editorial secretary Jennifer Wedderspoon holding a baby Bernard Levin (WR); printer John Thorpe (WR); Ralph Steadman self-portrait holding up coin bearing the image of Tony Rushton; (in profile at centre) Christopher Logue and Barry Fantoni (WR); small-ads seller Gillian Brooke (Ralph Steadman); (on mural within mural at top) Gerald Scarfe self-portrait among political figures; Peter Usborne (by Barry Fantoni) holding magazine featuring Christopher Booker; (in front, in boaters) distributor Charles Harness, Willie Rushton and John Wells (WR); (with halo) Richard Ingrams (BF); Mary Ingrams and their son Fred (BF).

Tom (L) and Nev (R):
like Ant and Dec, they
always stand the
right way round for
photos for ease of
identification

and we started our writing partnership after *Week Ending* folded.

Nev: When we started doing radio we were doing lots of shows, *Loose Ends*, the *News Quiz*, we were doing *Dead Ringers*, and we just thought we'd put our elbows out in every direction we could think of.

Tom: We basically just lobbed some copy in [the *Eye*'s] direction. It was in September 1999.

Nev: We wrote about ten articles – I remember one was about Carol Vorderman – and we sent them in. And then Ian [Hislop] wrote us this nice note back saying –

Tom: Thanks but no thanks.

Nev: "No, we don't take stuff from freelancers, nice though this stuff is …"

Tom: So we wrote another load of stuff for the next issue, and got another nice letter saying "Thank you for your very excellent copy, but no." And then we wrote *another* load of stuff and got one thing in. It shows the power of annoying people!

Nev: I don't know why we did it.

Tom: Why did we do it? We wouldn't do it now. This is the problem of when you become battle-hardened, you just give up, don't you? When you're new and young you're just stupid.

Nev: Persistency is a good trait in people who can actually do it. For the nutters, persistency is bad. But you never know if you're a nutter or not.

Ian Hislop: Given how many joke pages there are, the team was not filling it. And Nick and I could and did fill a lot, but you just want some other voices really. You just want some more to choose from. From outside I use Richard Jolley a lot [☞ RGJ]. There's a bloke called Nick Tolson who occasionally gets stuff in, mostly visual stuff like the Twin Towers made out of sandwiches, odd things – he's slightly more off the wall. Matt Owen sends in stuff. Tom and Nev sort of work at a tangent really. They've got a slightly different set of interests which they send in on their own and have done for ten years or more. They're terrifically solid, funny.

Nev: It's been an absolute bedrock of our writing career, always there in the background. In a time when writing is short-term and people just turn their backs on you the minute you stop being useful, the *Eye* has been extremely faithful to us. Once you're in, you're looked after, and we really appreciate that.

Tom: And every other aspect of our business – which is fair enough – is youth, youth, youth, what's the new thing, who's the new person we're excited about? That's every other aspect of comedy writing, and the *Eye* has been very different.

At first – just as Richard Ingrams had done with him – Ian Hislop kept the new contributors a secret from the old guard until they were well established.

Tom: We remember the levels, from being secret, to having a nickname, to being in the office.

Nev: Richard Ingrams used to call us Mutt and Jeff.

Tom: That was the breakthrough, when Richard gave us a nickname and actually acknowledged our presence.

Ian Hislop: They were furious. Scornful. They referred to them as "Mutt and Jeff", which I believe is a reference to something in the music hall in 1904 or something! And then Barry started referring to himself and Richard as Fant and Dick. But I think it's conceded now that they are pretty funny.

"NEASDEN" - CENTRE

CAM. 1
MS RUSHTON

Piano live

CAMS. 2 & 3 as dir.
(shots 99 - 109)

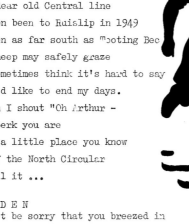

NASTY NIP
IN THE AIR,
LOBETHRUST

I've been as far as Orpington
Tufnell Park and Golders Green
Seen the northern lights of Harlesden
And visited East Sheen.
I've travelled out to Ongar
On the dear old Central line
I've even been to Ruislip in 1949
I've been as far south as Tooting Bec
Where sheep may safely graze
And I sometimes think it's hard to say
Where I'd like to end my days.
But then I shout "Oh Arthur -
What a berk you are
There's a little place you know
Just off the North Circular
They call it ...

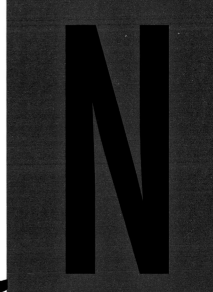

N E A S D E N
You won't be sorry that you breezed in
The traffic lights and yellow lines
And the illuminated signs
All say welcome to the borough
That everybody's pleased in.
Neasden
Where the birds sing in the breeze-den
You can hear the blackbirds coo
So why not take the Bakerloo
It'll work out that much cheaper
If you buy a seasden.

Tape:
Orch back

OCCER
TALK IN

A Song
r Neasden

THE NEW BOYS (22)
Dr Gordon Brown

THE new Labour Member for Dunfermline
East, Dr Gordon Brown, is typical of the new
brand of mediocre,
middle-class
careerists who make
up an increasing pro-
portion of the un-
distinguished lobby-
fodder which Labour
habitually returns
from Scotland, though
he has greater acade...
pretens...

BARE BARE BARE BARE BARE BARE

PRIVATE EYE

.. and where was
he standing ?

GAZINE
T BENDS OVER

NAMES, rejected for magazine

A name for the new organ was hammered out over the course of a number of nights in the pub in the autumn of 1961, with helpful suggestions from friends.

Bent

"It was Bruce Page's idea to call it 'Bent'," sniffs Christopher Booker of his *Liberal News* colleague. "I never liked that idea."

Tumbril

Presumably referring to the favoured transport for the guillotine-bound during the French Revolution, although the alternative, "a cart that tips to empty its load, esp. one carrying dung" (OED), seems equally appropriate.

The Flesh's Weekly

A good pun, but one that might have lost its effect over five decades.

The British Letter

Because it was meant to be a bit like *Le Canard Enchaîné*, the French satirical magazine which had been running since 1915. And French gives you French Letter, which is a bit rude, so, British Letter … no, you're right, it's rubbish. Whose round is it?

The Yellow Press

Co-founder Peter Usborne had the idea of making the magazine stand out, just as the pink *Financial Times* does, by printing it on yellow paper. But no one liked the name. Nor were they bothered that he had gone ahead and purchased reams of yellow paper in preparation.

The Bladder

Richard Ingrams proposed "The Bladder". "It combined an element of coarseness with a reference to the Court Jester. Unfortunately, [Willie] Rushton's grandmother, who was at that time staying with him, suffered from a severe bladder complaint. He explained that it would be most embarrassing to return home of an evening to be greeted with cries of 'How's "The Bladder"?' and suchlike."[153]

Finger

One from the other co-founder Andrew Osmond. "I had been looking at the Lord Kitchener recruiting poster. We would be putting the finger on people. Then I looked at Kitchener's eye …"

Private Eye

"It was Osmond who suggested 'Private Eye'," remembers Ingrams. John Wells wasn't sure. "I remember thinking it sounded too American, and too much to do with private investigation." But as Ingrams puts it, "by that time everyone was so bored with trying to think up titles that they fell in with his conviction that Private Eye was far and away the best idea".[154]

NATIONAL SERVICE, Near misses during

1956, Korea: Lieutenant **John Wells** visits the Sergeants' Mess and spots "an incongruous baboon-like figure at the harmonium". He doesn't bother to talk to him. It is **Richard Ingrams**, his future writing partner.

1957, Malaya: Ingrams, who has become "more of a Bolshevik" serving in the ranks, spots a Gurkha officer "strutting about in these silly shorts, and I thought 'There goes a real shit'". It is **Andrew Osmond** who will become his friend at Oxford and provide the start-up cash for *Private Eye*.

1958, Cyprus: Coronet **Auberon Waugh** shoots himself in the chest with his own machine-gun. He is visited regularly in hospital by the wife of the island's governor, who "told me many times how much she hoped I would get together with her son at Oxford". The son in question is his future *Eye* roommate **Paul Foot**.

NEASDEN, Origin of *Eye's* obsession with

The first four issues of *Private Eye* were printed by a small off-print litho operation called Huprint discovered by Peter Usborne. Lord Rank, the owner of its parent company, then found out and banned the magazine. But by then the postal address of the printers had sunk into the collective minds of the editorial staff. "Osmond and I used to go off to Neasden with the copy," says Booker. "That's how the Neasden joke arose, because we thought it was a very dim and obscure part of outer London, the epitome of mediocrity. Although it's probably changed dramatically now."

The joke hasn't.

NEASDEN FC

Neasden FC first made an impression on the *Eye* when ashen-faced supremo Ron Knee led them to a series of glorious defeats during the 1970 season: a time when such sporting giants as Bert O'Relli, Dave 'Baldy' Pevsner and one-legged goalkeeper Wally Foot bestrode the hallowed turf. The 1980s brought hooligan excesses as legions of out-of-control fans (Sid and Doris Bonkers) roamed the stadia of Europe engaging in pitched battles with massed police (PC Ned Strangelove) in scenes described as "the actions of human savages running amok like a pack of hungry okapis". Even this paled alongside the 1995 controversy when striker Eddie Depardieu launched a chainsaw attack on a fan who taunted him from the sidelines as a "useless French git".

In recent years the team have plunged out of the North Circular League and the pages of *Private Eye* alike. "I was sorry to see Neasden go," says ashen-faced Barry Fantoni, who remains a devoted fan. "Ian seemed not to be interested in, and certainly not to know much about, football." As the seasons roll on with "The Premiershits" lifting the trophies – Paul Wood won Sports Cartoonist of the Year in 2010 for his regular strip – it does indeed appear that referee Hislop has blown his whistle for full time.

NEILL, Andrew, Gratuitous excuse to print photograph of

NEWMAN, Nick, on his early cartoon strips

"I finished at university in '79 [☞ *PASSING WIND*]. And then I was working as a serious journalist – I'd got on the Haymarket Training Scheme and had a job on *Management Today* writing very long boring pieces about the future of the steel industry. And Ian would come up once a week and we'd have lunch and then he'd go and do the *Eye*. I was full of admiration for him having the nerve, because it was quite a scary place to go in to.

"Sorry, didn't we tell you? We changed it to best out of three . . ."

I gave stuff to Ian to pass on to the mag, and I think the first cartoon I got in was an idea that Richard had, and asked me to draw up, and of course I was absolutely over the moon. And then it becomes easier once you've got in, because they're aware of your stuff, and I started selling one or two a month.

1981: Richard suggested I started doing a cartoon strip, "Bod". Which was very bad! Strips are very hard things to do. Much

BOD   by Hislop & Newman

harder than spot cartoons. If they're good, you build character into them, and character is the hard thing to do.

1982: Then Richard encouraged Ian and I to do a strip called "Forbidden Alliance", which was a parody of a sort of teenage magazine, about the Liberals and the SDP. It was completely out of my comfort zone of drawing.

1983: We did another strip called "Battle for Britain" by Monty Stubble (a pun which no one understood right up until the last panel when it said "I was Monty Stubble").

1987: I particularly liked "Dan Dire" – it just lent itself to good jokes about sci-fi – David Owen becoming Doctor Who the Waste of Time Lord, and Nigel Lawson being Blubba the Hut. It was a huge amount of work – it took me a day to draw those things, and then we had to get it to a lettering person on the other side of London. Incredibly time consuming, a fantastic amount of work. And gradually as Ian and I did more jokes for the magazine, and when Ian took over as editor, we sort of ran out of time for doing that sort of thing."

Since 1986, Newman has been part of the regular joke-writing team on the magazine (☞ JOKE-WRITING TEAMS, Extraordinary longevity of). He has, however, found time to chronicle the adventures of both "Prehistoric First Family the Clintstones" and "Dave Snooty and his Pals" ("I love the Snooty strip, it makes me laugh endlessly," says Hislop), as well as publishers "Snipcock and Tweed" (☞ STRIPS, Longest-running).

NEWS QUIZ

Radio 4's *News Quiz* started out in 1977 with two opposing teams made up of staff from *Private Eye* and *Punch*. They were led by respective editors Richard Ingrams and Alan Coren. Former chairman Barry Took remembered his favourite episodes as those when Peter Cook would appear for the *Eye*. "Richard and Peter would emerge to be greeted by the audience looking as if they'd drifted into the studio from cardboard city. In my introduction I'd say thinks like 'Please don't laugh, they've made a special effort,' while the audience, who loved them, cheered, applauded and roared with laughter."[155] Ian Hislop remembers the best double act as being Ingrams and John Wells: "They were hysterical together – just brilliant, that was always the top team you hoped for when you switched on." Later he

inherited the captaincy as a double-act with his predecessor – "We used to do a sort of 'You're very old, I'm not' double act for ages" – before being recruited for the TV version, *Have I Got News for You* (☞).

Thirty-four years on, the *Eye* is still represented on the programme by the only series regular from the world of journalism rather than stand-up comedy, Francis Wheen.

NIGHT SHIFT, strange goings-on at the *Eye* after hours

Barry Fantoni's night time antics (☞) and Michael Gillard's unsociable hours (☞ SLICKER) are far from the only odd activity to occur after the office has closed for the day. In the early 1960s Richard Ingrams invited itinerant poet Michael Horovitz to make use of the office whenever he needed; five decades and several office moves later he still pops up at odd hours to use the photocopier and phones, occasionally leaving behind small gifts of organic vegetables which are some way past their best.

For some time in the late 1970s and early 1980s – including the period when the "Wimmin" column of "loony feminist nonsense" was a regular feature in the magazine – advertising manager Celia Boggis used the office in the evenings as a venue for Women in Publishing meetings. "Occasionally I'd forgotten something and I'd go back to the office and there would be all these militant women sitting around – 'aargh, there's a man in the place!'" remembers Steve Mann fondly. Boggis's partner, a voluminously-bearded crop circle enthusiast, also used the office after hours to put together pamphlets on unexplained phenomena.

Impressively, editorial assistant Rowan Pelling, later to become editrix of the *Erotic Review* and agony aunt for the *Mail on Sunday*, spent some time in the early 1990s actually living in the *Eye* office, sleeping on the sofa in reception. "At the weekends it was pretty much me watching movies on Ian's TV, but in the weekdays there was a steady flow of traffic. The day troops would filter out around 6ish, then a second shadowy force emerged in the manner of Mary Norton's Borrowers," she recalled.[156]

She was not, however, present for the most spectacular out-of-hours culture clash, which occurred one Sunday in 1995. During the lengthy period between the death of Peter Cook and the establishment of exactly who now owned *Private Eye* (☞ WILL, Peter Cook's), his widow Lin made a number of tours of inspection of the magazine's offices. She was not impressed by what she found. "She claimed there were 'signs that some people had been drinking in the office – there was a half-empty bottle in a filing cabinet or something," recalls Francis Wheen. "But on the most famous occasion she was horrified to find there was a piano in the editor's room – a sign of frivolity – and worse still, there was someone playing the piano and Christopher Silvester singing beside it."

"Why was *she* there?" retorts keen part-time crooner Silvester. "I would often come in at weekends and use the office, just to work, you know. And because there was a piano I thought this was a good place to rehearse our musicians, to save money and everything. The six of them would come in with all their instruments, not disturbing anyone…"

NINETY-FOUR, Page
☞ p. 94

NOOKS AND CORNERS
☞ PILOTI.

NOOKS AND CORNERS,
of the New Barbarism

John Betjeman, the poet who invited friendly bombs to fall on Slough, was the *Eye*'s first architecture correspondent. He had become friends with Richard Ingrams through his daughter Candida, who had been at Oxford with the future *Eye* editor and nursed a hopeless crush on him. "He never showed any sign of knowing about my love for him. Once I saw him when I was on my bike and I fell off, but he did not notice."[157]

Betjeman kicked off the grandly titled "Nooks and Corners of the New Barbarism" column in 1971. It was a very different beast to the version which followed under a curtailed title (☞ PILOTI). Betjeman would bash out an ironic appreciation of some concrete monstrosity lately thrown up in the name of modernism and town planning. "Perhaps it was thought that the Portland Stone of the Church Commissioners' new buildings would show up the needless decoration of Wren's Portland Stone, and by its stark simplicity put to shame the extravagance of the Renaissance," he enthused over the notorious Paternoster Square development adjacent to St Paul's Cathedral.

Of the fourteen buildings targeted by Betjeman during his brief stewardship of the column, four have been demolished, five refurbished beyond all recognition, and two – St Catherine's College, Oxford and Brunswick Square in Bloomsbury – listed Grades I and II respectively.

NORTH LONDON, It's Grim Up

☞ STRIPS, Longest-running

NOT.COM

The *Eye*'s attitude to the web revolution can probably best be expressed by the reply offered to a reader who asked in June 1995 about the newly launched "WWW page".

> "Sir – I was just wondering if you had any plans to put further sections of the *Eye* on the net?
> … No. Go *and buy the mag. Ed.*"

It took Rupert Murdoch exactly fifteen more years to come round to this point of view.

"Well done, guys, our greatest competitor is our own website"

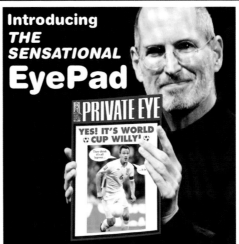
Eye views of new technology from 2000 and 2010

"I couldn't see what the advantages were," says Ian Hislop now. "The culture of everything being free isn't mine. It's the hippy base of the net moving on to the next generation who don't want to pay for anything. Well, that's not me. I don't see why if you pay journalists and writers anyone should get it for free. And I thought 'This isn't going to help.'"

So apart from a slightly peculiar early and temporary alliance with MSN for a bells-and-whistles animated *Eye* website in 1998 – "We were so ignorant about technology we didn't realise they were the great evil," laughs Hislop – the magazine has only ever used its website, private-eye.co.uk, as a sales and marketing tool. "We had a very, very early website, set up by a guy called Nick Rosen who was Maxwell's nephew, so we thought that was quite amusing to get involved with him," recalls former IT boffin Steve Mann, "and Ian said 'Oh, if it sells one subscription it will be worth it,' and if you think about it now probably the bulk of our subs are coming online." And since pressure from users of Twitter helped stave off the Trafigura superinjunction (☞) the magazine has had a presence there too. "Even I noticed that had a huge effect," jokes Hislop. "I thought straight after that we should be saying to those people who read Twitter 'You've just heard of Trafigura. If you'd like to have read about it previously, there's this magazine called *Private Eye*.' I would imagine that most people think the *Eye*'s Twitter posts are basically spam now. What I can't see is that it's an alternative. I'm not putting the whole magazine up, or saying 'I'm going to give this to you for free.'"

As a result, the *Eye* was celebrating its highest circulation figures in eighteen years in 2010, while newspapers like the *Guardian* which had spent the previous two decades enthusiastically seeking out new and expensive ways to give away all their content and more online have seen their sales drop by around a third in the same period.

NOT ENOUGH – ED

"It must have been for the thirtieth anniversary we all had to pose for a photo," recalls Francis Wheen, "John Wells, and probably Cookie, and Booker and Ingrams and Ian and me and

one or two other people, and when this photo appeared I said to Ian 'There are all of the old boys all with their full heads of hair looking incredibly youthful and there's you and I letting the side down looking about twice as old as any of the oldies.' So I constructed this theory that there must be something about the old original gang that made them so indestructible and so impervious to baldness, they just seemed ageless – and then quite soon after that they started toppling over. Willie Rushton, John Wells, Peter Cook, none of them particularly old."

The late 1990s were not a good period for *Eye* contributors. Cook was the first to go, his body finally surrendering to the effects of decades of epic alcohol consumption in January 1995. "I always thought he was indestructible," a devastated Ian Hislop told the *Guardian*. Then, without telling anyone, Willie Rushton went into hospital for a heart operation in December 1996 – and never came out. "His sudden death came as a terrible shock," said Richard Ingrams. In January 1998, John Wells succumbed to cancer.

John Wells, Peter Cook and Willie Rushton pictured in 1985

Can't Wait to properly yet, but Soon will! Just to say hello, & thanks

love

Paul

Be properly addressed POSTCODE IT

Foot's writing career
resumes after his
aortic aneurysm

"I'm beginning to feel a bit lonely," pointed out Ingrams in his address at Wells's memorial service. Finally, in April 1999, Andrew Osmond died of a brain tumour.

For a while that month it looked like the *Eye* was about to lose Paul Foot too. He suffered an aortic aneurysm, complicated by subsequent kidney failure and pneumonia, and doctors warned his family that, if he did survive, it was likely to be in a vegetative state. Footy, characteristically, surveyed the evidence for himself, took a view completely at odds with the prevailing opinion and went on to prove it correct, battling his way back to full mental (if not physical) health. He was back at his desk by the end of the year, celebrating his return to the *Eye* with a full-page attack on Jeffrey Archer. Life went on as normal.

NOT FOR PUBLICATION

The following letter was published in *Private Eye* in January 1985, beneath the headline "Not For Publication":

"Sir – I enclose by way of service upon you sealed writ and form of Acknowledgement of Service which I have issued on behalf of

my client ... I should just like to say that I regret not extending to you the courtesy of a letter before action. The last time I did this my letter was partially published in *Private Eye* without my permission. I do not propose to run the risk of this happening again.
Yours truly, Richard C. M. Sykes, Solicitor, London."

NOT PRIVATE EYE

☞ MIRROR BUILDING, Peter Cook leads *Eye* raid on

NUMBER 10, Richard
Ingrams's visits to
In 1970, Richard and Mary Ingrams were invited to an evening reception at Downing Street, which is bizarre. Even more bizarrely, they went. "I was very shocked," says Ian Hislop. "If I was invited, I wouldn't go."

"We were introduced to Wilson by Gerald Kaufman," recalled Ingrams. "Kaufman muttered my name into the air, and he shook hands and started off by saying 'You know

Jack Kennedy's parties at the White House had nothing on this – there are people here from all walks of life: artists, composers, sculptors – look around.' And then I think he suddenly clicked my name, who he was talking to – it was quite late at night, he'd obviously had a lot to drink – and he stopped that completely, but it was pure 'Mrs Wilson's Diary', I could not have improved on it. Particularly as the people there, the artists and composers, were people like Morecambe and Wise and Cliff Michelmore."[158]

Wilson's spin-doctor Joe Haines swiftly came up with his own version of the reception, in which a jovial Mary Wilson who "rather enjoyed" her portrayal in *Private Eye* "turned to a waiter and said 'Please bring Mr Ingrams a glass of Wincarnis'". "Quite wrong," Ingrams informed the BBC. "I've certainly never met Mrs Wilson, and I don't think she wants to meet me at all."

He has, however, met Sarah Brown. He went to Downing Street again in March 2010, for a reception celebrating progress in cancer research. "I've got no idea why they asked me." The only other celebrity guest he recognised was the ginger one from Girls Aloud.

☞ PRIME MINISTERIAL PARODIES, moments they become reality

NUMBER CRUNCHING

The hack who has compiled the majority of the "Number Crunching" items since 1998 (me) actually took a GCSE in Statistics. And failed.

IS THIS FAIR TO THE PRESS ? shouts
Lunchtime O'Booze

FOR TWO WEEKS I HAVE BEEN TRYING TO EFFECT AN ENTRY INTO GORDONSTOUN, SCOTLAND'S HUSH-HUSH ACADEMY, WHERE OUR YOUNG CROWN PRINCE IS BEING TAUGHT SAILING, ROCK-CLIMBING, POLO AND ALL THOSE OTHER SKILLS WHICH WILL EQUIP HIM FOR HIS VITAL ROLE AS A TWENTIETH CENTURY MONARCH.

But this School is as difficult to penetrate as Liz Taylor's bedroom.

Surrounded by a two-fold 12 foot high electric fence patrolled by Gestapo-trained bloodhounds, Gordonstoun is a challenge to any honest reporter.

BLOODY

I personally accept the challenge. The Duke of Edinburgh has used regrettable language about me, smacking more of the Tar than of the Consort, but I bear him no grudge. Though as I sit here in Elgin's Station Hotel, along with several of my colleagues, nursing a broken leg and an arm bitten to shreds by the Gestapo

trained bloodhounds I must confess, as the locals say, "I hae me doots".

RUGGER

And my colleagues will bear me out. Rex Froth, trying to obtain an exclusive interview with Prince Charles' matron was beaten over the head with a polo-stick by the young fencing instructor Von Grips. Arthur Bellylaugh, caught trying to photograph a game of Rugger in which the young prince was playing, was set upon by both teams and fed to the hounds. He is not well. Is this a right and proper way to treat the Press, I ask myself ?

O'Booze as a keen cub reporter in 1962 . . .

O'BOOZE, Lunchtime

"Lunchtime O'Booze was a Rushtonism," says former editor Christopher Booker. The bibulous hack filed his first report, on "the season" and the debutantes of 1962, in issue 9. His reward for successfully locating both Liz Taylor and the Loch Ness Monster that summer was to be assigned to cover every major news story of the decade – although he conceded coverage of the Paris riots and Vietnam War to his cousins, Lunchtime O'Boulevards and Lun Tai O'Booze respectively. He continues to contribute to the magazine to this day, when capable.

. . . and in the more familiar state he was in by 1966

OFFENSIVE, Most, items
published in *Private Eye*

● The cover of issue 73 in October 1964 featured not only a free record (☞ FLEXIDISCOGRAPHY) but a photograph beneath it of the prime minister **Alec Douglas-Home sitting on a toilet** (*right*).

It elicited the following anguished response from the principal of Buckingham College:

"I write to voice a strong protest … whatever one's political views, and whoever the picture represented, it is crude and in the poorest tastes of English journalism. Furthermore, all our leaders have a responsible and difficult task to perform and should be entitled to the respect that the responsibility of their post demands.

This particular issue came to my notice through one of the boys in the school, and it seems to me an appalling thing that young people can pick up such trash as this which insults our national leaders and is certainly in no way humorous.

Crude vulgarity just tends to deprave our young generation and add to the already sizeable problem of general attitudes in Britain today.

Yours faithfully
E. Ivor Hughes, Principal."

In the interests of political balance, the next issue of the *Eye* provided Mr Hughes and its other readers with a picture of Harold Wilson on the toilet as well.

● In 1970, several readers objected that **jokes about the Queen Mother** made them "want to vomit" and were "revolting, vulgar and disgraceful, unbecoming public opinion and loyalty to the Throne". One expressed his hope that "you are prosecuted by the Police. You richly deserve it."

In 1974 an Edith Simpson wrote to inform the *Eye* that they had lost a reader due to Auberon Waugh's description of **Captain Mark Phillips** – "by any normal standards, an excitingly good-looking man" as "hideous". Two years later she wrote again, to complain about further insulting references in Waugh's column. "Mrs Simpson seems to have forgotten a promise she made herself (and us)," complained another reader. "If only this lady would have the decency to carry out her threat, maybe the rest of us could enjoy Waugh's ramblings unmolested."

In 1977, Auberon Waugh had his revenge on **Nora Beloff**, the *Observer* journalist who had sued the *Eye* six years earlier (☞ BALLSOFF MEMORANDUM), on the occasion of her marriage.

"I had hoped I would be asked to be best man at Nora Beloff's wedding today, since I imagine it was I who supplied a large part of the bride's dowry. It makes me happy to think that the £3,000 I gave her in libel damages a few years ago might have helped her find such a suitable husband as Clifford Makins, the well-known journalist … For 56 summers, Nora has resisted the advantages of the coarser sex. Nothing will ever be the same again. Even as I write, I imagine that Clifford Makins is exploring the unimaginable delight of her body, never sweeter than when first sampled. If I had been best man, I would have given Clifford the advice I always give bridegrooms on these occasions – take things gently at first, there's no rush. A new bride should be treated like a new car. Keep her steady on the straight, watch out for warning lights on the ignition and lubrication panels and when you reckon she's run in, give her all you've got."

The letters pages of the subsequent two issues were crammed with readers calling Waugh's helpful note "cruel and utterly tasteless", "moral corruption", "obscene" and "sickening and the first reason for press censorship I've ever seen". Beloff and Makins went on to enjoy a long and presumably fulfilling marriage.

In 1979, the "Grovel" column waited until six weeks after the murder of **Louis Mountbatten** by the IRA to point out that he was "a raging queen with a preference for young servicemen". Hordes of readers complained that "your remarks are as base and hurtful as any I can recall" and "such drivel we can do without".

September 1981 saw the first of many letters complaining about the magazine's claim that the right-wing Tory MP Harvey Proctor was homosexual. Readers continued to maintain that this was "left-wing propaganda" and a "monstrous slur" right up until the MP resigned and pleaded guilty to gross indecency with two teenage boys in May 1987.

In 1982 John Kent designed his own **memorial to the Falklands War dead**.

Patriotic readers objected that this was "tasteless and mindless", "untrue, dishonest and of an abysmal bad taste … an insult to the dead and a stab in the heart to their relatives" and, er, "the best comment on the Falklands episode so far".

The original is now held in the collection of the National Army Museum.

NEW WAR MEMORIAL

● In 1986 a V. M. Taylor (Mrs) was one of many to complain about the use of **swear words**.

"On reading *Private Eye* I am filled with embarrassment knowing I have purchased it for another person. I can now understand why we have football hooliganism, mugging and foul language, which the youngsters of today have no hesitation in using when magazines like these are allowed to be printed. In the 'Colour Section', F--- is used – and on several other pages. It is just a disgusting magazine destined to reduce British people to the lowest scum. I might add my husband shares my sentiments."

● The *Eye*'s take on the coverage of the death of **Princess Diana** prompted one of the biggest postbags ever (☞ DIANA, Princess, Death of and subsequent lunacy).

● **Issue 969** in February 1999 proved particularly controversial:

Two subscriptions were cancelled over the cover, one over a joke about the late Linda McCartney, one over a rude joke in the "Eye TV" column and another over an Ed McLachlan cartoon of the Grim Reaper in a hospital ward.

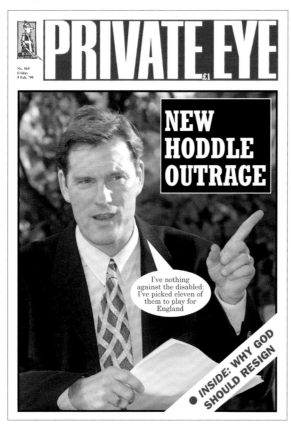

● A cover referring to the **Paddington rail disaster** later the same year prompted several subscription cancellations – as well as letters of praise for how it "eloquently highlights UK railway operators' and Railtrack's gross negligence of safety to increase profit".

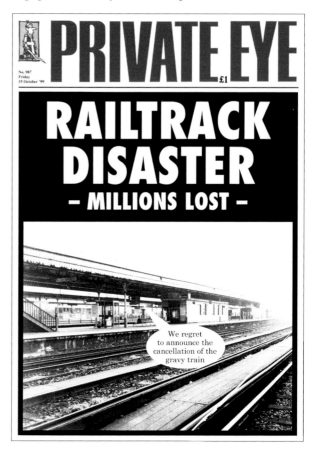

● One copy of the "Armageddon Out of Here" cover after the **11 September attacks** (☞ TERRORISM, as subject of jokes) was returned with the addition of the message "Pathetic under-6th form sick humour – for God's sake act like grown-ups" scrawled across the cover, which isn't nearly such a good gag. "To make fun of the death of some 6,000 people and their president in such dreadful circumstances is unforgivable. You should apologise," demanded another reader. According to Michael Oakley of Sutton Coldfield the actual terror attacks themselves were the *Eye*'s fault: "Your blatantly prejudiced feature the Book of Sharon, and previous similar, has long been a blot on your mission to attack hypocrisy on both sides equally. This week we've seen the consequences of, obliquely, such hypocrisy by you. For the first time ever, I hope you're ashamed."

Thankfully, the *Eye* had pre-empted the complaints by providing a "special cut-out-and-keep subscription cancellation form" in the previous issue. The magazine got plenty of them back.

✂ -

SPECIAL CUT-OUT-AND-KEEP
SUBSCRIPTION CANCELLATION FORM

Dear Sir,
   I was shocked and appalled by the cover/cartoon/article/crossword *(delete as applicable)* in the latest issue of Private Eye. I have been a reader for .... years and have never been so offended. Please cancel my subscription at once.

Name: . . . .

Address: . . . .

. . . .

- -

● Readers filled an entire page of the letters section in March 2001 with complaints about the *Eye* accepting **pro-hunting adverts from the Countryside Alliance**. Others objected to a series of 2004 ads for Sky TV, something Ian Hislop had pre-empted by instructing his hacks to look for especially uncomplimentary stories about Rupert Murdoch to offset them.

● In December 2004 the *Eye* had a special Christmas cover (*below, left*) alluding to the recent surprising revelations about the home secretary's sex life.

A horde of readers rushed to accuse the magazine of **blasphemy**. "To say I find the cover gratuitously offensive is an understatement ... you witless, gutless buggers wouldn't dare mock Islam ... Is it your editorial policy to crucify the Christ?... You don't deserve a happy Christmas."

"It made me laugh because I think there were four of us who'd done that cover, Nick [Newman] who's fairly atheist, and then the other three – me, Richard [Ingrams] and Barry [Fantoni], who are almost the only church-goers left in the country," chuckles Ian Hislop.

● Proving the royal family are still an issue in the twenty-first century, many readers objected to the *Eye*'s commemoration of the **Queen's eightieth birthday** in 2006.

It was, apparently, "tasteless and UNKIND ... SILLY, VERY POOR TASTE", and several loyal subjects were "no longer purchasers of *Private Eye*".

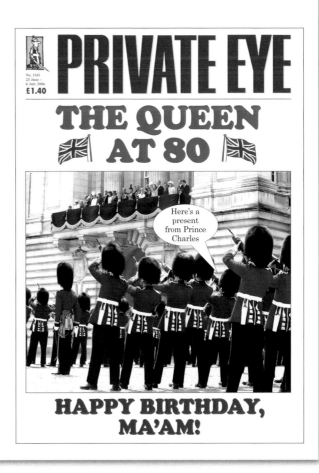

● Issue 1256 was another bonanza of tasteless-ness, with readers objecting to both the "outrageously stupid, heartless and unfunny" and "disgusting" cover featuring Gordon Brown's pre-election celeb-style confessional TV interview and a Nick Newman cartoon about the death of a competitor at the winter Olympics. "Just NO," yelled one reader. "You have really sunk to the gutter," observed another.

● Last word goes to reader Philip Harris, who wrote in 2007: "Sir – I would like to sympathise with your correspondents' predicament on finding a potentially tasteless joke in a satirical magazine. I recently bought a copy of *Tractors Weekly* only to find it full of stuff about tractors. I was gutted."

☞ FIRST SUBSCRIPTION CANCELLATION

OFFICES

Private Eye has had several homes.

October 1961–January 1962:
28 Scarsdale Villas, Kensington
Willie Rushton's mother's house.

February–June 1962:
41 Neal Street, Covent Garden
Spare warehouse loaned by Gareth Powell (☞ PRESSDRAM) on condition the team locked the doors every night. They forgot to.

June–August 1962:
18 Greek Street, Soho
Peter Cook's Establishment Club. ☞ RICH OWNER, Search for a

August 1962–February 1969:
22 Greek Street, Soho
Building shared with a striptease joint and betting shop. Offices so small that the boxwallahs (☞) had to stay two doors up the road. Room was however found for a pinball machine.
☞ MURAL

February 1969–March 1984:
34 Greek Street, Soho
"Another revolting office with exactly the same atmosphere," remembered secretary Tessa Fantoni. "The street door was unlocked, so you'd go into the lavatory and there'd be some junkie fixing themselves up."[159]

March 1984–present:
6 Carlisle Street, Soho
Former hackette Sarah Shannon describes the four-storey building as "shambolic, with bits of paper piled up on noticeboards and teetering piles of paper and books under the table and sometimes classified advertising people lying under there".

OLDIE, The

Magazine for distressed gentlefolk, edited by a man whose name for the moment escapes me.

O'NEILL, Terry, Gratuitous excuse to print photograph taken by

OZ AND UZ, founding fathers of *Private Eye*

Peter Usborne's and Andrew Osmond's names have long been overshadowed by those of subsequent celebrity proprietors and editors. But, without them, *Private Eye* would never have happened.

"The key man was Peter Usborne," says first editor Christopher Booker. "He was the man who said 'An end to pub talk, let's make it a proposition.' He deserves a huge pat on the back." Ingrams agrees: "Once Usborne got involved I thought it would happen. Usborne was a very dynamic character. We needed a boxwallah to get things going."

Usborne was working for an advertising agency, "and I kept on thinking about this suggestion that maybe we should do *Mesopotamia* [☞] in real life. I was starting effectively to do the research for setting up a new magazine in my lunch hours, going out to phone boxes and ringing up printers. We discovered this newish technique called off-set litho which involved typing text on a typewriter and sticking it down and the printer would then photograph

"Andrew, Chris Booker, Willie Rushton and me were enough to get the thing going", remembers Peter Usborne. "And we did some of it in my flat in Islington." Glamorous assistants also pictured

it, and that was it." This was a pivotal moment in two ways. Off-set litho bypassed the need for expensive and unwieldy newspaper hot-metal techniques and made a magazine financially possible. And the "little printers" were located in NW2 (☞ NEASDEN, Origin of *Eye*'s obsession with).

Someone – Usborne thinks it must have been Willie Rushton – told him he should talk to "a very good writer called Chris Booker". Booker quickly realised how seriously the young entrepreneur was taking things. "He sent me this very long memo, which I wish I still had, really setting out the business plan for how we were going to do it."

It had a rather glaring hole in it. The minimum amount that Usborne reckoned they could get away with to set a magazine up was £300. And they didn't have £300.

"I remember sitting in my flat in Kensington with Usborne and perhaps Willie, and we said 'Where the hell are we going to get three hundred quid?'" says Booker. "And Usborne said 'I know! Andrew Osmond. His dad owns a supermarket chain in Lincolnshire and he's got a bit of money.'"

"That was the day my life changed," Osmond recalled. "I had gone to Paris to learn French before taking the Foreign Office exam. This telegraph arrived. It read, '*Mespot.* rides again. Come home. Uz.'"[160] And so he immediately did. "By the time I got back and had found which pub they had moved to, they had completely forgotten about the telegram. Anyway, I had £450 and I agreed to back them with it. I became the original Lord Gnome."

"Osmond was the man who made it possible with the money," says Booker. "And Usborne's real contribution was sending me that letter saying 'Stop playing around, let's get real, and this is what we should do.' I would give him great honour for that. If *Private Eye*'s worth having, without that it would never have got going. He was the one who tied the knot."

☞ PRESSDRAM

PRIVATE EYE

ARLES IN SECURITY REVIEW

"Feel lucky, punk?"

"Would you like a cup of tea before you start the exorcism, Vicar?"

Star Letter

P45

We would be most grateful if you would send us response to the news that PUNCH is re-launching in mber. The first issue has a letters page in need ing and I am sure you have a view on the matter.

Yours sincerely,
SUZANNAH HUSEY,

CRISIS:
ON TO ACT

DON'T TELL US YOU'RE A POOVE TOO?

PRIVATE EYE

CKSON/PRESLEY BABY LATEST

you want a boy?

No comment

P

PAD, Brillo, Gratuitous use of photograph of

PAEDIATRICIANS, not to be confused with paedophiles

In August 2000, as the *News of the World*'s Name and Shame campaign was in full spate, the *Eye* ran this cartoon by Noel Watson.

"I'm a paediatrician!"

One week later, trainee consultant paediatrician Dr Yvette Cloete was forced to move out of her home in Newport, South Wales, after vandals painted the word "paedo" on her front door. "It looks as though it was just a question of confusing the job title for something else – I suppose I'm really a victim of ignorance," she told the BBC. The *Eye* printed the news in its following issue, beneath the headline "Life Imitates Art, Part 94".

It also began a handy guide for wannabe angry mobs.

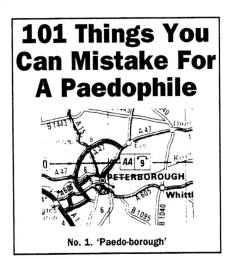

101 Things You Can Mistake For A Paedophile

No. 1. 'Paedo-borough'

PARKINSON, Cecil, his part in Nigel Dempster's downfall

In 1983, the "Grovel" column ( ) scored one of its increasingly rare victories.

"Grovel", 7 October 1983:

Why was Cecil Parkinson asked to step down as Tory Party Chairman? I can assure readers that it had nothing whatever to do with his marital difficulties which have recently caused raised eyebrows in Tory circles. Now comes the news that Parkinson's fun-loving secretary Ms Sara Keays is expecting a baby in 3 months time …

BBC News, 14 October 1983:

Cecil Parkinson, Secretary of State for Trade and Industry, has resigned. The decision comes as fresh details were revealed about his extramarital affair with his former secretary Sara Keays. Prime Minister Margaret Thatcher had initially stood by her Trade and Industry Secretary, but accepted his offer of resignation early this morning …

The story had been subject to the usual scrupulous research.

Richard Ingrams: I remember putting in the original Sara Keays story which came in through the post, and I think I rang up [Nigel] Dempster and said 'I've got this thing, do you know anything?' and he said 'Well, I've heard something like that.' 'Probably true then' – and I just put it in."[161]

In February 1985, another anonymous letter arrived at the Eye office. Twenty-five-year-old Ian Hislop was editing at the time.

Ingrams: I was away. I had an operation on my spine and Ian took over. I was away for three or four issues, I guess, and there was quite a lot of muttering from the hacks.

Ian Hislop: I filled in, and almost closed the mag down. The way I remember it happening was a story came in, an anonymous tip-off about Parkinson. I was technically in charge, I thought "I will give this story to Dempster and he will sort out whether it is true or not." It was an anonymous tip-off. I just didn't have the apparatus to know whether I should run that or not. I thought that's how you do it, you give it to the person who runs the "Grovel" column.

Nigel Dempster: I was playing squash at the RAC. Liz Elliott rang me up and said "look, we haven't got a Grovel column." I said "Aah, I don't want to do one." She said "You've got to do it, we're relying on it. We've got a blank page." So I left the squash court, went to *Private Eye*, sat down at a typewriter and wrote the thing. I inserted a story which was in the "Grovel" folder about Cecil Parkinson and his new secretary.[162]

Hislop: "Grovel" was very much his thing. He delivered it. Absolutely. He ran the column, and what he said when he turned up on Monday to deliver it, I thought, went. So I gave it to him, he wrote it up, or I assumed checked it out, did whatever he was supposed to do, and we ran it in the mag.

"Grovel", 8 March 1985 (on sale 6 March):

For some weeks Fleet Street, chastened by failing to crack the former Secretary of State for Trade and Industry's lengthy liaison with his onetime amanuensis, Sara Keays, has been investigating new reports of an outbreak of libidinous behaviour …

Dempster: I handed the Grovel copy over, and

for the first time in my life, Hislop was there. I said, "Look, these stories I can vouch for, but this one about Parkinson I know nothing about."

Paul Halloran: He said "I told Hislop it wouldn't work and that he shouldn't put it in," which was a lie, he said quite the reverse. I fuckin' asked him. Ian mentioned it to me, and I went to Dempster, and asked "How does this stand up?" He said "I asked this guy and that." On what Dempster said, Ingrams would have run that story.[163]

Hislop: And then an injunction came in. Parkinson's lawyers were tipped off that the story was coming.

Dempster: Someone in *Private Eye* perhaps leaked the story to Parkinson.

Hislop: Dempster had either told someone or he'd tipped them off himself.

Peter McKay: The Parkinson story had been investigated at the *Daily Mail*, where Dempster had been writing a gossip column for more than ten years. Parkinson was tipped off by a *Daily Mail* reporter that the story was about to appear, which is how he was able to go swiftly into action with an injunction.[164]

Hislop: I remember I was working at *Spitting Image*, writing jokes with Nick, and I got a call from the lawyers saying "We've got an injunction, the mag's going to be pulled." Oh God, I couldn't believe it. I thought "I've been given this mag for five minutes and I've fucked it up completely."

Times, 6 March 1985:

Lawyers acting for Mr Cecil Parkinson were yesterday granted a High Court injunction after references to him in the forthcoming issue of *Private Eye*. Writs seeking injunctions and damages against *Private Eye* will be issued today, Mr Parkinson's solicitor Peter Carter-Ruck said last night … Of the 368,000 copies of *Private Eye* printed on Monday night, 60 percent had already been distributed. 145,000 were withdrawn from sale after the interim injunction was granted on Tuesday night. Mr David Cash, managing director of Pressdram, said "We will lose at least £45,000 in revenue …"

Christopher Silvester: One thing Dempster did was unforgivable. I remember it vividly. He said to the *Sunday Times*, "I saw that item before it was published and I told Ian Hislop not to put it in the magazine." He shouldn't have said anything. He didn't have to say anything.

Hislop: Dempster denied it! He said that not only was the story nothing to do with him, but it was not true.

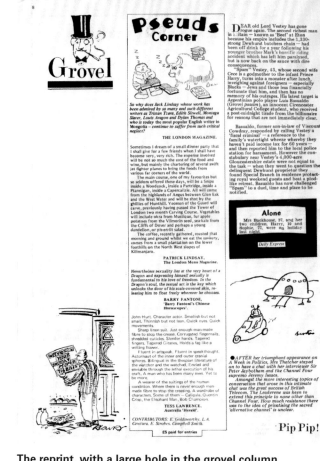

The reprint, with a large hole in the grovel column

So I was completely and utterly in the shit. I went back to talk to the lawyers and they said "Part of the reason you're completely screwed is this interview with Dempster." The lawyers were perfectly nice about it but they just said "You haven't got a leg to stand on." I looked a complete idiot, and I thought the only way to get round this is to print the whole mag again without the offending article and a very funny cover. We recouped it – with the publicity, that copy did all right.

Ingrams returned to work the following week.

Ingrams: I was very impressed by Hislop's amazing feat of having a whole issue of *Private Eye* withdrawn.[165]

Hislop: Oh, he just loved the trouble! But he was then in a genuine dilemma, because he was Dempster's friend, and I think it clashed with attempting to support me and that was difficult for him. Richard believed my version of events and not Dempster's. He's very decisive when he takes your side. It would have been very odd at that

age if I'd positively decided to run a really tough gossip story about a senior cabinet minister without asking anyone – I just wouldn't have done it.

Silvester: Richard, quite rightly, said it was an appalling thing to do and fired Dempster. That's basically what happened. Ian felt he had been betrayed, and he *had* been betrayed.

McKay: It appeared to Ingrams that *Private Eye* had been used to float a story so that Parkinson's reaction could be solicited without danger to the *Daily Mail*.

Ingrams: Dempster behaved very badly, and he told a lot of lies about it.

Ingrams – not Hislop, as Dempster believed – wrote a message from Lord Gnome in the following issue.

Lord Gnome, 22 March 1985:

I would like to take the opportunity to point out, with regard to the disgraceful references to Mr Cecil Parkinson in the most recent issue of my organ, that I myself was on holiday at the time the offending item was printed. Normally I fully appreciate the need to protect those anonymous informers who contribute to my pages. On this occasion however I have no hesitation whatsoever in naming Mr Nigel Dempster as the sole author of the offending paragraph. Were Mr Parkinson to sue Mr Dempster personally for libel I would certainly not attempt to dissuade him from doing so. On the contrary he would have my full support.

Dempster: It was what I most feared: a disgraceful act. Ian Hislop had told the world that I wrote the story. I walked in and screamed at Hislop, "You know nothing about journalism. You're a little shit. I never want to have anything to do with you again. This has just gone to prove everything I've said to Ingrams about you. You have no knowledge of journalism whatsoever and I'm not going to put my reputation on the line for you."

Hislop: He was screaming about "You'll find I'm the iron fist in the glove, you'll never work in this town again, you cross me, people find ..." He absolutely bawled me out, and I had very little comeback at the time. I was dumbfounded. He just screamed in a rather psychotic way, and read this full riot act.

McKay: Dempster told Ingrams he would not work for the *Eye* again unless Hislop was fired. Ingrams refused to do this.

Ingrams: I've always thought what happened was that his editor at the *Mail* David English knew perfectly well that he was doing the Grovel column, and he didn't object to that until the Parkinson story, because Parkinson was a friend of his. I think – this is my supposition – that he told Dempster that he had to stop doing it. And instead of admitting that, Dempster picked a quarrel with Ian in a very clumsy way, and made a situation where he couldn't carry on.

Hislop: I think Dempster felt betrayed by Richard. In a slightly sort of lover's way. I think he felt he was the real apple of his eye. To be Richard's favourite was what people wanted. And the sunshine of his smile was very warming, and when it went, you got very cross. Richard would arrive, and Dempster would say [puts on snotty voice], "Ah, Lord Gnome, Lord Gnome, how marvellous." People like Paul [Foot] and [Christopher] Booker and Barry [Fantoni] didn't say "Ah, your Gnomeship," they said "Oh, Richard, it's you again."

Dempster: I wish Ingrams nothing but ill. I shall dance on his grave. I have nothing but contempt for him.[166]

Ingrams: He became an unpleasant character. He wasn't that at all to begin with. I sometimes wonder if it wasn't due to the fact he became ill.

Francis Wheen: No, it was long before he fell ill. He was very pleased with himself. It was odd because socially he was quite shy and gauche and awkward in many ways. But professionally he was tremendously full of himself. He launched glossy magazines, called *Dempster's*! And published books, *Dempster's Diary*. He got madder and madder, poor chap.

Dempster: I was working for *Private Eye* out of a sense of mischief and a sense of love for Richard Ingrams. Clearly I was a very great selling point, and the acceptable face of *Private Eye*. People used to look on *Private Eye* as a rabble who poked fun at their betters. I was the only person who had any position in society. "Grovel" of *Private Eye* worked on a decent newspaper, his wife was a duke's daughter, he appeared on television and was a public person ... No one could have invented a better gossip columnist than me ... I think there are very few stories in our world in the last twenty years that I haven't started ...

Nigel Dempster died in 2007 after a long battle with the brain disorder Progressive Supranuclear Palsy. He and the Eye *were never reconciled.*

☞ HAPPY SHIP, Not a; MARQUESA

PARSON'S PLEASURE

Parson's Pleasure was a pocket-sized gossip magazine founded by Adrian Berry, the undergraduate son of the *Daily Telegraph*'s proprietor, which had been running for a couple of years before Richard Ingrams arrived at Oxford University. It was, recalled Ingrams, "filled with estoteric gossip quite unintelligible to people outside the wealthy public school set at Christ Church".[167]

Berry was preparing for his finals and was only too happy to pass *Parson's Pleasure* on to anyone who looked keen. And so it was that Ingrams and Paul Foot produced their first magazine under their own auspices, starting as they meant to go on, adding parodies and a cast of comedy characters to Berry's gossip. "It was the true forerunner of *Private Eye*," noted Andrew Osmond.[168] The team were hit with their first libel writ after one issue and the magazine was banned from W. H. Smith.

☞ *MESOPOTAMIA*

PASSING WIND

Nick Newman and Simon Park set up their magazine *Passing Wind* at Ardingly (☞) and then took it with them to Oxford. It was in a slightly sorry state when, two years later, Ian Hislop followed them there. "Simon had sort of lost interest in it; I'd just about managed to keep it going and thankfully when Ian arrived he was interested in taking it over," says Newman. Hislop bought the title for £400 after borrowing the cash from "the Old Etonian in my tutorial group. I paid him back, I'm glad to say."[169] He continued to employ Newman to write and draw cartoons.

There had been a very specific model for the magazine. "At the back of our minds was the fact that Richard Ingrams had done this magazine when he was at Oxford, *Mesopotamia* [☞], which is fantastic," says Newman. "I got them all out of the Bodleian when I was there, and they're wonderful. We did our own parody of *Private Eye* in about issue 3, and made up a load of stories about Richard."

They also used the mag, which was sold

"We were pretty obsessed." *Passing Wind*'s parody of *Private Eye,* and (*right*) the edition documenting Hislop's attempt to interview Peter Cook

around colleges and certain shops in Oxford for the bargain price of 15p, as a blatant excuse to meet their comic heroes. "We tried to have an interview every issue, to make it more interesting. We interviewed Michael Palin, bought him a beer, and he told us the whole plot of *The Life of Brian*. And we interviewed Willie Rushton when he came up to talk to the Union. And we interviewed Auberon Waugh – we were pretty obsessed with *Private Eye*, as you can see. When we sent him a copy of the interview I remember he wrote back and said 'I wasn't aware that I spoke with so many spelling mistakes.'"

Hislop kept up the tradition when he took over, interviewing Richard Ingrams for issue 8 (☞ QUESTIONS, asked by Ian Hislop of Richard Ingrams at their first meeting). "I tried to make him laugh, because when you're that young you're very arrogant – 'You think you guys are funny? Hey, we're students, and we're *really* funny.'"[170] Hedging his bets, in the same issue he also interviewed *Punch* editor Alan Coren, who, in a spooky premonition, informed him that what the *Eye* really needed was to "get a twenty-five-year-old editor and some young cartoonists".

Then for issue 11 he travelled down to London again, to meet Peter Cook and interview him – or at least that was the intention. Instead, they went for lunch, which for Cook at that stage of his life was an entirely liquid affair. "Having laughed and drunk more than I thought possible, I managed to ask him no questions at all. By the end of the lunch I was so drunk he kindly told me to come back when I had sobered up." Hislop did so, and managed to get a good four pages for the magazine out of a gossipy chat that covered *Derek and Clive*, Dudley Moore's film career, what happened to the Royal Shit after the Queen went to the lavatory, and the deep mutual relationship between Norman Scott's next-door neighbour's pig and a man from Chagford. He didn't get close to discovering the Real Peter Cook, but then no one ever did. "I never know quite what this quest to find out 'the Real So-and-So' is," Cook told him. "I feel the real whatever-it-is may be a very dull find. This pursuit of the real Peter Cook is futile because I haven't bothered to find out myself."

He was, however, rather impressed by the Real Ian Hislop (even if he did describe himself in the contributors' list thus: "Ian's interests are roller disco and editing humorous undergraduate magazines. His hobbies are gals and gals and early Bay City Rollers.") Cook was delighted not long afterwards to find his young interviewer in residence at the *Eye* office (☞ HISLOP, Ian, arrival at *Private Eye*).

PEDANTS(') CORNER

"Pedants Corner" was inaugurated on the letters page in 2002, and can best be summed up by the following exchange:

"Sir – Might I point out that Pedants Corner does not require the apostrophe you stuck on it. Pedants, in this sense, is adjectival. Tom Cutler."

"Sir – Mr Cutler asserts that Pedants is not a possessive form but is adjectival. In a sense all possessive forms are 'adjectival' in that they describe, or add information to, a noun; but this is not to accept his argument which is based on false premises. In English, adjectives do not agree in number or gender, so if 'Pedants' was indeed an adjectival

Passing Wind No 11 20p

'Ere...Pete
Yes Dud?
Is it true you were done for "*Passing Wind*"?

form, it would, of necessity, be used thus: 'Pedant Corner', English adjectives being singular. Glyn Austen."

"Sir – Strictly speaking, Glyn Austen is right. But English syntax has its own vagaries. We write 'sports field' and 'games room' with never a possessive apostrophe in sight. During World War Two, the BBC ran the Forces Programme. No apostrophe was used, even though there were three armed forces whose programme this was. However, the Boys' Brigade always spell themselves with an apostrophe. Brian White."

"Sir – If Pedants Corner stretches the full length of the page, it is a column, not a corner. Ben Stanley."

PERSIA, Shit of

So exercised was Parviz Radji, the ambassador of the Shah of Iran, by *Private Eye*'s insistence on referring to his ruler as "The Shit of Persia" that he consulted diplomatic colleagues about the possibility of both bribing the magazine to stop and suing them for "defamation against a Head of State". In July 1976 he was called to an audience with the Shah, which he recorded in his diary:

"His Imperial Majesty says he understands that every patriotic Iranian must feel insulted by the magazine's offensive comments. Would he permit it if some trusted friends arranged a meeting on neutral territory so that some kind of dialogue might be established with the editorial staff? One might perhaps hope for a toning down of the language and even ultimately for an end to their offensive allusions to His Imperial Majesty. I add that I am convinced that to try to 'buy' them would be disastrous, because they seem to adhere to *some* principles. 'Principles?' asks His Imperial Majesty angrily, with an expression of bewilderment on his face as he turns on me the full glare of his wrath. 'Principles?' he repeats. He continues to pace the room in ruminative silence. After what seems to me an indecent interval, with his face averted, he says in a soft voice, void of anger, 'It's not worth it.'"[171]

The Shah was deposed in favour of the Ayatollah Khomeini three years later, which suggests that both men would have been better off concentrating on more important things.

PHALLUS, taken from *Punch*
by Malcolm Muggeridge

Malcolm Muggeridge's most significant contribution to the *Eye* when he guest-edited an edition in August 1964 was to dig out a detail of an illustration from the "Charivari" section of *Punch*, the magazine he had edited from 1953 to 1957, and have Gerald Scarfe (☞) blow it up big for the cover of the *Eye*. "The detail in question, despite its appearance week by week over so many years, may well have escaped due notice. It has been a privilege to rescue it from undeserved obscurity."

The following month *Punch*'s editor Bernard Hollowood hastily removed the phallus from its pages, a victory which the *Eye* recorded beneath the headline "Hollowood Withdraws Prick". It has had pride of place on the first editorial page of *Private Eye* ever since.

PILOTI

"This column is serious," declared Piloti, aka Gavin Stamp, custodian of the *Nooks and Corners* column, in 1988. "We are interested in buildings because Architecture is the Mother of the Arts – a pity that these days she is usually a single parent after artificial insemination. We defend old buildings not because they look pretty in colour photographs, or make the world of television more real, or encourage nostalgia, or because they make money, but because a civilised society must be in contact with its past, otherwise it becomes as barbaric and hellish as Ceaucescu's Romania, or Birmingham."

"I was very keen to keep Gavin," says Ian Hislop of the academic, conservationist and founder of the campaigning Twentieth Century Society who took over the *Eye*'s architecture coverage in 1978 and was the model for the other expert columnists like M.D. (☞) and Dr B. Ching the incoming editor subsequently recruited. "The people who do it have a love for the area that's not necessarily journalistic. So Piloti writes very well, but what he loves is architecture. And what he hates is architects! That's what you need. Gavin cares, he's passionate about it. And if you look at what annoys the readers most, most weeks there are three or four letters about Piloti. He continually stirs people up, which I like."

Since 1982, Piloti (a piloti, by the way, is "one of several columns or piers supporting a building over the ground, thereby elevating the lowest floor to the first-floor level and leaving an open area below the building")[172] has awarded an annual Sir Hugh Casson Award for the worst new building of the year. The full list of winners:

1982 The Ismaili Cultural Centre, Kensington, by the Casson Conder Partnership
1983 Shaftesbury Avenue Fire Station, Westminster, by Richard Seifert and Partners
1984 The Renault Centre, Swindon, by Norman Foster
1985 Lloyd's Building, City of London, by Richard Rogers
1986 Clore Gallery for Turner Collection, Tate Gallery, by James Stirling
1987 Buckingham Palace Police Station,

Buckingham Gate, by the Property Services Agency, Department of the Environment
1988 "Skylines", Marsh Wall, Isle of Dogs, by Maxwell Hutchinson
1989 "All-weather public space" on Mound, Edinburgh, by Allies & Morrison
1990 Glasgow Concert Hall by Leslie Martin
1991 Sainsbury Wing, National Gallery, by Venturi, Scott Brown and Associates
1992 United Kingdom Pavilion at Expo '92, Seville, by Nick Grimshaw
1993 The Maitland Robinson Library, Downing College, Cambridge, by Quinlan Terry
1994 Principal's Lodge, Manchester and Harris College, by Peter Yiangou
1995 Law Faculty, Cambridge, by Sir Norman Foster and Partners
1996 House for an Art Lover, Glasgow, by Charles Rennie Mackintosh, completed by Andy Macmillan
1997 The Armadillo, Glasgow, by Norman Foster
1998 Buchanan Galleries Shopping Centre, Glasgow, by Jenkins and Marr
1999 The Millennium Dome, Greenwich, by Richard Rogers
2000 Falklands Islands Memorial Chapel, Pangbourne College, by Crispin Wride Architectural Design Studio
2001 The Forum, Norwich, by Michael Hopkins and Partners
2002 Manchester City Art Gallery extension and refurbishment by Michael Hopkins and Partners
2003 Juxon House, Paternoster Square, City of London, by William Whitfield
2004 The Sage, Gateshead, by Sir Norman Foster
2005 Women of World War II Memorial, Whitehall, by John W. Mills
2006 Palestra Building, Blackfriars Road, London, by Will Alsop
2007 The Meeting Place sculpture, St Pancras Eurostar terminal, by Paul Day
2008 "The Public", West Bromwich, by Will Alsop
2009 One Hyde Park, London, by Rogers Stirk Harbour and Partners
2010 One New Change, London, by Jean Nouvel

POOVES, Richard Ingrams's peculiar attitude to

Richard Ingrams adores homosexuals. He can't get enough of them. "I remember [Paul] Foot once saying to him 'What is it with you, Richard?'" says Ian Hislop. "'I turned up to your birthday party, and the only people there were homosexuals and lesbians. Maggi Hambling and her girlfriend who's a friend of yours, Tom Driberg [☞], Peter Ackroyd ...' Footy said 'It was an entire house full of homosexuals.'" And yet, as Hislop readily concedes, it is "an odd attribute of the old man" that as editor of the *Eye*, and afterwards, he took every opportunity to denigrate what he liked to call "pooves", "homosexualists" or "sads" in print. At one point in the early 1980s his magazine was outing gays in public life with infinitely more enthusiasm, and considerably less justification, than Peter Tatchell's Outrage were applying from precisely the opposite direction (☞ HAPPY SHIP, Not a).

"It's the thing with Richard that is always there," says Hislop. "I think he thinks it's like Swift, you know, individually he loves humanity but as a general thing he hates them all. It's something that, obviously, we never shared, and I always find slightly embarrassing." Paul Foot reckoned Ingrams was "quite grossly prejudiced against gay people: there is no excuse for his attitude, I find it exceedingly offensive and irrational".[173] A perplexed Barry Fantoni accepts the existence of his friend's "homophobia, so it's called", but says "I don't know where it comes from." He too, reaches for a more generalised misanthropy to explain, if not excuse, it: "I don't think Richard likes anything in excess. It would be anybody who ate too much, had too much sex, did anything which was in excess – you know, a flashy car, a pullover that didn't have holes in it. Shoes that were polished. Thinking too much. Having opinions."

Certainly Ingrams is so constitutionally incapable of talking about his own personal life that he regards anyone else giving away anything at all about their own as beyond the pale. Some of his closest colleagues at the *Eye* only learned that he was getting married for a second time from press reports. But much of the *Eye*'s coverage of matters homosexual probably came down to Ingrams's innate desire to find things you're not allowed to say and shout them instead (☞ SEMITISM, Alleged anti-) as much as his natural distaste for the more vocal gays who were the only ones making themselves visible in the 1970s and 1980s. "One must never forget the importance of mischief as a motivating force in any of Ingrams's pronouncements," cautioned his biographer Harry Thompson.

The editor's prejudices certainly remained on a theoretical rather than practical level in the office. He employed and enjoyed the company of Tom Driberg among others, and the mag happily carried ads for *The Boys in the Band* even as it was being mercilessly spoofed in the jokes pages, as well as ads for both "HIM – the Gay Guy's Top Magazine" and "Gayway: the only personal dating service for homosexual men and women" in the mid-1970s. (A later ban on gay contact ads was part of one of the periodic attempts to de-smut the small ads: it was short lived, and Hislop points out that "There was actually an ad section called 'Pink Eye' at one point which was deliberately set up to counter that question.") In fact when younger Ingrams sometimes seemed to, er, swing in the contrary direction: his measure of a politician after the legalisation of homosexuality in 1967 was always to ask "which way he voted on the pooves": if he'd voted to keep gay sex illegal he was dismissed as unacceptably right wing, whereas those who had voted to do away with the law were "fundamentally decent".

It must also be admitted that from the "Poove Power Mass Mince through Hyde Park and pretty candlelit demo" of 1969 to "The Gays" strip by Michael Heath (☞) in the early 1980s, Ingrams's *Eye* produced some rather good jokes on the topic of homosexuality alongside the bad journalism.

Despite occasional protests from the humorously challenged, Ian Hislop remains

THE GAYS   by Heath

happy to put in gay jokes "when they're funny". But he has deliberately and successfully excised any form of homophobia from the *Eye*. I can testify personally to that, and if you don't believe me, you can ask my boyfriend who's been enthusiastically welcomed to every staff party since we got together. Ben Summerskill, *Eye* hack turned chief executive of gay-rights charity Stonewall, adds "I started writing for the *Eye* in 1994 and the two things that impressed me about Ian were his insistence on factual accuracy, which I thought hugely refreshing, and his relaxedness about the gay thing."

POULSON, scandal brings down home secretary

In April 1970 *Private Eye* printed a three-page investigation by Paul Foot beneath the headline "The Slicker of Wakefield". It told of John Poulson, an unqualified architect who had nevertheless become a millionaire through property development. He had gone into business with a PR man and Labour councillor from Newcastle-upon-Tyne, T. Dan Smith, who had persuaded many local authorities across the North-East to engage Poulson to put up hospitals, schools, council houses and shoddy system-built tower blocks of the sort that were springing up across Britain in the 1960s. From 1967 to 1969, the deputy leader of the Conservative party Reginald Maudling had been on the board of one of his many companies. And now those companies were in trouble. "Pessimists close to the Poulson empire over the past few years are praying that whatever happens its affairs will be conducted with the minimum of publicity, and that if Mr Poulson goes down, he goes down alone," wrote Foot.

It was the biggest story the magazine had yet uncovered. Not that you'd have known that from the reception it received. Richard Ingrams recalled that "It was our first experience of a familiar pattern, the exposure by the *Eye* of what looked like a truly sensational story, only for us to find that it was completely ignored by the national press, which only began to take an interest in Poulson when he was later declared a bankrupt."[174]

This did not happen until the summer of 1972. "When Maudling's connections with Poulson were revealed in the bankruptcy hearings, the press responded with surprise and shock," noted Michael Gillard laconically (☞ SLICKER). By that point Foot and Martin Tomkinson had printed many more articles detailing Poulson and Dan Smith's bribery and corruption of surveyors, lawyers and civil servants and both Labour and Conservative councillors across dozens of local authorities, at every turn reminding readers of the connection to the man who became home secretary in June 1970. Gillard had uncovered Maudling's involvement with another dodgy company, the Real Estate Fund of America, run by the fraudster Jerome Hoffman, which he had joined as a director in 1968 "hoping to build up a little pot of money for my old age". The company then collapsed, and Hoffman went on the run from police. Still the *Eye* had been the only paper to pursue either tale, in a series of articles entitled "Reggicide". "See next week's exciting instalment," "Footnotes" promised in December 1970. "The series will continue until Mr Reginald Maudling resigns or sues."

He finally did the former eighteen months later, in July 1972, after police investigating Hoffman requested an interview with him. "It would not be appropriate for me to continue to hold this office while the investigations are being pursued," he announced. The *Eye* had pointed this out four months earlier: "This is believed to be the first investigation in the history of fraud where the principals of the company concerned have not been interviewed, and may have something to do with the fact that senior police officers might be a little embarrassed about interviewing the man who is responsible in this country for law and order."

In 1977, long after Poulson, Dan Smith, Hoffman and several corrupt councillors and officials had all been jailed, a parliamentary select committee finally got round to finding Maudling guilty of "conduct inconsistent with the standards which the House is entitled to expect from its members". The Commons promptly rallied round and declined to take any action against him, but his career was already over.

"No subsequent corruption scandal has rivalled Poulson's scope or impact," reckons Gillard. "Three decades have dimmed recognition of just how seismic were the shockwaves to British public life."
☞ BALLSOFF MEMORANDUM

PREDICTIONS, Most accurate, made at time of Ian Hislop's accession

"It's goodbye old-style, fuddy-duddy Ingrams and hello new-style, fuddy-duddy Hislop." – *Peter Cook, Observer*[175]

PREDICTIONS, Most optimistic, made at time of Richard Ingrams's accession

"In the early days, under Christopher Booker, some serious mistakes were made … Under Richard Ingrams's editorship, the libel record of *Private Eye* has been extremely good, and nothing serious has been incurred for 9 months now." – *Notes sent out to possible sources of finance, 1964*

PRESS COMPLAINTS COMMISSION

Private Eye is not governed by the media's laughably ineffective self-regulatory body the PCC. But the PCC is governed by *Private Eye*, at least in one respect. Its "Financial Journalism Best Practice Note" warns hacks that "Many publications apply what they describe as the '*Private Eye* Test': if it would embarrass a journalist to read about his or her actions in *Private Eye*, and at the same time undermine the integrity of the newspaper, then don't do it."

The rule was brought in in 2005, as a result of Piers Moron (☞) embarrassing himself and undermining the integrity of his newspaper with his share dealing.

PRESSDRAM

Pressdram Limited is the company which publishes *Private Eye*. Andrew Osmond bought it, name and all, as a readymade company off "a bloke in Fleet Street" at the end of 1961. He kept ninety-nine shares in the new publisher for himself and gave the other one to Peter Usborne.

It was all part of the boxwallahs' professionalization of what had until then been a fairly ramshackle operation. "We thought it would die after about four or five weeks," claimed Willie Rushton. "Then it would slowly decline and vanish, and at the same time the *Observer* would come along and say 'My word, you're a clever young satirical person, you must do a page for us a week for a thousand pounds.'"[176] Peter Usborne, however, was in it for the long term. "We sent the third one out to people whose opinions we thought were worth listening to. Kenneth Tynan and one or two others, I forget their names, wrote back and said 'This is absolutely brilliant; for God's sake keep going.' And because we got these encouraging letters from bigwigs I decided to give up my job."

Usborne found a new printer, John Thorpe & Son, in Wembley, which was at least *near* Neasden. The elder Thorpe printed one issue, decided it wasn't really the sort of thing he wanted to be associated with, and set up another company in & Son's name: Leo Thorpe Ltd. "We jumped the print run from about 500 to 5,000," recalls Uz. They also found an office in Covent Garden thanks to the generosity of publisher Gareth Powell, who was wildly enthusiastic about the magazine and even attempted (unsuccessfully) to persuade his fellow directors of the Seymour Press to buy it outright. And Christopher Booker's and Rushton's wages were agreed: ten pounds a fortnight, which, as Booker points out "was a lot less than I'd been earning as a dogsbody for Lord Goodman (☞) before university five years earlier".

☞ BOXWALLAHS; FAMOUS FRIENDS; FORTNIGHTLY APPEARANCE; OZ AND UZ; RICH OWNER, Search for a; WILL, Peter Cook's

PRIME MINISTERIAL PARODY, Evolution of a

"Mrs Wilson's Diary". "Heathco." "Dear Bill". "The Secret Diary of John Major". "St Albion Parish News". "The Supreme Leader". And in 2010? The process that led to "The New Coalition Academy" was about as clear-cut as the one that put its subjects in Downing Street.

1 June 2009

Gordon Brown has just been hit by a rash of ministerial resignations, dreadful local election results and calls to quit.

Ian Hislop: Unfortunately it looks like we won't get much chance to develop "The Supreme Leader" any further.

Adam Macqueen: The prime minister parody is a really essential part of the magazine, isn't it?

Hislop: *God* yes.

AM: So do you know what you're doing for Cameron yet?

Hislop: No. Not a clue. I never know in advance, and journalists, because we all like shorthand, say "So what's the next thing gonna be?" And if you don't know, then presumably the *Eye*'s finished! With any luck between everyone who's working here at the moment, something will turn up. You don't know who it will be – the old guard were a bit miffed when it was just [John] Wells and Richard [Ingrams] doing "Dear Bill" and no one else – but, as editor, I don't care at all, ha ha. As long as the best thing comes out, I'll run it and take the credit for it obviously!

10 May 2010

The general election four days ago returned a hung parliament. Coalition talks are continuing. It is press day. Gordon Brown resigns as Labour leader at 5pm, but remains prime minister. The magazine is being rewritten right up to the very latest possible printers' deadline at 8pm.

At around 7pm, Hislop rewrites "The Supreme Leader" page to have Brown being administered "a potentially lethal dose of his medication, 100 Millibands of Bonkazapam".

12 May 2010

Cameron moved into Downing Street yesterday evening, in coalition with the Lib Dems, whose leader Nick Clegg is deputy prime minister. It's the Wednesday of an off-week.

From: <Adam Macqueen>
To: <Ian Hislop>

It's probably the question you are most sick of being asked this week, but it would be great to have an account of the process in the book: where are you at with coming up with the Cameron/Clegg equivalent of Supreme Leader/St Albions/Secret Diary etc?

Are you having special joke meetings to discuss it, or will it just arise out of usual sessions? Or have you discussed it with Richard, Nick, Barry etc already?

All best
Adam

From: <Ian Hislop>
To: <Adam Macqueen>

No – have had no meetings and have got no ideas. ian

13 May 2010

Hislop is refusing to stress about having to get things right first time. "With Blair, as well as 'St Albion' there was also 'Blairzone', which Nick [Newman] and I did together. I ran the two of them essentially to see which one would work best, and it became obvious that it was the vicar. The other one was as if it was a terrible boyband, I thought it was quite funny, but it came to an end more obviously. But that's the brilliant thing about magazines, you can try stuff, and then if it doesn't work terribly well and it goes, people don't mind."

19 May 2010

The usual Wednesday-morning jokes meeting with Hislop, Ingrams, Barry Fantoni and Christopher Booker. Various ideas are discussed. "'They look like they're in a civil partnership' was the first joke everyone was making," says

Hislop. "Which they do, and that's quite funny. But once you've said that, what would they be doing? His wife's pregnant again – how would that fit? People kept saying 'He was a PR man, you should do it as a press release.' But I'm not sure most people know or care about press releases. Or doing Samantha Cameron's diary. But I'm a fifty-year-old bloke – I'm not terribly good at imitating the voice of a thirty-year-old woman. And I don't terribly want to, although I'm very happy to pretend to be Polly Filler."

Then inspiration arrived. "We were looking through the pictures of the election campaign, and they were all of Cameron in schools, talking to children. The whole election seemed to be aimed at people who can't vote, which was rather peculiar. I remember Richard pointed out how much he looked like a headmaster in one of them. And then they did the press conference in the [Number 10] rose garden, and that was the moment where you thought, 'They've both got the lectern, he's here with his deputy, that's what it is: they're addressing the parents.' I – we – I can never quite remember how these things turn out – said 'That is Parents' Day.'"

From that came the all-important format of a school newsletter. "The things that work best are when you do other literary formats. Just saying 'Here are some thoughts about what the prime minister might be thinking' – it would be a stand-up routine. There aren't that many formats – there's diaries, there's letters, there's magazines … there are school magazines!"

At 1pm a thick wodge of pink pages – handwritten by Booker, with amendments by Hislop – emerge and are taken downstairs to typist Sally Farrimond.

26 May 2010

Edition 1263 of *Private Eye* goes on sale with the first Headmaster's Letter from the New Coalition Academy – tweaked and updated at the regular jokes meeting on Monday morning – inside. Helpfully, the news bulletins that morning are leading with letters sent by coalition education secretary Michael Gove to every school in England inviting them to become academies.

PRIME MINISTERIAL PARODIES, moments when they become reality

"Dear Bill": Asked by journalists in November 1980 what he did all day now that his wife had been in Downing Street for eighteen months, Denis Thatcher obligingly replied "When I'm not paralytic, I like to play golf."

"The Secret Diary of John Major": John Major unveiled his political legacy in July 1991, when he had been prime minister for eight months: "The Citizen's Charter initiative will be fundamental to this Government's policies for the 1990s. It will be a milestone for us."

The big idea? The Cones Hotline, which allowed road users to report the unnecessary use of traffic cones.

"St Albion Parish News": Tony Blair launched his 2001 general election campaign at St Saviour's and St Olave's School, Southwark. Days later, on *Newsnight*, Jeremy Paxman asked him "How soon did you realise it was a mistake?... Come on! Seriously, there must have been a point where you are there in front of the stained-glass windows and you thought you were the vicar of St Albion's."

"The Supreme Leader": Gordon Brown had been in Number 10 for five months and had begun to manifest the amazing anti-Midas touch that characterised his premiership when Lib Dem deputy leader Vince Cable stood up in the Commons and informed him that "The House has noticed the prime minister's remarkable

transformation in the last few weeks from Stalin to Mr Bean."

"Dig for LibTory": In the edition dated 1 October 2010, Fountain, Jamieson and cartoonist Henry Davies [☞ MUTT AND JEFF] had David Cameron adopt a Churchillian tone in their "Dig for LibTory" strip.

Five days later, Cameron told the Conservative party conference that "We will play our part – but the part you play will mean even more meaningful. Your country needs you."

☞ NUMBER 10, Richard Ingrams's visits to

PRIVATE SPY

Thirty-three years after the resignation of Harold Wilson as prime minister, it was finally officially confirmed that MI5 had held a file on him, under the codename "Norman Worthington".[177] This came thirteen years after his former cabinet secretary Lord Hunt had outlined his belief that "There is absolutely no doubt at all that a few, a very few, malcontents in MI5, people who should not have been there in the first place – a lot of them like Peter Wright who were right wing, malicious and had serious personal grudges – gave vent to these and spread damaging malicious stories about that Labour government."[178]

Did they use *Private Eye* to do so? Opinions are divided. Richard Ingrams says that "I don't go along with that at all," although he concedes that "I think if there was any connection to MI5 it would have been through Bron. Because the sort of clubs that he went to, he would have met people in MI5." Auberon Waugh himself said in 1987 "I think the *Eye* probably was used by MI5."[179] Certainly a number of the semi-fictional fantasies floated in his "Diary" () bear an astonishing resemblance to those the rogue MI5 man Peter Wright claimed in *Spycatcher* that he and his colleagues had been propagating. "Mr Cord Meyer, the CIA's gifted and agreeable new station chief in London, should take a long hard look at these repeated attempts by Iron Curtain countries to secure Harold Wilson's re-election," Waugh mused in May 1973. "I am not, of course, suggesting that Wislon may be a Russian agent,

which would be completely absurd, or that there could be any connection between these events and his close relations with various Russian leaders after Mr Wilson's numerous visits to Moscow as 'economic consultant' to Montague Meyer, the timber merchant." By September 1975 he was less cautious: "I have never attempted to disguise my belief that Harold Wilson was a Soviet agent."[180]

Waugh, of course, always insisted that nothing in his "Diary" was meant to be taken seriously. But the hacks working on the factual side of the magazine were getting plenty of material on Wilson and his associates too. Martin Tomkinson has said he had a Security Service contact who "hinted that Wilson was far too interested in promoting Anglo-Soviet trade".[181] And Patrick Marnham described a series of "Secret Service information packs" about Wilson and his political associates which had arrived anonymously at the offices from 1974 onwards. "As we sorted through this material, we were directed back over the years to the 'Groundnut Scheme', the Lynskey Tribunal, the export to Russia of top-secret Rolls-Royce engines, the Leipzig Trade Fair and the opening of the Soviet Trade Delegation in London – after a quarry whose name changed on every other page," he recalled. "Was it the KGB? Was it the Israeli Intelligence Service? Was it some dark alliance of both?"

One document sent to the *Eye* and other publications – a photostat of statements from a Swiss bank account supposedly held by Labour deputy leader Ted Short – was later confirmed by Peter Wright as a forgery circulated by

The name is Bron, Bron Waugh: Ingrams says "I think if there was any connection to MI5, it would have been through Bron."

MI5 dissidents engaged in their own personal war against Wilson. That was just the tip of the iceberg, according to Marnham: "It was a story on a vast scale, stretching back over 30 years and moving from London to Moscow to East Berlin to Bucharest to Tel Aviv. It would have tested the resources of a national newspaper, and it was well beyond the powers of *Private Eye* to investigate it as thoroughly as it deserved."[182] That wasn't for want of trying. Ingrams even called in the cavalry – "following on from the Wilson resignation in '76, Paul Foot started coming into the *Eye* again because there was a general feeling that there was a big story behind Wilson's resignation and Paul, Gillard, Marnham and myself, we had regular meetings as a sort of special committee set up to try to get to the bottom of it." They never did. "Our investigations ground to a halt for lack of corroborative evidence," said Marnham. "The paper is frequently accused of failing to check its stories. Here was a case where the failure of its inquiries caused it to keep silence. We were unable to discover whether or not the KGB had infiltrated Downing Street."

"It's fairly clear now that Wilson had decided to resign because he thought he was getting Alzheimer's. Which he was. So there was really no more to it than that," sighs Ingrams now. But in his latter days in Downing Street and afterwards, the prime minister certainly believed someone was out to get him, calling in police to investigate the "theft" of his tax records ("I never had any doubt as to where they had gone – into the wastepaper basket," wrote his close colleague Joe Haines)[183] and briefing BBC journalists Roger Courtiour and Barrie Penrose that a number of different secret services from various countries were plotting against him and Jeremy Thorpe – although he also told them "I might tell you to go to the Charing Cross Road and kick a blind man standing on the corner. That blind man may tell you something, lead you somewhere," which suggests he might not have been the most reliable source in the world.

Another twist came with Paul Foot's championing of Colin Wallace, whom the *Eye* had been happy to call a "lunatic and killer" when he was wrongly convicted of manslaughter in 1981, but whose work on black propaganda in Northern Ireland as a Ministry of Defence press officer in the 1970s Foot subsequently detailed at length in the magazine's pages – including his claim that he had been ordered to disseminate the idea Harold Wilson was a KGB agent.

One figure from the *Eye*'s early days who has been convincingly accused of involvement with the secret services is Tom Driberg (☞). His biographer Francis Wheen pooh-poohed claims that Driberg was ever a full-fledged MI5 agent – he was the last person to be trusted with state secrets – but points out that when he was a member of the Communist party in the 1930s he had been cultivated by Max Knight, who definitely did work for the security service. Driberg's subsequent career on Fleet Street and in Parliament could have made him a useful source of information to the security service – Wheen points out that he was "a man who gossiped compulsively about everyone and everything". It's possible he was smuggling information back from the *Eye* lunches as well as taking it to them. Marnham noted that when Driberg left for Malta for a while to avoid a scandal over frolics with guardsmen, an MI5 man and Tory MP Captain Henry Kerby suddenly started taking an interest in the *Eye* and coming to the lunches. Another figure who took a keen interest in the magazine was Colonel Sammy Lohan, the secretary of the D-Notice Committee who had summoned the young *Eye* team for a telling-off in 1963 (☞ COCKBURN, Claud). After falling out with Harold Wilson he "took to dropping in at Greek Street and drinking a great deal of whisky" with the hacks. It would be thirty years before papers released by the Public Record Office revealed that Lohan had been on a £500-a-year retainer from MI5 "for titbits of information he brought them from Fleet Street".[184]

But MI5 may not have been the only agency to which Driberg reported. A 1999 book by KGB defector Vasili Mitrokhin claims that Driberg was blackmailed into working for the Russian secret service after falling for the compromising-photos trick when enjoying himself in a Moscow toilet he described as "frequented by hundreds of questing Slav homosexuals".[185] "There can't, I think, be any doubt that he knowingly passed on government information," a former head of the Joint Intelligence Committee told the BBC in 2009.[186] "I think Driberg was very blackmailable because of his activities, so it would be perfectly possible that he would have been used," says Ingrams. Whether he ever passed any KGB propaganda on to the *Eye* – or vice versa – we will probably never know. Maybe he just smuggled in subversive crossword clues.

Only one thing can we know for sure – spies from both sides of the cold war were keen *Eye* readers. KGB defector Kim Philby took out an overseas subscription and had it sent to Moscow for many years. And when journalists toured the old MI5 building in Gower Street in 1995, after the secret servicemen had decamped to a new HQ in Thames House, they found decorating the walls framed *Private Eye* covers depicting John Major.[187]

☞ BLUNT, Anthony, extremely displeased to be outed as spy; REGRETS, few had by eds

PROFUMO SCANDAL

☞ WARD, Stephen; COCKBURN, Claud

PROPRIETORS' RULE,
breaking of by 'Street of Shame'

For decades under press giants such as Beaverbrook and Rothermere, there was a tradition that newspaper proprietors did not report on one another's bad behaviour. Since 1970 – when it splashed the new owner of the *Sun* all over its cover and promised full coverage of "Rupert 'Digger' Murdoch, the man who made a fortune out of filth" – *Private Eye* drove a coach and horses through this rule.

"There used to be a dog didn't eat dog thing – that just ended with *Private Eye*, *Private Eye* just stopped it, dogs ate dog all over the place," says Peter McKay. "And also media gossip – prior to *Private Eye* there were no media columns – the media just never wrote about the media. *Private Eye* changed that completely, to this day."

Or did it? In March 2009 the magazine reported that McKay's boss, the 4th Baron Rothermere, owner of that most proudly British of newspapers the *Daily Mail*, was non-domiciled for tax purposes and channelled "hundreds of millions of pounds" of dividends from his newspaper business through the tax haven of Bermuda. To date not one other paper has followed the story up.

PROVEN LAWYER

Robin Shaw of Davenport Lyons is *Private Eye*'s lawyer, and reads each edition for libel. He finds quite a lot. "If I were to try to make an issue of the *Eye* non-libellous, it would just be blank pages. My job is to help them get away with as much as they can," he says.[188]

He's very good at it. "He understands perfectly what we're trying to do," says appreciative hack Tim Minogue. "He understands that our job is to tell the story as best we can, without it costing us a fortune because we used the wrong bloody word. Whereas there are lawyers who come in when Robin's not there who look at it in a very nervous, anxious, defensive way and hold up their hands and say 'No, you can't do that!'"

Robin Shaw in the *Eye* office, 2010

"There used to be this chap called Barry who came in and read the magazine for libel back in the 1980s," remembers Francis Wheen. "He'd just sit there and say 'This is all libel from beginning to end, you can't publish that.' And I'd say 'Let's take it one sentence at a time. Word one, "The". Do you think that's libellous?'"

Shaw, by contrast, sees his job as facilitating journalists to say what they need to say. And usually giggling along with them as he suggests just how to do so. Like most of the hacks, he's been a fan of the magazine since his teenage years, and it shows. "I think it's essential publications like it exist. I am astonished by the sleaziness and corruption of some of the people they expose. These people need to find their nemesis."

He is the master of a legal device which Ian Hislop calls the "Fuck Off letter". These go out to lawyers whose clients are chancing their arm with an initial accusation of libel. And they are things of beauty, as these extracts from one sent to weirdo businessmen the Barclay Brothers after they objected to a joke in June 2010 demonstrate:

> "The contents of your letter are really quite astonishing. Is it the case that, between you and your clients, you have all failed to realise that the 'article' on page 21 of which you complain is a spoof?
>
> Even to those unfamiliar with *Private Eye* there are a number of features of the article, on the page on which it appears, and on those surrounding it, that would suggest to such readers that the articles and material on these pages are not genuine … Would any reader studying the 'Disillusion Honours List' on page 22 believe that John Prescott had been ennobled for 'services to his secretary' or Michael Howard for 'services to the Transylvanian Community and the Involuntary Blood Transfusion Authority?' …
>
> The law of libel recognises that statements made in jest are not actionable … The overall position was most recently summarised by the Master of the Rolls in *Jeynes v. News Magazine* (2008), in a passage which Tugendhat J. cited and relied on only a few days ago in *Thornton v. Telegraph Media Group* (16 June 2010) arising out of allegedly defamatory material published in the *Daily Telegraph*, i.e. your clients' publication …
>
> In these circumstances, we would suggest that you reconsider whether this is a claim that your clients wish to maintain."

Nothing further was heard from the Barclays on the matter.

☞ ARKELL v. PRESSDRAM; JOBS, unlikely subsequent ones of *Eye* contributors

PSEUD, The

The Oxford English Dictionary defines Pseud as an adjective "used of the pretentious or insincere generally", and cites its first use as being in the *Spectator* in October 1962.

The Oxford English Dictionary is wrong. The Pseud made his first appearance in school magazine *The Salopian* in 1954, courtesy of 'Otis', aka Richard Ingrams.

THE PSEUD

There is a tribe that in the world exists
Who might be called the pseudo-culturists.
Who think they can to heavenly realms aspire
By warbling Handel in the concert choir ;
He who acclaims as masterpieces all
The tawdry paintings of the mad Chagall
Who quotes from Blake or from Professor Freud,
This man I label with the title " Pseud."

OTIS.

It would not be appended to a Corner until 1968. The OED at least manages to get that right.

☞ SHREWSBURY

PSEUDO-NAMES

The *Eye*'s pseudo-names correspondence began in September 2009 when Carl Isleunited wrote to warn the magazine of the danger of football fans infiltrating its pages (a sentiment quickly echoed by Ray Throvers and Lew Tontown among others). The piles of entries stacked next to chief sub-editor Tristan Davies's desk suggest it is not going to stop any time soon.

PSEUDS, Britain's ten biggest

By number of entries in "Pseuds Corner" identified in the *Eye*'s archive:

10. Damien Hirst

9. Paul Johnson

8. Tracey Emin

7. James Wood, chief literary critic on the *Guardian*

6. Hans Keller, music critic

5. Sir Roy Strong

4. Clive James, who once complained that "*Private Eye*'s crusade against barbarism is decisively hobbled by its own philistinism, and even though its editor undeniably knows how to put one of his own sentences together, it doesn't necessarily follow that he's equipped to criticise one of mine."[189]

3. Martin Amis

2. Simon Barnes, chief sports writer on the *Times*, *with* thirty-eight entries, more than double the number of his closest competitor

---

PSEUDS' CORNER
£1 prize for entries

■ If the essence of Bach, Mozart and the Beatles has bitten into a person, that person today will, barring prejudice and narrowness of interest, listen delightedly to The Incredible String Band and Tyrannosaurrus Rex, Bob Dylan, Jacques Loussier, Simon and Garfunkel, T-Bone Walker, Julian Bream, Ewan MacColl and Stockhausen - all music irrespective of irrelevant old-style categorisations.

> William Mann
> '*The Times*'

■ The Redfern (Gallery) where Peter Sedgley is showing a number of rotating discs ('video-rotors') whose concentric patterning and fluorescent colour come to life when ultra-violet and stroboscopic light is focused on them. They're quite pretty, very lightweight, not interesting for more than a minute or two ...

> Bryan Robertson
> '*The Spectator*'

■ Why did John Braine become a *Coronation Street* addict? Because "it has heart" he says.
> TV Times

■ It is already becoming clear that one of the themes which will proccupy modern art in the Seventies is that of technology.

> Edward Lucie Smith
> '*Sunday Times*'

The first corner, 1968

BRITAIN'S BIGGEST PSEUD: Will Self, with a staggering forty-one entries, including an entire "Corner" to himself in September 1996

Honourable mentions go to *Guardian* art critic Adrian Searle, Dr Jonathan Miller and Julie Burchill, all hovering just outside the top ten, and Russell Brand, who despite only making his debut in 2006, has already racked up eight appearances in "Pseuds Corner".

Britain's pseudiest publication is, by quite some distance, the *Guardian*.

PYNE, Ken

Ken Pyne's cartoons first appeared in the *Eye* in 1975. Like Willie Rushton, whose slot on the "Literary Review" page he took over, he has the ability to dash off a caricature which somehow manages to look more like the subject than they do themselves.

☞ STRIPS, Longest-running

QUEEN, Ian Hislop turns down invitation from

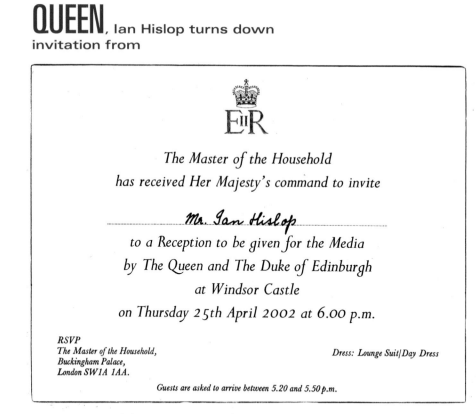

*The Master of the Household
has received Her Majesty's command to invite*

Mr. Ian Hislop

*to a Reception to be given for the Media
by The Queen and The Duke of Edinburgh
at Windsor Castle
on Thursday 25th April 2002 at 6.00 p.m.*

*RSVP
The Master of the Household,
Buckingham Palace,
London SW1A 1AA.*   *Dress: Lounge Suit/Day Dress*

Guests are asked to arrive between 5.20 and 5.50 p.m.

IAN HISLOP: I didn't go. A step too far.

☞ NUMBER 10, Ingrams's visits to

QUESTIONS, asked by Ian Hislop of Richard Ingrams at their first meeting

Undergraduate Ian Hislop interviewed Richard Ingrams for his student mag *Passing Wind* (☞) in 1980. "It was a bit stalkery," he admitted later.[190]

These are the questions he asked him.

- *Do you have a political stance?*
- *Is the idea to expose people for a moral purpose or for its own sake?*
- *Do you justify this form of 'muck-raking'?*
- *Do you think Journalism is a bitchy world?*
- *Do you censor yourself?*
- *The essence of your gossip pages is to be funny?*
- *What do you gain from the Libel cases, apart from publicity?*
- *Do you know for certain that Reginald Bosanquet wears a wig?*
- *Do you believe that there's a possibility of you being put in prison?*
- *Does your attitude to the Royal Family get you into trouble?*
- *What sort of market is the* Eye *aimed at?*
- *People have claimed that much of the magazine is of little general interest – the City pages for example.*
- *You haven't changed the format in a very long time. Do you feel it becoming staid as some people claim?*
- *Are you interested in expanding the magazine?*
- *Is Peter Cook still as funny?*
- *Have you heard Derek and Clive live?*
- *What do you think of* Punch*?*
- *You don't seem to like John Cleese?*
- *Would you define yourself as a journalist?*

In return Ingrams told him that yes, Reginald Bosanquet definitely did wear a wig.

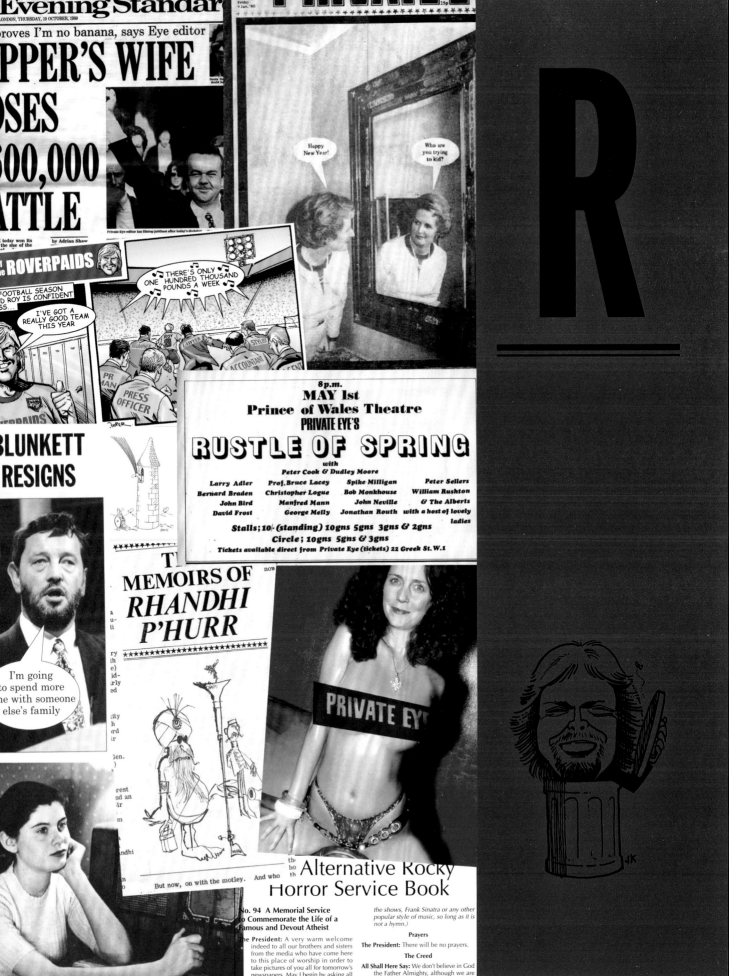

R

Evening Standard

LONDON, THURSDAY, 19 OCTOBER, 1989

...roves I'm no banana, says Eye editor

...PPER'S WIFE

...OSES

...00,000

...TTLE

...today won its ...the size of the

by Adrian Shaw

Private Eye editor Ian Hislop jubilant after today's decision

...e ROVERPAIDS

FOOTBALL SEASON ...D ROY IS CONFIDENT ...S...

I'VE GOT A REALLY GOOD TEAM THIS YEAR

THERE'S ONLY ONE HUNDRED THOUSAND POUNDS A WEEK

PR MAN

PRESS OFFICER

BIOGRAPHER / LAWYER / STYLIST / ACCOUNTANT

Happy New Year!

Who are you trying to kid?

...BLUNKETT RESIGNS

I'm going to spend more ...me with someone else's family

8 p.m.
MAY 1st
Prince of Wales Theatre
PRIVATE EYE'S

RUSTLE OF SPRING

with
Peter Cook & Dudley Moore

Larry Adler	Prof. Bruce Lacey	Spike Milligan	Peter Sellers
Bernard Braden	Christopher Logue	Bob Monkhouse	William Rushton
John Bird	Manfred Mann	John Neville	& The Alberts
David Frost	George Melly	Jonathan Routh	with a host of lovely ladies

Stalls; 10/- (standing) 10gns 5gns 3gns & 2gns
Circle; 10gns 5gns & 3gns
Tickets available direct from Private Eye (tickets) 22 Greek St. W.1

THE MEMOIRS OF RHANDHI P'HURR

But now, on with the motley. And who...

PRIVATE EYE

Alternative Rocky Horror Service Book

No. 94 A Memorial Service to Commemorate the Life of a Famous and Devout Atheist

The President: A very warm welcome indeed to all our brothers and sisters from the media who have come here to this place of worship in order to take pictures of you all for tomorrow's newspapers. May I begin by asking all...

...the shows, Frank Sinatra or any other popular style of music, so long as it is not a hymn.)

Prayers

The President: There will be no prayers.

The Creed

All Shall Here Say: We don't believe in God the Father Almighty, although we are...

READER SURVEYS

"We don't aim at a particular market; we certainly would not sit around here discussing who's going to read it," said Richard Ingrams in 1980. "I see people reading it on the trains and things and they look like a strange lot."[191]

Actually, his advertising staff did a fair bit of research into who was reading the *Eye*; they just knew better than to tell him about it. Opposite are some of the exciting findings of readership surveys conducted in 1962, 1968 and 2010.

Typical *Eye* readers as seen by Ralph Steadman in 1965 . . .

	1962	1968	2010
Sex	80% male	92% male	69% male
Age	Young – 72% of readers under 34, and 2% under 16	Even younger – 62% were aged 16-24	Average age 48
Education	24% were students	28% had gone to public school, and 49% to grammars	66% have a degree
Earnings	Majority "over £1,000 a year"	19% "£2,000 p.a. and over", 31% "under £11 per week"	Average household income £50,169
Work	9% described themselves as politicians; 47% were "in a profession"	7% described themselves as "artisans", more than the 4% who were journalists	"*Private Eye* readers account for 7% of all chairmen/CEOs and 5% of all MDs"
Best fact	Asked "Do your suits cost over £20?", exactly half said yes	"79% of our readers approve of the increase in *Private Eye* of serious political comment"	"*Private Eye* readers are 27% more likely to drink every day than all AB adults"
Cost of a full page ad	£150	£120	£5,550
Cost of a copy	One shilling	1/6	£1.50

READERS, Mutually beneficial relationship with

"Because our readers are about as tolerant as I am, they let you know if they think you've got a story wrong," says Ian Hislop. "If it's in an area they know about, you just get a flood of letters straight away. It's like it's their club."[192]

Francis Wheen agrees. "Some weeks you get a blizzard of rather good tip-offs. That's one of the great assets of the *Eye*, that people write in to a degree that they don't with other publications."

If your local council is up to no good, or the bloke who lives down the road who happens to be an MP has been seen with large bundles of brown envelopes full of five pound notes you then naturally write to *Private Eye*. One of the things that appealed to me from the moment I started reading it aged thirteen was this sense of being in on something."

This is, of course, exactly the sort of relationship with readers that most media companies are investing millions in trying to create via their websites, Twitter feeds and Have

... and by Nick Newman in 2007

Your Say initiatives, and twenty-somethings with words like "Community" in their job titles are insisting is a new and revolutionary concept. But it's been going on at the *Eye* since the days of fountain pens and 6d first-class stamps. "Each postbag bulged with marvellous stories," remembered Paul Foot of his first stint at the mag in the 1960s. "Disaffected and disorientated middle-class and professional people mischievously, usually anonymously, provided inside information about their employers, their competitors, their jilted lovers or their heroes." When he got to the *Mirror* in 1979, the letters and calls were of a totally different order. "The sense of mischief had almost vanished."

Back at the *Eye*, things were as good as ever. Christopher Silvester remembers when he joined in 1983 that "The postbag was like the spoils that would be shared out among the in-house hacks by Richard [Ingrams], writing our names on the top." The system remains unchanged to this day, save for the addition of hundreds of emails – all neatly printed out, the *Eye* being about as far from a paperless office as it is possible to imagine. And there's still gold in them there piles. "Vast amounts – so much stuff!" enthuses current full-time hack Jane Mackenzie of the material that floods in from readers. "Probably about 30 percent is good stories – you could actually get enough stuff out of the postbag for most issues. And I don't think that's true of many places."

On one rule you can always rely. "One of the astonishing things with Ian is when he's going through the mail, you'll get the odd thing where he's written 'Francis – AMAZING!'" says Wheen. "And the moment you see a phrase like that, or 'This Looks Promising' or 'Astonishing Tale', you know it's a complete dud and you can throw it away without doing anything. It's odd because it seems to me editorially, by and large, he has good judgement. But I've never known that rule to fail. It's quite uncanny."

☞ UNSUNG HEROES

Jane

opinion

Loon ?

Heather.

will you have a look at this and give me a view ?

Loon-seeming but He does occasionally have a point/story.

Adam

How about his love-child?

REEVE, Tony

Surreal twists on domestic or office life have been the specialities of Tony Reeve since he started contributing in the early 1990s.

REGRETS, few had by Eds

"It would be very hard to discuss in the abstract the question of whether we've ever gone too far," said Richard Ingrams not long after relinquishing the editorship. "There is one regret I have from a long way back. After the Conservative MP Commander Courtney was photographed in bed with a woman in Moscow, the KGB circulated the pictures to various newspapers. The fact that this happened was mentioned in *Private Eye* and as a result he was dropped by his constituency and his political career brought to an end. That was a clear case where we were wrong to do as we did since we were really playing the KGB game."[193] Ingrams also admitted to feeling "uneasy about one or two of Bron's [Auberon Waugh's] personal campaigns against individuals, and I think probably I should have been stricter with my blue pencil looking back on it".[194]

And Ian Hislop? "If you ask me hand on heart which of the things which we have done that I feel least comfortable about I would say pretty much that Bryn Estyn is there," he says. This was the coverage during the 1990s of a paedophile network centred on a children's home in North Wales: while six suspects were jailed for sex abuse, one man named in *Private Eye* (as well as on television and in the *Observer*) successfully sued for libel. "It turned into this sort of terrible case, which unlike a lot of the *Eye* cases had no sort of redeeming humorous features at all," says a visibly discomfited Hislop. "It was miserable. The *Eye* had three of the boys as witnesses, all of whom I believed, and our counsel believed them. By the time they were in the witness box they were very damaged young men. And they were easily picked apart by the other side: they couldn't remember anything, the dates didn't hold up. Their subsequent lives of alcohol, drugs, rent and whatever gave little sympathy to a jury." One of the witnesses committed suicide a few months later.

Tony Blair called the report of a subsequent government inquiry into abuse, covered extensively in the *Eye*, "an appalling catalogue of terror and tragedy inflicted on some of the most vulnerable children in our society". But questions were subsequently raised about the methods of police "trawling" for witnesses and the reliability of the evidence it turned up. "There is no pattern: for instance I thought we'd done a very good job with the Orkney cases [where nine children were removed from their families amid claims of ritualistic abuse, only to be returned after legal action was ruled out] of saying this stuff is made up, this satanic abuse is bollocks," says Hislop. "But in that particular case there was definitely some sloppy journalism of which I'm not very proud and a slight mass hysteria ... yeah, I would say that that case is still grey."

☞ MMR

RESIGNATION, Richard Ingrams's, as recalled by those who were there

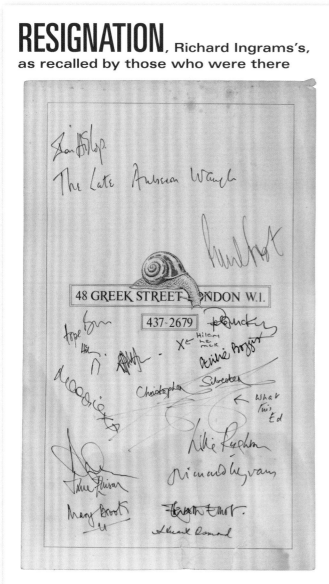

48 GREEK STREET, LONDON W.1.

437-2679

Auberon Waugh: When I resigned from the *Eye* after 16 years a small luncheon party was given in my honour at a Soho restaurant.[195]

Peter McKay: The staff assembled at L'Escargot on Friday 14 March 1986 in happy anticipation of an entertaining lunch. Bron sat next to Ingrams. Others present were Willie Rushton, Christopher Silvester, Tony Rushton, Elizabeth Elliott, Jane Ellison, Sheila Molnar, Mary Brooks, Hilary [Lowinger], Maggie [Lunn] and myself. Hislop arrived just after the lunch had started and, from the three empty seats available, took the one next to Ingrams – a move that did not escape teasing comment about his "sitting next to teacher". Ingrams gave a gently witty speech about Bron's contribution to the *Eye*, laughingly quoting readers who said his

departure was a good thing. Then he took everyone by surprise.[196]

Richard Ingrams: I have decided I should hand over to a younger and shorter man …

Auberon Waugh: Richard Ingrams chose to use this occasion to announce his own retirement as editor, and his appointment of Ian Hislop as his successor (☞ INGRAMS, Richard, decision to retire).

Tony Rushton: It was a bombshell. Richard at his absolute worst, totally disgraceful. A big table of people saying goodbye to Bron, it was an occasion to say thanks for everything, and then he gets up and said "Well, I think now I'm going to make an announcement." It was just … flabbergasting.

Ian Hislop: It was a *catastrophic* decision of Richard's to make the announcement at the end of Bron's leaving do. It infuriated Bron because it stole his thunder, a really bad bit of upstaging, and it meant that the entire story was about upset, shock, horror, fury.

Peter McKay: There was a shocked silence, broken by Willie Rushton, who said "About time too!", before striding out of the room. There was a growing chorus of disbelief.

Ian Hislop: Liz Elliott weeping. Sheila always claims she wasn't weeping. I think Liz Elliott probably was, because she was very attached to Richard and very unattached to me, ha ha! And then the wonderful moment when Silvester leaned over …

Christopher Silvester: I said, "Allow me to be the first to suck up to you."

Ian Hislop: And then ran for the phone. Which, again, was all very funny.

Sheila Molnar: McKay was pissed as a newt, and filing his copy – it was like a farce.

Maggie Lunn: It was chaos. Bron was sitting there gobsmacked. Ian was in a frenzy of keeping his end up. And I sat back and thought, "Yet again, he's got the whole thing in turmoil."[197]

Auberon Waugh: My own reaction was to try to dissuade him from resigning, but it took the form of saying "Who is this extraordinary fellow Hislop?" He'd been around for about two years but I hadn't really noticed him much at all. I thought it was unnecessary and a great shame, and I thought the magazine would collapse without him.[198]

Christopher Silvester: A lot of people were already talking about Ian as an heir apparent, that is true, but nobody expected it to happen for at least another ten or fifteen years. Most people expected Richard to go on for ever.

Tony Rushton: We'd seen a lot of Ian. I could see that he was a very talented guy. I realised that it was very good that these young people should be coming in. I think his great strength was that he was as strong on good stories for the "Colour Section" [the news pages which opened each edition of the magazine] and "In the Back" as he was on producing very original comedy. He had a much wider spectrum. Richard's decision was absolutely bang on, but it was a tragedy given that we were a supposedly democratic organisation that he hadn't taken us into his confidence.

Christopher Booker: Richard should have explained "Perhaps not all of you realise this, but actually Ian has fitted in like nobody did since Barry Fantoni walked in off the street twenty years ago."

Sheila Molnar: It was a shock to everybody. We all knew Richard just wasn't interested any more, and we weren't against Ian – Ian was incredibly funny, we liked him, you knew he was special, there was something about him – but it felt like you couldn't be sad about Richard going without being opposed to Ian. It became like these opposed camps.

Auberon Waugh: In his acceptance speech, Hislop made some hurtful remarks about the importance of youth, the need to find younger readers or whatever.

Jane Ellison: Hislop rose with an expression of triumph. He announced grandly that Ingrams was "the funniest person round this table" and added "I'm grateful to him for going." The *Eye*, he said, would be a different magazine from now on. "Some people aren't going to like it," he said, looking round the table with an expression of menace.[199]

Ian Hislop: I remained calm and told them of my intentions to find satirical targets to appeal to younger readers. I also pointed out that if the old guard didn't like me as editor that's their funeral. I revealed my plans to cut the spiralling costs of libel actions and I hinted at certain exciting future plans for the *Eye*.[200]

A press mob descended on Carlisle Street. As Eye *contributor Harry Thompson put it, "You might have been forgiven for thinking it was the Archbishop of Canterbury who had passed on his job to a twenty-six-year-old, not a mere magazine editor."*

Ian Hislop: I had no idea of the shitstorm that was about to hit, not a clue. And I went off on a skiing holiday. I'd booked to go, and I thought, "That'll be fine, I'll go." And I remember I was at Gatwick Airport with my friend Charlie Fletcher, and the front page of the *Guardian* was a picture of *me*. And I thought "Shit. This is going to be quite a story."

Guardian, 15 March 1986:

Mr Ingrams's decision came as a surprise to the staff. None of the directors had been consulted. *Eye* insiders are predicting that Mr Hislop's appointment will be strongly contested … The dispute could put the ownership of *Private Eye* in doubt. One main shareholder wants to sell his shares, and the Murdoch empire has already expressed an interest in buying *Private Eye* … The lunch broke up amid further acrimony from the old *Eye* hand Mr Peter McKay …

Ian Hislop: I'd underestimated how obsessed journalists are with themselves and each other, I just didn't know. And in the story there were endless quotes from everyone putting the boot in, and [journalist] Henry Porter said: "He's gone off on a skiing holiday, probably the worst decision he'll ever make."

Nick Newman: I don't know how Ian coped with all that animosity. He wasn't cowed by any of it.

Ian Hislop: Victoria didn't go on the holiday, and I remember ringing home and her saying "There's quite a lot of stuff here; do you want to hear it?" And I said, "How bad is it?" It was tough on her, she was slightly bewildered by it all. We weren't engaged at that age or anything. And I was away for about a week or so, and when I came back the press vitriol had really kicked in.

TURMOIL AT *PRIVATE EYE*
– Headline in Sunday Mail, *Australia*

**SATIRICAL U.K. MAGAZINE
MIRED IN STAFF REBELLION OVER
CHOICE OF EDITOR**
– Headline in Globe and Mail, *Canada*

Ian Hislop: It took ages. They had a lot of outlets. It was an extraordinary baptism of fire. I remember I had lunch with my old friend Marcus Berkmann after about six months or a year, and he looked at me in a very curious way, and said "You're going to get through this, aren't you?" And I said "Yeah, I am." Ha ha.

It came early and it wasn't the way anyone would have wanted, but maybe that's just for the best. Because I was certainly never worried again after that.

☞ INGRAMS, Richard, decision to retire and appoint Ian Hislop as successor; WORST COUP EVER

REVOLUTIONARY CADRE (left wing), *Eye* run by a

In December 1972, some time after Paul Foot had left to edit the *Socialist Worker*, the *Eye* was anonymously sent a memo which warned that "The International Socialist Group is to make a determined challenge to take over the editorial side of the magazine completely in the early part of 1972." It identified Willie Rushton as one of those whom "the recent magazine revolves around". The *Eye* pointed out that "News of this takeover will come as a particular blow to Mr William Rushton who left the *Eye*'s editorial board in 1966."

REVOLUTIONARY CADRE (right wing), *Eye* run by a

Private Eye was, the general secretary of printer's union Natsopa informed his members in 1973, "the official organ of the British Department of Dirty Tricks and Court Jesters. There is a large money fund backing the paper ... They have sought to defame our officers, our members and our Society. It is their front of the 'destroy the trade unions from within' activity."

RGJ

Richard Jolley, who began contributing in 1990, is an out-and-out gag man. So prolific a gag man, in fact, that he has expanded out of the cartoon slots: "RGJ sends in so much stuff that sometimes he just sends in ideas which we turn into jokes because there's not room for twenty-eight of his cartoons," says Ian Hislop. "Pieces, or ideas for photo bubbles. He's very good. Loads of ideas."

MAXIMVS, YOU LOST. HOW'S IT FEEL?

I'M GUTTED

POST-GLADIATORIAL SPORTS INTERVIEWS

REVOLUTIONARY LEFTISTS, Figures claimed as

by Paul Foot include:

- Shelley
- Shakespeare
- Peter Cook
- The old man who ran the sandwich bar round the corner from *Private Eye*

RICH OWNER, Search for a

Christopher Booker: You could see *Private Eye* wasn't quite what Osmond expected. And in May 1962 he comes to us with a long face and says "I think I'm going to have to leave, I have to get a proper job."

Andrew Osmond: I passed my Foreign Office exam and had to face the final board. Nine men sat round a crescent-shaped table. As I walked in they turned up a copy of *Private Eye* and said "Are you responsible for this?" and tittered. I knew then that I was in. The only thing I needed was a buyer.[201]

NUMBER CRUNCHING

£450 = amount Andrew Osmond invested in *Private Eye* in October 1961

£1,500 = amount he sold it for eight months later

Peter Usborne: When I was looking for money, my most vivid memory is of going to the offices of the *Daily Mirror* and asking the proprietor Cecil King, and he sat on a high chair in this rather grand office on a sort of dais, and I remember him saying "Well, my boy, I'm not going to back you, but I can tell you that money is never really the problem." And I thought, you bastard!

Tony Rushton: Clive Labovitch and Michael Heseltine invited us to Haymarket Press, which produced just *About Town* then, before becoming this huge empire that it is today. But they insultingly wanted us to run a section of their magazine. They would buy our talent and *Private Eye* would close. We thought "No, we don't want to be that."

Booker: I said I think the answer is the Establishment nightclub, which was then at its zenith. I used to see my old friend Peter Cook from time to time. It was an amazing place, the Establishment. For about a year it was really quite exciting to be there, and then it lost its way. Basically when Cookie and the *Beyond the Fringe* lads went off to the States.

At twenty-five, Peter Cook had already written a West End revue for Kenneth Williams; been one-quarter of the immensely successful show Beyond the Fringe, *which had run at the Edinburgh Festival, sold out houses in London for a year and was now transferring to Broadway; become a huge celebrity, and opened Britain's first satirical nightclub, the Establishment. It was an attempt to ape the political cabarets of 1930s Berlin which, as he points out, "did so much to prevent the rise of Adolf Hitler". The building also contained a cellar jazz bar in which the Dudley Moore Trio performed, a photographic studio where Lewis Morley took* that *photo of Christine Keeler straddling a chair, and a waiters' changing room which was the home of* Private Eye *for three issues until they found other premises two doors down Greek Street.*

Usborne: Peter flew over from New York as soon as he heard that *Private Eye* needed money – it was amazingly quick; he flew over straight away – and basically agreed to buy the magazine from Andrew Osmond.
Peter Cook: I was actually very annoyed when the *Eye* had come out. I'd wanted to start a practically identical magazine, then bloody *Private Eye* came out and I was really pissed off.[202]
Booker: It happened with remarkable speed.
Usborne: Peter Cook having bought *Private Eye* went back to America and *Beyond the Fringe* on Broadway, and left Nick Luard as kind of his representative on earth.

☞ LUARD, Nicholas, opinion of own role in *Private Eye*; LUARD, Nicholas, others' opinion of role in *Private Eye*

RING OF TRUTH, The

ROTTEN BOROUGHS

One of the defining characteristics of the *Eye* is that it is less Londoncentric than the rest of the media. This is helped by the fact that very few of its journalists live in the capital – the regular contributors range from the Isle of Wight to Cumbria and Somerset to Sussex – but it is also the result of a determined effort by Ian Hislop to extend the scope of its investigations beyond the boundaries of London Underground's Circle Line, outside of which most national newspapers believe nothing exists. "One of the bits of journalism I did before I was editor was a thing called 'London Calling'," says Hislop of his days

"Rotten Boroughs" illustrations provided by Rupert Redway

chronicling Ken Livingstone's Greater London Council. "And I remember consciously thinking then, 'We should do this about everyone.'"

The "Rotten Boroughs" heading had been used occasionally on Paul Foot's column since the 1960s – the T. Dan Smith story (☞ POULSON, scandal brings down home secretary) was probably the premier example of the genre – but it got its own fortnightly berth in 1986, and has now expanded to a full page of the magazine every fortnight. The column has prompted resignations, walk-outs and furious denunciations in council chambers across the land: countless contracts have been ripped up after the cosy relationships between councillors and contractors were detailed in full, and any number of seats have been lost after the *Eye* put electors in full possession of the facts about their representatives.

Tim Minogue, the third person to helm the column after Ed Glinert and Sarah Shannon, says he never ceases to be amazed at the scale of the scandals which are left to the *Eye* to uncover. "We've got room for five or six items each issue, and these are selected and checked out from around 100 to 150 tips or leads every time. The majority are just from members of the public who are pissed off. I'd say each fortnight we get tipped off about sixty or seventy or so things that if you had the time and the manpower you could turn into proper stories." This journalistic goldmine is all but ignored by the rest of the media. "Unless it's some really sort of egregious bit of corruption, or its Boris or a mate of Boris's, the national papers just aren't interested," says Minogue. "There are some honourable exceptions – some local papers do it, but they should beat us all the time because they're there. I don't know anybody in Aberdeen or Exeter or wherever. I think local papers have always been very cautious about some of this stuff because you don't want to rock the boat: some councils have withdrawn job advertising from local papers when they've criticised them, and put it in their own papers instead, so there's a sort of economic fear. And then of course local papers are absolutely terrified of getting any lawyers' bills. So there's all sorts of reasons why they won't rock the boat."

Occasionally a story erupts into the national consciousness when it balloons to an extent the rest of the media can't ignore. Minogue recalls "Donnygate", the extreme corruption of the local authority in Doncaster in the 1990s which led to the imprisonment of more than twenty councillors: "It came about because of a very honourable councillor called Ron Rose who realised that all his colleagues were on the fiddle. And he tried to raise this at local and regional level, and was ignored. And then he managed to get it to Tony Blair, who did nothing about it. So eventually Ron went to Christian Wolmar at the *Independent* and *Private Eye*, and we both broke it."

After Minogue's own twelve years (and several electoral cycles) overseeing the column, he has had the satisfaction of watching many chickens come home to roost. "We were in early with the Bath Spa stuff and got outraged letters from the chief executive of Bath and North East Somerset Council saying it was going to be a big success and they would invite us when it opened in six months' time. And then it didn't open for another three years! And he said 'How dare you say it's going to be five million over budget,' and it ended up being twenty or thirty million pounds over budget!"

☞ READERS, Mutually beneficial relationship with

RUBBISH, stolen and passed to Mohammed Fayed

Birthday card by Nick Newman sent to Ian Hislop, 1999

In the summer of 1999, Mohamed Fayed's magazine *Punch* ran a sneering piece about Ian Hislop's relations with his staff, based on a scathing memo he had sent to investigative hack Solomon Hughes. Except he hadn't.

"I quite often write notes to people and then think 'No, I'm not going to send that,' and then throw them away," says Hislop. "I threw this one away, and then it appeared in *Punch*."

The magazine had carefully tried to disguise the origin of its scoop, printing fulsome thanks to a supposed source in the *Eye* office. But the editor never had any doubt. "I know who's in the building, and when pieces appear about the *Eye* you know if someone leaked it. I know if I read a piece in Peter McKay's column whether Richard's had lunch with him. It's not a big office."

This came as a relief to Hughes, who had double reason to fear the finger of blame: not only had he done some work for *Punch* himself in the past, he hadn't quite got round to telling the boss at his day-job that he was moonlighting as a journalist yet. "I thought 'Oh God, this is really bad.' But then, obviously, I realised nobody was going to read *Punch*."

Ed McLachlan's take on the relaunch of the *Eye*'s old competitor in 1996

Hislop swiftly set up a security camera outside the office which revealed that Benji "The Binman" Pell, a peculiar individual who made a living rifling through the bins outside lawyers' chambers, talent agencies and other businesses and flogging off whatever he found to newspapers, had added the *Eye* to his rounds. Security measures were introduced. Staff took care to dispense teabags and the leftovers from smelly lunches equally around each wastepaper basket, wrote epically scurrilous notes about Fayed especially to throw them away, and, slightly more practically, purchased a shredder. "I have always known that *Punch* was full of rubbish and that its proprietor deals in rubbish, but I had not realised before that this was the literal truth," wrote Hislop in a lengthy piece for the *Eye*. And Pell himself was arrested in possession of fifteen sacks of rubbish he had picked up from various addresses around Soho. When James Goldsmith had employed private detectives to rifle through the *Eye*'s rubbish at the height of his war with the magazine (☞ GOLDENBALLS) they had taken the precaution of photocopying whatever they found and then returning it, so they could not be charged with theft. Pell hadn't, and was. Didn't that make his clients guilty of handling stolen goods, the *Eye* asked?

Apparently not. No one else was ever charged in relation to the case, and Pell managed successfully to convince a jury that he suffered from "a severe debilitating illness … an obsession with waste and rubbish", which meant he should only be fined £20. The other distressing symptom of his condition, compulsively selling relevant bits of the rubbish to journalists for thousands of pounds, was not considered relevant.

Punch itself disappeared into the dustbin of history in 2002. Fayed is not thought to have taken up the generous offers by several *Eye* readers – some with children still in nappies – who wrote in and offered to forward their own rubbish directly to Harrods if he liked it so much.

☞ FRASER, Jason; MORON, Piers

RUSHTON, Tony, Sacking of (failed)

The Ballsachers: 1

The ghastly world of Sydney Nothing

BY LUNCHTIME O'BOOZE

Tone takes a starring role in an *Eye* photostory, 1965

Willie Rushton's cousin Tone joined the *Eye* in June 1962 – "on Peter Usborne's invitation, not on William's invitation. I always make a point of telling people I didn't get in through the back door." He started off as a "sort of general dogsbody", but swiftly added the

layout to his duties thanks to his experience in the area: "Letraset, the transfer lettering, had been launched the previous year, and I'd used some samples to write my name in one of my diaries."

He too was a Shrewsbury boy, but "a year younger than William, Richard, Booker and Foot, and a year makes a huge difference at that age, so I never really knew them at school". They have continued to treat him like disdainful sixth-formers ever since.

Rushton soon added the advertising department to his kingdom too. And for a brief period that it clearly still pains the former editor to recall, he was the *Eye*'s managing director. "I can't remember how that happened." Ingrams's brow creases in bafflement. "I can't *imagine* how that happened."

"He just sort of acquired the role when Uz went off," says his eventual successor Dave Cash. "Tone's a nice enough bloke, but in certain aspects he doesn't have … I don't like to put Tone down actually. I'm soppy. Tone's all right. He wasn't suited to that at all."

"It was the biggest mistake he made in his life really," Rushton cheerfully confirms of Ingrams allowing him to take the job. "I wasn't really very good with figures. And it was obviously impossible to do advertising, management and layout all at the same time. There was only so much time in the day. I lasted for quite a few years, possibly four or five. I enjoyed it. I probably wasn't spending as much time and trouble on the accounts as they would think proper. And in hindsight they were completely right."

Fortunately, at this point – part way through 1969 – Andrew Osmond reappeared on the scene, having changed his mind again about his career (☞ RICH OWNER, Search for a), and started writing political thrillers in collaboration with a Foreign Office colleague, Douglas Hurd. While Hurd relied on politics for the day job that enabled him to maintain their four-novel collaboration, Osmond decided a part-time post as managing director of *Private Eye* would be ideal. "I always thought he was a very good businessman, Andrew, if he put his mind to something," says Ingrams. "He was called in at various points when things had got in a mess, to sort it all out."

All that remained was to sack Tone to make

Andrew Osmond, having rejoined the *Eye,* **plans for the future**

way for him, a task which the editor bent himself to with glee. "Richard was always cursing Tone, all the bloody time," says Cash. "At 34 Greek Street I was in one office on the second floor and Tone was next door, where the mag used to be laid out. And Tone had this dreadful sneeze. And he used to sneeze and then – *thump*, *thump*, *thump* – Ingrams was banging on the ceiling, and this happened every bloody day. Tone used to drive Ingrams absolutely mad, he used to come down and complain to me and anyone else within earshot all the time about what Tone was doing on the layout and all the rest of it, and how he wanted to get rid of him. So it was an ongoing thing that Richard had. It wasn't just his management skills."

"I was sacked – ha ha!" cackles Rushton. "I have letters which I have put in my 'not to be opened till after death file' from Richard to me, saying 'I think you should hand over.'" But Ingrams had made a serious mistake: he had only sliced off one of the Hydra's heads. "I continued to do the advertising and I continued to do the layout," says Tone calmly. "In a way I was still managing, because I was telling people what to do, and when to do it and so on."

"Richard wanted him to go altogether," confirms Cash. "But it was just a sort of shrug of the shoulders." Ingrams, who is about as capable of confronting someone directly as he is of walking on water, elected to deal with the situation by ignoring it and just continuing to

grumble. The only person rude enough to ask why Tone was still coming to the building every day was Norman Balon from the Coach and Horses, who used to greet Rushton with the words "I thought they sacked you?" Eventually, in 2006, Balon retired too. Forty-two years, one editor and four managing directors later, Tone is still very much in residence.

☞ BOXWALLAHS; WREATH, Funeral, delivered by editor to art director

Tone at work in Greek Street: dagger added by affectionate colleagues

RUSHTON, Willie, leaving present from

When she left the *Eye* in 1985, hackette Liz Elliott was presented with a version of Botticelli's *Venus* as seen by the magazine's longest-serving cartoonist.

Clockwise from centre: Liz Elliott, Richard Ingrams, a canine Barry Fantoni, Willie Rushton, Christopher Booker and Tony Rushton, Ian Hislop.

POWER MAN

ULTRA MAN

TOKEN WOMAN

TOM MAN

MEYRICK JONES

105-106 Great Russell Street London WC1B 3LJ
Tel 01-580 2746 Telex 261026 Adlib G Fax 01-631-3253 Cables Adlib London WC1

Ian Hislop
PRIVATE EYE
6 Carlisle Street
LONDON W1

BY FAX

CONGRATULATIONS!

All the best from everyone here.

Tom Rosenthal

PRIVATE EYE
50p

SAS INQUEST SHOCK

Why did you shoot him 16 times?

I ran out of bullets

mummy

SCHOOL

KEVIN WOODCOCK

1.

"My wife! Say I'm busy - in conference, tell her anything".

2.

"He's on the couch with Miss Burnham".

S

THE ALTERNATIVE VOICE

SANDY LANE, Gratuitous
excuse to print picture taken in

SECRET DIARY
OF JOHN MAJOR, The

"The Secret Diary of John Major" arrived well ahead of its subject's ascension to Downing Street. "When he was foreign secretary he made a trip and we wrote him up as a silly Pooter figure, and then when he became prime minister we thought 'That's funny,'" recalls Ian Hislop. "I can't remember which person, or whether it was all of us – I suppose I must have made the final decision as the editor – I thought 'That's funny, that'll work.'"

After eleven years of Ingrams and Wells writing "Dear Bill" (☞) alone – which Hislop says "the old guard were a bit miffed" about – the whole team got involved with the "Secret Diary". "Of all the things we've ever done in the *Eye*, the John Major diary is my favourite," enthuses Barry Fantoni. "That whole world is

SCARFE, Gerald

Gerald Scarfe, who made his debut in December 1962, credits the *Eye* with giving him the confidence to develop his style: "I worked as a commercial artist for a while, which felt like I'd sold my soul to the devil. Peter Cook and William Rushton encouraged my political cartooning and it was then that I could let myself fly."[203]

"There was a period of great savagery in *Private*

Eye at that time, particularly with Scarfe," remembers Ingrams, who enjoyed their collaborations. "I always thought that political cartoons worked better if you discussed the idea with them. Scarfe and Steadman would come in every fortnight and we'd talk for about half an hour, an hour. Then [Scarfe] got very grand and didn't like being given ideas."

22

Now, Exclusive to Private Eye

The Diary of a Private Foreign Secretary

(aged 30¼)

——— Tuesday 29 September ———

TODAY I went in an aeroplane to a place called America. They gave us sweets on the aeroplane, and there was a film. It was called *Indiana Jones*. I liked it.

Then we landed at a big airport called New York. We went in a car to the hotel. There are very tall buildings here called skyscrapers. I sent a postcard to Mrs Thatcher. It was of the Empire State Building which is one of the tallest buildings in the world. All the taxis here are yellow and there are lots of Chinese people like in Hong Kong.

called Mr Sheverdnasty or something like that. He was very kind to me although I think he thought I came from Canada. I tried to explain that I was English, but he had already moved on to talk to someone else.

I was looking round for someone else to talk to and then a very nice American came up to me and said he was called Mr Bush. He...

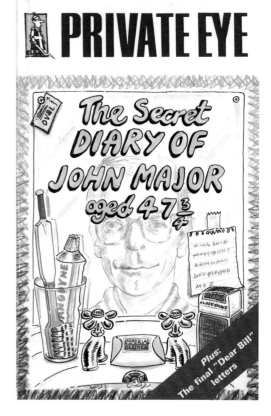

majestic, it made the most wonderful – his brother turning up, and his wife Norman, it was perfect! When Heseltine finally usurped and he had to knock on the door before he was allowed in … I don't think he ever fully recovered from that, his image." Along with Steve Bell's depiction of the prime minister wearing grey Y-fronts over his suit, it probably did more to seal the image of John Major as an ineffective nonentity than anything he ever said or did in real life (☞ PRIME MINISTERIAL PARODIES, moments they become reality).

"*Adrian Mole* was a very funny and 'in' book," says Hislop. "And a very, very obvious thing [for us] to do!" The magazine was helped in its conceit by having the same illustrator as the original Adrian Mole books, Caroline Holden. Its author, Sue Townsend, pronounced herself less impressed in 1997. "I was enormously flattered of course. People just assume I write it. I just wish theirs had been as funny. I particularly don't like their Norma/Norman confusion joke going on and on so long."

She was not alone in her objection to the persistent swapping of Norma Major's and chancellor Norman Lamont's first names. In 1996 reader J. C. Q. Coaker wrote from South Africa to berate the *Eye*: "I do not appreciate your calling Major's wife Norman. This makes it sound as if he, Major, is married to a queer – which is not the case."

SEMITISM, Alleged anti-

One debate which still crops up every so often is whether the *Eye* is, or was, or might be, anti-Semitic. It is a particular bone of contention among editors for the magazine's Wikipedia entry, who were divided over whether "the fact that *Private Eye* is anti-Semitic is received wisdom – whether or not it's true", and should therefore be recorded despite "an awkward lack of evidence to cite", or whether, as another averred, "the allegation really is complete cock". Names offered as evidence in a recent online slanging match where the topic came up were Esther Rantzen, James Goldsmith, Robert Maxwell and Richard Desmond:[204] as other commenters were quick to point out, there were

"Lord Gnome himself is quite obviously Jewish.
A caricature of a Jew. I don't think at the time it
was ever considered to be in questionable taste"

Tony Rushton

rather more convincing reasons for targeting each of them than their religious beliefs.

"How could they be anti-Semitic? I'm working there," demands Barry Fantoni – a fact which, along with the magazine's enthusiastic patronage of the Coach and Horses (☞ LUNCH), owned by the just-as-Jewish Norman Balon, would appear to settle the matter. Fantoni does, however, express reservations about the mock-biblical coverage of the conflict between Israel and the Palestinians in the jokes pages he co-writes: "I've almost absented myself completely from 'The Book of Whoever', though I'll hypocritically add a joke if I can think of one. I think they've got a one-sided view of Israel, most of them have no idea what Jews are, what it is to be Jewish, what it's like to live there." He would not, however, want the magazine to lose the feature: "I support the reason for doing the attack on Israel, insofar as I don't think there should be anybody who's let off."

Being opposed to the actions of the Israeli regime is, of course, a completely different thing to being opposed to Jews, although the two are often muddled. Richard Ingrams, who has written regularly in recent years about the Middle East in his columns in the *Observer* and *Independent*, has long since got used to being called an anti-Semite. It was under Ingrams's editorship that the strongest accusations – "What are you trying to achieve? See thousands of Jews killed? Turn the youth of this country into murderous thugs? Yourself finish up on the gallows the same way the Nazi leaders did?" a reader demanded in 1978 – were levelled at the *Eye*. "There was just a residue of that country-house anti-Semitism that had been allowed to creep in," concedes his successor Ian Hislop of the *Eye* of the 1960s and 1970s. "I don't think Richard has any of it himself, and in my own time I didn't see it."

"Lord Gnome himself is quite obviously Jewish," points out Tony Rushton. "A caricature of a Jew. I don't think at the time it was ever considered to be in questionable taste." A contemporary of Ingrams from the same school, he points to the difference age makes:

"I didn't know that Jews existed until I got to *Private Eye*. I don't know whether there were Jews at Shrewsbury, it was never anything I was aware of. There was quite a lot of respectable anti-Semitism before the war, among people that Richard came into contact with, because Richard was forty-five when he was twenty. He was much more interested in Claud Cockburn and Osbert Lancaster, and he admired Hilaire Belloc, and there were periods where people that today you never think were anti-Semitic – T. S. Eliot! – but at the time they were, quite." Hislop agrees, seeing the *Eye*'s early attitude as on a "sort of continuum" with some of Ingrams's literary heroes: "Chesterton, Belloc, they've all got some very dodgy bits in there."

What definitely applies is the first rule of *Private Eye* under Ingrams: if anyone told them they weren't allowed to say something, they said it more loudly. Accusations of bigotry were seized upon gleefully by contributors such as Auberon Waugh, with what he described as "my own small gift for making the comment, at any given time, which people least wish to hear".[205] He and his colleagues found ample opportunity for this during Harold Wilson's 1974-76 administration, and the crowd of chancers and charlatans the prime minister gathered around himself. The Israeli paper *Ha'aretz* claimed in September 1974 that "the only paper that stresses the Jewishness of the businessmen, shady land developers or bankrupts is *Private Eye*, a marginal paper which combines Trotskyism with Antisemitism". A month later the magazine demonstrated this in practice by pointing out that Labour donor Sigmund Sternberg, "like Wislon's ennobled business friends Sir 'Gannex' Kagan, Lord Harry Kissin, Sir Rudi Sternberg, John Mayer CBE and Montague L. Meyer, is from a middle-European Jewish background", which prompted a reader to come at them from the opposite direction and accuse the magazine of being in the pay of the National Front, an organisation which was frequently attacked in its pages. "Our purpose was merely to draw attention to one of many examples of supporters of the Labour party who are themselves members of the wealthier section of the community," the *Eye* limply protested. But while the magazine put in plenty of its own admirable investigative work on the real dodginess of Wilson's associates, two of whom died while being investigated by the Fraud Squad and one of whom, Kagan, was imprisoned for theft, its objectionable preoccupation with their Jewishness – in 1979 the "Grovel" column referred to the "Kosher Nostra" – gave them an easy get-out clause which could be loudly exploited.

James Goldsmith, for instance, had little difficulty in convincing mainstream journalists that his battle with the *Eye* was prompted by its anti-Semitism, though Chaim Bermant was sceptical in the *Jewish Chronicle*: "Goldsmith was only vaguely aware of his Jewishness until *Private Eye* began what he regarded as a personal vendetta against him. Scratch a semi-Jew and one will discover a full one."

In 1980 Ingrams himself was interviewed by the same paper. "I would absolutely and entirely agree with you as far as Jews are concerned that obviously their contribution to everything has been terrific," he told David Nathan. As for Goldsmith, "I certainly never looked upon him as being a Jew at all. If anything, I always regarded him as a German." He also took the opportunity to deny another widely circulating fiction which originated with Goldsmith, that the *Eye* "receives large subsidies from Arab sources – it is completely untrue".[206]

"The anti-Semitism tag is a dangerous one and I don't want it sticking to the *Eye*," Ian Hislop pointed out after the old accusations were dragged out once again in the early 1990s. "We have Jewish reporters, Jewish humorists, Jewish cartoonists and Jewish lawyers and accountants. From Lord Kagan to Maxwell, if they are crooked and Jewish they go in. But this is equally true if they're not Jewish – Profumo to Asil Nadir, or Poulson to Barlow Clowes … you get the point."[207]

One footnote: the cartoon strip "Snipcock and Tweed". Yes, the *Eye*'s resident publishers started out (long before they were illustrated) as a spoof of Weidenfeld and Nicolson, and yes, Weidenfeld was Jewish. But they always called the hotel chain Trusthouse Foreskin too, and the Forte family are about as Catholic as they come: it probably says more about their schoolboy humour than anything else. Certainly the interpretation some have put on the name came as a surprise to cartoonist Nick Newman. "It never occurred to me – I just thought it was a funny name. I've never made any reference to it, it never featured in the strip."

SHREWSBURY

No fewer than four of the key figures of Private Eye *met at Shrewsbury School at the age of thirteen.*

"I want him to have all the disadvantages I never had, Headmaster …"

Willie Rushton looks back to his schooldays in issue 8 of *Private Eye*, April 1962

Christopher Booker: I went up for the scholarship exam. The first person I met was Paul Foot.

Willie Rushton: I arrived on the same day as Richard Ingrams.[208]

Richard Ingrams: Willie and I were very close, because he was in my house. I wasn't really friends with Booker. I didn't really know him.

Booker: Ingrams and I sang in the choir together. So that's how I would have met him, trilling away.

Ingrams: The reason I knew Footy was that we did Classics.

Paul Foot: At Shrewsbury I was on Ingrams's coat tails. I worshipped him and wanted to be near him. I was in a position of *total* hero-worship to him.[209]

Rushton and Ingrams as schoolboys

Ingrams: He was widely suspected of taking things too seriously.[210]

Foot: We had a debate against the landed gentry, and of course I spoke out against the landed gentry, but I didn't actually know what the landed gentry was. Ingrams delivered the most ferocious attack on me, saying that the world was full of weeds and wets, and that I was one of them.

Ingrams: It would be nice to say that the harsh authoritarian air of public-school life nurtured the first seeds of savage indignation in the breasts of the young satirists, but this was not really the case. The school was no worse than most public schools at that time, and we conformed with the other pupils.[211]

Booker: It was intensely traditional in many ways and hierarchical: you weren't allowed to speak to boys a year ahead of you, privileges for the elite, you were allowed to have your coat open and things. It had its merits, that kind of system, but there was a lot of bullying and once people got to the top of the hierarchy they could treat people pretty badly. We'd just been through World War Two, which all of us remembered, and what won World War Two was a version of the old values: discipline, tradition, respect. And those were very much the values of the Shrewsbury that we came into in the early 1950s.

Ingrams: There was the usual public-school emphasis on sport, which I was never any good at.[212] I spent most of my time translating Housman into Latin verse – that was the sort of thing you did.[213]

Rushton: The thing missing at Shrewsbury, apart from women, was any awareness that there was anything else except the *Daily Telegraph* and the Tories.

Ingrams: We were all told at school that we were the leaders of the future.[214]

John Peterson, headmaster: These people were quite unnoticed when they were at Shrewsbury. Ingrams was a very able boy, a classical scholar, no trouble at all, a model boy. Christopher Booker was an extraordinarily staid young man, reserved and studious, who used to spend his Sundays collecting fossils. Paul Foot had all the makings of an angry young man, but he was not in fact a difficult boy at school. William Rushton was undistinguished until he took the part of Lord Loam in *The Admirable Crichton*. He was an enormous success and after that experience of the limelight never recovered. But he had one talent: he was a good cartoonist. They were pillars of happy citizenship compared to the generation that followed them at Shrewsbury.[215]

The school magazine team, including Rushton on banjo, Foot on cornet, and master Laurence LeQuesne on drum

Ingrams: My brother edited the school magazine and he roped me into that. The *Salopian* had been terribly boring until then; every single football or cricket match had to be covered in full, and there was endless news of old boys, and very few illustrations. But at the back there was a section where people could put their attempts at writing. I was very keen to write funny things, parodies and poems, and I remember the terrific excitement I got from seeing something I'd written being in print.[216]

Laurence LeQuesne, master with responsibility for the magazine: They were a most amusing bunch to be in charge of. I didn't realise – I suppose people in my position rarely do – just how remarkable that group of people was. My strong impression is that none of them has changed very much. At heart Paul was already the crusader, William the humorist, Christopher the ideas man and Richard the satirist, whose basic inspiration was a deep-rooted hostility to taking things seriously. Rushton's cartoons were brilliant. Certainly the best schoolboy cartoons I've ever seen.[217]

Ingrams: I've always worked best with other people and having Willie as a collaborator – which he went on being until he died, basically – it was a wonderful, God-given opportunity.[218]

Booker: There were two terms when Willie and I were sort of pretty key figures in running the magazine. I used to write the editorials, which were very irreverent. I attacked all the school institutions: I attacked the Corps and I attacked the Chapel and I attacked Speech Day.

John Peel, Old Salopian and DJ: It was effectively

the first *Private Eye*. I submitted what I thought was a hilariously funny piece, written very much in clumsy imitation of J. B. Morton, "Beachcomber" of the *Express*. My attempt was rejected by the editorial team. They were very senior boys and probably wouldn't have spoken to me anyway.[219]

Ingrams: My brother wrote a piece entitled "If God Came to the School Chapel, What Would He Think of It, and Where Would He Sit?" This caused a tremendous row, for some reason. Old boys complained that it was blasphemous, and we were told we now had to submit everything to the headmaster beforehand.

LeQuesne: Richard's occasional clashes with authority were never serious. He was not at all actually subversive. It was all for the fun of the thing: for seeing just how far you could put your toe over the line and get away with it. Things weren't evil, they were absurd, and their absurdity was to be enjoyed.[220]

☞ ARDINGLY; CAKE'S, St; PSEUD, The

SLAGG, Glenda,
the Gal You Can't Gag

Glenda Slagg – née Slag – is the last of the First Ladies of Fleet Street. She made her *Eye* debut in 1969 and has long outlived her initial inspirations Jean Rook and Lynda Lee-Potter. These days she looks on young pretenders like Jane Moore, Amanda Platell, Polly Filler and Mary-Ann Bighead with a mixture of scornful pity and generous encouragement. Mind you, she looks at everything that way.

She has always courted controversy. Her forthright advice to the pregnant Bernadette Devlin in 1971 – "Why don't you be a sensible girl and take a trip down to Harley Street during your lunchbreak? I know Aunty Glenda's always sticking her neck out when she shouldn't. But that's because I CARE. Desperately. (Oh my God. Ed.)" – caused her colleague Dave Spart to threaten to resign from the magazine. Four decades later her observations on the death of Bogzone singer Seamus Gayfeller – "Who did he think he was, a-mincin' and a-wincin', a-preenin' and a-queenin' with his boyfriend (sorry, Mr PC, 'civil partner'). No wonder the gay brigade all end up dead" – resulted in over two million complaints to the Press Complaints Commission, the Race Relations Board and the UN Security Council and a Twitter campaign to have Slagg tried for war crimes.

She declined to be interviewed for this book, despite having enthusiastically agreed a few minutes earlier.

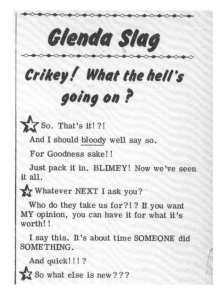

Glenda Slag

Crikey! What the hell's going on ?

⭐ So. That's it! ?!

And I should <u>bloody</u> well say so.

For Goodness sake!!

Just pack it in. BLIMEY! Now we've seen it all.

⭐ Whatever NEXT I ask you?

Who do they take us for?!? If you want MY opinion, you can have it for what it's worth!!

I say this. It's about time SOMEONE did SOMETHING.

And quick!!!?

⭐ So what else is new???

Glenda makes a little go a long way: April 1972

SLICKER

One morning, after I had been working at *Private Eye* on and off for nearly a decade, I walked past a door at the top of the building which I had always assumed led to a stationery cupboard or other cubbyhole. I had never seen it open. This morning, however, it was ajar. I looked inside and … no. I can't tell you. It wasn't quite Bluebeard's Castle. Let's leave it at that.

When I mentioned it to the managing director, half thinking I'd dreamed the whole thing, she just said "Oh yes, that's Gillard's office." The door has never been left unlocked again, although in recent years strange cracks have started to appear in the walls and ceiling of the room below.

When Michael Gillard, who has been writing the "In the City" column under the byline Slicker since August 1969, actually uses the office, is a bit of a mystery. He is very seldom seen in the building during daylight hours – he is thought to be nocturnal – but the copies of the *Wall Street Journal* which are delivered for him regularly disappear from his pigeonhole. Francis Wheen claims to have caught him late at night watching boxing on the TV in the editor's office. Some of us think he might actually live in that attic room and only emerge when we have all left.

His editors are scarcely any wiser. "Only very recently did I acquire Gillard's telephone number," Ingrams told me almost exactly forty years after he recruited him from the City desk at the *Daily Express*. "He's amazingly reclusive. I was amused to find there was even a jokey message on the answer machine. It's extraordinary." "He's a genuine enigma. I know very little about him, have almost no contact numbers," confirms Ian Hislop. "He spends a lot of time in America. I was amused to find that someone I thought had been living with him for five years didn't have his home number or any way of contacting him either." He is tall, has a long moustache and often wears dark glasses, but we are fairly sure he is not Lord Lucan.

One thing, however, we do know: he is by some distance the best business journalist in Britain. "His column is read at every level in the City of London," declared *Management Today* in 2000. "It is a must-read for those who police the markets – the Bank of England, the Stock Exchange, the Securities & Exchange Commission in Washington. It is read in City coffee shops and in executive dining rooms, where the movers and shakers either laugh or cringe, depending on who Slicker is roasting. The column has become an institution used today by many City professionals to pick up on gossip and to help them

separate the good from the bad." Gillard was pursuing Robert Maxwell way back in the tycoon's book-publishing days; he was pouring scorn on BCCI over a decade before its eventual collapse; he was several years ahead of what he calls the Serious Farce Office on Asil Nadir; and he tore apart the claims of the Fayed brothers as quickly as they could come up with them during the House of Fraser takeover in the mid-1980s. The collapse of the sub-prime markets and subsequent credit crunch would not have taken Slicker readers unawares. Knowing that crooks are very good at conning investors with impressive PR and glossy promotional material – and that most journalists are only too happy to take it at face value – Gillard specialises in digging deep into accounts, annual returns, historical records and his own extraordinary memory to come up with the real facts about companies and their directors, and presenting them in uncompromising terms.

"My strength is in detail, a crushing weight of detail," Gillard said in a rare public excursion in 1982. "And there is no concession made to the layman. The column is aimed at professional readers. Others can understand it, it is not written in jargon, but the layman must make an effort. It is better to have it this way round than bore the experts by spelling it out."[221] His editors have never been among those experts. "I don't understand it all," says Hislop. "I try. I always read it all, and I take a lot of it on trust. It's very dense."

Gillard's thoroughness even awed Paul Foot. "The level of his accuracy is uncanny. The Slicker index of stories is one of the most valuable documents the *Eye* has produced. In his way he is a genius. He has a memory like a filing cabinet. He could have made a fortune in the City. But he sticks to his last. He has been lucky in the sense that he could never have got his stuff published anywhere else if Richard had not published it." Certainly Gillard exited the *Express* fairly rapidly after some of his targets complained to his proprietor about him doing his job and sticking his nose into their businesses. He went on to work for many years on the long-running ITV investigative series *World in Action*, where he had exactly the same set-up, locked room and all. The boss of Granada eventually got so cross about it that he ordered the door be broken down.

"There are a great many misunderstandings about how, why and with whom I operate," Gillard told Dominic Prince when he requested an interview for that *Management Today* piece a decade ago. "I believe in freedom of expression, so I will not seek to stop you doing it, but I am not interested in promoting myself under any circumstances."

SMALL ADS,
Stories from the

THE SMALL ADS WERE THE LAST STRAW that finally persuaded founding managing director Peter Usborne to move on in 1965. "Trailing through the bloody small ads trying to work out which were code for perverted sexual practices. It was one evening when I realised I was spending all my time trying to work out whether an ad for motorcycling gear was actually rubber fetishism or real motorcycling gear and I thought 'Fuck this for a way of life, this is ridiculous.' I was twenty-four, twenty-five, something like that, and I just thought: 'I'm not going to go on doing this for the rest of my life.'"

"I STILL HAVE TO TALK TO THE ODD PROSTITUTE, saying 'Why won't you take my ad?'" admitted ad manager Steve Tiernan in 2010. "They're quite aggressive, some of them. But then, I suppose people pay for that."

A THRIVING TRADE IN MEN offering themselves as husbands for hire sprang up in the Eye's small ads in the mid-1970s. It was not all it seemed. One unlucky bachelor who placed an ad offering marriage to the highest bidder received four replies – from journalists on BBC News, the *Sunday Telegraph*, *Paris-Match* and the *Sunday Times*, all of whom were preparing articles on the subject.

IN 1985 THE EDITORS OF *VIZ*, then an obscure fanzine sold only in the North-East, placed an ad in *Private Eye*: "Bum rates paid for top cartoonists." Simon Thorp replied, was recruited, and went on to draw such legendary characters as Student Grant, Eight Ace and Mrs Brady Old Lady.

JOSEPH CHALMERS, A GLASWEGIAN LAWYER, joined the Carmelites after spotting an advert for a retreat in Private Eye in 1975. Twenty years later, Father Joseph was elected as prior general, the worldwide leader of the monastic order.

Michael Gillard hides his identity

He revelled in his anonymity for many years before he was eventually forced into the public eye by a vengeful James Goldsmith. "If the bankers that give me information knew I was Slicker then it would be a quick fitting of concrete boots for a walk across the Thames," he wrote in the *Eye* in April 1970. I spoke to him twice while I was researching this book, by lying in wait in his natural habitat. Both times he expressed his approval of the project, offered useful tips and promised he would be in touch very soon to arrange an interview. Then he left the building.

ESCAPE

Lonn

Novelties

Make Money

Wine & Dine

Announcements

Eye Buys

Eye Love

Services

Fr Sale

Wanted

Entertainment

Reads

Available

WHEN THE *EYE* WAS ATTACKED for the "superficial, cheap, shallow and depressing" content of its small ads in 1999, an enthusiastic patron wrote in their defence: "Sir – I should like to point out that through the medium of *Eye* Love I was fortunate enough to meet the finest husband a woman could want. As the husband in question is not of course my own, I will remain yours anonymously."

SPIKE MILLIGAN once placed an advertisement reading "Spike Milligan seeks rich, well-insured widow. Intention: murder." He got forty-eight replies.

IN 1972 LIEUTENANT-COLONEL JOHN ELLIOTT BROOKS sued the *People* for libel in 1972 after a nineteen-year-old student he had recruited through an *Eye* small ad for "good-natured young ladies" to crew his motor-yacht sold the story of how he had paid her £15 for regular spanking sessions in between lock gates. He was awarded damages of one halfpenny.

ARTIST JOHN MYATT advertised his services providing "genuine fakes – your own renaissance impressionist modern painting" in 1986 and was recruited by conman John Drewe as part of the biggest art fraud of the century. After fooling galleries including the Tate into purchasing Myatt canvases, both men were eventually jailed.

THE MILLION-DOLLAR QUESTION: do those ads begging for money in the "*Eye* Need" section actually work? *Money Marketing* magazine concluded in 1991

that they did – if you counted "three replies, one for a mailing-list scheme a bit like a chain letter, some literature from a chap involved in selling the unlikely combination of burglar alarms and skincare products" and the mysterious offer of "two days' work – unconventional and challenging but not illegal – for which you could earn up to £500" as a result. A similar effort by *Campaign* magazine netted them a host of chain letters, a 50p coin and a puncture-repair kit.[222] "The same people keep coming back and booking them, so they must get a result," points out Tiernan.

SMUG, W. H.

PRIVATE EYE INTRODUCES
W.H.SMUGG
PERSECUTION WEEK
June 2–9
in aid of Private Eye

WHAT YOU CAN DO

CALL at your local branch of W.H.Smugg and say "Have you a copy of Private Eye?". The assistant will say "No".
You may then say "You are a c**** !" and walk out.

A thousand people doing this in the course of a week will cause Lord Hambleden, the bloated chairman of W.H.Smugg, to go mad.

* chump

W. H. Smith's refusal to stock *Private Eye*, depriving it of tens of thousands of potential sales, was a source of rancour for decades. "It was an ongoing battle," remembers managing director Dave Cash. "I was in constant correspondence with Smiths and Menzies. The reason they gave, which was true, was that under the laws of libel as the distributor they were just as liable as the publisher. And Goldsmith and Maxwell later both used that as a factor."

What solved the problem? Cold hard cash (from cold hard Cash). "I think this was 1984 or '85, John Menzies and I made a deal that they would distribute *Private Eye* if I gave them an indemnity of a hundred thousand pounds. And just after that I arranged to see Sir Simon Hornby, who was the chairman

STEADman
with much respect
to
H.M. BATEMAN.

The man who asked for Private Eye at W.H.Smiths

Far left: an *Eye* campaign in May 1963 and *left:* how Ralph Steadman saw it in 1967

of W. H. Smith, with Richard shuffling along in his best corduroys. And he said 'Give it six months – if Menzies doesn't have any problem we'll take *Private Eye* on.' Because obviously, with Menzies taking it on, they were going to start losing out. It was quite a good ploy. So that was a great breakthrough. I remember we printed over 400,000 the first few issues Smiths took, which is absolutely massive, because we didn't know how many we were going to sell. The print order then settled down to 250, 300 thousand, which was incredible."

☞ DIANA, Princess, Death of, and subsequent lunacy

SNOWDON, LORD, offers
editorial feedback

Lord Snowdon, the Queen's brother-in-law, once found himself seated near Richard Ingrams and Willie Rushton at a party in the 1960s, and took the opportunity of telling them at great

Cracks in the royal marriage as seen by the *Eye* in August 1970

length what he thought of his portrayal in the *Eye*. Rushton claimed that "Ingrams lay there rumbling like Krakatoa, then pronounced 'You must remember, Snowdon, that you are a very unimportant person. Utterly insignificant.' Princess Margaret sank beneath the table like a U-boat."[223]

☞ JAWN

SPART, Dave

Dave Spart has been the *Eye*'s resident polemicist since December 1971 when he was recruited as spokesman for the National Amalgamated Union of Sixth Form Operatives and Allied Trades, one of many, many pressure groups to which he still belongs (the *Eye* pays his subs).

He declined to be interviewed for this book on the grounds that "the celebration of anniversaries is an inherently militaristic act and as such totally unacceptable while Britain retains its illegal, repressive and imperialist presence in Iraq, Afghanistan and the Falkland Islands". He did, however, give us permission to reprint the views of his sister Deirdre Spart, written for the 500th edition in 1981 (a decision she described as "typically phallocentric"):

DEIRDRE SPART writes:

FOR DAYS now the Tory media (e.g. the *Guardian*, *Observer* etc) have been filled with nauseating articles about the 500th issue of the so-called "satirical" magazine *Private Eye*, totally ignoring the fact that *Eye* is a suppository of all that is typical of public-school sexism directed against the feminist movement, ethnic minorities (i.e. blacks, coloureds), the gay movement and what is more is totally anti-Semitic, recalling the excesses of Nazi Germany, Julius Sturmer and the like. Their twisted minds (contd. p. 94).

SPIEGLS, Fritz's

Fritz Spiegl may be most famous as the composer of the patriotic 'UK Theme' controversially axed from its dawn airing by Radio 4 in 2006, but he was also the man who came up with the idea of printing amusing newspaper misprints and ambiguous headlines in *Private Eye*. Later on, when they were gathered in book form, they became known as "Boobs", but they made their debut in November 1962 as "Fritz's Spiegls".

SIBELIUS DIES
As he hears Sargent conducting his Fifth Symphony
From Daily Mail Correspondent: Helsinki, Friday.

SPOONS

Nothing amusing has ever happened at *Private Eye* in connection with a spoon.

ST ALBION PARISH NEWS

"I remember the exact moment," says Ian Hislop of his decision to turn Tony Blair into a vicar. "It was when I saw him going into Number 10 with a guitar, and I just said 'That's the new curate.' He's a bit evangelical, he's a bit of a straight kind of guy. And then I talked to the others and Richard [Ingrams] told me Malcolm Muggeridge said 'All prime ministers are either bookies or vicars,' and it's true, you can divide them up. It was beginning to look right."

The team was particularly well qualified to bash out a fortnightly parish newsletter. "Vicars I'm pretty good at, I've listened to a lot of them. I think [Christopher] Booker wrote his local parish newsletter, Barry [Fantoni] was certainly involved in producing and distributing his when he went through a very churchgoing phase, Richard plays the organ at his local church – we thought here's a literary form, to put a grand word on it, that we all knew fairly well. There was a huge amount you could do with it."

The format also broke away from "Dear Bill" and "The Secret Diary of John Major" (), which for the previous eighteen years had rooted the *Eye*'s prime ministerial slot in a fantastical but recognisable Downing Street. The parish, like the Soviet state and the educational institution which followed it, was by contrast a strange world somewhere parallel to Number 10. "I prefer taking it on a step," says Hislop. "Rather than just saying 'This is the person.' I think it's because you've seen so many impressionists do prime ministers. And after doing *Spitting Image*, which was as good a version of 'this is them' as you were going to get really, not tweaking the world a little bit seems a bit dull. Just writing a thing that says 'This week the Prime Minister says …'"

That congregation in full:

Vicar: The Reverend A. P. R. Blair M.A. (Oxon)

Churchwarden: Mr Mandelson

Editor of the parish newsletter: Mr Campbell
(no outside contributions welcome)

Parish Treasurer: Mr Brown from the bank on the High Street

Organist and leader of the social chapter: Mr Cook

Leader of the Mission to St Gerry of the Peacemakers, Northern Ireland: Ms Mowlam

Leader of the Outreach Programme for the Third World: Ms Short

Warden of the St Albion Home for Distressed Gentlefolk: Ms Jay

Chair of Governors, St Albion Primary School: Mr Blunkett

Chair of the Neighbourhood Watch: Mr Straw

Representative of the Working Men's Club: Mr Prescott

Organiser, Millennium Marquee: Mr Falconer

Conductor, Welsh Male Voice choir: Mr Michael (sadly pipping Mr Morgan to the post!)

Lead in the St Albion's Amateur Dramatic Society Panto, *Dick Whittington, Mayor of London*:
Mr Dobson (and not Mr Livingstone from the Newts "R" Us Aquatic Centre on the High Street,
whatever he may say)

'Hands Across the Water'
Reverend William Jefferson Clinton
of the Church of the Seven Day Fornicators
Reverend Dubya Bush of the Church of the
Latter Day Morons (and Sister Condi!)

☞ EYE TV; PRIME MINISTERIAL PARODIES,
moments they became reality

STEADMAN, Ralph

"*Punch* were rejecting my drawings like dodgy transplant organs," Ralph Steadman remembered. "They felt, maybe rightly, that mean and bitter social comment was not *Punch*'s bag. Richard Ingrams thought differently and bought one of my rejects, Plastic People. 'Here's a fiver,' he wrote, 'more power to your elbow!'"[224]

STORIES YOU CAN'T PRINT

"People say to us, 'You must know stuff that you don't print,' and I say, 'Well, if it's any good then I'd put it in,'" Ian Hislop told an interviewer in 2008. "If I don't believe it I don't put it in, because otherwise why would people buy you?"[225]

If a story is good and the *Eye* can stand it up, it will print it, and fight any legal barrier that is put in its way, sometimes at great expense. That same year Hislop spent a great deal of time and money establishing the media's right to report the fact that BBC presenter and regular writer on the ethics of journalism Andrew Marr had obtained an injunction banning the media from reporting facts about his private life, even though he had no interest in printing the facts in question. What Hislop objected to on principle was that the "superinjunction" also banned any mention of its own existence. "I can see

Sheila [Molnar, the managing director] thinking 'So, you got a paragraph ... and you spent six figures. That's a terrifically good use of the *Eye*'s resources in a downturn.' But I think it probably is," he says.

Still, many people remain convinced that there are plenty of stories out there that are true but remain mysteriously unreported. The fictions most frequently cited by pub bores include the paternity of Prince Harry, a gay affair between two members of John Major's cabinet and a straitlaced BBC presenter who was supposedly recorded demanding that a colleague "fuck me till I fart". The *Eye* has sometimes even appealed for evidence of these urban myths: "A rumour is circulating among BBC engineers about a bootleg videotape involving Noel Edmonds, *Big Breakfast* presenter Chris Evans and *Baywatch*," the magazine announced in 1993. "Would anyone like to send this tape to the *Eye* to allay fears that it is merely an empty hoax?" Unsurprisingly, no one did.

☞ INJUNCTION; TRAFIGURA

STRIPS, Longest-running

11 years and ongoing: "It's Grim Up North London". Knife and Packer (aka Duncan McCoshan and Jem Packer) first strolled through Islington in 2000. "The characters actually look like us," admits McCoshan. "I did the first one and my wife said 'That's you and Jem isn't it?' I said 'No! No!… Have your latte and shut up!'"[226]

11 years and ongoing: "Young British Artists". Andrew Birch first swapped science for art – he is a biology graduate – in 2000.

14 years: "Directors". Peter Dredge wrote and drew the strip alone from 1995 to 1999, when Peter Rigg joined him on the writing side for another decade.

15 years and ongoing: "Apparently". Mike Barfield is a qualified zoologist who has worked on *Location, Location, Location* and *Who Wants to Be a Millionaire?*. His *Eye* strip began in 1996.

18 years and ongoing: "Supermodels". Most modelling careers last a decade at most. Neil Kerber's strip has been running since 1993.

23 years: Ken Pyne's TV slot: From 1986 to 1994 Ken Pyne drew the medialand soap opera "Corporation Street" on the TV review page. For the following fifteen years he used the slot for his own, unbranded take on the fortnight's TV.

24 years and ongoing: "Celeb". The misadventures of rock has-been Gary Bloke have been documented since 1987 – almost without interruption. A furious Pete Townshend of the Who wrote to *Private Eye* in October 1999, "Where was fucking 'Celeb' last issue? I'm lost now. I don't know how to act, what to say or do. Please don't upset my life again in this careless manner."

Cartoonists Charles Peattie and Mark Warren

apologised in the following issue. "On completion of the strip, to add extra authenticity, we smashed up our equipment (drawing board and biro) and then set fire to it. The artwork was, unfortunately, totally destroyed."

25 years and ongoing: "Snipcock and Tweed".
Snipcock and Tweed made their first appearance in the *Eye*'s pages during the 1970s, but they did not find their faces until February 1986 when Richard Ingrams suggested that Nick Newman start a strip on the brand new "Literary Review" page (☞). Both characters have real-life models. "I based Tweed on Richard. And Richard suggested I model Snipcock on Tom Rosenthal who was then running André Deutsch," says Newman. "He said 'Make him rather small with a beard, and wearing a bow tie.' Richard likes men with beards, he's always amused by beards. And eventually

Tom Rosenthal realised it was him, and I had lunch with him – I didn't realise how exactly I'd got him until he walked into the room."

PRIVATE EYE

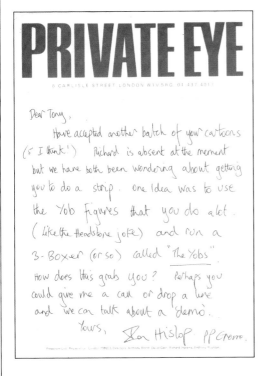

Dear Tony,

Have accepted another batch of your cartoons (5 I think!) Richard is absent at the moment but we have both been wondering about getting you to do a strip. One idea was to use the Yob figures that you do a lot. (Like the headstone joke) and run a 3-Boxer (or so) called "The Yobs". How does this grab you? Perhaps you could give me a call or drop a line and we can talk about a 'demo'.

Yours,
Ian Hislop. PP Grover.

HUSBAND

26 **years and ongoing: "Yobs".** Tony Husband has been writing and drawing the strip – with occasional diversions into "Yobettes" and, when the House of Lords was being reformed, "Nobs" – since 1985. "I was beaten up by a bunch of skinheads, so maybe this was my way of getting back at them," he says.[227]

The main character himself was even longer lived. As a classically educated reader pointed out in 1987, he managed to work for Julius Caesar (100–44 BC), Nero (AD 37–68) and Tacitus (AD 55–120), although not in that order.

35 **years: "Hom Sap".** David Austin's Ancient Roman saga ran from 1970 until his death in 2005. The final strip was finished by friends: fellow cartoonist Kipper Williams recalls "Four days before he died, David rang our studio from his hospital bed and dictated what was to be the final instalment. As requested, the cartoonist Nick Newman adapted David's original drawings and the strip duly met Friday's deadline."[228]

STYLE BOOK, as followed
by *Private Eye* sub-editors

- Andrew Neil should always be spelt "Andrew Neill", because it annoys him.
- Mohamed Fayed is never to be referred to as Mohamed Al Fayed, because that is not his name. It is permissible to refer to him as Mohamed "Al" Fayed.
- All references to Michael Cole, spokesman for Mohamed Fayed, must contain the detail that he has "pompadoured" hair, because he always rises to it and writes a cross letter.

- Articles referring to David Blunkett should, where possible, contain the phrase "Buck up, Beardie!"
- While editor of the *Sun*'s "Bizarre" column in the 1980s Piers Morgan personally requested that the *Eye* desist from describing him as "gormless" on the grounds that it upset his mother: he should therefore always be described as "Piers Moron" (☞ CARTER-FUCK, Peter).
- Any right of reply offered to figures being criticised should be followed by the phrase "So that's all right then" or similar.

- Weirdo *Sun* editor Rebekah Wade prefers, since her promotion and second marriage, to be referred to as "Weirdo News International boss Rebekah Brooks".
- Number Crunching: decimals above .5 are rounded up, below .5 are rounded down, and figures which nearly but don't quite match are ruthlessly rounded in whichever direction will make them read better.
- Any new technology terms should be placed in quote marks, so geeks have something to complain about on Twitter. Viz: "schiaparelli: I see *Private Eye* refers to 'Tweets' with heavily ironic inverted commas. This is the TIP of the 'why I cancelled my subscription' iceberg. 25 June 2009."
- The use of "Shome mishtake shurely", "er", "That's enough – Ed", and "Trebles all round" is strictly controlled. Chief sub-editor Tristan Davies has been known to impose a cliché moratorium on entire issues.

SUNDAY TIMES, former
editor, Gratuitous excuse to print picture of

SUPREME LEADER, The

The joke-writing team were well qualified to document the dangers of the Bullingdonite–Cameroonian–Borisite claque from the Desk, subsequently the Sickbed and ultimately the Bunker of Supreme Leader Gordon Brown. "For sheer boring Communist jargon, Christopher's quite difficult to beat," says Ian Hislop. "But it's a voice that more than one of us can do, so we were competing there. Christopher is very logical, he likes the structure of a piece, so by the time he's finished it will come back and make sense and there will be a line and the pure silliness will tend to be tempered by him so that it will end up with a point."

The original idea, however, came from outside the office. "It was a reader's suggestion," admits Hislop. "I can't even remember what his name was. He wrote in and said 'Why don't you do him as Stalin?' I did write to him and say 'This is very good, do you mind if we take you up on this, we've written one, what do you think?' and he said 'It looks good.' And then we never heard from him again. Maybe he thought it was crap after the first one and didn't want to tell us."

Ultimately, the format didn't have the legs to run long term. Fortunately, neither did Gordon Brown. "It was very restrictive, and it was very one-tone in the end – because he was! If he'd gone on, I'm not sure it would have gone on. It was about enough."

☞ PRIME MINISTERIAL PARODIES, moments they became reality; PRIME MINISTERIAL PARODY, Evolution of a; UNSUNG HEROES

SUTCLIFFE, Sonia, sues *Eye*
for libel
☞ BANANA, I'm a

The entire Politburo rally behind the Supreme Leader, 2010

CAST LIST

E MILLIGAN
BIRD
NOR BRON
IAM RUSHTON
WELLS
AN CHAGRIN
FORTUNE
Y FANTONI
ARD INGRAMS
SNAGGE
NWY JENN

T

"PRIVATE EYE T.V."

POP SCENE

BY MAUREEN CLEAVAGE

Introducing the TURDS

I want you to meet four very yo...
and very exciting Turds.

They're from the new Beat Cen...

SO. AREWE THEN.

and Other Poe by J. Thribb

eword by Richard

his ever-widening readership, this
ob's genius will be a work of const...
inspiration.' Melvyn Ba...

EYE 21 GLORIOUS YEARS

R-82

"There's not much on the television tonight"

Fantoni

We've got taste...

BAD taste

T SHIRTS

BE WARY, MADAM, I HAVE A TIGER IN MY TROUSER

I AM A POOVE

The Duke of Argyll

Nothing like him

TAKE THAT v. PRIVATE EYE

In 1995, eighty-year-old pop fan Peter Carter-Fuck (☞) demanded from the *Eye* "an undertaking not to say anything negative about Take That or any of its distinguished members ever again".

TALBOT!

Less than two years after dropping his many legal actions against *Private Eye* (☞ GOLDENBALLS), having been turned down in his attempts to buy every single newspaper company he had expressed an interest in, James Goldsmith decided he would achieve his ambition of becoming a press baron by starting his own publication, *Now!*. *Private Eye* promptly rebranded it *Talbot!*: the ailing Chrysler company had just done the same thing with its European models in the hope that no one would notice

they were still the same rubbish cars. Goldsmith boasted he was selling 243,000 copies a week; the *Eye* said he was selling 90,000. Goldsmith sued; *Eye* hack Jack Lundin phoned up W. H. Smith's wholesale department who cheerfully confirmed the lower number.

By the summer of 1980 *Eye* readers were taking photographs of unsold piles of *Talbot!* in their local newsagents and sending them in to be printed, and the magazine launched a competition for "the newsagent who has most reduced his order for *Now!* magazine". The prize of a holiday for two in the Canary Islands went to Mr Sydney Smith from Wigan, who was presented with his prize by a large cardboard cut-out of Sir James which for decades afterwards lurked in the *Eye*'s editorial office, frightening visitors: it's now been banished to the cellar where it is kept company by an equally disconcerting life-size version of Richard Ingrams.

Talbot! finally limped to closure in May 1981.

TAXMAN and the Mapeley affair

The *Eye*'s Richard Brooks – no relation to the *Sunday Times* hack of the same name – came to journalism late, after sixteen years as a tax inspector. In many ways he's the ultimate whistleblower. After several years as a case director with the Inland Revenue, he came to the realisation that the information which was being put out to the public about tax avoidance was simply not true. "It was sort of Orwellian, because there was what was really going on and the official version of what's going on, and it drives you mad after a while. There's a point where the spin, which you sort of get used to, trips over into outright bollocks."

"I'd raised all these concerns internally. They said 'Oh, don't be so silly.' And I thought 'Well really, people ought to know this.' I was an *Eye* reader, and I could tell it was right up Paul Foot's street. I sent him a wodge of information."

It was material that was already in the public domain, but which only a specialist could hope to make sense of. And that's exactly what Brooks did for Foot. "I wasn't leaking, it was stuff that was technically out there, but wouldn't have been picked up. Paul was no great financial expert but his understanding of what it really meant was just phenomenal. He wrote this piece saying 'Look, there's this big business-friendliness push going on in the Revenue that you haven't heard about.' It didn't spark any recriminations internally. It was commented on. But none of my colleagues knew it was me. Nobody knew about anything until about two weeks before I left."

By this point, however, the *Eye*'s new Deep Throat – or Taxman, as he was rather less sexily codenamed – had stumbled across something even bigger. The tax office in which he worked – along with all the Revenue's other properties – had been contracted out to an outside company as part of an enormous PFI deal. The Private Finance Initiative was already a particular bugbear of the *Eye*. "The new people were just crap from day one. Whereas before if you had a meeting one of the secretaries would bring in some coffees for your guests, you'd have to ring somebody in Milton Keynes, and then it would go wrong and you'd be on the phone to bloody Nottingham. Just madness. That kind of thing prompted me to think 'Who are these people?' Mapeley – no one had ever heard of them. So I then started – not using the Revenue's records, because that's a big no-no, if you look at people's tax records that aren't your business they really do nail you – using Companies House records I found Mapeley, and it was pretty easy to establish that they were owned in Bermuda. I thought 'Whoa – the bloody tax offices going to a tax haven!' I wasn't a journalist, and I didn't have a great nose for a story – but to me it seemed absolutely amazing."

He wasn't wrong. Like many of Brooks's subsequent scoops – the man in charge of saving taxpayer's money spending huge amounts of it on his own foreign trips and posh dinners (☞ BOURN, Sir John) or CDC, the publicly owned development fund designed to help people around the world out of poverty rejecting that in favour of turning its executives back home into millionaires (☞ GELDOF, Bob) – it was a tale that could be told in a single, gasp-provoking line. And Foot could see quite how valuable this new contact could be. "He took me for lunch once, it must have been Christmas 2003. He was trying to warn me not to be too reckless, not to get into trouble, but if you do, I'll try to find you some work."

> *"Using Companies House records I found Mapeley, and it was pretty easy to establish that they were owned in Bermuda. I thought 'Whoa – the bloody tax offices going to a tax haven!' I wasn't a journalist, and I didn't have a great nose for a story – but to me it seemed absolutely amazing."*
> Richard Brooks

He did exactly that – although sadly Brooks, who was looking to move on anyway ("I was thirty-eight, thirty-nine, and you either think 'God, I've got what I'm doing now for the next twenty years,' or I make a break now"), did not make his career change until after Foot's death in July 2004. "The week after Paul died Ian was on holiday so I was in charge and suddenly there was this two-page gap in the magazine where Footy's stuff should have been," says Francis Wheen. "I thought of Taxman as he was known, and I sent him an email saying 'You don't know me but Paul always spoke very highly of you: I just wondered if you might have the odd story?' And back came a thing from Richard with about seven *tremendous* stories, all perfectly written, didn't need a word changed. Ever since then I've thought he was Footy's greatest bequest to the *Eye*. Every time I read one of Richard's pieces I think how proud Paul would be."

Brooks has been one of the team of office-based regular hacks since the autumn of 2004 (the *Eye* was subject to its first and only tax inspection not long after poaching him, which was an astonishing coincidence). "He has a brilliant ability which we hadn't had here really to analyse economic data and understand balance sheets. He's just brilliant at that stuff," says Ian Hislop. Knowing the workings of Whitehall from inside, Brooks is also an expert wielder of the Freedom of Information Act. "Some of these departments and government bodies don't appreciate that they do themselves more harm than good by stringing you along, because the agony just gets prolonged."

About his writing abilities, Brooks remains modest. "I spent a year at the Treasury doing policy advice for ministers and it's not that different to basic journalism really, because you've got to keep it very simple or they're not going to understand it. Janet and John stuff."

TECHNICOLOUR, Glorious

Private Eye went full colour in May 1998, after a run of practice covers in migraine-inducing hues.

The new printing process was not an immediate success. "I have just received my latest subscription copy," wrote reader John Dean, "but the 3-D glasses seem to have fallen out en route. Please advise."

TERRORISM, as subject of jokes

Ian Hislop – who has "a feeling I overlapped with a young Bin Laden" when he was at primary school in Jeddah – knew exactly what to do when his old school pal perpetrated the worst terrorist attack on American soil in history on 11 September 2001. "I put the Armageddon joke on the cover. A real music-hall special! I think what was needed then was levity."

It was a counterpoint to the unquestioning coverage elsewhere of "the biggest thing that had happened anywhere ever", as Hislop puts it. "Without trying to diminish the human suffering, we had a bombing campaign *here*. This is the first time it's happened to the Americans, it hurts a lot. But a dear friend who I was at college with died in the Harrods bombing [in 1983], that's what happened in this country for a while and it wasn't the end of the world. That definitely influenced – not a sense of 'Oh, we've seen it all before' but you have to be careful before you define things as the apocalypse."

When London suffered its own terror attacks four years later, he identified the opposite problem. "I remember thinking that that wasn't a surprise, and there was a certain reticence, and lots of policemen trying not to use the word Islamic in terms of who'd done it, and suggesting that this was terrorism based on thin air as opposed to an extreme version of a religion, which you have to notice and put in. And then we got a lot of rather Sparty people saying 'Well, you never said they were Catholic bombers when it was the IRA,' and you think 'Well, they weren't asking for an international caliphate based in Rome with the pontiff, there is a difference here.' I was keen to point out all that bullshit quite quickly. Because that was a bombing where people were trying to underreact, I think."

The *Eye* was not always so bold. A proposed Christmas cover in 1980 depicted one of the hunger strikers in Northern Ireland's Maze prison with the speech bubble "Oi tink oi moit fancy a bit o'd Christmas pudden." It was rejected, in the words of contributor Patrick Marnham, "lest it draw unwelcome attention from the IRA".

☞ OFFENSIVE, Most, items published in *Private Eye*; WHERE'S BIN LADEN?

TESCO, *Eye rescues Grauniad from*

In April 2008, Tesco sued the *Guardian* for libel and malicious falsehood over a mistake it had made in a series of stories about the supermarket giant's tax avoidance schemes. It aroused the interest of the *Eye*'s tax specialist, Richard Brooks, who quickly discovered "a couple of companies they had that looked a bit dodgy", and, working with a journalist in Switzerland, established that Tesco were indeed avoiding tax through a complex web of offshore operations. The *Eye*'s story was eagerly seized on by the *Guardian* as it prepared its defence. "We were entering an immensely complex area of commercial life which very few people understand," admitted its sheepish editor Alan Rusbridger. "*Private Eye* has the sense to employ a former Inland Revenue inspector and got the tax schemes right."[229]

"I still think it's the funniest single thing that's happened in my editorship," cackles Ian Hislop. "I remember Rusbridger doing a *What the Papers Say* when I became editor saying 'He's no good, useless old *Eye*, gets it all wrong.' Twenty years later the *Eye* has to bail out the *Guardian* from a hole caused by *sloppy journalism*! The most hysterical turnaround."

☞ TAXMAN

THAMES, Pages thrown in

Inquiring as to the whereabouts of the "Letter from" column one press day in the late 1980s, Ian Hislop was surprised to be told by the sub-editor that he had "thrown it in the Thames". Shortly afterwards the same man enlivened an editorial meeting by calling Hislop a "balding cunt" and then leaping on him and attempting to throttle him. He was wrestled off the editor by the crack fighting team of Christopher Silvester and Francis Wheen and subdued. His family later confirmed that he had stopped taking his medication and believed his brother to be the Antichrist. He no longer works at *Private Eye*.

THAT WAS THE WEEK THAT spoiled everything

FOCUS ON FACT— *The Frost Story*
By BARTY FENTON & STUART HARRIS (8)

The *Eye* delves deep into Frost's past in August 1976

That Was the Week That Was has achieved the sort of legendary reputation only possible for a show broadcast when there were only two channels and which has never been repeated so that people had the chance to realise it wasn't actually that good. "It was so bogus, *TW3*, because it was the first time that satire had been mass-marketed," admits chief scriptwriter Christopher Booker.

He was recruited by producer Ned Sherrin,

How Barry Fantoni saw the TV phenomenon in April 1963

Ingrams, each plop and splash clearly still etched in his memory. "Traumatic experience for me. I seem to remember there were people like Henry VIII who used to receive people when they were sitting on the toilet. It's a good way to humiliate people. An early sign of Frost's power-mania." "He always did that," confirms Booker. Booker stuck around anyway, and still speaks fondly of "Frostie". Ingrams didn't, and doesn't.

Back at a considerably quieter *Private Eye* office, he may have brooded a little. Sherrin had even recruited his old Tomorrow's Audience (☞) partner, Jack Duncan, to direct *TW3*, as the programme quickly became known. And worst of all, the BBC scheduled the first show to go out live on 24 November 1962 – the very day that Ingrams was due to marry Mary Morgan. Even best man Willie Rushton had to make his excuses and spend all day rehearsing instead.

"The big rift started with *TW3*," Booker admits. "It caused a bit of grief with Richard." He insists he continued to generate "absolutely" as much material for the magazine, despite the BBC offering him eighty guineas a week as opposed to the fifteen quid the *Eye* could manage, but Ingrams merely sniffs that he supposes Booker and Rushton "must have come in at some point". "Very soon after the *Eye* started Willie became a TV personality, went off and did all these programmes, and that became his main interest in life," says Ingrams sadly. "He had his career mapped out. He always wanted to be in showbiz and regarded the *Eye* as a stepping stone."[230]

The first series of *TW3* was brought to a close after five record-breaking months in April 1963. *Eye* 37 noted its passing: "The death took place quietly yesterday of Mr David Frost, one of the most brilliant and outspoken critics and commentators of his generation. The cause of death was believed to have been overstrain of the talent."

Then Peter Cook got back from America. Before he had departed for the Broadway run of *Beyond the Fringe*, he had had several meetings with the BBC about a possible Saturday-night satire show. So he was less than delighted that they had gone ahead and set up exactly such a show in his absence. Worse, Frost had been recruited on the strength of his turn at the Blue Angel Club – which consisted almost entirely of Peter Cook jokes. "Cook was pissed off

who was busy hoovering up everyone he could from the so-called Satire Boom all the newspapers kept writing about. Booker's inspiration, Bernard Levin, was hired as an on-screen interviewer and part-time punchbag. Timothy Birdsall was put on the payroll and given a sketching spot in the middle of the show. John Wells was asked to submit material. Willie Rushton was hired as a performer alongside Roy Kinnear, Lance Percival and Millicent Martin. And Richard Ingrams was invited round to presenter David Frost's flat to write some sketches with the up-and-coming star.

It was not a successful collaboration. They had barely got past the hello, good evening and welcomes before Frost departed for the toilet – and invited Ingrams to accompany him, so that he could continue to dictate jokes as he emptied his bowels. "I've never forgotten it," shudders because Frostie was using his cabaret material," confirms Ingrams. He somehow also contrived to be introduced by the compere as "the man who is responsible for the Establishment Club and various other concerns of that kind that have become so popular".[231]

Having famously failed to let Frost drown when they met in America – something he later described as his only regret in life – Cook had his revenge on his return. In May 1964 the *Eye* printed an excoriating full-page report beneath the headline "THE BUBONIC PLAGIARIST". It detailed Frost's history of appropriation and the enormous number of uncredited writers behind the "script by David Frost" for his new show which, according to the magazine, was called *Not So Much a Frost, More a Shower of Shit*. "After this latest show 400 people rang up the BooBooC – 3 in favour, 4 against and 393 to say they wrote the script."

Frost might have gone on to be a transatlantic media star, political interviewer, knight of the realm and, most impressively, host of *Through the Keyhole*, but the *Eye* has never forgiven him.

"It's all rubbish – my old man smoked 300 a day, and he lived to be seven"

THOMPSON, Robert

Robert Thompson's cartoons have featured in the *Eye* since 1989. He specialises in extreme anthropomorphism and wordplay.

THORPE, Jeremy

☞ DITTO MAN, The; VOTE *PRIVATE EYE*

THREE-DAY WEEK, *Eye* can take it

The three-day week ordered by prime minister Edward Heath in January 1974 did not stand in the way of the *Eye* coming out. All right, it had to produce three issues in a severely curtailed form and on funny paper, but it remained defiant even at sixteen pages.

With the electricity supply to individual businesses drastically limited, the *Eye* implemented its own emergency measures. "There was one press day when we had no power in the office and we couldn't run the IBM Composer we typeset the whole thing on, so Tone [Rushton (☞)] and I literally lugged it over to the upstairs room at Norm's [the Coach and Horses (☞)] across the road and ensconced ourselves up there and carried on up there," remembers Steve Mann.

Typesetter Steve Mann works at one of the IBM composers used to make up the *Eye*'s pages in the mid-1970s

THRIBB, E. J.

Eric Jarvis Thribb had his first poem published in *Private Eye* at the age of sixteen in September 1971. It was a moving tribute to the murdered Black Panther George Jackson which began "So they have got you at last, the Fascist Pigs." Critics feel he had not really found his voice at this point. In November of the same year Thribb penned "Buenos Dias, Signor Picasso" on the occasion of the painter's ninetieth birthday, and celebrated his own seventeenth. He turned seventeen and a half in June 1972 and has stayed there ever since.

CLERIHEW CORNER
E.J. Thribb
Has a lyrical nib.
Yes. His grasp of caesura
Is a miracle of adolescent bravura.

"It was a collaborative thing with Richard. I think I thought up the name," says Barry Fantoni. "And later Ian brought the idea of a joke to it, rather than Richard and I who preferred just the whimsical ending. Either way it worked."

"Thribb is everyone, we've all written loads of Thribb. It's a voice you can do, it's one you can tap into," says Ian Hislop. Fantoni seized possession of Thribb for a while during the 1970s and took him on tour, prompting a jealous Ingrams to kill the poet off for a while. "I went out on the road with [Liverpool poet] Roger McGough, and he'd do the first half and I'd do the second. We did Hay a couple of times and lots and lots of little literary festivals." In 1996, Thribb's poetry was performed alongside that of Heathcote Williams and Carol Ann Duffy at the Poetry Olympics in the Albert Hall, a feat which none of the *Eye*'s other resident poets – John Betjeperson, Ted Who-hes or William Rees-McGonagall – have managed. His "minimalist clarity and compression" have been hailed by no less an authority than the *Times Literary Supplement*.

IN MEMORIAM
VLADIMIR NABOKOV, 1977

So. Farewell
Then Vladimir
Nabokov.

Author of *Lolita*
A name that
Has passed into
The language.

You read in
The paper of
"Lolita Girl
in Love Drama"
For example.

Yet how
Many people
I wonder
Have read
The original book?

I have not
For one.

It is not the
Type of book
That interests me

Particularly.

IN MEMORIAM
KENNETH WOOD, 1997

So. Farewell then
Ken Wood.

Inventor of the
Reversible
Toaster.

Reversible the of
Inventor
Wood Ken.

Then farewell
So.

IN MEMORIAM
SIR ALEC ISSIGONIS,
AUTO ENGINEER, 1988

So. Farewell
Then
Sir Alec
Issigonis.

Inventor of
The Mini.

"Mounting the engine
Transversely across
The Frame,

"And driving
The front wheels
Through an integral
Transmission."

Yes, that was your catchphrase.

IN MEMORIAM
FRANK MUIR, 1998

So. Farewell then
Frank Muir

With your white hair,
Pink bow tie and
Funny
Way of talking.

"Everyone's a
Fruit and nut case."

That was your
Catchphrase.

But now you have been
Taken From Here.

This last poem earned a letter of thanks from Muir's son Jamie: "He was a life-long fan of the Eye *and would have considered it an honour."*

TOMORROW'S AUDIENCE

"I liked going on the stage," says Richard Ingrams of his Oxford acting days. "There was a kind of camaraderie."

Actually, he liked it so much he bought the company. When fellow student Jack Duncan proposed that the two of them go into business together as Tomorrow's Audience (even Duncan later admitted the name was "cringe-making") and tour schools performing youth-orientated anthologies to a soundtrack of jazz and Elvis, Ingrams not only signed up but also volunteered as start-up cash the bulk of the generous inheritance he had received on turning twenty-one. He now pooh-poohs the idea that he ever expected the company to last. But that might just be because he's embarrassed about the Elvis records.

They got their big break in February 1962, with a full-scale production in Canterbury of *The Bed Sitting Room*, a new play by former Goon Spike Milligan. It become a major hit, hailed by the critics, and went on to enjoy no fewer than three West End runs and a film adaptation starring Ralph Richardson, Arthur Lowe, Peter Cook and Harry Secombe. And Ingrams and Duncan didn't make a penny from it. "We commissioned that and first produced it, but we got swindled by Milligan," says Duncan. "We put it on first, and we got cheated. Kenneth Tynan put us above the London openings, because he thought the thing was so significant. The money we should have had from it …"[232]

A considerably poorer Ingrams – who claims not to have "minded all that much" losing his entire inheritance – headed back to *Private Eye* to see what his friends were up to.
☞ BOOKER, Christopher, Editorship of

TOPES, Spiggy, Life and times of

1964 – Turds introduced to world by pop columnist Maureen Cleavage. Their leader, Spiggy Topes, tells her "actually we don't have a leader. In our eyes all Turds are equal." They are declared foremost practitioners of swinging Rochdale sound.

1965 – "I Want a Lungful of Tongue" follows "I'm a Red-Hot Swinging Perve" to number one. Topes turns down peerage from Harold Wilson.

1966 – Turds travel to Tibet to take guidance from guru the Veryrishi Lotsa Moni Yogi Bear.

1967 – Turd anthem "Love Is the Thing. Hate Isn't" released. Topes and girlfriend Madeleine Grutt undertake three-day "bore-in" in paddling pool off Rockall.

1968 – Release of animated film *Subnormal*. Critics stunned at exhibition by Topes's girlfriend Okay Yoni when she drops a ton of concrete on their heads.

1969 – Recently sacked Turd Enoch Hogg dies in own swimming pool. Three people die and four are born during Turds' performance at open-air freak-out on sheep farm in New Zealand.

1970 – Topes announces departure from Turds due to "personal, musical, artistic, ethical, psychological and tax reasons".

1972 – Topes denies accusation by Mary Whitehouse that lyrics of his single "I dig that mainline needle when I need some kicks, man" encourage drug use.

1974 – Heavily bearded Topes received by President Thargs at White House. Asks president "Do you have any grass?" and is shown lawn in Rose Garden.

1977 – Topes claims to know "absolutely nothing" about twelve sacks of cocaine found in his custom-built Rolls-Royce after concert in Neasden. Then becomes confused and confesses to Munich Massacre and Reichstag fire.

1978 –Topes is divorced by wife Bronco on grounds of "irreconcilable breakdown of trousers".

1980 – After shooting, Topes hailed as "voice of twentieth century" by world media, "Who?" by teenagers.

1985 – Fellow Turd Paul McCantsing hits out at the "Cult of Spiggy", describing his former colleage as "a complete Turd".

1986 – Following death of founder of Signhereology, Topes pays tribute: "I owe everything to L. Ron Neasden. Before that I owed it to the Inland Revenue."

1988 – Controversial biography by Albert Goldman reveals that Topes was actually gay mass-murderer.

1995 – New Turds single based on lost recording, "Hello, You Have Reached the Home of Spiggy Topes".

2009 – Whole new generation introduced to Turdmania with launch of new "You Are a Turd" videogame by Fuwatascorcha Karaoke company.

☞ COOK, Peter, begins regular editorial contributions to *Private Eye*

TRAFIGURA

In September 2009, the oil giant Trafigura obtained a superinjunction banning the *Guardian* from using a leaked report which the company had commissioned into the grim health implications of the toxic waste it had dumped near homes in the Ivory Coast. Moreover, it banned "the publication of all information relating to these proceedings or of information describing them", and required all media outlets to "conceal the identity of the Applicants" on pain of being "imprisoned, fined or having their assets seized".

Trafigura's laywers being Carter-Fuck (☞), they figured that this did not go quite far enough, and the following month tried to ban anyone from reporting the fact that MP Paul Farrelly had asked a question about the injunction under parliamentary privilege. At which point online social network Twitter went batshit crazy.

"One tweet and that legal edifice crumbled,"

Claim No HQ09X04132

IN THE HIGH COURT OF JUSTICE
QUEEN'S BENCH DIVISION

Before the Honourable Mr Justice Tugendhat on 13 October 2009

BETWEEN:

(1) RJW
(2) SJW

- and -

(1) GUARDIAN NEWS AND MEDIA LIMITED
(2) THE PERSON OR PERSONS UNKNOWN

who in or about September 2009 offered or supplied to the publishers of *The Guardian* and/or to David Leigh a copy of, or information contained in or derived from, the document described in the Confidential Schedule C to this Order relating to the operations or affairs of the First Applicant and/or the Second Applicant

Defendants

ORDER

The learned judge having read correspondence between the Claimants and the First Defendant on 13 October 2009 agreeing to a variation of the Order of Mr Justice Sweeney of 18 September 2009 which extended the Order of Mr Justice Maddison of 11 September 2009.

IT IS ORDERED BY CONSENT that

1. Nothing in the Order of Maddison J of 11 September 2009 and/or the Sweeney J of 18 September 2009 shall prevent the First Defendant or any other person from reporting or publishing information relating to:

    i. any proceedings of the United Kingdom Parliament, including any information or matter published on the website www.parliament.uk

    ii. any proceedings of the Scottish Parliament, including any information or matter published on the website www.scottish.parliament.uk

    iii. any proceedings of the National Assembly for Wales including any information or matter published on the website www.assemblywales.org; or

    iv. any proceedings of the Northern Ireland Assembly and any information or matter published on the website www.niassembly.gov.uk

2. The costs are reserved.

Dated this 13th day of October 2009

boasted *Guardian* editor Alan Rusbridger a few months later. "Within 12 hours of my tweeting a suitably gnomic post saying we had been gagged Trafigura became the most popular subject on Twitter in Europe. Within hours Trafigura had thrown in the towel on the injunction and dropped any pretence that they could enforce a ban on parliamentary reporting. The mass collaboration of strangers had achieved something it would have taken huge amounts of time and money to achieve through conventional journalism or law."[233]

Except that the defiantly old-school *Private Eye* had gone to press the day before, with the full text of Farrelly's question as the lead item in its "HP Sauce" section.

"There is an emerging culture of anonymity in which justice is not even seen to be done, and that is an unfortunate, rather dangerous, trend. I thought *Private Eye*'s job was to expose this," said Ian Hislop, who had been banging on about superinjunctions for a while by this point. "It is a legal technique which shuts stories down very quickly so that now it is not a question of publish and be damned, as it used to be: we are now finding that we can't even publish at all."[234]

☞ CONTEMPT OF COURT; INJUNCTION; STORIES YOU CAN'T PRINT

TRIUMVIRATE, joke-writing group
formed after return of Christopher Booker

Part-way through 1965, with Peter Cook's energies now largely taken up by his TV series Not Only But Also *and Willie Rushton also busy elsewhere, a familiar face returned to the* Eye.

Christopher Booker: I think it must have been a bit of a shock to Richard [Ingrams], realising that he needed little friends to help him write it. Richard was hopelessly unclued up, he knew nothing about politics. They went through '64 with Richard's shambolic presiding. I didn't actually read it, but when I saw it I thought this isn't going to last, it's terrible. I was pretty pissed off, and the upside from my point of view was to see what a mess they made of it – but we can save that for my memoirs, I will put it in my own words.

Richard Ingrams: Booker came back when, in '65? And started writing these profiles.

Booker: I can't remember who made the first move: I think it must have been Richard. He must have been pretty desperate at that stage. And Cookie must have been pretty desperate. The way I came back was I think Richard said "Would you like to write some profiles?" and in '65 I did a series called "Pillars of Society".

These scathing pen-portraits of such quitessentially 1960s figures as Paul Johnson, Anthony Wedgwood Benn and Marc Boxer were each given a full page of the magazine – but no byline.

Ingrams: I think he was a changed man to a great extent. He went through – it wasn't a conversion, because he'd been a Christian all his life, but a re-version. And Booker had become very friendly with [Barry] Fantoni, and then he and Fantoni were born again, together. They were both of them big jazz fiends, and with the conversion they suddenly started being interested in Mozart as well as God.

Booker: I was going through quite a big change of life at that stage. I switched off completely from the swinging London scene as it were, having been very much part of it. I really turned totally upside down about it all.

Barry Fantoni: Booker was completely obsessed by it and then had a reversal of the epiphany and decided that he should hate himself for liking anything that was jazz or pop, and then has decided that he only

likes music up to 1828, when Beethoven died. He's a complete madman.

Booker: So I was coming in to the magazine, and inevitably I would do a piece and then Richard would say, "Why don't you do some jokes?" So by the middle of '65 as I remember I was back as part of the show.

Ingrams: We'd established a framework by then into which he could be fitted. It was just a case of changing the seating plan as it were. John Wells was very involved at one stage.

John Wells: If there are two of the Shrewsbury mafia in Greek Street no one else gets listened to. They kept a lot of my jokes out of the paper when I was on the editorial board.[235] The rivalry was intense. Joint writing sessions with the Shrewsbury mob involved a great deal of eye-gouging, knee-in-the-groin work to get a joke in edgeways. When Peter Cook appeared he was absorbed into the public-school changing room atmosphere.[236]

Booker: There wasn't much Cookie at that stage. There would be months when we wouldn't see him at all and then he'd come in for a couple of issues and sit around, and he was sort of all right. He was obviously very funny, but he was pretty dominating and sometimes his ideas were absolutely useless. So he never really fitted in. Fantoni, who's amazing, was part of the collaborative group fairly early.

With Wells's departure from full-time duties in 1966, the central joke-writing trio of Ingrams, Booker and Fantoni was established. They worked together until Fantoni's retirement at the end of 2010, getting more and more like Last of the Summer Wine *with every passing year.*

Fantoni: There was a continual battle in my own mind I must say about the fact that the two great pillars of the magazine were based on very strong personalities with very strong editorial thoughts, and my problem was who to be loyal to, what to be loyal to. Fortunately it solved itself in a way by Booker writing himself out of it by writing all these huge books.

Booker: It's not the magazine that I would have had. But I'm delighted to be shot of it. Don't get me wrong. I think it's the best thing that ever happened to me, that I didn't have to stick with it in an editorial role. I was going too serious, I was becoming very very profound and boring. I'm quite a nerdy thinker about the world, and people think I'm pretty mad and boring. I've had a long life and I'm actually doing now what I've been preparing for all these years which is writing proper serious books. And I've got several more that I've got in mind to do. But I still love going into London once a fortnight.

TROG

Wally Fawkes, jazz clarinettist and artist behind the "Flook" strip which ran in the *Daily Mail* from 1949 to 1984, had this cartoon about abortion rejected as too controversial by the *Spectator* in March 1962.

He brought it straight round to *Private Eye*, which promptly hired him to provide a political cartoon for every issue for the next two years. His drawings usually took pride of place on page 3 each fortnight.

I'm sorry but the ethical position is quite clear. Thalidomide was a legal prescription, but what you suggest is an illegal operation.

ivate Eye
a Apology

We regrit that owing to an Industrial Dispote
s poge of Private Eye is only being pronted
one editin.
The dispote arosed fillowing some very
sonable propisols mad by the membrs of the
tinal Graphical Astociaton who are osking
more dibs to bring them into line with
l Getty.

McLACHLAN

PRIVATE EYE
CONFERENCE UNITY SPECIAL

No. 830
Friday
8 Oct. '93

It's time
to make thugs
up

All right, John.
I'll say I support
you

BUMPER AUTUMN NUMBER
ONLY 80p

PRIVATE

an't scrap
r. THINK OF
MPLOYMENT!

RIVATE EYE
N STRIKE

1/6

NORMAL COVERS
WILL BE RESUMED
AS SOON AS POSSIBLE

TOBLERONE   U.K   U.S.A   WORLD ATLAS

UPFRONTERS
At The Private Eye
1000th Issue Party

○ Watch out, Dave!
Hilary's after your
Cash! She's
certainly Loweringer
sights to make a
pass at you!!? But
I don't think she'll
get much of a
reception!?!

○ Stop lowering the Tone, Mr Rushton!! She'll tell
you to Ciar off any minute!! If you're looking for a layout you'll get your fingers Byrne-t!!

TUC NEWS

HEATH

I can reveal that the expression "talking about Uganda" has acquired a new meaning.

I first heard it myself at a fashionable party given recently by media-people Neal and Corinna Ascherson.

As I was sipping my Campari on the ground floor I was informed by my charming hostess that I was missing out on a meaningful confrontation upstairs where a former cabinet colleague of President Obote was "talking about Uganda".

Eager, as ever, to learn the latest news from the Dark Continent I rushed upstairs to discover the dusky statesman "talking about Uganda" in a highly compromising manner to vivacious former-features editor Mary Kenny. Mrs. Ron "Badger" Hall was also present, though she was not participating in the 'talk-in'.

I understand that 'Long John' and Miss Kenny both rang up later to ascertain each other's names.

UGANDA, Talking about

The *Eye*'s long-standing euphemism for sexual intercourse all stems from a "Grovel" (☞) piece way back in March 1973.

Notes for Younger Readers:

Neal and Corinna Ascherson – *married journalists on* Observer *and* New Statesman

Campari – *alcoholic beverage from Luton Airport, popular at the time*

President Obote – *former president of Uganda, deposed by Idi Amin in 1971*

Dusky statesman – *he was actually the former electricity minister and had a wooden leg, but Ingrams agreed to cut this intriguing detail because he would have been identified immediately and "he was already on the run from Amin's death squads"*

Mary Kenny – *journalist and former good-time girl. Subsequent to this incident she married the* Eye *contributor Richard West (which perhaps explains why her name became detached from this story in subsequent tellings) and became a sternly moral writer on Catholic issues (which makes it even funnier to drag it up again)*

Ron "Badger" Hall – *far too well known to need explanation*

UNIVERSITY CHALLENGE

The team, as seen by Nick Newman. L-R: Berkmann, Wheen, Hislop and Booker

In 2005 a *Private Eye* team took on one from *Debrett's* in the first round of *University Challenge: The Professionals*. Ian Hislop, Francis Wheen, Christopher Booker and Marcus Berkmann trounced the etiquette experts 160 points to 135 (it would have been embarrassing if they hadn't: apart from anything else, Berkmann compiles the "Dumb Britain" column).

Unfortunately, only the four highest-scoring teams from the series progressed to the second round, which meant the *Eye* didn't get anywhere near the final in which the Privy Council Office beat the Romantic Novelists Association.

UNSUNG HEROES

● "My favourite 'Colemanism' has always been: 'You can tell how bright the sun is by the length of the shadows.'"

R. A. House, Nuneaton, January 1977.

"**Colemanballs**" has been running ever since.

● "May I suggest a new column for the *Eye*? 'Livewatch', for the most pointless of the generally pointless segments of the TV news where they insist on going 'live' to a reporter at a place where something is either going to happen several hours in the future, or has already happened several hours in the past. In both scenarios, there is nothing to see or report!"

Nick Pycraft, Woking, June 2000.

"**Going Live**" has been running ever since.

● "I wondered if you might start a new 'spotter' column – along the lines of Luvvies etc. – for the increasingly prevalent, already clichéd, and somehow pretentious use of 'Solutions' in company titles and subtitles. For example not cardboard boxes, but Packaging Solutions, not a diet, but Slimming Solutions …"

Anna C., via email, October 2004.

"**Solutions**" ran until the end of 2007.

IE VERIRISHI
y loot
d

Veririshi Lotsa Moni
Bear TALKS TO PERISHING WORTHLESS, 32

in *the...er*, ten pound. Me -

e. Boozed ? Well, perhaps. But I
for one reason: to see if they were
d, as treacherous and uneasy as I
ht. They were. My handwriting is
ery good, if you want to make one of
witty jokes about it. But there it is:
't bore or amuse you with the true
n. In the meantime, do you think
t of view would help you ? I think not.
er, you really should learn not to
when you accuse others of this sin.
        JOHN OSBORNE

I may be litigious, but I would never

PRIVATE EYE
No. 970 Friday 19 Feb '99

GENETICALLY MODIFIED FOOD
BLAIR SPEAKS OUT

> There is
> absolutely no
> danger at all

TORIES
NEW CARING FACE

> I can't speak to
> you now. The sun's
> coming up

"*Let me through! I'm the victim!*"   HENNET

"I'm sure it was the
Viagra that killed him"

McLACHLAN

To the voters of Kinross and West Perthshire

My name is **William Rushton, and I am asking you to vote
for me in the by-election on November 7th. I am asking
you to do so for one reason, and one reason only**—as a
protest against the way in which Lord Home, of all people,
has been foisted upon the country and the Conservative Party
and this constituency.

Let me explain:—

During the days of intrigue and manoeuvre which followed
Mr. Macmillan's announcement that he intended to resign,
it became rapidly clear that some Conservatives wanted Lord
Hailsham, some wanted Mr. Butler, and some wanted Mr.
Maudling.

But one thing was clear from the start, and remained clear
until the end—**practically nobody wanted Lord Home.**

Oh, yes—many Conservatives said they would 'put up with
him' if a good Prime Minister could not be found instead.
But practically nobody got up and said 'Lord Home would
be the best Prime Minister—let's choose him'.

How could they, after all, have said it with a straight face?

Home is the best man to lead your party into the final months
of this Parliament and the election—and beyond?

And if you are happy, why do you think Mr. Macleod and
Mr. Powell, two of the most brilliant Cabinet Ministers, have
refused to serve in Lord Home's Cabinet? **Why do you
think that in addition to Lord Home, two other Conservatives
are standing at this election?**

But secondly, the man chosen in this case was chosen not
only to be a Party Leader; he was also chosen to be Prime
Minister of the whole country.

And anyone who can be entirely happy at the prospect of
his or her country being led by this man is very easily
pleased indeed.

His political record is one of wretched insignificance.
Before the last war he was one of Neville Chamberlain's
most fanatical supporters (and his Parliamentary Secretary)
in the terrible policies that led to war. And to Britain's
shocking state of unreadiness.

Later his patient mediocrity was rewarded with a job in the

"I lived among
miners for 20 years"

Lord Home B.B.C T.V.
Monday 21ST Oct 63

Astonishing Revelation by Scottish Newspaper

THE PROV

PROVOST KNOWLES   BAILLIE VASS

Mod terror not

spirit

THE new pr
unruly te
"They must h
Provost Fre
less than t
Every
teenage b
areas.
The i
little to
most

'DOUGLAS-HOME' an Impostor

In an amazing report, the Aberdeen Evening Express last week revealed that the man known to the country as 'Sir Alec Douglas Home' is none other than the notorious Scottish impostor Baillie Vass.

VASS, Baillie

One of the *Eye*'s most enduring nicknames – a pub-quiz favourite to this day – arose from a simple printing mistake in the *Aberdeen Evening Express* in the spring of 1964.

A baillie is, as any fule kno, a "municipal officer and magistrate in Scotland". As the *Eye* put it, "Sir Alec (or Baillie Vass) last night said, 'I have no idea who this Vass fellow is. All I can say is I don't envy him his job as Prime Minister.' When it was pointed out that Sir Alec (or Vass) was in fact Prime Minister he replied, 'Don't bore me with statistics. I can't be expected to know everything.'"

☞ VOTE *PRIVATE EYE*

VASS, Mass for

A CONSTABLE POINTS THE WAY TO SMITH SQUARE

"Now is the time for all 'guid men and true' to come to the aid of the Baillie," declared *Private Eye* on 16 April 1965, inviting its readers to join a "Mass for Vass" to declare their allegiance to Sir Alec Douglas-Home a fortnight hence. Much to the editor's shock, they actually did. On 1 May, John Wells recalled, "Ingrams looked out of the first-floor windows of the offices on Greek Street at the collection of beards and pushchairs, socks and sandals, pipes and baggy sweaters, and seemed genuinely appalled."[237]

It was left to Peter Cook, in a wheelchair after breaking his ankle, to lead the procession to Conservative Central Office. Douglas-Home was deposed as leader two months later.

MEMBERS OF THE MILITARY BAND PAUSE FOR A "SMOKE" BEFORE THE DEMONSTRATION BEGINS

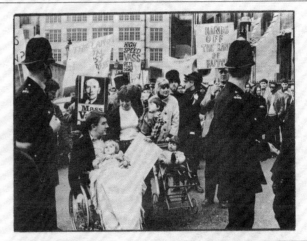

A DISABLED MUSIC HALL ENTERTAINER WITH HIS YOUNG FRIENDS PREPARES TO LEAD THE PROCESSION

WATCHED BY A CURIOUS CONSTABLE, THE EDITORIAL STAFF PRESENTS THE PETITION AT THE CONSERVATIVE PARTY CENTRAL OFFICE

VOTE PRIVATE EYE

Private Eye has fielded candidates in two elections.

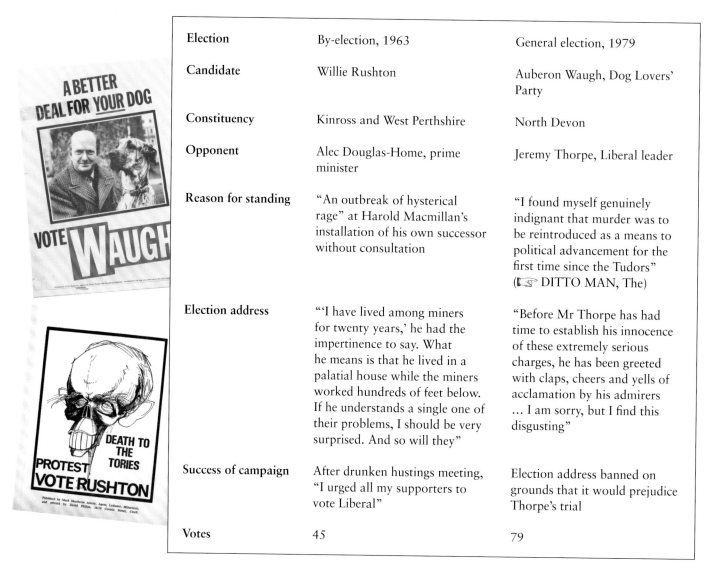

	By-election, 1963	General election, 1979
Election	By-election, 1963	General election, 1979
Candidate	Willie Rushton	Auberon Waugh, Dog Lovers' Party
Constituency	Kinross and West Perthshire	North Devon
Opponent	Alec Douglas-Home, prime minister	Jeremy Thorpe, Liberal leader
Reason for standing	"An outbreak of hysterical rage" at Harold Macmillan's installation of his own successor without consultation	"I found myself genuinely indignant that murder was to be reintroduced as a means to political advancement for the first time since the Tudors" (☞ DITTO MAN, The)
Election address	"'I have lived among miners for twenty years,' he had the impertinence to say. What he means is that he lived in a palatial house while the miners worked hundreds of feet below. If he understands a single one of their problems, I should be very surprised. And so will they"	"Before Mr Thorpe has had time to establish his innocence of these extremely serious charges, he has been greeted with claps, cheers and yells of acclamation by his admirers … I am sorry, but I find this disgusting"
Success of campaign	After drunken hustings meeting, "I urged all my supporters to vote Liberal"	Election address banned on grounds that it would prejudice Thorpe's trial
Votes	45	79

**OSTAGES:
ARTER'S SHOCK
NITIATIVE**

But Mr President, there's no such person as Wonderwoman

That Honorary Fellowship Citation In Full

SALUTAMUS FRANCISCUM WHEENUM ALUMN
HARROVIANUS ET LOOKALIKUS IANUS DUNCAN
SMITHO COLUMNISTICUS MULTOS ANNOS
GRAUNIADO INDEPENDENTEQUE ET PRIVATO OCU
QUOQUE SCRIPTOR MULTORUM LIBRORU
INCLUDANS BIOGRAPHICOS TOMASO DRIBERC
NOTORIUS PREDATOR HOMOSEXU

FURNITURE DEPT.

HONEYSETT

"We'd like to see some wardrobes please"

WIMMIN

I got my wife through Private Eye

RIVATE EYE

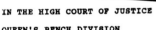

WILSON SUES PRIVATE EYE

PRI

W

KEVIN WOODCOCK

WARD, Stephen

The basic facts about what became known as the Profumo affair are these: Christine Keeler and Mandy Rice-Davies were call-girls living at the flat of an osteopath and orgy-organiser, Stephen Ward, who had an awful lot of famous friends, as well as contacts in the security services. At a party at Lord Astor's country estate, Ward introduced Keeler to the secretary of state for war, John Profumo, who had an affair with her. She was also sleeping with Eugene Ivanov, the naval attaché at the Soviet embassy – all during a particularly chilly period of the cold war. Hardly any of which anyone at Private Eye *knew.*

Christopher Booker: We knew a little tiny bit about it. The rumours were swirling around in all directions.

Richard Ingrams: We were little better informed of the situation than anyone else, though we printed on 22 March 1963 under the heading "Idle Talk" a summary of the current rumours which went further than any of the national papers.

Private Eye, *issue 33:*

Lunchtime O'Booze reveals: Gay, funloving Miss Gaye Funloving, a 21-year-old "model", has disappeared. One of Miss Funloving's close "friends", Dr Spook of Harley Street, revealed that night that he could add nothing to what had already been insinuated. Dr Spook is believed to have "more than half the cabinet on his list of patients". He also has a "weekend" cottage on the Berkshire estate of Lord *, and is believed to have attended many "parties" in the neighbourhood. Among those believed to have attended "parties" of this type are Mr Vladimir Bolokhov, the well-known Soviet spy attached to the Russian Embassy, and a well-known Cabinet Minister.

Ingrams: The day that article appeared, George Wigg first raised the matter in the House of Commons.

George Wigg (Lab.): There is not an hon. member in this house, nor a journalist in the press gallery, who, in the last few days, has not heard rumour upon

Timothy Birdsall's fortuitous cartoon, April 1963

rumour involving a member of the Government front bench. The press has got as near as it could – it has shown itself willing to wound but afraid to strike. That being the case, I rightly use the Privilege of the House of Commons – that is what it is given to me for – to ask the Home Secretary to go to the Dispatch Box. He knows that the rumour to which I refer relates to Miss Christine Keeler … and, on behalf of the Government, categorically deny the truth of these rumours.

After a thorough interrogation by the minister without portfolio, a young chap by the name of Bill Deedes, Profumo made a personal statement to the Commons.

John Profumo (Con.): There was no impropriety whatsoever in my acquaintanceship with Miss Keeler.

Ingrams: Profumo's peccadillo might have been quickly forgotten if it had not been for the behaviour of the Home Secretary Henry Brooke and the police force. It was Brooke who, perhaps unintentionally, instigated the police inquiries about Stephen Ward which led to Ward's hamfisted attempt to blackmail the government with a threat to reveal the truth about Profumo, which in turn led to Profumo's admission that he had lied to the House of Commons. The subsequent trial of Ward bore all the appearance of a primitive act of vengeance by the authorities and had the effect of implicating the police and the judiciary in the scandal.

Willie Rushton: We were the first people to actually get on to the Profumo business at all. And then as the other papers began to realize something was amiss, I remember Stephen Ward coming round to the offices to spill the beans: "I'd like to put my side of the story." Which of course, no one else got.[238]

Booker: One of the puns I am most proud of in all my years of *Private Eye*, having written millions of them, is in that Birdsall cartoon 'The last days of Macmillian', and there's a little thing above the swimming pool, 'Per Wardua Ad Astor', and that's what got Stephen Ward thinking 'Oh, they know more about it' and triggered him coming in.

Rushton: He said 'I see you know everything,' so we said, 'Just refresh our memories.'[239]

Ingrams: That was a time when he was still friendly with Profumo. Later when they started investigating he blew the gaff, I think, but at that time he was still backing up Profumo. I think Profumo had sent him round. The 'per Wardua' joke made them think that the *Eye* knew a lot about it. And Ward was basically trying to pump me, but we didn't know anything.

Booker: I find Stephen Ward a terrifically tragic figure, above all because I don't recollect a shred of evidence at that trial of his to suggest he was living off immoral earnings, which was what he was found guilty for. And then he topped himself. It was a classic scapegoat.

Ingrams: The Profumo affair kindled a lot of indignation. It was the first time that I remember that anyone had shown that the police and the justice system were not these wonderful institutions we'd been brought up to believe. From my point of view it was an eye-opener. It revealed that politicians could be involved in skulduggery, using Ward as a scapegoat and putting him on trial. It was a very kind of what-d'you-ma-call-it moment.

☞ COCKBURN, Claud

Scarfe puts Macmillan in the Christine Keeler pose, June 1963

WHEEN, Francis

Francis Wheen first arrived at *Private Eye* at the age of fifteen. "A friend of mine at school called Steve Parkes had *Private Eye* delivered every fortnight, and he always had any extras, books and annuals and the floppy singles they used to have on the covers, and it was because Venetia Parkes, his stepmother, worked on the front desk at *Private Eye*. So I started reading it in his room and I said 'Oh, this is very good.' And one holiday he said 'Why don't you come with me and we'll go to the

Private Eye office in London.' So he took me in to Greek Street, and I met Ingrams and I thought it was wonderful. There were piles of paper and newspapers scattered around the place and people wandering in and out. Piles of unwanted cartoons stacked in corners waiting to be sent back. Richard was terrifically friendly. He asked us if we had any good jokes, and he showed us a picture in a newspaper and asked if we had any good bubbles for it. I thought 'That seems like a nice place to work.'"

A decade and a half later in 1987, having left in turn Harrow, mainstream society, the alternative society, Royal Holloway College, the *Guardian* post room, an office at the *New Statesman* shared with Martin Amis and Christopher Hitchens and the *Independent*, he discovered it was. "Getting Francis was a very important early thing," says Ian Hislop of his early days in the editor's chair. "He was always, I thought, streets ahead. And that made a huge difference, because it gave it a weight and authority, and you could give him stories that were difficult or controversial or tough without him thinking 'Ooh, well, I can't really make the phonecall' or 'I'm a bit worried about my anonymity'. Rather like Bron Waugh, he has an amazing ability – everyone knows he's worked for the *Eye* for years, and everyone thinks he's great. He's sort of charming and it's a great skill. They know he'll be fair in the end. He won't make it up. He will say to someone, 'Now, the spanking, we really need to talk about that,' and

out it would come. When he joined it was a real turning point."

"He was desperate for copy, poor chap, because quite a few of his contributors had defected or deserted in a huff," remembers Wheen (☞ WORST COUP EVER). Wheen was meant to be writing a book at the time, but "Ian was on the phone saying 'You'll need some more work, I can't believe you'll be able to live on a book advance. A couple of days a fortnight would be really helpful – go on.'"

He's now the longest-serving hack in the *Eye* office after Michael Gillard (☞ SLICKER) and, nominally at least, the deputy editor, although he doesn't like being called it. "Nobody has a job title. I'm deputy in the sense that when Ian goes on holiday then I step in. More often than not I tend to do it in August or some ghastly time like that so you try ringing people and you discover that all your contributors are away at the same time and no one's around, it's like the *Marie Céleste*. But normally, on other publications, the deputy is someone who is week to week saying to the editor 'What are we going to do on page 6 here?' whereas in fact, when Ian's around, he jealously guards all that himself to the extent of still hanging on late on Monday evening when everyone's desperate to go home, tinkering with a page or two saying 'Actually I think we might put that here' as they're all screaming. I think my greatest contribution has been to give everyone an early press day when Ian goes on holiday."

WHERE'S BIN LADEN?

October 2001: As NATO forces enter Afghanistan, *Private Eye* publish cartoon "Where's Bin Laden?"

WHERE'S OZZIE?

Osama bin Laden is hiding somewhere in this jolly scene. Can YOU find him without turning the whole area into a smouldering pile of ash?

2006–2010: Xavier Waterkeyn and Daniel Lalic publish books *Where's Bin Laden?*, *Where's Bin Laden 3D Edition*, *Where's Bin Laden CIA Undercover Edition*, plus jigsaw puzzles *Where's Bin Laden?*, *Where's Bin Laden in London?*, *Where's Bin Laden in California?* and *Where's Bin Laden in Sydney?* The joke does not get any funnier.

WHISTLEBLOWERS,
Best

"Academics put together beautiful tip-offs," says Jane Mackenzie. "All the 'High Principals' stories. They put in all the details, plus links to the University Council minutes, and citations."

WHISTLEBLOWERS,
Worst

Journalists are terrible tale-tellers. The juiciest bits of the gossip directed at the "Street of Shame" column can generally be relied upon to have been round the office canteen four times, and "improved" beyond all recognition, and fall down at the first check. BBC hacks are particularly flaky.

WIKIPEDIA, Rules of,
changed thanks to *Eye*

In 2008, "Street of Shame" carried a story about the collaborative and notoriously inaccurate online encyclopaedia site Wikipedia, to which a saboteur had added various made-up details about a Cypriot football team ("a small but loyal group of fans are lovingly called 'the Zany Ones' – they like to wear hats made from discarded shoes") only to find them reproduced in a match report in the *Daily Mirror* when the team played Manchester City.

The *Eye* noted that "brilliantly, by the rules of Wikipedia – which relies on 'verifiability – whether readers are able to check that material added has already been published by a reliable third party source' such as 'mainstream newspapers' – this is now officially true".

Within a week, after a solemn exchange of emails between Wikipedia administrators and the *Eye* hack who wrote the story (me) the website's guidelines had been amended. "To avoid this indirect self-referencing, editors should ensure that material from news organisations is not *the only existing source* outside of Wikipedia."

This put an end to Wikipedia relying on newspapers for facts. It has certainly not stopped newspapers from relying on Wikipedia for facts.

WILL, Peter Cook's

After Peter Cook's death in January 1995, everybody assumed that *Private Eye* belonged to his fiercely devoted widow, Lin Cook. She did nothing to disabuse them of this idea. "She gave us that impression," says Dave Cash. "She said, or implied – she didn't correct us, that she had inherited all the shares. And what she wanted was for her and her brother Yinn, a Geneva-based accountant fellow, to be directors. They were refused point blank."

Just as in Paris six years previously (☞ HONEYMOON, Presence of Dave Cash on Peter Cook's), Mrs Cook had failed to understand the unique way that *Private Eye* functions. "The shareholding bit doesn't really make any odds," explains Ian Hislop firmly. "It really isn't any of their business what's going on here. They get a perfectly decent dividend. They're just not involved in the decision-making process, that's always been taken as read."

Besides, the situation was actually very different, as Peter's sisters Sarah and Elizabeth soon discovered. "In his will, he named Private Eye Productions and Pressdram Ltd, I leave in equal thirds to my sisters and to my wife," says Elizabeth Cook. "So that was pretty unambiguous. The intention is very clear – that he didn't want to give *any* of us particular power over the *Eye*. I think he was just trusting that we would continue to support it, really." Cook had owned 66 percent of *Private Eye*: this arrangement would give all three women 22 per cent, more than any of the minor shareholders (☞ FAMOUS FRIENDS) but not enough for any of them to be able to start throwing their weight around.

But things were more complicated than that. At some point after making his will – during a period of "some kind of financial anxiety", his sister speculates – Cook created a new company called Peter Cook Productions and transferred some of his Pressdram shares to it. Because that company wasn't specifically named in the will, it fell within the residue of the estate, which went to his wife.

"So Peter's intention didn't happen, essentially," says Cash sadly. "Lin finished up owning 40% and the reside divided between Elizabeth and Sarah. It's not a majority, but a 40% holding has got some clout."

All this, however, took months, and the involvement of several lawyers, to emerge. In the meantime things got very messy, and there was some rather unedifying behaviour on all sides. Hislop threatened to leave and take his whole team with him if Cook sold her share to an outsider: "If the existing people walked out then the magazine would be worth bugger all."[240] When it was rumoured that she was talking to Mohamed Fayed he went a step further and threatened to burn the building down as well. Millionaire publisher Owen Oyston made an approach: it came to nothing before he was convicted of rape and jailed in 1996. Lin barred both Peter's sisters, as well as his daughters and two ex-wives, from his memorial service, and then expunged all record of Richard Ingrams' oration at it from the book she published afterwards. Ingrams put a Chinese sign up above the door of the office. Lin wrote a letter to Peter's sister Sarah calling her "the most unpleasant person I have come across in a long time"; Sarah gave it to Peter's biographer to quote in full. Each twist and turn was extensively and gleefully covered by newspapers more used to having their dirty linen exposed in the pages of the *Eye* than the other way round.

In 1997 Lin declared her intention to sell her shares. "Over the two years I sort of thought Peter would not have wanted me to sell the *Eye*," she told the *Observer*. "But because of their totally careless attitude towards me, I just feel that Peter loves me and my welfare would mean more to him than anything else and it would be ok."[241] Cash and Hislop immediately made it clear to her that if she did, she was bound by Pressdram's articles of association to offer them to the existing shareholders first: "no share shall be transferred to a person who is not a member so long as any member is willing to purchase the same at a fair value." And there, slightly uneasily, things have rested ever since. Cash's successor as managing director Sheila Molnar says relations between the magazine and its biggest shareholder have been much calmer and more cordial over the past decade. When I spoke to Lin Cook early in 2011, she was keen to stress that she felt no animosity to anyone at the *Eye*, and that she regretted things that have appeared in the press in the past about her relationship with the magazine. The only article she wholeheartedly approves of appeared in the *New Yorker* in September 1995. It quoted her as saying "I have never been involved in *Private Eye*; I would not begin to know how to be involved. So there's no question of me wanting to take over the *Eye* and change things. Why would I? Why should I?" and stated that all she wanted was to get an income from the magazine. And so she now does – along with all the other shareholders, Cook gets a dividend at the end of each financial year.

"Shareholding is one of those unfortunate necessities: it happens, it's capitalism," sighs Peter Usborne, whose 8 per cent share of the magazine suddenly turned into an important factor as a result in the whole affair. "If it had been a socialist state we'd never have started *Private Eye* so there you go. I hope it can become some sort of foundation one day, some sort of charitable, *Guardian*-like ownership structure, but it's very awkward."

WINNERS, Paul Foot Award

The Paul Foot Award for investigative and campaigning journalism was set up by *Private Eye* and the *Guardian* after Foot's death in 2004.

The winners so far:

2005: John Sweeney, *Daily Mail*, for his investigation into Shaken Baby Syndrome which led to the freeing of three wrongly imprisoned mothers.

2006: David Willcocks, *Sunday Telegraph*, on Eastern European sex trafficking.

2007: Joint prize: David Leigh and Rob Evans, the *Guardian*, for their work on bribery in the British arms trade.
Deborah Wain, *Doncaster Free Press*, for her exposé of corruption in the Doncaster Education City project.

2008: Joint prize: Camilla Cavendish, the *Times*, for her investigation into the many injustices which have resulted from the Children Act 1989 and the professional cultures that have grown up around child 'protection'.
Richard Brooks, *Private Eye*, on the mismanagement and financial irregularities surrounding the sale of the UK government's international development business, Actis (☞ TAXMAN).

2009: Ian Cobain, the *Guardian*, for exposing Britain's involvement in the torture of terror suspects detained overseas.

2010: Claire Sambrook, for reports on the imprisonment of asylum-seeking families in harmful conditions.

WOODCOCK, Kevin

First drew for the *Eye* in 1972 and contributed for more than three decades, during which time he never visited or spoke to anyone from the office. He had no telephone.

He specialised in surreal architectural fantasies and people meeting gruesome ends. When he died in 2007, his body was not discovered for some time.

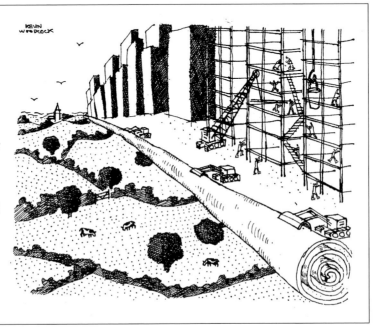

WORST COUP EVER

In the wake of Richard Ingrams's unilateral declaration in March 1986 that Ian Hislop would be succeeding him as editor (☞ RESIGNATION), tensions were running high.

Richard Ingrams: It caused a terrific fuss. And in a way you could understand that, because Dave Cash and … they didn't know Ian particularly well. They obviously thought he was very young, and they thought "Who is this guy?" And Cash was always prone to panic.

Dave Cash: Typical bloody Ingrams. He did Hislop no favours at all. None. And he should have talked to Cook about it. That really got to him – I remember Peter phoning me up, we had long conversations with Peter saying 'I like Ian very much, but what is Richard doing?' The first person Ingrams should have spoken to was Cook, the proprietor. He was very pissed off.

Ingrams: He was very upset about it. He thought I should have consulted him, but I just thought if I started consulting people it would never have happened.[242]

Auberon Waugh: An opposition group formed under Peter McKay. It included Nigel Dempster. I was roped in and Peter Cook, to everyone's surprise, was inveigled into attending our emergency meeting.[243]

Cash: Dempster and McKay had been plotting and silly McKay thought he should be editor, which was all bollocks. They organized a lunch at the Gay Hussar [in Greek Street], and they were getting various bods there and they wanted Peter to come, and Peter phoned me and said he wanted me to come along as well to listen. It wasn't a plot or anything – he just wanted me to hear what McKay and Dempster had to say.

Ian Hislop: Dave was certainly extremely ambivalent – he went to this lunch with Cook and had got it into his head that for the future of the magazine it was important for me not to do it.

Peter McKay, writing in 1986: We assembled in the top floor private room of the Gay Hussar – Peter Cook, Auberon Waugh, Patrick Marnham, David Cash, Nigel Dempster, Dick West and myself. Dempster then made what was generally believed afterwards to have been a crucial mistake. He invited Waugh to choose the wine. After fastidiously studying the list, Bron opted for Gressier Grand Poujeaux Haut Médoc at twenty-five pounds a bottle. Cook's enthusiasm for the wine was no greater, but certainly no less, than everyone else's.

The general view was that Hislop could not fill Ingrams' shoes. Waugh reiterated his view that under Hislop jokes would be calculated to appeal to a yobbo audience, and that the successful *Private Eye* had no need of such people. Dempster urged the view that Hislop was not a proper journalist, and did not understand how stories were gathered, written and used to proper advantage. He should be fired. Dick West raised the suspicion that Hislop might seek to suck up to minorities such as feminists and homosexuals, whose proselytizing activities had long provided *Private Eye* with targets for satire.

My own expressed view was that it was undesirable for Ingrams to have been allowed to choose his successor, and certainly not without reference to his fellow directors, shareholders and senior colleagues. Dick West suggested that Hislop should be put in charge of the "funnies" and that I be appointed editor of the rest of the magazine. Cash asked if I would serve if I were called, and I said I would.[244]

Cash: That's bollocks. Absolute tosh.

McKay, 1986: There was a call for a show of hands, and I was happy to receive the unanimous blessing of my merry luncheon friends.

That electorate in full: a man who had resigned from the magazine some months previously; a man who had left under a cloud four years previously; a man who had been sacked a year previously; a man whose involvement with the magazine had ceased several years before and man who describes himself as having been "not properly involved with the Eye" at the time. Viva democracy!

Jane Ellison: No one else remembered McKay agreeing to 'serve if called'.[245]

McKay, speaking in 2009: Ha ha! Well, a great deal of wine was taken. Myself and Marnham were the candidates, as I remember. I think I remember that I – oh, it's lost in the mists of antiquity. Marnham might say that he got more votes than I did. But it's nonsense, anyway, it wasn't a question, it was just a lark. No one took it seriously. It was madness. Cook was just treating it as a joke – I don't think he was anti-Ian, he just wanted an opportunity for trouble. It was never – no one was ever going to do anything about it, what could we do about it, it's an institution, who can say who was to be – I don't know how on earth anything is approved at *Private Eye*, is there a board as such?

Waugh: My memory of the event is as hazy as that of everyone else who attended, but the consensus appears to be that at lunch we decided that Peter Cook should go and confront Ingrams, with the support of David Cash, and demand the sacking of Hislop and the appointment in his place of Peter McKay.

Cash: I sat there, I had a few drinks there actually, and Peter had a lot to drink, and the plan was to go back and talk to Richard.

Hislop: The two of them came back from the lunch – the conspirators were still there – and they were convinced that they had changed Cookie's mind. And he literally came up to me, *fantastically* pissed, and said "Welcome aboard!" Two words I will never forget. Basically Cook had had the wine, he'd enjoyed the lunch, and ignored them entirely.

Peter Cook: The idea of having *Private Eye* run by McKay is a joke. If Richard had appointed Christine Keeler I might have intervened, but Ian was the ideal choice.[246]

Hislop: I spoke to him afterwards on a different occasion, and he said: "Richard's chosen you, Richard's made the decision. It was very rude of him not to mention it to me" – Cookie was slightly hurt that he hadn't been consulted – but he said it was absolutely no reason to change what had happened. I'd spent enough time with Cookie by then for him to just say "Let's get on with it."

Cash: Peter and I then went and saw Richard, and Richard being Richard he doesn't say anything. It's very unnerving, he just sort of sits there. Which he did with us. And Cook was leaving it to me to say something, and there wasn't really very much to say other than "I think you should have possibly told a few more people." And the outcome was nil really.

Hislop: The worst, most pathetic, incredibly botched coup in history! But they were absolutely serious.

Christopher Silvester: The whole point about Cook's proprietorship, if that's what you'd call it, was that he didn't want any power of that nature. He was perfectly happy to help the magazine out if it was under threat from an outsider, but he wasn't going to get involved in office politics.

Waugh: It was perhaps the most ludicrous of our joint enterprises. Hislop remains editor to this day, and the *Eye* flourishes.

Hislop: Richard was very gracious, he wrote me a letter afterwards saying "I really botched this one." Which he had.

☞ PARKINSON, Cecil, his part in Nigel Dempster's downfall

WREATH, Funeral, delivered
by editor to art director

One Christmas in the mid-2000s, Ian Hislop instructed his secretary Hilary Lowinger to go out and buy a funeral wreath and deliver it to the desk of Tony Rushton. Because she's almost supernaturally efficient, she rustled one up within ten minutes ("I ran round to the flower stall on Berwick Street market, and asked them to take the pinecones off a Christmas one and put lilies on instead"). "He was saying 'This Christmas schedule is a nail in my coffin' and I thought 'Bloody hell, that's outrageous, you're here on sufferance at your age and you're not complaining about the bloody schedule,'" giggles Hislop.

This is not recommended as a management method.

Ian Hislop's deepest sympathies, as sent to Tony Rushton on the occasion of a bumper Christmas issue, and *below* his amendments to Tone's original artwork

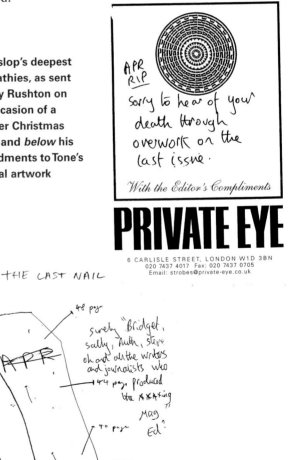

ÆSOP revisited

OVER NOW to the factory in Suffolk, where the keel has just been laid of the 500-volume Official Biography of the Greatest Dying Englishman. The Great Bumpkin himself, Rudolph Rednose, is enthroned . . .

It's not me that's the hack – it's the people who write my books

Here beginneth the First War

W.S.C.

. . . never was so much written by so many for so little. But, as the Bumpkin and his hirelings pay nightly homage with readings from the Great Book, as fat offers for serialisation flow in from the scoop-hungry Sunday Telegraph – a dreadful doubt arises. That like all Official Portraits this one too will bear little resemblance to the original . . .

WRITS, First of many

The very first person to issue a libel writ against *Private Eye* was the little-known author Colin Watson, who objected to being called "the little-known author Colin What's-'is-name" in issue 25. He was eventually paid £750 to go away. The second was Alderman L. J. Tarbit, a former mayor of Rotherham who was standing for Parliament, and who was described as being "keener on the Good Things of Life than the bad things in Rotherham". He promptly proved not to be that keen on life at all, dropping dead not long after his writ arrived and giving rise to the legend of the Curse of Gnome. The third arrived courtesy of Randolph Churchill – as did the fourth, and the fifth through twelfth as well.

He objected to the "Aesop Revisited" (☞) strip in issue 30, which suggested that his official biography of his father Winston was being written by a team of hacks and would gloss over incidents like Churchill senior sending in the army to tackle striking miners in Tonypandy in 1911. Individual writs were personally addressed to "every single person connected with *Private Eye*, right down to the girls in the office" by Churchill's solicitor Peter Carter-Fuck, then a mere stripling of forty-nine.[247]

"The issuing of the writs was treated by us as a colossal joke," recalled Richard Ingrams. "In the display window outside the office we mounted a collection of exhibits – the offending article, the writ and a special Rushton cartoon called The Great Boar of Suffolk showing Randolph as a pig." Less amused was Churchill, who, never a man to do things by halves, had hired private detectives to keep an eye on 22 Greek Street. "Within a few hours, an injunction was issued compelling the removal of the exhibits from public display. Our lawyers, already spluttering with rage at the thought of anyone stooping so low as to attack Sir Winston Churchill, could now scarcely contain themselves. 'You did not inform us that the pig was excreting,' they wrote." The window display was replaced by a handwritten sign: "Killjoy was here."

"That was the grand moment," chortles co-founder Peter Usborne. "We were front page on the *Evening Standard*: 'It's Randolph v. Private Eye', we were headline news. Just an amazing boost. And that contributed to our incredible rise to a print run of 150,000 copies."

The law, however, did require some kind of sensible response – and this, like all the other boring bits, fell to Usborne. "I was doing jolly well I thought," he recalls. He found out the names of the various dons Churchill had engaged to research his book and went round to visit them all individually. "And I'd found out various things. And I spent the night in

Willie Rushton's original window display, long lost but recently returned to Richard Ingrams by a stranger

the rooms of one of them, with my little red notebook, and when I got back to the office on Monday my little red notebook was not there any longer. And it came through two days later from Randolph Churchill, with a note saying 'Yours, I believe.' At that point we decided to settle, because we couldn't bloody win."

This cock-up wasn't their only problem. Attending court over the window injunction Willie Rushton had managed to make the judge laugh by counting out the steps of Churchill's counsel into the courtroom – "TEN guineas, TWENTY guineas, THIRTY guineas" – but when the bill arrived it turned out he had been underestimating. And that hearing had lasted only ten minutes. They simply couldn't afford to defend the libel action. "In those days we could never have raised the money if he had stood on his rights," recalled Rushton. "Apart from anything else he seemed to have retained every available lawyer in the country. We couldn't find anyone notable who was free."[248]

Nick Luard (☞) was summoned back from his honeymoon at the Paris Ritz – he had just married *Eye* secretary Elisabeth Longmore – and dispatched to visit Churchill at his Suffolk home to hammer out a settlement. Willie Rushton went with him on the off-chance some jokes would help.

"No one's going to have a drink until we've settled this," Churchill announced when the pair arrived at 11.30 in the morning. This swiftly

We the undersigned wish to withdraw unreservedly the false allegations we made and implied against Sir Winston and Mr. Randolph Churchill and the latter's research assistants in the issue of Private Eye of February 8.

Nicholas Luard	*Mrs. O'Morgo Ingrams*
Christopher Booker	*Anne Chisholm*
William Rushton	*Sir Charles Harness*
Richard Ingrams	*Brian Moore*
Peter Usborne	*Pressdram Ltd.*
Tony Rushton	*Leo Thorpe Ltd.*

The withdrawal published in the *Evening Standard*

turned out to be more of a problem for him than it was for them, as Luard recalled. "As the hours passed he started to sweat. He was clearly in poor shape and needed some refreshment. Finally at 4.45 we reached a settlement. We would withdraw on a full page of the *Evening Standard*. There would be no apology. It was all we had hoped to get out of him. He then relaxed, brought out the whisky and even introduced the hacks – or 'researchers' – who were arranged around the premises very much in the way that we had suggested."[249]

The full-page withdrawal appeared on Valentine's Day 1963. It accepted that the *Eye*'s cartoon strip was "abominable", "exceptionally gross and offensive" and, for good measure, contained "the vilest libel I have ever seen". "It cost us twelve hundred quid," remembers Usborne. Just as Churchill had insisted, the names of all the staff were listed exactly as they had appeared in the magazine, granting one of the distributors a knighthood and recording Mary Morgan's nickname for prosperity.

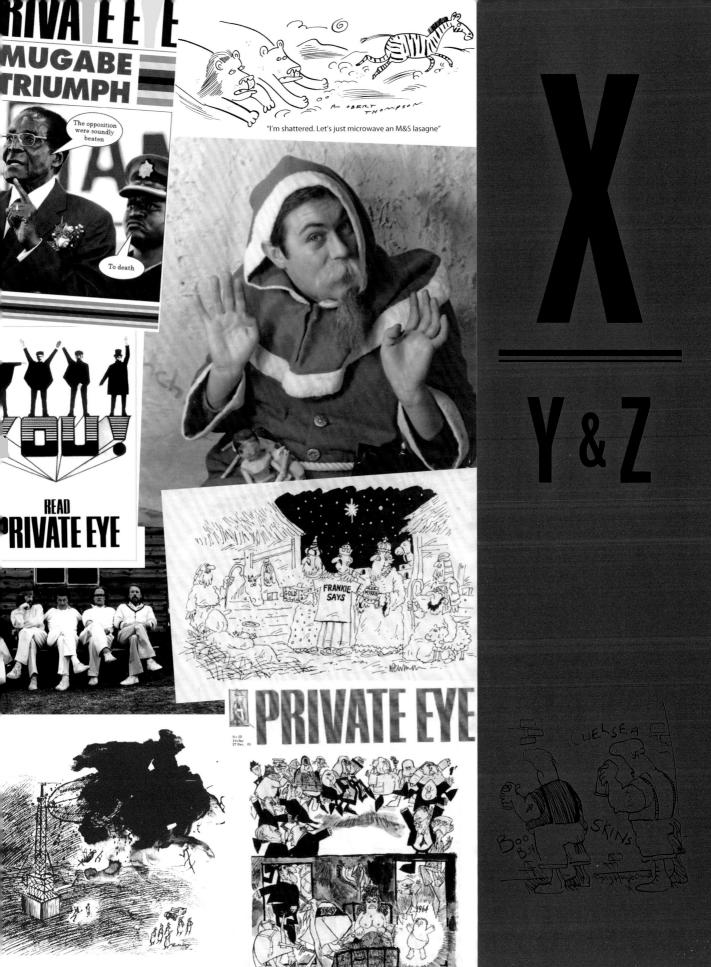

RIVATE EYE

MUGABE TRIUMPH

The opposition were soundly beaten

To death

"I'm shattered. Let's just microwave an M&S lasagne"

READ PRIVATE EYE

FRANKIE SAYS

GOLD

MYRRH

PRIVATE EYE

No 53
Friday
27 Dec. 85

X
Y & Z

CHELSEA

BOO BOY

SKINS

"Does anybody know whether they're supposed to do that?"

XMAS covers by Steve Bell

Steve Bell, best known for his cartoons in the *Guardian*, provided special glossy covers for *Private Eye* every Christmas from 1992 to 1996.

☞ COOK, Beryl, Cover by; FLUCK AND LAW

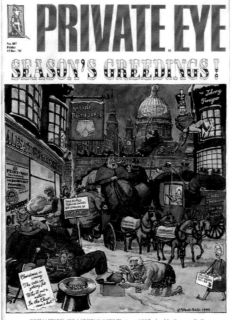

PRIVATISED COACHING SCENE circa 1895 *by Mr Steven Bell*

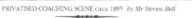

And a Happy New Labour!

YESTERDAY'S MEN

In 1971 David Dimbleby interviewed the former prime minster Harold Wilson for a BBC documentary unflatteringly titled *Yesterday's Men*. Infuriated by questions about media reports on his personal finances, the leader of the opposition halted filming. "The interview's off, the whole programme's off," he raged. "I think we'll have a new piece of film in and start all over again. If this film is used or if this is leaked then there's going to be a hell of a row … There are [sic] plenty of personal stuff you can ask without this kind of *Private Eye* level …"

Inevitably, a full transcript of his rant appeared in *Private Eye*. But, for once, Wilson's suspicions were correct. Some months earlier the team behind the programme had attempted to recruit a researcher from the *Eye*, to look for "sexual dirt" on politicians at arm's length from the BBC. They were refused. Not on any moral grounds, but because they were offering "the paltry sum of £25".

YOBS

☞ STRIPS, Longest-running

YORKSHIRE RIPPER, wife

sues *Private Eye*

☞ BANANA, I'm a

YOUNG PRODIGIES

The *Eye* has a talent for spotting them young.

March 1967 – The *Eye* has a pop at a student journalist at Oxford University, "Miss **Polly Toynbee**, the very well-connected daughter of Philip, literary critic of the *Observer*, and grand-daughter of Arnold".

May 1969 – While an undergraduate at University College London, young debater **David Irving** "closed his speech by greeting the audience with a Heil Hitler salute".

July 1969 – The *Sunday Times* has turned down a piece from "**Simon Schama**, a Cambridge don" for being insufficiently reverent towards the monarchy.

November 1969 – A piece about the sharp practices of Don Arden, manager of bands including the Small Faces, notes that one of his businesses is set up in the name of his teenage daughter Sharon Levy, who would go on to be **Sharon Osbourne**.

December 1969 – Paul Foot trains his sights on the newly elected member for Louth, who has been forced to pay back £1,700 in expenses to a former employer, and has set up a company using paperwork with a forged signature. It is the first of many, many appearances by **Jeffrey Archer**.

January 1970 – "**Richard Branson**, the presiding boy genius of *Student* magazine", comes under fire for underpaying his staff while feathering his own nest. He is nineteen.

June 1971 – "Little is known about the appalling **Gyles Brandreth**, except that he is thought to have been the first person to employ a literary agent while still at university."

March 1972 – A young parliamentary secretary, Christine Holman, demands that the *Eye* print a photograph of her at the wheel of a car containing her boss Gerald Nabarro MP, to prove he is driven by his secretaries as he has claimed during his trial for dangerous driving. The *Eye* obliges, pointing out that they are "not displaying the required road tax certificate". She will later marry another MP and become **Christine Hamilton**.

July 1974 – "Mr **Michael Mansfield**, 29" has been given a dressing-down for making "excessive pay demands" of £200 per day from the legal aid fund, notes legal columnist Justinian Forthemoney. The *Eye* also notes that "young Mr Mansfield is also apparently a time traveller", given that he is engaged upon two cases at the same time.

May 1984 – "His ambition has outstripped his ability … It appears that he lacks certain essential social graces," points out the *Eye* of the recently elected MP for Dunfermline East, **Gordon Brown**.

January 1987 – The cover of issue 654 features Neil Kinnock posing with a baby. She is **Georgia Gould**, and twenty-two years later she will cause controversy when Labour attempt to "parachute her in" as a candidate in the upcoming general election.

YOUTH, Voices of

The last "official" history of *Private Eye*, published for the twenty-first anniversary in 1982, mentions in its penultimate pages "Ian Hislop, a recent graduate of Oxford. He now contributes regularly, possibly the first of a new generation of satirists to join the original collaborators."

As this book is published, he has been editor for exactly half the *Eye*'s lifespan, beating Richard Ingrams's record by two years ("I'm very, very aware of the fact it will annoy him. So I'll certainly be here then!"). In all that time, only one other publication has tried to poach him: "I was offered the editorship of *Punch* once, by a headhunter. And I said 'You really must go and read your brief more carefully.'" His increasing TV stardom means he gets offered

every gig going – "*Celebrity Big Brother*, the jungle, *Strictly* … I get offered all that rubbish. *Celebrity Detox* was my low. But no seats on major boards, no Blair-style mediating roles – it's an incredible shortage of offers. That's why I'm still here!"

So how long does he think he will stay for? "What d'you think's the maximum time that would annoy people who want the story about me leaving?" he muses, a copy of that morning's *Independent* open on his desk at a story suggesting that "the anniversary would be a fitting moment for Mr Hislop to hand over to a younger man". "Another thirty years should just about see 'em off, ha ha! I have no plans at all to leave."

He has, however, fostered a younger generation of talent at the *Eye*. Plenty of the thirty-something hacks who got their big break with the *Eye* are still around and contributing – Sarah Shannon, Jane Mackenzie, Ed Howker, er, me – and in 2010 Nev Fountain and Tom Jamieson moved into the office to conduct their fortnightly joke-writing session, the first comic duo to work from the office since Newman and Hislop twenty-five years earlier. They share a room – in a more dreadful workplace it would be called hot-desking – with, among others, Andy Murray (not that one), a twenty-three-year-old Oxford graduate and comedy performer who does a couple of days per issue.

"I actually don't know what would happen if Ian fell under a bus: I think it's jolly awkward," says Francis Wheen, the man who is at least nominally deputy editor. "It would be hopeless giving it to me. You need someone who can do the whole magazine which is quite tricky: straddling the jokes and the libels and the 'In the Back'. I suppose what you really need is for Ian to find some work experience person and detect something in them, and then resign and give them the job."

Of course there is another option. "If Ian went I think there's a lot to be said for making Booker editor," chuckles Wheen. "Because he's been waiting for however many years it is, since 1963, ever since that embarrassing business of the honeymoon …"

ZIONIST PLOT, *Eye* outed as part of a

In February 2011, after the *Eye* had run a lengthy piece about the involvement of raving anti-Semite Israel Shamir with the whistleblowing website Wikileaks, its figurehead Julian Assange phoned editor Ian Hislop to tell him the article – which he hadn't read – was "crap."

He went on to accuse the *Eye* of being part of an international conspiracy to smear him and his organisation, led by figures at the *Guardian* who were Jewish. Hislop pointed out that not all the people he named were actually Jewish, but Assange insisted they were "sort of Jewish" and sometimes went to the same parties, and insisted that it was the magazine's job to reveal this sort of thing (rather than, say, the fact that his own associate Shamir was a holocaust denier). Assange – then fighting extradition from Britain on sexual assault charges – also informed the editor that journalists at the *Guardian* "failed my masculinity test."

When Hislop printed an account of this conversation in the following edition of *Private Eye*, Assange accused him of having "distorted, invented or misremembered almost every significant claim and phrase," and allied himself with those other well-known crusaders for truth and justice Robert Maxwell, Jonathan Aitken and Sonia Sutcliffe (☞) by pointing out that "he has a reputation for this, and is famed to have received more libel suits in the UK than any other journalist as a result."

That isn't true either.

ZZZ, that's enough – Ed
(cont. 2094)

WHO'S WHO?

Various long-standing friends and enemies of the Eye *are quoted or referred to in passing in entries other than their own. This is a quick reference guide for the confused reader:*

Balon, Norman – landlord of *Eye* pub the Coach and Horses, Greek Street, 1943-2006

Bernard, Jeffrey – *Eye* contributor, 1977-80

Booker, Christopher – *Eye* editor, 1961-63 and member of jokes team, 1964-present

Brooks, Richard – hack, 2004-present

Brown, Craig – contributor, 1988-present

Cash, Dave – accountant, 1963-74, managing director, 1974-2000

Carter-Fuck, Peter – solicitor who handled multiple litigations against *Eye*, 1963-2003

Cockburn, Claud – hack, 1963-81

Cook, Peter – owner of *Private Eye*, 1962-95 and member of jokes team

Davies, Tristan – sub-editor, 1987-present

Dempster, Nigel – hack, 1970-85

Driberg, Tom – contributor and crossword compiler, 1969-76

Elliott, Liz – editorial secretary and hack, 1976-1985

Ellison, Jane – hack, 1982-86

Fantoni, Barry – member of jokes team, 1963-2010

Foot, Paul – hack, 1967-2004

Fountain and Jamieson, Nev and Tom – joke-writers, 1999-present

Gillard, Michael – hack, 1969-present

Goldsmith, Sir James – serial litigant, 1970s-80s

Halloran, Paul – hack, 1981-92

Hislop, Ian – member of jokes team, 1981-86 and *Eye* editor 1986-present

Hughes, Solomon – hack, 1995-present

Ingrams, Richard – *Eye* editor, 1963-86 and member of jokes team, 1986-present

Lowinger, Hilary – editorial secretary and office manager, 1986-present

Lunn, Maggie – editorial secretary, 1985-1991

Mackenzie, Jane – hack, 2002-present

Macqueen, Adam – hack, 1997-present and author of this book

Marnham, Patrick – hack, 1966-82

McKay, Peter – hack, 1970-86

Maxwell, Robert – serial litigant, 1970s-90s

Mills, Heather – hack, 1998-present

Minogue, Tim – hack, 1997-present

Molnar, Sheila – accountant 1976-2001, managing director, 2001-present

Newman, Nick – cartoonist from 1981, member of jokes team, 1986-present

Osmond, Andrew – owner of *Private Eye*, 1961-2, managing director 1969-74

Roccelli, Sue – editorial secretary, 1996-present

Rushton, Tony (Tone) – art director and sometime advertising manager and managing director, 1962-present

Rushton, Willie – member of jokes team from 1961-1964, cartoonist from 1961-1996

Shannon, Sarah – hack, 1994-99

Silvester, Christopher – hack, 1983-1995

Tomkinson, Martin – hack, 1973-81

Usborne, Peter – managing director, 1961-1965

Waugh, Auberon – contributor, 1970-1986

Wells, John – member of jokes team, 1961-64 and co-author of *Mrs Wilson's Diary* and *Dear Bill*

Wheen, Francis – hack, 1987-present

ACKNOWLEDGEMENTS

For their generosity with time and memories, I am grateful to everyone who agreed to be interviewed at length for this book: Christopher Booker, Richard Brooks, Dave Cash, Elizabeth Cook, Tristan Davies, Barry Fantoni, Nev Fountain, Michael Gillard, Ian Hislop, Solomon Hughes, Richard Ingrams, Tom Jamieson, Peter McKay, Jane Mackenzie, Steve Mann, Heather Mills, Tim Minogue, Sheila Molnar, Andy Murray, Nick Newman, Matt Owen, Tony Rushton, Sarah Shannon, Christopher Silvester, Peter Usborne, and Francis Wheen.

I picked the brains of many others, some of them probably not even realising I was doing it at the time: thanks to Mary Aylmer, Norman Balon, Joan Bakewell, Marcus Berkmann, Cecilia Boggis, Ciar Byrne, Lin Cook, Geoff Elwell, Sally Farrimond, Phil Hammond, Eric Hands, Tony Husband, Grizelda Grizlingham, Ed Howker, Graham Lord, Hilary Lowinger, Patrick Marnham, Lewis Morley, Stuart Osmond, Alice Pitman, Libby Purves, Sue Roccelli, Ben Summerskill, DJ Taylor, Steve Tiernan, Ben Tisdall, Bridget Tisdall, Megan Trudell, Andrew Wilson and a smattering of people whose names cannot be mentioned in association with the *Eye*. Stephen Buckley, Shonali Chapman, Adam Curtis, Damian Daunt, Dave McLeod, Andy Murray, James Price and Camilla Wright provided invaluable research help, as did all those who commented on the '*Private Eye* at 50' blog at private-eye.co.uk.

Photo credits: Page 7, colour: Toby Madden, Page 7 (black and white), 44, 71, 141, 149, 151, 170, 173, 201, 279, 283, 286, 291: Eric Hands. 8-11, office photos: Paul Kerley/Radio 4 Today programme. 29: Beatles: Paul Popper/Popperphoto. 61, 232: Press Association. 62: Jeremy Selwyn. 85: Cook outside Establishment Club, 123, Ingrams with machine gun, 255, Father Christmas 301 and various other photographs from early editions of the *Eye*: Lewis Morley. 100, 125: John Lawrence Jones/Fluck and Law. 110: News International. 21, 133, 233: Rex. 166: Jane Bown. 219: Ingrams and Cook: Getty. 236: *Financial Times* 270: Photographers Direct.

Every reasonable effort has been made to trace copyright holders, but if there are errors or omissions, Private Eye Productions will be pleased to insert the appropriate acknowledgement in any subsequent edition. Thanks to all the contributors, cartoonists and photographers whose work has been reproduced in these pages.

A complete library of *Private Eye* covers can be viewed at private-eye.co.uk

Bridget Tisdall worked tirelessly compiling the illustrations and photographs, and Peter Ward was responsible for a superb design job. Peter James copy-edited wisely. Henry Davies drew a special Gnittie for the cover.

Especial thanks are also due to Louis Barfe, the very definition of a gentleman, and to my partner Michael Tierney for putting up with me.

The job would have been much, much harder if a lot of the groundwork had not already been done for me by Patrick Marnham in *The Private Eye Story* and Harry Thompson in his brilliant biographies of Richard Ingrams and Peter Cook. I am indebted to both of them. The fact that I was mining Harry's books for quotes from those key figures – Cook, Willie Rushton, John Wells, Andrew Osmond – who are no longer around to speak for themselves makes his own death at the ridiculously young age of 45 seem even more poignant. I never met him. I wish I had.

I was lucky enough to know and work with Paul Foot. Talking to others who had that privilege brought back just how much I miss him.

NOTES

1   *Independent on Sunday,* 12 August 2001
2   *Times,* 14 January 1995
3   *Observer,* 17 August 1997
4   *The Goldfish Bowl: Married to the Prime Minister* by Cherie Booth and Cate Haste, Chatto & Windus 2004
5   *Below the Parapet: The Biography of Denis Thatcher* by Carol Thatcher, HarperCollins 1996
6   *Independent,* 20 November 1994
7   *Stick It Up Your Punter* by Peter Chippindale and Chris Horrie, Simon & Schuster 1999
8   Archive material in *Thirty Years of Satire,* BBC Radio 4, October 1991
9   *The Private Eye Story*
10 To aristocrat Emma Tennant, who told friends she had "met a satirist and decided then and there to ally myself with this new movement". It didn't last.
11 sajata.net
12 *Total Politics,* May 2010
13 *Guardian,* 25 April 2005
14 *Trust Me, I'm (Still) a Doctor* by Dr Phil Hammond, Black & White Publishing 2009
15 *The Lost Diaries* by Craig Brown, Fourth Estate 2010
16 *Guardian,* 27 November 1999
17 Ibid, 25 January 2003
18 Ibid, 2 October 2010
19 *Peter Cook: A Biography* by Harry Thompson, Hodder & Stoughton 1997
20 *The Pythons: Autobiography by the Pythons,* ed. Bob McCabe, Orion 2004
21 Turner-Samuels even managed to get the name of the publication wrong: he was actually quoting the *Times Literary Supplement.*
22 *Cockburn Sums Up* by Claud Cockburn, Quartet Books 1981
23 Press Association report, 15 February 2000
24 *Mark Lawson Talks to Ian Hislop,* BBC Four, May 2009
25 *Richard Ingrams: Lord of the Gnomes* by Harry Thompson, William Heinemann, 1994
26 *Times,* 5 October 1991
27 *So Farewell Then, Peter Cook* by Wendy E. Cook, HarperCollins 2006
28 *Heroes of Comedy: Peter Cook,* Channel 4, January 1998
29 *Desert Island Discs,* BBC Radio 4, August 2008
30 *Loving Peter: My Life with Peter Cook and Dudley Moore* by Judy Cook with Angela Levin, Piatkus Books 2008
31 *Passing Wind,* no. 11, 1980
32 *Aspel and Company,* ITV, January 1988
33 *The Private Eye Story*
34 *Will This Do? An Autobiography* by Auberon Waugh, Arrow 1992
35 *Peter Cook: A Biography*
36 *So Farewell Then, Peter Cook*
37 *Publisher,* no. 10, October 1964
38 *Doctor Who: The Chase,* DVD extras, 2 Entertain, 2010
39 *Below the Parapet*
40 *The Goldfish Bowl*
41 *Evening Standard,* 6 May 1998
42 *Guardian,* 7 October 1991
43 *The Remarkable Lives of Bill Deedes* by Stephen Robinson, Little, Brown 2008
44 *Not Many Dead* by Nicholas Garland, Hutchinson 1990
45 *Granta,* issue 60, Winter 1997
46 *Independent,* 19 October 1997
47 *Observer,* 7 September 1997
48 *Desert Island Discs*
49 *Lord of the Gnomes*
50 *Independent,* 10 August 2003
51 *Mark Lawson Talks to Ian Hislop*
52 *Observer,* 8 December 2002
53 *British Journalism Review,* vol. 13, no. 4, 2002
54 *Ever, Dirk: The Bogarde Letters* ed. John Coldstream, Weidenfeld & Nicolson 2008
55 *Peter Cook: A Biography*
56 *The Private Eye Story*
57 Ibid.
58 *Lord of the Gnomes*
59 *Thirty Years of Satire,* BBC Radio 4, October 1991
60 *The Penguin Book of Journalism* ed. Stephen Glover, Penguin 2000
61 *My Friend Footy: A Memoir of Paul Foot* by Richard Ingrams, Private Eye Productions 2005
62 *Private Eye, Public Interest?,* BBC Radio 4, October 1976
63 *The Penguin Book of Journalism*
64 *UK Press Gazette,* 13 June 1988
65 *My Friend Footy*
66 *Will This Do?*
67 *The Writing on the Wall: Britain in the Seventies* by Phillip Whitehead, Michael Joseph 1985
68 *New York* magazine, February 1974
69 *Lord of the Gnomes*
70 *The Penguin Book of Journalism*
71 *Lord of the Gnomes*
72 *The Penguin Book of Journalism*
73 *Mark Lawson Talks to Ian Hislop*
74 *Goldenballs* by Richard Ingrams, Private Eye Productions/André Deutsch 1979
75 *Glimmers of Twilight* by Joe Haines, Politico's 2003
76 *Goldenballs*
77 *Trail of Havoc: In The Steps of Lord Lucan* by Patrick Marnham, Penguin 1987
78 *The Private Eye Story*
79 *Lord of the Gnomes*
80 Archive interview included in *Thirty Years of Satire*
81 *Observer,* 5 March 2006
82 *Western Mail,* 8 February 1977
83 *Downing Street Diary: With Harold Wilson in Number 10* by Bernard Donoughue, Jonathan Cape 2005
84 *Guardian,* 20 January 1999
85 *Lord Goodman* by Brian Brivati, Richard Cohen Books 1999
86 *Independent,* 14 June 1990
87 *Lord of the Gnomes*
88 *The Private Eye Story*
89 *Independent,* 16 February 1992
90 *Times,* 6 November 1986
91 *Observer,* 30 October 1999
92 *Independent,* 16 February 1992. Wilson – who once called a fellow journalist a "painted whore" in print and was bewildered when she cut him dead at a party the following week – is eminently qualified to make this point.
93 *Goldenballs*
94 *Lord of the Gnomes*
95 *London Review of Books,* 2 December 1982
96 *The Private Eye Story*
97 *Will This Do?*
98 *Guardian,* 1 June 1989
99 *Tatler,* December 1986
100 *Singular Encounters,* Naim Attallah, Quartet Books 1990
101 *Guardian,* 1 June 1989
102 *Independent,* 27 March 1999
103 *Redbrick,* 27 October 1997
104 *Independent,* 20 November 1994
105 *Sunday Telegraph,* 9 February 2003
106 *Mail on Sunday,* 8 April 2001
107 *Will This Do?*
108 Introduction to *The Diaries of Auberon Waugh,* Akadine Press 1998
109 *The Private Eye Story*
110 *Lord of the Gnomes*
111 *Desert Island Discs*
112 *Thirty Years of Satire*
113 *Guardian,* 1 June 1989

114 *Home Truths: Life Around My Father* by Penny Junor, HarperCollins 2002
115 *Paul Foot and the Eye*, a tribute enclosed in issue 1116, 1 October 2004
116 *The Penguin Book of Journalism*
117 The correspondence was uncovered by Nicholas de Jongh in *Politics, Prudery and Perversions: The Censoring of the English Stage 1901–1968*, Methuen 2001
118 *Something Like Fire: Peter Cook Remembered* ed. Lin Cook, Methuen 1996
119 *Peter Cook: A Biography*
120 *You're Barred, You Bastards* by Norman Balon with Spencer Bright, Sidgwick & Jackson 1991
121 *Times*, 18 February 1983
122 *Desert Island Discs*
123 *Lord of the Gnomes*
124 *Just the One: The Life and Times of Jeffrey Bernard* by Graham Lord, Sinclair-Stevenson 1992
125 *Not Many Dead*
126 *Oldie*, Summer 2010
127 *Margrave of the Marshes* by John Peel, Bantam Press 2005
128 Interview by Nick Newman in *Passing Wind*, 'Best of' edition, 1980
129 *Daily Mirror*, 14 May 2001
130 *Goldenballs*
131 *Peter Cook: A Biography*
132 *More Please: An Autobiography* by Barry Humphries, Penguin 1992
133 *Sunday Times*, 16 August 2009
134 *Hot Press* (Ireland), 27 October 1999
135 *Mark Lawson Talks to Ian Hislop*
136 *Lord of the Gnomes*
137 *Trust Me I'm (Still) A Doctor*
138 *The Graduates* by Edward Whitley, Hamish Hamilton 1986
139 *Lord of the Gnomes*
140 *Dear John: A Tribute to John Wells*, BBC2, December 1998
141 *Times*, 1 March 1996
142 *The Private Eye Story*
143 *Singular Encounters*
144 *FT Weekend*, 6 September 2008
145 *Parkinson*, BBC1, March 2002
146 *Listener*, 17 March 1988
147 *Peter Cook: A Biography*
148 *Spectator*, 29 May 1976
149 *The South Bank Show: Private Eye*, ITV, October 1991
150 *Lord of the Gnomes*
151 *The Goldfish Bowl*
152 Ibid.
153 *Publisher*, no. 10, October 1964
154 *The Life and Times of Private Eye 1961–71* ed. Richard Ingrams, Penguin 1971
155 *Something Like Fire*
156 *Independent on Sunday*, 12 August 2001

157 *The Private Eye Story*
158 *Tonight*, BBC1, October 1976
159 *Lord of the Gnomes*
160 *The Private Eye Story*
161 *The South Bank Show: Private Eye*, ITV, October 1991
162 *Singular Encounters*
163 *Lord of the Gnomes*
164 *Inside Private Eye* by Peter McKay, Fourth Estate 1986
165 *Lord of the Gnomes*
166 *Sunday Times*, 19 October 1986
167 *My Friend Footy*
168 *Lord of the Gnomes*
169 *Oxford Today*, vol. 22, no. 1, Michaelmas 2009
170 *Lord of the Gnomes*
171 *In the Service of the Peacock Throne* by Parviz Radji, Hamish Hamilton 1983
172 *Dictionary of Architecture and Landscape Architecture* by James Stevens Curl, Oxford University Press 2000
173 *Lord of the Gnomes*
174 *Paul Foot and the Eye*
175 *Observer*, 21 September 1986
176 *Claud Cockburn: One Pair of Eyes*, BBC2, April 1968
177 *The Defence of the Realm: The Authorized History of MI5* by Christopher Andrew, Allen Lane 2009
178 *Secret History*, Channel 4, 15 August 1996
179 *Guardian*, 15 May 1987
180 These are just two examples of many such references, which are exhaustively catalogued in *Smear! Wilson and the Secret State* by Stephen Dorril and Robin Ramsay, Fourth Estate 1991
181 *Guardian*, 15 May 1987
182 *Trail of Havoc*
183 *Glimmers of Twilight*
184 *Guardian*, 13 April 1999
185 *The Soul of Indiscretion: Tom Driberg* by Francis Wheen, Fourth Estate 2001
186 Sir Paul Lever interviewed on *Tom Driberg and Me: A Personal Portrait*, BBC Four, March 2009
187 *Guardian*, 25 October 1995
188 *FT Weekend*, 6 September 2008
189 *Times Literary Supplement*, November 1972
190 *Mark Lawson Talks to Ian Hislop*
191 Interview with Ian Hislop, *Passing Wind*, 1980
192 *Steve Wright in the Afternoon*, BBC Radio 2, November 2007
193 *Singular Encounters*
194 *The South Bank Show: Private Eye*
195 *Will This Do?*
196 *Inside Private Eye*
197 *Lord of the Gnomes*
198 *Thirty Years of Satire*
199 *Literary Review*, July 1986

200 *Mail on Sunday*, 8 June 1986
201 *The Private Eye Story*
202 *Peter Cook: A Biography*
203 *Guardian*, 27 September 2008
204 Comments on "*Private Eye* hits best sales since 1992", guardian.co.uk 11 February 2010
205 *Will This Do?*
206 *Jewish Chronicle*, February 1980
207 *Lord of the Gnomes*
208 *Singular Encounters*
209 *Lord of the Gnomes*
210 *Life and Times of Private Eye*
211 Ibid.
212 *Sunday Times*, 28 October 2001
213 *Lord of the Gnomes*
214 *Desert Island Discs*
215 Quoted in *The Private Eye Story*
216 *Sunday Times*, 28 October 2001
217 *Shrewsbury Chronicle*, 1 November 2001
218 *Desert Island Discs*
219 *Margrave of the Marshes*. Fifty years on, the school's sixth form produces its own satire sheet, called *Public Nose*.
220 *Lord of the Gnomes*
221 *The Private Eye Story*
222 *Campaign*, 29 June 1990
223 *Lord of the Gnomes*
224 *Private Eye at 45*, exhibition catalogue, Cartoon Museum, 2006
225 *Vice*, November 2008
226 Interview with *Welcome to the Fold* website, 9 November 2009
227 *Observer*, 14 January 2001
228 *Private Eye at 45*
229 Evidence to the House of Commons Culture, Media and Sport Committee, 5 May 2009
230 *Lord of the Gnomes*
231 *So Farewell Then, Peter Cook*
232 Unpublished interview conducted in November 2004 by Louis Barfe for his book *Turned Out Nice Again: The Story of British Light Entertainment*, Atlantic 2008.
233 Hugh Cudlipp Lecture, January 2010
234 *Guardian*, 13 October 2009
235 *The Private Eye Story*
236 *Something Like Fire*
237 *Times*, October 1982
238 *Satire in the Sixties*, BBC Radio 2, August 2001
239 *The Private Eye Story*
240 *Times*, 14 January 1995
241 *Observer*, 17 August 1997
242 *Peter Cook: A Biography*
243 *Something Like Fire*
244 *Inside Private Eye*
245 *Tatler*, December 1986
246 *Lord of the Gnomes*
247 *Life and Times of Private Eye*
248 *The Private Eye Story*
249 Ibid.

Thats enough Eds: Ian Hislop, Richard Ingrams, and Christopher Booker, photographed in the magazine's offices in 2010